English feminists
and their opponents
in the 1790s

MANCHESTER
UNIVERSITY PRESS

English feminists and their opponents in the 1790s

Unsex'd and proper females

William Stafford

Manchester University Press

Manchester and New York

distributed exclusively in the USA by Palgrave

Published by Manchester University Press
Oxford Road, Manchester M13 9NR, UK
and Room 400, 175 Fifth Avenue, New York, NY 10010, USA
www.manchesteruniversitypress.co.uk

Distributed exclusively in the USA by
Palgrave, 175 Fifth Avenue, New York,
NY 10010, USA

Distributed exclusively in Canada by
UBC Press, University of British Columbia, 2029 West Mall,
Vancouver, BC, Canada V6T 1Z2

British Library Cataloguing-in-Publication Data
A catalogue record for this book is available from the British Library

Library of Congress Cataloging-in-Publication Data applied for

ISBN 0 7190 6082 6 *hardback*

First published 2002

10 09 08 07 06 05 04 03 02   10 9 8 7 6 5 4 3 2 1

Typeset in Times
by Action Publishing Technology Ltd, Gloucester
Printed in Great Britain
by Biddles Ltd, Guildford and King's Lynn

For Edmund,
Benjamin and Eleanor Stafford

Contents

Acknowledgements

I am grateful to the University of Huddersfield for giving me a sabbatical semester, and to the Arts and Humanities Research Board for awarding me a matching semester so that I could complete the research for this book.

1

Unsex'd females and proper women writers

Intertextualities

There was a debate about women in the 1790s, addressing their nature, their
capacities and their roles. These issues had become increasingly topical in the
course of the eighteenth century, in medical and educational writings, in periodical essays from the *Tatler* onwards, in prose fiction and in the popular
genre of conduct literature giving advice to women about proper behaviour.
Increasingly women themselves contributed to the debate as a consequence of
the exponential growth of printed publications addressed to women and the
rising tide of female authorship. But the debate acquired a new urgency and
passion in the 1790s as a result of the French revolution and the ferment of
ideas it provoked. In France, the law was changed to permit civil marriage
and easy divorce; some women such as Olympe de Gouges went so far as to
demand the same civil and political rights as men. This book will take as its
subject the contribution of a selection of 1790s English women writers to the
debate. But how should the selection be made? This chapter will explore the
way in which the debate, and the contributors to it, were identified by
contemporaries; the beginning of the next will add a few more voices which
the hindsight of modern scholarship has considered of importance.

  Women writers were evidently being marshalled into rival camps in the
1790s. They were doing it themselves; writers we might label 'progressive'
or 'radical' – or even 'feminist' – developed a sense of solidarity under the
fire of often scurrilous vilification by conservatives. Male 'jacobins' identified and consorted with their female allies. Above all male antijacobin
writers set out to establish a contrast between 'proper',[1] approved women
writers and their detested antitypes. They strove to identify progressive ideas

---

[1] 'Proper' is not Polwhele's term, but it is a useful one. See Mary L. Poovey, *The
Proper Lady and the Woman Writer: Ideology as Style in the Works of Mary
Wollstonecraft, Mary Shelley, and Jane Austen* (Chicago, University of Chicago
Press, 1984).

about women with French revolutionary terror and social breakdown – perhaps because they believed that these phenomena were connected, perhaps because the mobilization of latent misogyny and fear of women stepping out of their traditional sphere was an effective propaganda ploy. Accordingly this chapter will be organized around the 1790s antijacobin categorization.

The most systematic, explicit and comprehensive sorting of women into the approved and the disapproved is to be found in *The Unsex'd Females: A Poem, Addressed to the Author of the Pursuits of Literature* which appeared anonymously in 1798.[2] The author, an Anglican clergyman called Richard Polwhele, did not long remain anonymous, and we may suspect that the *Anti-Jacobin Review*, to which he was a contributor, was in on the secret from the start. But the *British Critic*, the other major review founded to combat 'jacobinism', which normally recommended this conservative's poetry and writings on topography and religion, evidently did *not* know. Its reviewer took issue with Polwhele's insistence that botany was an indelicate subject of study for ladies – 'These over-refinements of delicacy are, in our opinion, most indelicate. They remind us of the prude, who would not speak some words because of their terminations, [e.g., album?] though quite innocent to other persons' – and while admiring the intention of the poem, condemned the language for bad taste.[3] Both the reviewer for and correspondents to the *Anti-Jacobin* leapt to the defence of Polwhele's poetic judgement.[4]

Polwhele's poem concentrates on the 'unsex'd females' but also invokes commendable ones by way of contrast. Four artists are mentioned (Angelica Kauffman and Emma Crewe – 'unsex'd': Lady Diana Beauclerk and Princess Elizabeth – approved) who will not be discussed here. I will merely list four approved women writers – Elizabeth Montague, Elizabeth Carter, Hester Chapone and Hester Lynch Piozzi – who either were not writing in the 1790s, or were not writing about women. That leaves four approved writers – Hannah More, Mme D'Arblay (Frances Burney), Ann Radcliffe and Anna Seward – and nine 'unsex'd' females – Mary Wollstonecraft, Mary Hays, Helen Maria Williams, Catharine Macaulay Graham, Charlotte Smith, Ann Yearsley, Mary Robinson, Anna Laetitia Barbauld and Anne Jebb.

Why did Polwhele select these women writers, and leave out others? Why did he divide them into sheep and goats in precisely this way? This chapter will explore the grounds of his judgements of propriety and impropriety. But before embarking on these tasks, it is important to notice that Polwhele did not produce his lists

[2] The Unsex'd Females: *A Poem, Addressed to the Author of the Pursuits of Literature* (London, Cadell & Davies, 1798).

[3] *British Critic*, 14 (1799) 70–1. This chapter makes considerable reference to contemporary reviews. I have consulted the two (*Anti-Jacobin* and *British Critic*) which were established in the aftermath of the French revolution to present an anti-revolutionary stance and, by way of contrast, the 'left of centre', Whiggish doyen of the reviews, the one with the largest circulation, the *Monthly Review*.

[4] *Anti-Jacobin Review & Magazine* (April–August 1799), 27; (August–December 1799), 468.

unaided. The debate we are about to consider involved more voices than those of Polwhele and his selected females. He draws this to our attention himself: 'The most sensible women (says Mr. Dyer) are more uniformly on the side of Liberty, than the other sex – witness a Macaulay, a Wollstonecraft, a Barbauld, a Jebb, a Williams, a Smith'.[5] George Dyer came from the opposite, 'jacobin' camp; he was a member of the circle around the philosopher and anarchist (and Wollstonecraft's husband) William Godwin. Polwhele is quoting from the notes to Dyer's Ode 'On Liberty' of 1792 welcoming the French revolution.[6] In that poem Dyer also mentions Mary Hays, and so in a sense the conservative Polwhele's list of 'unsex'd' female writers, with the exceptions of Yearsley and Robinson, was made up within the ranks of radicalism.

Polwhele's poem is 'Addressed to the Author of the Pursuits of Literature' and headed with a quotation from that work: 'Our unsex'd female writers now instruct, or confuse, us and themselves, in the labyrinth of politics, or turn us wild with Gallic frenzy'. *The Pursuits of Literature*, which came out in four parts between 1794 and 1796, was by T.J. Mathias; like Polwhele's poem it was a verse satire attacking other writers both for the quality of their writing and for their politics. The ultimate models for polemical poems of this kind were the Latin verse satires of Horace and Juvenal, classically imitated by Pope at the beginning of the eighteenth century in for example his *Dunciad* and *Epistle to Dr. Arbuthnot*. In case the reader should fail to recognize the targets, eighteenth-century imitations such as Polwhele's and Mathias's add lengthy footnotes. Mathias mostly attacks men, the usual 'Jacobin' suspects – Priestley, Paine, Thelwall, Horne Tooke, Godwin – but he also has a stab at Robinson and Kaufmann (as well as Charlotte Smith), thereby contributing two more to Polwhele's list of the 'unsex'd'. Just as Polwhele declared himself to be carrying on the good work of Mathias, so Mathias in turn refers back to a precursor in the same genre: 'The author of *The Baviad* has taken some pleasant trouble off my hands'.[7] *The Baviad*, published in 1791, was by William Gifford, later editor of the conservative *Quarterly Review*. Polwhele and Mathias are pompous and dull; Gifford is wickedly funny. His ostensible main target is not political but literary, namely the poetry of the so-called 'Della Cruscan' school, and Mary Robinson, as a member of that school, receives considerable attention. But at bottom, politics is still the issue; 'Della Crusca' was the pen-name of Robert Merry, and the *Baviad* attacks his poem, *The Wreath of Liberty* (correctly, *The Laurel of Liberty*), which welcomed the French revolution.[8]

5 Polwhele, *Unsex'd Females*, pp. 16–17.

6 George Dyer, *Poems* (London, J. Johnson, 1792), pp. 36–7.

7 Thomas James Mathias, *The Pursuits of Literature, or What You Will: a Satirical Poem in Dialogue, Part the First* (London, J. Owen, 1794), p. 7n.

8 William Gifford, *The Baviad, a Paraphrastic Imitation of the First Satire of Persius* (London, R. Faulder, 1791), pp. 9, 13. Mary Robinson herself alludes to the *Baviad*, and satirizes Robert Merry as 'Mr. Doleful' in her *Walsingham; or, The Pupil of Nature. A Domestic Story* (London, Longman, 1797), ii, 244; and Wollstonecraft criticizes the inflated language of his *Laurel of Liberty* in the *Analytical Review*, 8 (December 1790), 548.

Gender, writing and genre

Does Polwhele think that it is improper, unsexing, for women to write and publish certain kinds of literature, or even to write for publication at all? This question needs to be addressed at the very outset, for some recent scholars have argued that the very act of writing, or of writing for publication, was subversive at this time. The pen was a symbolic phallus, hence writing in itself was unsexing.[9] And *public*ation, it has been claimed, was transgressive in that the woman writer presented her thoughts and herself publicly, breaking out of her proper, private sphere.[10] Other scholars have thought that genres were strictly gendered; some kinds of writing were permitted to women, others were thought of as male terrain, protected by barriers and signs saying 'No entry'. It has been said that only those kinds of writing which were rooted in the private sphere, or which expressed expected 'feminine' characteristics such as sensibility, were approved for women – private diaries and letters (which might then be published), novels which, especially when in epistolary or first-person form appeared as extensions of letter and diary writing, conduct books and educational publications (because the education of children was a womanly duty), the poetry of feeling.[11] Were there such restrictions and inhibitions on women's writing at the end of the eighteenth century, and is this a basis for Polwhele's sorting of women into the 'unsex'd' and 'proper'?

[9] Sandra M. Gilbert & Susan Gubar, *The Madwoman in the Attic: the Woman Writer and the Nineteenth-Century Imagination* (New Haven, Yale University Press, 1979), pp. 3–16.

[10] Vivien Jones, *Women in the Eighteenth Century: Constructions of Femininity* (London, Routledge, 1990), p. 140.

[11] Kathryn Shevelow, *Women and Print Culture: the Construction of Femininity in the Early Periodical* (London, Routledge, 1989), pp. 90, 152; Julia Epstein, *The Iron Pen: Frances Burney and the Politics of Women's Writing* (Bristol, Bristol Classical Press, 1989), p. 48; Barbara Maria Zaczek, *Censored Sentiments: Letters and Censorship in Epistolary Novels and Conduct Materials* (Newark, University of Delaware press, 1997), pp. 14–15. That women were better at this kind of writing is not a discovery of present-day critics: 'Women have been allowed to possess, by a kind of prescription, the knack of epistolary writing; the talent of chatting on paper in that easy immethodical manner, which render [sic] letters dear to friends, and amusing to strangers. Who that has read Madame Sevigne's and Pope's letters, with an unprejudiced eye, can avoid giving the preference to the artless elegance of the former; interested by the eloquence of her heart, and the unstudied sallies of her imagination; whilst the florid periods of the latter appear, like state robes, grand and cumbersome, and his tenderness vapid vanity', Wollstonecraft writing in *Analytical Review*, 8 (December 1790), 431; 'The genius of living and dead languages differs so much, that the pains which are taken to write elegant Latin frequently spoil the English style. – Girls usually write much better than boys; they think and express their thoughts clearly at an age when young men can scarcely write an easy letter upon any common occasion', Maria Edgeworth, *Letters for Literary Ladies. To which is Added an Essay on the Noble Science of Self-Justification* (1795) (London, J. M. Dent, 1993), p. 26.

In part the answer is yes. Polwhele did not believe that women should be silent; he praises Mrs Montague as a 'female critic' and judges Mrs D'Arblay the best novel writer ever. He praises Barbauld, Seward, Robinson and Smith as poets. But he thinks that women are good at certain kinds of writing only, such as Poetry, Romances (i.e., what today would be called 'gothic' novels) and Novels (the 'realistic' novel set in the writer's own times). He implies that they are not suited to history and science, detecting 'numerous femalities' in Mrs Macaulay Graham's *History of England from the Accession of James I*, and remarking of Margaret Bryan's *Compendious System of Astronomy*, 'I am rather pleased with elegant illustration, than instructed by science'. Women writers should not be too assertive: 'The crimsoning blush of modesty, will be always more attractive, than the sparkle of confident intelligence'.[12] It cannot be doubted that such sentiments were part of the common coin; Charlotte Smith, one of his 'unsex'd' females, wrote in the 1792 Preface to her *Elegiac Sonnets*, 'notwithstanding I am thus frequently appearing as an Authoress, ... I am well aware that for a woman – "The Post of Honour is a Private Station"'.[13] But standing at the head of the sixth edition of her poems, and coming from an author who by the end of 1792 had published four novels, Smith's remark sounds like affected modesty, a ritual obeisance to a cliché which no longer carried much weight. We need to look a little further before we are entitled to conclude that there were real cultural obstacles to women engaging in certain sorts of writing, or even engaging in any writing at all for publication.

In order to answer this question we might look further at what women writers had to say about it, and also at the book reviews. There were weighty reviews devoted to literature at the end of the eighteenth century.[14] For example the *Monthly Review* and the *Critical Review* (which also appeared monthly) were very up-to-date and comprehensive in their coverage, and reviews could be several pages long, with extensive quotations. The *Analytical Review* was founded in 1789 in order to appraise literature from a progressive point of view – Mary Wollstonecraft was an editor and contributor. The conservatives responded by setting up the *British Critic* in 1793, and the *Anti-Jacobin Review* in 1797. In all of them less space was devoted to female than to male authors. The reviews divided their coverage into main items, often very long and in large print, and a 'catalogue' of short reviews in small print. Women's writing was mostly noticed in the catalogue, to which for example all but a handful of novels were consigned. But this downgrading was not total and systematic; the best poetry, novels and romances by women got main reviews, as on occasion did other women's

12 Polwhele, *Unsex'd Females*, pp. 16, 32, 34, 37.
13 *The Poems of Charlotte Smith*, ed. Stuart Curran (Oxford, Oxford University Press, 1993), p. 6.
14 For a history of the reviews at this time see Derek Roper, *Reviewing before the Edinburgh, 1788–1802* (London, Methuen, 1978).

writing – conduct books, travelogues, educational treatises. Still, the main section paid most attention to such fields as classics, philology, poetry, history, theology, philosophy and science. The organization of the reviews made manifest a hierarchy of genres with novels and romances a long way down.

Poetry and prose fiction were the genres most associated with women writers; but there was a degree of prejudice against writing prose fiction, which affected women *and men* alike. There was still a sense that writing mainly for money – not only novels but also articles in newspapers and periodicals – was not entirely compatible with gentility, hence the common practice of anonymous authorship which survived well into the nineteenth century.[15] Female authors of the 1790s acknowledge this prejudice. In her preface to *A Simple Story* Elizabeth Inchbald, actress, playwright and novelist, confronts it head on; necessity drove her to write, and 'I will not complain of any hardship thy [necessity's] commands require, so thou doest not urge my pen to prostitution'.[16] Are we being asked to excuse her writing on the grounds that she chose a more honourable route to independence than the oldest profession, with which actresses were so often associated? Marchmont, the hero of Charlotte Smith's novel of that title, is discouraged by his rich relations from becoming an author, and Warwick's uncle in Smith's *The Old Manor House* reinstates him as his heir in return for him giving up the trade of playwright. Smith herself, chronically short of money, was obsessed with the precariousness of her status as a gentlewoman, and several of her novels contain passages justifying her authorship as the only way of supporting her family.[17] Commendation as a good mother outweighs disdain for the mercenary writer. In all of this it is important to remember that anonymity might be chosen by men as well as women, and we cannot simply assume that their reasons for this choice differed.

Was the writing of novels in particular thought to be degrading and improper in other ways? The moral worth of novels was a matter of some urgency for 'unsex'd' and 'proper' females alike. In Hannah More's tract series *The Two Wealthy Farmers*, Farmer Bragwell's daughters are corrupted by the trash in marble covers for which they send Jack the ploughboy to the local bookshop; novels set parental authority at nought, make 'light of the sins of ADULTERY, GAMING, DUELS, and SELF-MURDER',[18] and give young women ideas above their station. Bragwell's daughter Polly, her head turned by the romances she has read, refuses to marry a sober, Christian, well-to-

[15] Joanne Shattock, *Politics and Reviewers: the* Edinburgh *and the* Quarterly *in the Early Victorian Age* (Leicester, Leicester University Press, 1989), pp. 5–6.

[16] Elizabeth Inchbald, *A Simple Story* (1791) (Oxford, Oxford University Press, 1988), p. 2.

[17] Charlotte Smith, *Desmond* (1792) (London, Pickering & Chatto, 1997), p. 6.

[18] Hannah More, *The Two Wealthy Farmers; or, the History of Mr. Bragwell* (London, Rivington, 1799), p. 18.

do grazier and runs off with a 'gentleman', Augustus Frederick Theodosius, who turns out to be Timothy Incle, a haberdasher's shopman. Other conservative women writers criticize novels for giving young women unrealistic expectations of undying love and perfect felicity in a companionate marriage, for trapping them in a fantasy world which unfits them for the humdrum duties of ordinary life. Novels, we are told, encourage young women to cultivate their feelings, their sensibility, at the expense of reason, judgement and self-control.[19]

But there is no clear division between 'unsex'd' and 'proper' female writers on this issue. Macaulay Graham is critical of novels because they propose that love is an ungovernable passion, and that it is possible for a woman to find the right man, with whom marriage will be effortlessly perfect. She would allow a young woman to read Cervantes, Fielding's *Joseph Andrews* and le Sage's *Gil Blas*, but very little else in the way of prose fiction; Richardson's *Pamela* is totally unfit for youth, Clarissa Harlowe is by no means a model of conduct and even Burney's *Cecilia* gives too vast an idea of the power of love.[20] Wollstonecraft's reviews of novels in the *Analytical* contain similar strictures.[21] Mary Hays defends novels of sensibility – *Clarissa* and *The Man of Feeling* – but is unhappy about the moral effect of Sterne and Rousseau.[22]

And if 'unsex'd' females had reservations about some novels, 'proper' females were not entirely hostile to the genre. In spite of her criticisms, More wrote a novel (*Coelebs in Search of a Wife,* 1808), and so did other conservatives. They and the radicals were in fact engaged in a common endeavour to reform the novel, both with regard to its moral influence and aesthetically, purging it of cliché and of unreality, as Smith insists in her 'Avis au lecteur' at the beginning of volume II of *The Banished Man.*[23] Of the 'unsex'd' females only Mary Robinson resists this reforming endeavour, defiantly persisting in writing novels with utterly improbable coincidences, novels which do not criticize sensibility and romantic love, in which heroes mark their heroism by fighting duels and in which the message is persistently conveyed that adultery is not an unforgivable sin.

Returning to the 'higher' genres we have to admit that women writers were greatly outnumbered by men. But absence from booksellers' lists, not the same as exclusion, resulted at least in part from lack of opportunities.

[19] Edgeworth, *Letters*, pp. 39–40, 45; Elizabeth Hamilton, *Translation of the Letters of a Hindoo Rajah* (1796) (Peterborough, Ontario, Broadview Press, 1999), pp. 190–2.

[20] Catharine Macaulay Graham, *Letters on Education. With Observations on Religious and Metaphysical Subjects* (London, C. Dilly, 1790), pp. 142–8.

[21] *Analytical Review*, 8 (October 1790), 222.

[22] Mary Hays, *Letters and Essays, Moral, and Miscellaneous* (London, T. Knott, 1793), pp. 95–6.

[23] Charlotte Smith, *The Banished Man* (London, T. Cadell, 1794), ii, pp. x–xi.

Few women received an education enabling them to translate books of the Bible from the Hebrew, or Gray's 'Elegy' into Greek. Access to Oxford and Cambridge libraries would be closed to them, though Mrs Macaulay Graham pursued her historical researches in the British Museum.[24] We cannot assume that a woman who had the necessary education would be told to 'keep off the grass'. Mrs Carter was an exceptional woman in her command of classical and European languages. Her translation of the Greco-Roman stoic philosopher Epictetus was celebrated, she published it by subscription (evidently a public endorsement of her work) in 1758, and made the very handsome sum of almost £1,000.[25] In spite of Polwhele, not only the Whiggish *Monthly Review*, but also the conservative *British Critic* and the *Anti-Jacobin Review* itself welcomed Margaret Bryan's *Compendious System of Astronomy* in 1798 and gave it full-length reviews.[26] The *Monthly Review*, indeed, remarked that 'there appears no reasonable argument to prove that the fair sex should not study philosophy and write upon it' (adding, it must be admitted, 'if a neglect of female duties does not ensue') and thought that it was better for women to study astronomy than to sew the alphabet on a sampler. The reviewer concluded that those who 'deem the powers of the male intellect alone adequate to the discussion of exalted science' did not deserve a serious answer.[27]

Large areas of the public realm of publishing and reading, then, were not closed to women; or at worst, the barriers were not insurmountable. But the critical area, the space where women were most likely to be denied access, was the bitterly contested terrain of public controversy in politics and religion. Even here, we should not think in terms of absolute and general prohibitions. Whether a woman writer's intervention would be resisted, would depend on who she was, what she wanted to say, and who was the gatekeeper.

The *Anti-Jacobin Review* regularly, and sometimes brutally, invoked presuppositions about the unsuitability of women for certain kinds of writing in order to discredit its opponents. For example in its review of her novel *Walsingham* Mary Robinson was advised to 'confine herself to the fashions and manners of the times, without any vain attempt to investigate their causes, and abstain from attempting political philosophy'; of her *False Friend* the review insisted that 'when she attempted to dive into moral and political causes, she went far *beyond her depth*'. Charlotte Smith's *The Young Philosopher* was unfavourably contrasted with Frances Burney's novels: 'we must whisper in her ear that she has not any depth in political philosophy. . . .

---

[24] The antijacobin writer Isaac D'Israeli accused her of tearing out manuscript pages favourable to the Tory side; *British Critic*, 3 (1794), 40.

[25] Sylvia Harcstark Myers, *The Bluestocking Circle* (Oxford, Oxford University Press, 1990), pp. 168–9.

[26] *British Critic*, 11 (1798), 535–9; *Anti-Jacobin Review* (September 1799), 58–62.

[27] *Monthly Review*, 26 (1798), 406–10.

The best of our female novelists interferes not with church nor state. There are no politics in Evelina or Cecilia'.[28] Mary Hays receives the following advice: 'As usefulness seems to be the watchword of this author and her friends, we will tell her how she can be much more useful than she can possibly make herself by devoting her time to literary labours – *to your distaff, Mary, to your distaff'*.[29] Traditional, longstanding gender conventions are invoked here to put down a woman who, from a conservative point of view, had gone just too far.

Though never quite so rude, the *British Critic* took a similar view. Implicitly it steered women towards poetry – 'In this branch ... we have chiefly had occasion to notice the efforts of the female sex' – and prose fiction – 'To female writers alone are we at present indebted for the Novels that seem most deserving of recommendation'.[30] A long review compared Charlotte Smith and Anna Seward as the leading composers of sonnets.[31] In its review of Wollstonecraft's *Letters Written during a Short Residence in Sweden*, it deplored the political and religious content, but welcomed the display of 'the finer sensibilities of a female', which it speculatively attributed to her recent experience of marriage and motherhood.[32] Mary Hays was advised that 'diffidence in decision, particularly in important points, is a great ornament to the female character' and to avoid 'spinning webs of feeble reasoning on such subjects as free-will, fore-knowledge, the origin of evil, etc.'.[33] The review of the *Appeal to the Men of Great Britain in Behalf of Women*, most likely by her, concludes 'the language is slovenly and incorrect, the reasoning weak and frivolous, and ... it abounds with grammatical errors'.[34] Helen Maria Williams, writing about French politics, is accused of a 'prompt, we had almost said pert, and decisive way of speaking, on matters far too perplexed for her sagacity, and far too abstruse for her acquirements'.[35] The reviewer of Mary Robinson's *Letter to the Women of England* agrees with her that women should acquire solid and useful learning, but doubts whether their 'interference in theological and political opinions would conduce much to the speedy adjustment of them'.[36]

Nevertheless, traditional conventions like these no longer had the field to themselves; the conservative reviews did not always wish to repress women's writing about politics and religion. Catherine D'Oyley's *History of the Life and Death of our Blessed Saviour* and Sarah Trimmer's *Sacred History, Selected from the Scriptures* both received enthusiastic reviews, and so did

[28] *Anti-Jacobin Review* (August 1798), 164, 189–90; (May 1799), 39.
[29] *Ibid.* (May 1799), 58.
[30] *British Critic*, 1 (1793), ix; 4 (1794), xiv.
[31] *Ibid.*, 14 (1799), 166–71.
[32] *Ibid.*, 7 (1796), 602–10.
[33] *Ibid.*, 1 (1793), 463.
[34] *Ibid.*, 13 (1799), 206.
[35] *Ibid.*, 6 (1795), 493.
[36] *Ibid.*, 14 (1799), 682.

the 'patriotic plan' of Hannah More's *Cheap Repository Tracts*.[37] Accusing women writers of stepping out of their proper sphere, and of logical and grammatical incompetence, were handy propaganda ploys for discrediting dissident voices; but the fact that such prohibitions could be lifted when approved women authors were reviewed suggests that gender/genre boundaries were fluid and uncertain.

In its review of Maria Edgeworth's *Letters for Literary Ladies* the *Monthly Review* thought that to educate women for an equal share in literary and political life was going too far; 'we can never be persuaded that the state of the world would be improved by converting all our affectionate wives, kind mothers, and lovely daughters, into studious philosophers, or busy politicians'.[38] But this remark is out of character for the *Monthly* in this decade, which normally takes a welcoming stand towards women writers. The review of Catharine Macaulay Graham's *Letters on Education* casts doubt on her abilities as a philosopher, but praises her as a historian, and the reviews of her and Wollstonecraft's replies to Burke do not even hint at disapproval of these female interventions in politics.[39] The reviewer of Wollstonecraft's *Vindication of the Rights of Woman* remarks that 'In the class of philosophers, the *author* of this treatise – whom we will not offend by styling authoress – has a right to a distinguished place', and he continues his reflections on the gendering of language by lamenting the absence in English of a general term as well as 'man' and 'woman'.[40] The review of Wollstonecraft's *Historical and Moral View of the French Revolution* praises her as a historian and philosopher; that of her *Swedish Letters* pays tribute to her strong 'or, if the fair traveller will accept the epithet as a compliment, [her] *masculine* mind'.[41] The fact that the reviewer goes on to praise her feelings and her heart, surely indicates that the use of the epithet 'masculine' is not meant to imply that Wollstonecraft is 'unsex'd'. The review of Charlotte Smith's *Desmond* praises its masculine tone and political discussions, 'being ... of the opinion, that the great events which are passing in the world are no less interesting to women than to men, and that in her solicitude to discharge her domestic duties, a woman ought not to forget that, in common with her father and husband, her brothers and sons, she is a citizen'.[42] The reviewer of Hawkins's *Letters on the Female Mind* is very hostile to her depreciation of female abilities and attempt to debar women from political writing.[43]

[37] *Ibid.*, 4 (1794), 299; 8 (1796), 499–502; 7 (1796), 569.

[38] *Monthly Review*, 21 (1796), 24.

[39] *Ibid.*, 3 (1790), 309; 4 (1791), 93–7. Though Macaulay's pamphlet was published anonymously, the review reveals her name.

[40] *Ibid.*, 8 (1792), 198–209; the reviewer was William Enfield, see Roper, *Reviewing before the* Edinburgh, p. 253.

[41] *Ibid.*, 16 (1795), 393–402; 20 (1796), 251.

[42] *Ibid.*, 9 (1792), 406.

[43] *Ibid.*, 12 (1793), 398–9.

It is often said that the *Monthly Review* became more cautious as the reaction against 'jacobinism' gathered strength;[44] but still in 1799 a (largely unfavourable) review of Mary Robinson's *Letter to the Women of England* could 'humbly beg this literary Thalestris to remember, that there is no restraint laid on female authors, either by the laws or the manners of the country; of which her list of distinguished female writers, and the publication of her pamphlet, are sufficient proofs'.[45] The *Monthly Review*'s stance towards women writers should come as no surprise. The review was Whig in its politics, and liberal and progressive in its opinions. Its cohort of reviewers included prominent unitarians such as William Taylor and William Enfield – and unitarianism was at this time hospitable to claims for the moral and intellectual equality of women.[46] Indeed five of Polwhele's 'unsex'd' females were or had been unitarians or had had significant contacts with unitarianism. In case we are inclined to think that women's writing on politics, philosophy and religion was encouraged only in limited, sectarian circles, we should remember that the *Monthly Review* was not a unitarian organ, and that it was the leading review with the largest circulation.

As the preceding discussion implies, by quoting from the reviews selectively, either of two opposite theses could be proposed: that women were debarred from certain genres of writing; or that the barriers were crumbling and ineffective. Perhaps the way of understanding this is to conclude that traditional gender stereotypes of a kind which degraded and disempowered women no longer held complete sway (if they ever had); a measure of uncertainty, or ambiguity, or fluidity in gender boundaries offered openings for women. Even conservative writers were prepared to accept female opportunites and demands in several areas: work, social and political engagement, education, writing, a more dignified and rational construction of femininity. But faced with the threat of what they saw as jacobinism, conservatives atavistically fell back upon simple, age-old stereotypes which served as handy rhetorical weapons. Their stance was incoherent and contradictory, torn between what we might label as progressive impulses and a tendency to relapse into the crudest binaries when it suited their polemical purposes.

What did 'unsex'd' and 'proper' females respectively think about prohibitions against women writing in certain genres? As we might expect, the 'unsex'd' wish to break down the fences. Smith and Robinson were well aware that a woman author was liable to attack, not because she was a woman but if her work expressed political dissidence.[47] In Robinson's *Angelina*, Sir Edward Clarendon declares that 'Women have no business

[44] Roper, *Reviewing before the* Edinburgh, p. 28.

[45] *Ibid.*, 29 (1799), 477–8.

[46] Ruth Watts, *Gender, Power and the Unitarians in England 1760–1860* (London, Longman, 1998).

[47] Charlotte Smith, *Marchmont* (London, Sampson Low, 1796), iv, p. 330; Robinson, *Walsingham*, ii, p. 212.

11

either to write or to read'.[48] The character of Sir Edward Clarendon is the butt of Robinson's humour throughout the novel; he is a stock reactionary from central casting. The fact that the reader is expected to laugh at his remarks implies that for Robinson, and for her readers as she second guesses them, barriers against women's writing have worn very thin. Another risible character, Dr. Pimpernel in her *Walsingham,* declares, 'Men should assert their rights – women grow saucy – must be taken down – only invented to amuse the lords of creation – no business to write. Arrogant husseys!'[49]

Even 'proper' females are reluctant to obey all of the signs saying 'Keep off the grass'. Hannah More (in spite of the fact that she wrote about politics herself) thought that women should not write on politics or law, satire or comedy; for such writing required a 'consummate knowledge of the world to which a delicate woman has no fair avenues, and which could she attain she would never be supposed to have come honestly by'.[50] She also thought classical learning problematic, because of the occurrence of indecent passages. But on the other hand, religion was not one of her tabooed subjects. Other conservative women writers of the decade were ready to write on religion and politics. Jane West includes a long debate on religion in her *Tale of the Times*, and justifies its inclusion.[51] Her heroine is advised not to engage in theological disputes, explicitly because she has not studied them, not because she is a woman.[52] Eliza Hamilton was aware that her *Letters of a Hindoo Rajah*, which treats of politics, religion and philosophy, might be censured by some 'as a presumptuous effort to wander out of that narrow and contracted path, which they have allotted to the female mind',[53] but one of her heroines is encouraged to write both to entertain and to instruct, in spite of her remark that 'you know how female writers are looked down upon. The women fear, and hate; the men ridicule, and dislike them'.[54] Above all Maria Edgeworth in her *Letters for Literary Ladies*, though she makes the standard obeisance to the wish that learning will not make women unpleasantly assertive and immodest, does not suggest that any field of learning is improper for a woman.

A final important point remains to be made. A firm gendering of genres would require genres to be distinct and writers to be specialists. In the eighteenth century, this was manifestly not the case. Hume wrote what we today

---

[48] Mary Robinson, *Angelina* (London, Hookham & Carpenter, 1796), i, p. 87.

[49] Robinson, *Walsingham*, ii, p. 279.

[50] Hannah More, *Strictures on the Modern System of Female Education. With a View of the Principles and Conduct Prevalent among Women of Rank and Fortune* (London, T. Cadell, 1799), ii, pp. 24–5.

[51] Jane West, *A Tale of the Times* (London, Longman & Rees, 1799), iii, pp. 386–7.

[52] *Ibid.,* iii, pp. 60–2.

[53] Hamilton, *Hindoo Rajah*, p. 72.

[54] *Ibid.,* p. 303.

would class as the distinct disciplines of philosophy, politics, history and economics as well as elegant essays; Rousseau wrote on political philosophy, economics, anthropology, education and music as well as a novel; Godwin wrote philosophy, politics, history, biography, plays and novels. What we would count as different genres often mingled promiscuously between the same covers – think, for example, of the range covered by Goldsmith's *Citizen of the World*, or in the constantly reprinted eight-volume sets of the *Spectator*. Rousseau's *Emile* was part novel, part treatise on education, morals and religion. Richardson's *Clarissa* was an ethical treatise as well as a novel. Conduct books could open out into morality and religion as well as education.

Boundaries between types of writing were fluid and permeable, giving the writer a freedom and a range which women too could exploit. So for example Macaulay Graham includes history, ethics, religion and philosophy in her *Letters on Education*; the Hays sisters' *Letters and Essays, Moral and Miscellaneous* has a vast *Spectator*-like range, adding stories and poems to religious and philosophical discussions. Wollstonecraft's *An Historical and Moral View of the Origin and Progress of the French Revolution* is ambitious, reflective philosophical history, and her *Letters Written During a Short Residence in Sweden, Norway and Denmark* embraces politics, economics, morality, society, culture and metaphysics. She comments that she was told on her travels that she asked men's questions.[55] Elizabeth Inchbald's *Nature and Art* is a philosophical novel, as is Hays's *Emma Courtney*, with its references to utilitarian moral philosophy and the associationist theory of mind. There are lengthy discussions of politics and society in novels by Charlotte Smith, especially *Desmond* and *The Young Philosopher*. The eminently 'proper' writer Jane West noted this fluidity of genres in 1799, lamenting the fact that female authors could smuggle attacks on government, filial obedience, religion and chastity into novels and books of travels, letters and education.[56] But it was not only radical writers who ignored genre boundaries; Hannah More's *Strictures on Female Education*, considering not only morality and devotion but also theological questions, often reads like a sermon and her *Tracts* are little stories with big religious, moral and political messages. The gendering of genres in this decade and the exclusion of women from certain types of writing, though obviously issues in that so many women writers pay attention to them, were by no means straightforward or absolute. Let Mary Robinson have the last word: 'The embargo upon words, the enforcement of tacit submission, has been productive of consequences highly honourable to the women of the present age. Since the sex have been condemned for exercising the powers of speech, they have successfully taken up the pen.'[57]

[55] Mary Wollstonecraft, *Letters Written During a Short Residence in Sweden, Norway and Denmark* (London, Joseph Johnson, 1796), p. 13.

[56] West, *A Tale of the Times*, iii, pp. 387–8.

[57] Mary Robinson, *Thoughts on the Condition of Women, and on the Injustice of Mental Subordination* (London, Longman & Rees, 1799), pp. 90–1.

'Unsex'd' females

So the sorting of women writers into approved and disapproved was not primarily based upon the genres to which they contributed. In order to identify the criteria in play, let us turn to Polwhele's lists and attempt to assess why he judged each woman as he did. At the head of his list of the 'unsex'd' stands Mary Wollstonecraft. In her classic *Vindication of the Rights of Woman* of 1792 she called for women to have the same education as men, demanded access to professions such as medicine which were closed to them so that they might escape from economic dependence upon men, and even hinted that they might have the same political rights as men. She herself had already (1791) intervened in the political arena with her reply to Burke's *Reflections on the Revolution in France*, her *Vindication of the Rights of Men*, defending that revolution and its democratic principles against his attack. Even more radically, in her *Vindication of the Rights of Woman* she launched a comprehensive assault on the construction of women as weak, passive, mindless sexual objects, insisting that there was a single standard of excellence for both women and men.

Given the extent to which she anticipated modern 'equality' feminism, that kind of feminism which insists upon the essential equality and identity of the sexes in all but reproductive function, her classic of 1792 might have been expected to provoke an immediate and hostile response; in fact with one exception it did not.[58] It has been suggested that this was because the book was perceived as a conduct book and treatise on female education rather than a political manifesto; also it was difficult to attack in that it had a pervasive moral tone, and was insistent upon sexual chastity and the duties of motherhood. Furthermore, the philosophical grounding of her argument was explicitly Christian; we shall see over and over again that it was easier to get away with radical ideas in texts cast in a pious mould. Religious ideas gradually disappeared from Wollstonecraft's later work; in effect she threw down her shield. But more simply, the major reviews in 1792, such as the *Monthly Review* were Whiggish and progressive; the *Monthly* gave her reviews which were on balance favourable – of her novel *Mary* of 1788, her history of the French revolution of 1794 and her Scandinavian letters of 1796 as well as of her two Vindications – right up to her death in 1797.

A crusading conservative review was lacking. It was the perception of this lack which led to the foundation of the *British Critic* in 1793 and the *Anti-Jacobin*, after its first year the *Anti-Jacobin Review and Magazine*, in 1797. These were always hostile to Wollstonecraft. The *British Critic* gave her history of the French revolution a long review, accusing her of plagiarism and deploring her politics, and also waxing indignant at its sexual immoral-

---

[58] R. M. Janes, 'The reception of Mary Wollstonecraft's *A Vindication of the Rights of Woman*', *Journal of the History of Ideas*, 39:2 (1978), 293.

ity; for she had argued that a woman should not be condemned for leaving an unhappy marriage to seek solace in 'a more congenial and humane bosom'.[59] This was an augury of what was soon to come; for the heroine of Wollstonecraft's last, unfinished novel, *Maria, or, the Wrongs of Woman,* pursues precisely this course of adultery, and moreover in the final scene is depicted defending her conduct in a court of law. Wollstonecraft's grieving husband, William Godwin, published this fragment in 1798 together with a frank biography. He revealed that she had fallen in love with the artist Fuseli and had not thought this wrong, even though he was already married; that she had lived unmarried with Gilbert Imlay, borne his child, and twice attempted the sin of suicide when he was unfaithful to her; that she had lived with Godwin but 'We did not marry' until she became pregnant; and that in her last illness 'not one word of a religious cast fell from her lips'.[60] *Maria*, a much more radical work than the *Vindication of the Rights of Woman*, contains only one religious remark. Godwin also published her passionate letters to Imlay.

These revelations were the material that the conservative reviews, and Polwhele, needed, and the present-day reader can sense the glee with which they seized upon them; they could use them to discredit Wollstonecraft and all who agreed with her, and to demonstrate that democratic principles led to sexual immorality and defiance of God. They presented an entirely false image of her as lascivious and promiscuous:

> She lived in a state of prostitution with *two other men*, the last of whom became her husband, and published this history of her amours, or at least of as much of them as she thought fit to entrust him; for many still remain untold which, if faithfully related, would make a book, in comparison with which the Adventures of *Moll Flanders* would be a model of purity. ... A sensuality far too gross to be characterized by any mind less impure than her own breathes through her letters.[61]

Polwhele and the reviewers drew attention to the Kingsborough affair to demonstrate the evil influence of her principles. In 1787 Wollstonecraft had been governess to the daughters of the Kingsboroughs in Ireland. In 1797 one of her former charges eloped; her father shot her lover dead, but was acquitted of murder in the Irish House of Lords on grounds of self-defence.[62]

Even the hitherto friendly *Monthly Review* was turned against Wollstonecraft and her associates by these posthumous publications:

[59] *British Critic*, 6 (1795), 29–36.
[60] William Godwin, *Memoirs of the Author of* A Vindication of the Rights of Woman (London, J. Johnson, 1798), pp. 90, 107, 114, 127, 132–4, 154, 190.
[61] *Anti-Jacobin Review* (January 1800), 93.
[62] Polwhele, *Unsex'd Females*, p. 29; Claire Tomalin, *The Life and Death of Mary Wollstonecraft* (Harmondsworth, Penguin, 1977), pp. 292–3; Janet Todd, *Mary Wollstonecraft: A Revolutionary Life* (London, Weidenfeld & Nicolson, 2000), p. 104.

Not only the general reader, but the most judicious and reflecting part of mankind, will arraign the prudence and the utility of these memoirs. ... Blushes would suffuse the cheeks of most husbands, if they were *forced* to relate those anecdotes of their wives which Mr. Godwin voluntarily proclaims to the world. ... He neither looks to marriage with respect, nor to suicide with horror.[63]

In the context of the 1790s, it is difficult not to agree with the reviewer. To call Godwin's *Memoirs of the Author of a Vindication of the Rights of Woman* a miscalculation would be an understatement: it was a propaganda disaster of the first magnitude. The community which had hitherto supported Godwin, Wollstonecraft and their allies was to a large extent a dissenting community, above all unitarian;[64] enlightened Christians outside the established church, who wanted a political reform which would challenge the dominance of the aristocracy and the Church of England. Indeed the radical views on marriage of Godwin, Wollstonecraft and Hays grew out of dissenting culture, with its individualism, its suspicion of established institutions and its concern for sincerity and authenticity. In the context of such beliefs it could seem dishonest to one's spouse and untrue to oneself to continue to live in a loveless marriage. But most dissenters, intensely moralistic, were not yet ready for such inferences and such behaviour. Where sex and marriage were concerned, they were more in tune with the rising tide of evangelicalism and its call for moral reform. Admittedly, the *Monthly Review* criticized the evangelical Hannah More's *Strictures on the Modern System of Female Education* for the doctrine that a woman who had fallen from virtue's path, but had repented, should not be readmitted to 'public society': 'Must society be severe that Heaven may be merciful? Does Mrs. More believe the story of the woman taken in adultery to be genuine? If she does, can she think that our Saviour's conduct justifies the treatment which she recommends?' But the reviewer's endorsement of 'virtue' and 'repentance' marks a gulf between this and the more radical views of Godwin and Wollstonecraft.[65]

Second only as a target for the conservatives came the unitarian Mary Hays, a friend and associate of Wollstonecraft who published two loyal obituaries of her in the *Annual Necrology for 1797–8* and in the *Monthly*

[63] *Monthly Review*, 28 (1798), 321–4.

[64] Unitarianism came out of presbyterianism; it was a Christianity of the enlightenment, a rational Christianity. Unitarians were so called because they found the doctrine of the trinity – of three persons in one God – not sensible, and so they argued that there was but one God, and Christ was no more than a divinely inspired man. The leading lights of unitarianism, Drs Priestley and Price, were distinguished representatives of the English enlightenment.

[65] *Monthly Review*, 30 (1799), 412. The story of the woman taken in adultery is from the New Testament; Christ saved a woman who was about to be stoned to death, saying, 'He that is without sin among you, let him first cast a stone at her' (John, 8:7).

Magazine. Her *Letters and Essays, Moral and Miscellaneous* of 1793 was influenced and commented on by Wollstonecraft, and it and articles published in the *Monthly Magazine* echo Wollstonecraftian themes. Like Polwhele she notices the passage from Dyer's poem listing female advocates of liberty, and speculates that women writers are more consistently for progress than men because of their experience of domestic oppression, and because they are not corrupted by patronage or place.66 She escapes with only a few lines of censure in Polwhele's poem – he charges her with being flippant, cynical, irreligious and politically inflammatory. But the *British Critic* and the *Anti-Jacobin Review* evidently found her a tempting target. The latter took strong exception to her obituary of Wollstonecraft in the *Annual Necrology*, and homed in on what it saw as a defence of Wollstonecraft's sexual immorality. Hays was short and had a squint; the reviewer declared, 'There are some women to whom, though sophistry has given the souls of prostitutes, nature has denied the attractions of successful prostitutes; who, as their figures are too hideous to entice men, can only labour by their writings to debauch women'.67

The same review remarked that Hays was the writer of 'some miserable novels', and in fact it was her novels which drew most fire. Like Godwin's *Memoir* of his dead wife, they challenge sexual conventions in what must have appeared a shocking manner at the time. *Memoirs of Emma Courtney* of 1796 tells the story of a woman who falls in love and declares it to the object of her affections, thereby violating the standard maxim of the conduct books that a woman should modestly conceal or even repress her feelings until the man had made the first move. Emma Courtney sends her man a series of letters, demanding to know whether he reciprocates her feelings; they were in fact based upon letters which Hays had herself sent out of an unrequited passion to William Frend.

Conservatives would have been offended also by the philosophy and the politics. There are hostile remarks about the established church, constant intimations that existing society is all wrong and in need of radical reform, and that advancing reason must clear away outdated prejudices. There are criticisms of slavery, social inequality and war. Hays's allegiance to the 'jacobin' philosophy of Godwin, Holcroft and Helvetius is made explicit. Hays's *Victim of Prejudice* of 1799 is affected by the attacks upon its author; in her 'Advertisement' she protests that *Emma Courtney* has been misunderstood, and that she is wholly in favour of female chastity.68 But in some ways her second novel is more challenging than her first; the heroine is a victim, ostracized from society because she is the bastard daughter of a prostitute and herself the victim of a rape. The novel rewrites the plot of Richardson's

66 Hays, *Letters & Essays*, pp. 10–11.
67 *Anti-Jacobin Review* (January 1800), 94.
68 Mary Hays, *The Victim of Prejudice* (1799) (Peterborough, Ontario, Broadview Press, 1994), p. 1.

Clarissa. Richardson intended to put the blame for Clarissa's tragedy on her rapist, Lovelace, on her family who tried to pressure her into an uncongenial marriage, but also on Clarissa herself for her disobedience and imprudence.[69] Hays places the blame for her heroine's downfall squarely upon society, its institutions and attitudes, and it was this that the reviewers could not forgive.

'There is something like an imitation of Clarissa,' remarked the *Anti-Jacobin Review*, 'but how unlike the original!', and, referring to the name of the heroine, Mary Vincent, to Hays and Wollstonecraft and to the heroines of the latter's two novels, Mary and Maria, it declared, 'we are sick of Mary'. Of *Emma Courtney* the reviewer exploded, 'What stuff is here! – but a little more, and we have done with the filthy labour'.

> 'Individuality of affection,' she says, 'constitutes chastity;' or, in other words, the mistress is, in all respects, as honourable as the wife, provided she hath but one lover. If such a sentiment does not strike at the root of everything that is virtuous, that is praise-worthy, that is valuable, in the female character, we are at a loss to discover by what wickedness they are to fall.[70]

The *British Critic* was hostile to Hays's writings from the outset;[71] the *Monthly Review*, true to its liberal stance, did not attack her *Letters and Essays* and was largely favourable about *Emma Courtney*. But by the time it came to review *The Victim of Prejudice* the Wollstonecraft scandal had broken, and the novel was criticized and dismissed in half a page.[72]

An Appeal to the Men of Great Britain in Behalf of Women of 1798 has usually been attributed to Hays, in part on the basis of a statement by the socialist and feminist William Thompson in the 1820s.[73] Similarities of ideas, examples and turns of phrase make it almost certain that it is by her, but there are artful attempts at concealment. For example the author hints that she is a married woman who has never published on this subject before. Perhaps the anonymity is simply a response to the developing climate of anti-jacobin hostility; and perhaps it is in this light that we should understand the rhetorical strategy of this work, so different from her other writings. The tone is witty and ironic; the reader is led quietly along, and then little mines of subversive ideas are exploded when least expected. It is all very cleverly done; the modest and unassuming tone insinuates the subversive message. The *Appeal* insists on the intellectual equality and moral superiority of women, calls for better education, criticizes the oppression of the law and of

69 Zaczek, *Censored Sentiments*, pp. 17, 36–7, 97.

70 *Anti-Jacobin Review* (May 1799), 54–8.

71 *British Critic*, 1 (1793), 463.

72 *Monthly Review*, 31 (1800), 82.

73 Gina M. Luria accepts this attribution; *Mary Hays: a Critical Biography* (New York, New York University dissertation, 1972), p. 190; but Gary Kelly, *Women, Writing and Revolution* (Oxford, Oxford University Press, 1993) p. 113, opines that it may have been by Hays's sister Elizabeth, who had contributed to *Letters and Essays*.

husbands and calls for enhanced employment opportunities for women. Significantly, the *Anti-Jacobin Review* gave it a long and not unfriendly notice, agreeing with much of what it had to say about female abilities, education and employment. The reviewer insisted that its appeal was not based on a Paineite or Wollstonecraftian philosophy of rights, and concluded that it contained nothing 'offensive to the feelings of delicacy, nor injurious to the interests of religion and morality'.[74] Given that at this time the review's attacks on Hays were at their most virulent, perhaps this casts doubt upon Hays's authorship; but more likely the reviewer simply made a rather ludicrous mistake, falling into the trap set by Hays's carefully calculated rhetorical strategy. In either case, it is a first and interesting indication of the common ground between the 'feminists' and their critics.

The only other woman writer who was consistently attacked by the conservative reviews with a violence akin to that meted out to Wollstonecraft and Hays was Helen Maria Williams, before the 1790s a respected bluestocking, poet and novelist. Her novel *Julia* of 1790 was really a pre-revolutionary work, with no more than one poem celebrating the fall of the Bastille. It depicted an utterly virtuous and chaste heroine, with whom the critics could find no fault. In that year she went to France to witness the revolution for herself, and between 1790 and 1796 she published eight volumes of *Letters from France* describing its progress. They systematically write the history of the great events from a woman's point of view, concentrating on how the revolution affected women and the part they played in it. She welcomed the revolution in its early stages, and then with mounting horror went on to describe the cruelty and tyranny of the reign of terror. Her sympathies were moderate, Girondist – the Jacobins imprisoned her. Politically she was close to English Whiggism, and accordingly the *Monthly Review* always gave her favourable and usually lengthy notices:

> Those who may expect to find the political ideas of this ingenious and well-informed young lady changed by the personal inconveniencies that befel her, in consequence of her residence in France, will, on perusing these letters, be convinced that she is as much as ever a friend to the original principle of the French revolution – that rational and manly principle from which that people ought never to have departed.[75]

To the conservatives this was precisely her offence; Polwhele attacks her for turning from poetry to politics, and for becoming 'an intemperate advocate for Gallic licentiousness'.[76] To the *British Critic*, 'our author seems to carry her complacency for her adopted friends, beyond the bounds of moderation, or of reason'. To antijacobin reviewers, any criticism of the established order in Britain was deeply offensive: 'As usual, the French are all wise, generous,

[74] *Anti-Jacobin Review* (October 1800), 150–8.
[75] *Monthly Review*, 19 (1796), 337.
[76] Polwhele, *Unsex'd Females*, p. 19.

good, great, etc. etc. etc. and every other nation, her own in particular, contemptible in the balance'. A long and hostile review of Williams's *Tour in Switzerland* of 1798 surveyed her career and her decline from respectability, adding sexual to political charges. It revealed that she was living with John Hurford Stone, 'who is, we are told, a married man, and has a wife living in this country'.[77] The *Anti-Jacobin Review* gleefully took up the refrain.[78]

There is just one more prime target of the conservative reviews, though she could on occasion attract their commendation. She was attacked so persistently in part because she was a successful, high-profile writer. Certainly there was never any hint of sexual scandal about her. Charlotte Smith was a gentlewoman who fell on hard times. She married young, making what looked like a good match; but when her father-in-law died ten years later in 1776, his will was so incompetently drafted that it became marooned in chancery; final payment to Smith's children was not made until after her death. Meanwhile her husband proved an incompetent businessman and fell into debt; they separated in 1787 and Smith was left with nine children out of twelve pregnancies to support on her own. She kept her family going and successfully launched her children by writing – though in accordance with the law, her husband could still call upon her earnings. Her *Elegiac Sonnets and Other Poems* came out in seven expanding and successful editions between 1784 and 1797, and between 1788 and 1798 she published nine novels.[79]

In her novel *Desmond* of 1792, Smith wrote extensively about politics, commending the French revolution (her first novel of the 1790s, *Celestina*, took the same stance). The Whiggish *Monthly Review* was accordingly very much in favour, of this and indeed of most of her writings. By the time of *The Banished Man* in 1794, the revolution had been sullied by the terror and the execution of the king and queen; furthermore one of her daughters had married a French emigré, and Smith wrote critically about contemporary events in France. But in 1798 the *Monthly Review*, which had been slightly sarcastic about her 'recantation' in 1794, remarked of *The Young Philosopher* that, 'Mrs. Smith cannot claim the praise of consistency in her political opinions. In the volumes before us they are of the *democratic* cast, widely different from those of *The Banished Man*; – which were equally opposite to the sentiments of *Desmond*'.[80]

The *Monthly* was right about *The Young Philosopher*, wrong about *The Banished Man*; Smith's stance as a moderate reformer and defender of the French revolution in its first phase never wavered. Her political radicalism

[77] *British Critic*, 2 (1973), 251; 8 (1796), 321; 12 (1798), 24–9.

[78] *Anti-Jacobin Review* (May 1799), 55; (January 1800), 94.

[79] For Smith's life see Lorraine Fletcher, *Charlotte Smith: a Critical Biography* (London, Macmillan, 1998).

[80] *Monthly Review*, 28 (1799), 346.

expressed itself, grumblingly and subversively, about England too, and it was no doubt this that most offended conservatives. She takes a cynical view of British society, and indeed of human nature. The concentrated essence of her venom is reserved for attorneys, at whose hands she had suffered; in her novels they are gothically wicked, more wicked than Robespierre and Danton,[81] with names of Dickensian vividness – Vampyre, Cancer, Loadsworth, Sir Appulby Gorges.

Clergymen come off badly too; they drink, gluttonize and hunt, they write conservative polemics in the hope of preferment, they have little feeling for the misery of the poor. A pure example of the type is the Rev. Philibert Hughson, Rector of Higginton cum Sillingbourn in *Montalbert*, ugly, vulgar, extravagant, in debt. The heroine of this novel is a bastard, and her mother's adultery is condoned by the author; she was married in the sight of God to the man she loved. There are hostile portraits of English peers, descended from 'heroes from whom [they] had so woefully degenerated'.[82] Smith is frequently unpatriotic, criticizes war, the law which imprisons debtors, and corrupt, antidemocratic politics. She doubts whether England is a land of liberty. *The Young Philosopher* is a thoroughly political novel, a successor to *Desmond* but reflecting the changed political climate of the late 1790s, systematically replying to the charges of the antijacobin press. There is a response to Burke's attack on the French revolution, a tribute to Wollstonecraft and a long defence of the British 'jacobins'; they are reformers not revolutionaries, and they are not advocates of sexual libertinism. It is impossible not to read one of the most unpleasant characters as a critique of Hannah More: Mrs Crewkherne is a conservative, methodistical bluestocking, fanatically prudish and interfering, a woman in whom the milk of Christian kindness has turned to gall. Throughout the novel, America is held up as freer and more equal than Britain and at the end the heroes and heroines emigrate there, disgusted by the persecution of political progressives. Clearly the attacks on *Desmond* and more generally on 'unsex'd females' completely failed to muzzle Smith.

The *British Critic* was even more divided about Smith than the *Monthly Review*. Its review of *The Banished Man* concludes:

> We must not close this article without congratulating the lovers of their king and constitution, in the acquisition of an associate like Mrs. Charlotte Smith. . . . She makes full atonement by the virtues of the Banished Man, for the errors of Desmond. Such a convert, gained by fair conviction, is a valuable prize to the commonwealth.[83]

But in this and other reviews, the *British Critic* objected to Smith's egotism in parading her private woes to all the world. She moved far too easily

---

[81] Smith, *Marchmont*, iv, p. 411.
[82] Charlotte Smith, *Celestina* (London, T. Cadell, 1791), i, p. 78.
[83] *British Critic*, 4 (1794), 623.

from lament about her own misfortunes, to complaint about the lot of the poor and about British institutions: 'But let us ask this author, are these the times, in which any one, who is a friend either to the rich or the poor, will *exaggerate* the hardships of the latter?'[84] Even the *Monthly Review* disliked the way she abused lawyers.[85] The *Anti-Jacobin Review*, though it insisted that it did not wish to condemn all of Smith's productions,[86] took the *British Critic*'s complaints much further; indeed its reviewer Robert Bisset seems to have found Smith particularly objectionable. She was an egotistical republican and a rank democrat, she delighted in abusing England and it was her wifely duty to conceal her husband's foibles and faults, not to blazen them abroad.[87] Polwhele himself was divided about Smith; unreservedly enthusiastic about her poetry, he complained, 'But why does she suffer her mind to be infected with the Gallic mania? I hope, ere this, she is completely recovered from a disorder, of which, indeed, I observed only a few slight symptoms'.[88]

It is an intriguing question why antijacobin polemic did not make more of Mary Robinson; for the charge of sexual immorality could have been levelled at her with far more justice than at Wollstonecraft, Hays or Williams. A woman of remarkable beauty, she had been an actress and fashion icon who came to public prominence when, a married woman and a mother, she had a year-long affair with the Prince of Wales. After a brief affair with Charles James Fox she lived with Banastre Tarleton and may have conducted other affairs simultaneously. She suffered partial and progressive paralysis for several years before her death, which may have been the consequence of syphilis.[89] But Polwhele, who praises her poetry, makes no more than a veiled allusion, calling on Robinson 'to think seriously of future retribution [i.e. Divine, after death]; and to communicate to the world, a recantation of errors that originated in levity, and have been nursed by pleasure!'[90] And the *Anti-Jacobin Review* goes no further than to refer obliquely to her fringe membership of the fast Whig set around Charles James Fox.

> Amidst her tragedy the author does not forget her politics. A very worthless Peer (Lord Arcot) is introduced as a specimen of the peerage in general; as the very worthless clergyman, Somerton, is represented as a sample of the Clergy. Though we cannot coincide in her reasoning, that because there are wicked Lords, or Clergymen, the majority of those orders are bad, yet we think it not unnatural for the author to have concluded so, as, perhaps, those Peers, or

84 *Ibid.*, 3 (1794), 679; 10 (1797), 379.
85 *Monthly Review*, 28 (1799), 346–7.
86 *Anti-Jacobin Review* (August 1799), 422.
87 *Ibid.* (August 1798), 187–90.
88 Polwhele, *Unsex'd Females*, p. 18.
89 A good modern biography of Robinson is lacking: see Robert D. Bass, *The Green Dragoon. The Lives of Banastre Tarleton and Mary Robinson* (London, Alvin Redman, 1957).
90 Polwhele, *Unsex'd Females*, p. 17.

Churchmen, who she might have an opportunity of intimately knowing, were not the best and most exemplary of mankind.[91]

Why no more than these hints, when the charges against Wollstonecraft, Hays and Williams are so blatant and crude? We may speculate that it was because Robinson did not in fact violate a sexual code. She became the mistress of aristocratic men, but then, it was tacitly accepted in their circle that such men would have mistresses. Though in her novels she occasionally paints sympathetic portraits of 'fallen' women, she was careful never to deliver an *explicit* critique of the *institution* of marriage.

Robinson was a prolific poet whose reputation, not as high as that of Smith or Seward, was nevertheless considerable.[92] Both the *Monthly Review* and the *British Critic* gave her poetry favourable or mixed notices. She wrote in several styles; her 'Della Cruscan' poems drew criticism for their inflated, artificial language. She wrote seven rather racy novels for money between 1792 and 1799; these too sometimes received favourable or mixed, occasionally long reviews, even in the antijacobin publications, though no one thought she was in the same league as Burney, Radcliffe or even Smith. Robinson wrote good comic scenes of a rather theatrical kind, with vivid dialogue and robust satire of high life, reminiscent of the prints of Gillray or Rowlandson. After her first, all of her novels have something to say about contemporary politics, and they all have a women's agenda, especially in relation to sex as we shall see. She defended the French revolution but not its later excesses, and she was careful to praise the British constitution. Her last novel, *The Natural Daughter*, contains fulsome tributes to the Duchess of Devonshire. This implicitly aligned her with the Foxite Whigs who had welcomed the French revolution and who remained enthusiastic for reform. Given the Duchess's notoriety, it was also a gesture of defiance against those antijacobins who sought to associate progressive politics with aristocratic debauchery.

In her last years she mixed with the radicals around the publisher Joseph Johnson, and became friendly with Godwin and Wollstonecraft. One of the minor heroes in *Walsingham*, the benevolent and progressive-minded Mr. Optic, is surely modelled on Godwin. Radical opinions became more overt in her novels, and the antijacobins grew more hostile to her. As the quotation above illustrates, they became increasingly displeased with her satires on the establishment and ruling classes, and her calls for political and social reform.

91 *Anti-Jacobin Review* (December 1798), 42; (July 1798), 163.
92 Present-day critics of the male canon have rediscovered her – see Stuart Curran, 'Romantic poetry: The I altered', in Anne K. Mellor (ed.), *Romanticism and Feminism* (Bloomington & Indianapolis, Indiana University Press, 1988); 'Mary Robinson's *Lyrical Tales* in context', in Carol Shiner Wilson & Joel Hafner (eds), *Re-visioning Romanticism: British Women Writers, 1776–1837* (Philadelphia, University of Philadelphia Press, 1994); Jerome McGann, *The Poetics of Sensibility: A Revolution in Literary Style* (Oxford, Oxford University Press, 1996).

Her novel *The False Friend* of 1799 contains Wollstonecraftian, even feminist passages about the rights and equality of women. But the *Anti-Jacobin Review* objected rather to its excesses of sensibility, all too likely to lead women to the concubinage, profligacy and attempted suicide of a Wollstonecraft: 'We doubt not, that even Newgate has considerable supplies from the *victims of sensibility*; or, in other words, from those who are propelled by present impulse instead of being guided by duty'.[93] *The Natural Daughter* drew the wrath of the *British Critic* for its heroine, 'a decidedly flippant female, apparently of the Woolstonecraft School'.

> Through the whole work, during all the vicissitudes of its heroine, we meet with no sentiment of religion, nor any moral derived from it; and the character of Morley seems to have been conceived purposely to show that an attention to religious duties, a regard for the subordinations of society, and a regular and decent conduct, are to be considered only as a mask for consummate vice. . . .
> It is of little use to lament or censure the French revolution, if the morals and manners which tended to produce it, are inculcated and held up for imitation.[94]

This novel has all the appearance of a veiled defence of Wollstonecraft's life. The secondary heroine, Mrs Sedgley, enters into a 'republican marriage' in Paris in order to avoid imprisonment and perhaps death, just as Wollstonecraft did; like Wollstonecraft, she bears a bastard child; like Wollstonecraft too she is in love with the man she 'marries' but is betrayed by him. The drift of the novel is to defend her as a wronged and indeed heroic woman – at the end she is reinstated with her aristocratic family. The man who betrayed her, Morley, the villain of the piece, is indeed depicted as a consummate hypocrite, a sexual libertine who hides behind a parade of propriety, a stickler for religious observances but uncharitable towards the poor, and a defender of the supremacy of husbands.

The remark at the end of the quotation from the *British Critic*, to the effect that Robinson censured the French revolution, suggests a further reason why she was not more attacked, or attacked earlier; she had in fact published a poem, *Monody to the Memory of the Late Queen of France*, in 1793, lamenting the execution of Marie Antoinette. Polwhele indeed applies Burke's celebrated words about Marie Antoinette to Robinson: 'I have seen her, "glittering like the morning-star, full of life, and splendor and joy!" Such, and more glorious, may I meet her again, when the just "shall shine forth as the brightness of the firmament, and as the stars for ever and ever!"'[95] Evidently there was a glamour and a charisma about Robinson, which to some extent protected her, the opposite to the situation of Hays whose plainness was gleefully exploited by her critics. But by 1800 the *Anti-Jacobin*

93 *Anti-Jacobin Review* (April 1799), 40.
94 *British Critic*, 16 (1800), 321.
95 Polwhele, *Unsex'd Females*, pp. 17–18; Edmund Burke, *Reflections on the Revolution in France* (1790) (Letchworth, Everyman, 1910), p. 73.

Review was lumping 'the trash of Mrs. Robinson' together with other 'jacobin' novels.[96]

Robinson's claim to be one of the few clear feminists of this period, along with Wollstonecraft and Hays, rests principally upon her *Letter to the Women of England on the Injustice of Mental Subordination*, published in 1799 under the name 'Anne Frances Randall', then almost immediately in a second edition as *Thoughts on the Condition of Women and on the Injustice of Mental Subordination* under her own name. It is a strong and witty production, influenced by Williams's *Letters from France*, and its main concern is to assert the intellectual equality of women, to call for better education for them and to insist that anything men can do, they can do too (including fighting). Robinson defiantly celebrates Wollstonecraft – surely a brave thing to do in the aftermath of Godwin's biography – and declares herself a disciple, 'For it requires a *legion of Wollstonecrafts* to undermine the poisons of prejudice and malevolence'.[97] The *Anti-Jacobin Review* evidently thought that a few quotations without comment were enough to condemn it, but it got off quite lightly in the *Monthly Review* and the *British Critic*, neither of which was inclined to dissent from its celebration of female intellect, responding with banter to its light and lively tone. Robinson had approvingly told the story of a woman who, the day before her wedding, was asked by her fiancé to anticipate the delights of the wedding night – why bother to wait? Incensed by this affront to her honour, she challenged him to a duel and shot him dead. The *Monthly Review* concluded: 'We forbear any further remarks on this vigorous and impatient writer; lest we should have occasion to exclaim, with the gentleman who was knocked down by an uncomplying mistress; "Those frowns are cruel, but that *fist* is death!"'[98]

Anna Laetitia Barbauld was an acclaimed poet, admired by Polwhele in that capacity, and a distinguished literary critic. She was also a unitarian who wrote political pamphlets calling for the repeal of the Test and Corporation Acts which deprived dissenters of certain civic rights, and more generally for political reform. As a moderate reformer, she was uniformly praised by the *Monthly Review*.[99] As a reformer who intervened in politics and religion, she was bound to attract the suspicions of the antijacobins. She published *Remarks on Mr. Gilbert Wakefield's Enquiry into the Expediency and Propriety of Public or Social Worship* (1792) and pamphlets with titles like those of published sermons, e.g., *Reasons for National Penitance, recommended for the Fast* (1794). A similar title, *Sins of Government, Sins of the Nation; or, a Discourse for the Fast appointed on April 19, 1793* greatly

96 *Anti-Jacobin Review* (February 1800), 152.
97 Robinson, *Thoughts*, p. 2.
98 *Monthly Review*, 29 (1799), 478; *British Critic*, 14 (1799), 682; *Anti-Jacobin Review* (June 1799), 144–6.
99 *Monthly Review*, 6 (1791), 226; 8 (1792), 429–31; 11 (1793), 237–40; 19 (1796), 26–8.

provoked the *British Critic*: 'Here we have *organ*, and *national will*, and all the jargon of French republicanism; and on this alone, stands all the argument of this discourse. Deny this, and the whole is blank paper, or worse than that, paper misused'. The reviewer rudely refers to her as a 'Fairy Queen', a 'politico-theological lady', 'this gallicised lady [attached to] the principles of that anarchical system'. The bitterness of this attack should not surprise; the *British Critic* had been founded by a group of Tory churchmen who were bound to be offended by Barbauld's scathing remarks about the established church.[100]

Ann Jebb, also a unitarian, gets into Polwhele's list of 'unsex'd females' on the same grounds. Like Barbauld, the reforms she called for were political and religious, not to do with gender; for this reason these two writers will not be discussed later in this book. She was no doubt offensive to Tories, not only for her opinions and because she dared to write about politics and religion, but also because she wrote very effective propaganda. Her *Two-penny worth of truth for a penny; or a true state of facts: with an apology for Tom Bull in a letter to Brother John* is a pamphlet with similar qualities to those of Hannah More on the Tory side. The pamphlet is mildly republican, and an attack on the 'church-and-king' mobs which had terrorized dissenters and political reformers in Birmingham and elsewhere.[101] Jebb was less well known than Barbauld, and she escaped the notice of the antijacobin reviews.

So did Catharine Macaulay Graham, very briefly mentioned by Polwhele, if we except the correspondence about her tearing of Tory pages in the British Museum. The reason she was not attacked in 1790s reviews is simple: she died in 1790.[102] Two chapters in her *Letters on Education* anticipate some of Wollstonecraft's themes, such as the artificial construction of a disempowering femininity and the possibility and desirability of women developing the same intellectual and moral qualities as the best men.[103] Macaulay had attracted some disapproval by marrying William Graham when she was a comfortably-off 47-year-old widow and he was only 21 and of limited means; such conduct suggested more passion than was thought appropriate in a modest woman. But it is doubtful whether it was these gender issues that earned her a place in Polwhele's list. She was from the well-heeled Whig mercantile gentry,[104] a bluestocking and a noted republican; she

100 *British Critic*, 2 (1793), 81–5. For the foundation of the review, see Roper, *Reviewing before the* Edinburgh, p. 23.

101 Ann Jebb, *Two-Penny Worth of Truth for a Penny; or a True State of Facts: with an Apology for Tom Bull in a Letter to Brother John* , 2nd edn. (London, 1793).

102 For Macaulay Graham's biography see Bridget Hill, *The Republican Virago: the Life and Times of Catharine Macaulay, Historian* (Oxford, Oxford University Press, 1992).

103 Macaulay Graham, *Letters on Education*, pp. 203–15.

104 J. G. A. Pocock, 'Catharine Macaulay: patriot historian', in Hilda L. Smith (ed.), *Women Writers and the Early Modern British Political Tradition* (Cambridge, Cambridge University Press, 1998), p. 248.

wrote a history of England under the Stuarts from the point of view of the good old parliamentary, antimonarchist cause. And just before her death, she published an effective reply, patently and defiantly 'unsex'd' in its assertively masculine voice, to Burke's *Reflections on the Revolution in France*. A target because of her politics, her *Letters on Education* were to some extent protected by their strong religious message.

There remains Ann Yearsley, a milkwoman and labourer's wife who became noted as a poet 'who ... warbled, Nature's child, / Midst twilight dews, her minstrel ditties wild'. Her political sentiments, her 'Gallic wanderings', were suspect to Polwhele; but it seems that her main offence was uppitiness and a lack of the deference and gratitude thought appropriate in a woman from the lower echelons of society who had been noticed and assisted by her betters. Her first publications were aided by Hannah More, who tried to manage her; but Yearsley was not willing to remain More's humble dependant, and a public quarrel ensued.[105]

That completes Polwhele's list of 'unsex'd females'; would other Tory writers have added to it? A survey of the reviews demonstrates that Polwhele had selected all of the principal targets; but some lesser ones could have been added if he had been aiming at completeness. For example, the *Anti-Jacobin Review* surmised that *Geraldina: a Novel* of 1798 was by a woman:

> The leading object of the work is, to shew, that if a woman has been compelled, or even induced, to sacrifice her affections to the commands or wishes of a parent, she may, without deviating from the most perfect virtue, leave the husband to whom she has plighted her faith, and betake herself to the arms of a favourite man. This is ... perfectly consistent with the opinions of Mrs. Woolstonecroft [*sic*].
>
> The author, now and then, aims at political discussion, and introduces much hacknied cant on the distresses of the poor, distresses of which a great part exist in the invention only of the abler Jacobins.[106]

Perhaps it would be difficult to list an anonymous, indeed speculatively female, author among the 'unsex'd'. A similar anonymity protected Eliza Fenwick, another member of the Godwin–Wollstonecraft circle, who in 1795 published her novel *Secresy; or, The Ruin on the Rock* 'By a Woman'. The *British Critic* thought it 'One of the wildest romances we have met with',[107] and it is easy to see why. The novel depicts the tragic consequences of the power of parents and guardians over the marital choices of women, and the heroine gives herself to the man she loves, judging that they are married in the eyes of heaven.

That Elizabeth Inchbald escaped Polwhele's list is, however, surprising. In a footnote the *Anti-Jacobin Review* excoriated 'that most impudent,

---

[105] Polwhele, *Unsex'd Females*, pp. 19–20.
[106] *Anti-Jacobin Review* (December 1798), 668–9.
[107] *British Critic*, 6 (1795), 545.

malignant, and audacious heap of absurdity by Mrs. Inchbald, called "Nature and Art" ... we are compelled to leave her in possession of the rank she has chosen for herself, *the scavenger of democracy*'.[108] The *British Critic* found *Nature and Art* (1796) thoroughly objectionable because it exhibited 'the errors or weaknesses of those in exalted rank, in the most odious and exaggerated representations', thereby giving encouragement to social revolt.[109] It is easy to see why the reviews were so offended. Inchbald writes explicitly from the point of view of the unprivileged; unusually for novels of the period, the happy ending does not leave the hero and heroine ennobled, or living in genteel affluence. The corrupting effects of inequality of wealth and status are mocked with gentle irony. Only the poor are good: all members of the upper classes and the church are depicted in an unfavourable light. The most striking episode is the story of Hannah Primrose, an innocent country girl seduced and abandoned by William Norwynne, driven from the village into prostitution and eventually condemned to death for forgery by Norwynne, now a judge. The tendency of the novel is to blame William, not Hannah, and also the cruel unforgivingness of a society which could require 'fallen' women to do penance in public in church, clad in a white sheet.

But though she was a member of the Godwin–Wollstonecraft circle, Inchbald had hitherto given no offence. In spite of a speech impediment, she had had a moderately successful career as an actress, and was even more successful as a playwright. Women of the theatre had a bad reputation, but Inchbald, like Mrs Siddons, in spite of outstanding beauty which brought her many admirers, was scrupulously careful of hers. When Wollstonecraft married Godwin, thereby revealing to the world that she had not after all been married to Imlay, both Siddons and Inchbald dropped her. Inchbald was cautious; the second edition of *Nature and Art* of 1797 toned down the ironic ending of the first of 1796, which suggested that professional men and politicians would not be permitted to enter the kingdom of heaven. Even Inchbald's famous translation of Kotzebue's *Lovers' Vows*, the improper play in *Mansfield Park*, received a wholly favourable review in the *British Critic*.[110] *Nature and Art* was an important 'jacobin' novel: but her *Simple Story* of 1791 is even more interesting as the work of a woman writing about women.

How then should we categorize the 'unsex'd females'? What was it about all of them that Polwhele and the conservative reviews so much disliked? As we have seen it was not 'feminism' because not all of them were attacked for opinions meriting that appellation. Primarily it was their support for progressive politics. They all of them criticized British social, political and religious institutions, or called for reform, or praised certain aspects of the French revolution. Secondarily, and in the case of the major targets, Wollstonecraft,

[108] *Anti-Jacobin Review* (February 1800), 152.
[109] *British Critic*, 7 (1796), 261–5.
[110] *Ibid.*, 12 (1798), 598–600.

Hays and Williams, it was perceived sexual immorality and disregard for or criticism of the conventions of marital fidelity and female chastity. The anti-jacobins ferociously defended the authority of parents over their daughters, and the sanctity and permanence of the marriage bond. They insisted upon that which Wollstonecraft and her followers rejected: that chastity was the principal index of female honour and worth. If measured by the heat of the rhetoric, this was their main concern, but one cannot help feeling that their passion about this was overdetermined and partly strategic; sexual immorality was the perfect stick with which to beat jacobin women. Other 'feminist' issues attracted much less attention. Of course the conservatives did not agree that women should have political rights, and they did not think gender differences should be completely blurred. But they did not altogether dissent from the views that the intellectual abilities of women had been insufficiently recognized in the past, that women could shine in all or most fields of intellectual endeavour, that they should be better educated and should have more employment opportunities. If at times they suggested that women should not write, or should not write on certain subjects, it is difficult not to regard such protestations as insincere. When women expressed 'correct' opinions, the conservatives were perfectly happy for them to write about religion, politics and society, as we shall see as we turn to Polwhele's list of 'proper' women writers.

'Proper' women writers

At the end and as the culmination of the list of the 'proper' stands Hannah More, evangelical anglican associated with William Wilberforce, bluestocking, playwright, novelist and poet. She also wrote an educational treatise and many writings dealing with contemporary social problems. The most famous of the last were her *Cheap Repository Tracts*, written as propaganda against the spread of French revolutionary ideas to Britain in a lively and popular style, aimed at a mass audience. In them for example working men discuss the issues of the day, and of course the church-and-king man persuades the incipient radical to see sense every time. They are socially conservative too, advising common people not to aspire to rise above their station, and teaching servants not to lie, or gossip about their employers, or cheat them, or leave them for better-paid jobs, or become saucy and familiar. Poachers of course come to a bad end. The tracts were enormously successful, according to the reviews selling two million copies.[111] Polwhele esteems her 'as a character, in all points, diametrically opposite to Miss Wollstonecraft', and praises her genius and literary attainments.[112] The *British Critic* called her tracts 'the most benevolent and judicious undertak-

[111] *British Critic*, 7 (1796), 569.
[112] Polwhele, *Unsex'd Females*, pp. 35–6.

ing. ... Most heartily do we wish continuance of success to this patriotic plan',[113] and remarked of her *Strictures on Female Education* that 'To the female *Illuminism* of Mrs. Wollstonecraft, and her disciples, it forms a striking and glorious contrast'.[114]

An antijacobin, then, and at first sight an antifeminist. But in fact More shares important common ground with Polwhele's 'unsex'd' females. For example she insists that at the profoundest level men and women are equal, because the immortal soul, the divine part in each human being, is unsexed. In language strongly reminiscent of Wollstonecraft she criticizes a degrading construction of femininity as weak and shallow, and calls for better, more serious education for women. Implicitly she repudiates the notion that women are primarily sex objects for the use of men.[115] Obviously she has sharp disagreements with the 'unsex'd'. More defends the gender difference, in terms both of selfhood and of spheres of activity. She wishes to raise the status of women, and implicitly to increase their social influence, but these advances are to be firmly grounded in the domestic role. Nevertheless, from the bastion of domestic femininity, More can launch forays into territory which, if not political in name, is so in reality – for example, her involvement in the campaign for the abolition of the slave trade.

Do the contemporary reviews suggest that there was any recognition of More as a woman's advocate in this sense? Certainly she was a controversial figure. As might be expected, the Whiggish *Monthly Review*, in a largely favourable review of her *Strictures*, did have words of criticism – of her harshness towards fallen women as we have seen, and more generally of her narrow, methodistical religiosity. But the reviewer was very much in agreement with her attacks on the dissipation of high society.[116] To criticize high society was to come close to that 'knocking' attitude which conservative reviews found so subversive in 'jacobin' writers; and it may be that the *Anti-Jacobin Review* felt she was guilty of class prejudice when it called upon her to turn her attention to the middle classes next. This review of her *Strictures*, though full of praise, took issue with her interpretation of St Paul's epistle. More was writing about religion, and the *Anti-Jacobin Review* was not entirely pleased.[117] Though as we have seen the *British Critic* saw More as a valuable ally, its review of the *Strictures* contains a revealing criticism:

> The first chapter treats on the subject of female influence. Here perhaps it may be contended, that the writer extends her position somewhat too far; the fact perhaps is, that the female character derives its features and colours from that of the male, rather than the contrary.[118]

113 *British Critic*, 7 (1796), 569.
114 *Ibid.*, 13 (1799), iv.
115 More, *Strictures*, i, pp. 66, 163ff., ii, pp. 9, 30.
116 *Monthly Review*, 30 (1799), 411–12.
117 *Anti-Jacobin Review* (October 1799), 190–9.
118 *British Critic*, 13 (1799), 644.

More's lack of soundness from a conservative point of view was most clearly revealed by the Blagdon controversy of 1801–2. The curate of Blagdon accused the master of More's Sunday school in the village of being a methodist, and her schools of promoting subversion against the established church and the constitution.[119] More was viciously and repeatedly attacked in the *Anti-Jacobin Review* for her religious and political transgressions. But the *British Critic* continued to defend her, and in due course the *Anti-Jacobin Review* reinstated her in its pantheon of 'proper' women writers. What the incident reveals is a fuzziness in the boundary line dividing 'unsex'd' from 'proper' females.

Polwhele judged Frances Burney the finest of all novelists, and the *British Critic* gave *Camilla* a long and enthusiastic review. Burney was a conservative who never aligned herself with 'unsex'd females'. She does depict worthless aristocrats, but carefully balances them with worthy ones, insisting that it is more difficult and therefore more praiseworthy to be virtuous amidst the temptations of high life. The two clergymen in her cast list are perfectly admirable. Ann Radcliffe's novels received long and enthusiastic reviews in the *Monthly Review* and the *British Critic*; she was judged to be the queen of the Gothic romance, and the reviewers, like Polwhele, referred to her as a 'genius'. The *British Critic* thought that *The Mysteries of Udolpho* 'inculcates the purest morality'.[120] Her own politics – or at least her husband's – were mildly progressive, but are barely evident in her romances. Polwhele thought that Anna Seward was the first among the British female poets, and that her name would be immortalized by her works. Seward, the 'swan of Lichfield', was a bluestocking who lived most of her life in the Bishop's palace in the cathedral close. The *Anti-Jacobin Review*, comparing her sonnets with Charlotte Smith's, thought that the latter moaned too much: 'we scruple not to adjudge the palm of poetic genius to the delightful muse of Litchfield'.[121]

Would contemporary conservatives have thought that Polwhele had provided a complete list of significant, 'proper' female writers? According to the *British Critic*, 'In speaking of females who do honour to their sex, by their talents, the author might easily have increased the number. Mrs. Trimmer certainly should not have been omitted.'[122] Mrs Trimmer had provided an inspiration for Hannah More's philanthropic and educational work among the poor, being a leading advocate of Sunday schools. But who else could have increased the number? The *British Critic* would surely have added Jane West, who published three novels in the 1790s; moreover, 'we are assured that, though she writes so much, her domestic duties suffer no

---

119 Beth Fowkes Tobin, *Superintending the Poor: Charitable Ladies and Paternal Landlords in British Fiction, 1770–1860* (New Haven, Yale University Press, 1993), pp. 110–11.
120 *British Critic*, 4 (1794), 110.
121 *Anti-Jacobin Review* (November 1799), 330.
122 *British Critic*, 14 (1799), 71.

kind of neglect'.[123] Significantly, the *Monthly Review* criticised her *Tale of the Times* for killing off a repentant fallen woman; here was a place where the battle lines were drawn between reformers and conservatives.[124] West did not immediately step forward as an antijacobin champion; her three novels track the rising tide of conservatism. *The Advantages of Education* of 1793 was not obviously antijacobin, or concerned with 'unsex'd' females. It was committed to down-to-earth sober realism, in response to the extravagant unreality of popular novels. It was conservative in its relentless emphasis on traditional and Christian virtues, and in its acceptance of class distinctions; like Hannah More, West insisted that different stations in society bring different duties. It was careful to rebut the charge of being anti-aristocratic, but in fact good aristocrats are conspicuous by their absence. *A Gossip's Story* of 1796 was a 'sense and sensibility' novel; the heroine of excessive sensibility comes unstuck, though there is no suggestion here that sensibility has any tendency to lead her into sexual impropriety. The novel was written before the breaking of the Wollstonecraft scandal, that crucial event which enabled the antijacobins to project an imbrication of radical politics, sensibility and sexual immorality.

This cluster had come together in West's full-dress explicitly antijacobin novel of 1799, her *Tale of the Times*. The political agenda is clearly in evidence; lack of respect for female chastity and filial obedience is explicitly connected with revolution and national ruin. 'Democratic' principles are caricatured, and there is a monstrous jacobin villain, Fitzosborne, who destroys the heroine Geraldine. But even in this novel the distance between West and the 'unsex'd' females should not be exaggerated, and the differences misconceived; on women, as opposed to general politics, it would be difficult to put a cigarette paper between this and the *Vindication of the Rights of Woman*, between West and Wollstonecraft while the latter still rested her argument upon Christian foundations. For Geraldine is ruined, not because she is politically radical, or irreligious, or unchaste; she falls because of deficiencies in her education and strength of mind. The novel is politically conservative, but mildly socially progressive in its hostility to snobbery and over-rigid social distinctions, its critique of the privileged who abdicate from their responsibilities towards the poor, its implied critique of primogeniture and its support for 'the cause of real candour, true philosophy, and judicious liberality'.[125]

By 1800, when she published her *Memoirs of Modern Philosophers*, the *Anti-Jacobin Review* would certainly have added Eliza Hamilton, for her attack on Mary Hays and on 'the voluptuous dogmas of Mary Godwin'; Hamilton 'deserves the honour of being classed with the most unexceptionable female writer of the times ... Hannah More'.[126] But her work of 1796,

123 *Ibid.*, 13 (1799), xvi.
124 *Monthly Review*, 29 (1799), 90.
125 West, *Tale of the Times*, ii, p. 386.
126 *Anti-Jacobin Review* (December 1800), 374, 376.

her *Translations of the Letters of a Hindoo Rajah*, did not immediately give her a reputation as a scourge of the 'unsex'd females'. Her book is in the style of Montesquieu's *Persian Letters* – a spoof account of the observations of an outsider on British society, whose naive remarks ironically expose its absurdities. *Hindoo Rajah* in fact shares a great deal of common ground with 'unsex'd females'; there are attacks on political corruption, the game laws, impressment into the armed forces, the failure of the rich to care for the poor, the prevailing and disabling construction of femininity, and the doctrine that women should receive a less strenuous education than men. So how did Hamilton escape being lumped together with the 'unsex'd'? The ironic mode is a good defence, a well-chosen rhetorical strategy; the ironic is always more difficult to attack than the earnest. Hamilton is also protected by where she comes from; like Hannah More she is devastatingly critical of existing society and manners, but from a strong and pervasive Christian standpoint. Anyone who attacked Hamilton would run the risk of appearing to attack Christianity itself. But above all, Hamilton has other targets against which conservatives would have welcomed her darts. She satirizes women who affect a masculine style, or who arrogantly parade their learning, or who exhibit an excessive, narcissistic sensibility. She targets 'jacobin' critiques of marriage and the tolerance of suicide in novels. And she takes on 'jacobin' philosophy, or rather a caricature of progressive ideas, which she depicts as atheistic and morally relativistic. There is a delightful parody of extreme Godwinian environmentalism; in order to demonstrate that nurture is all-powerful over nature, the philosophers set up a sparrow hive wherein to condition young sparrows to make honey like bees. The fledglings are all found dead and stinking in the bottom of the hive.

Perhaps Maria Edgeworth too would have been included after her publication of *Belinda* in 1801, but her role as a champion of traditional family values was less in evidence in the 1790s when her writing career was in its early stages. Nevertheless both the *Monthly Review* and the *British Critic* praised her anonymously published *Letters for Literary Ladies*, in which she explicitly distanced herself from Wollstonecraft and her followers while calling, like Wollstonecraft, for better education and a more serious and dignified construction of femininity. But the *British Critic* took strong exception to *Practical Education*, which she wrote jointly with her father: 'Here, readers, is education *à-la-mode*, in the true style of modern Philosophy; nearly 800 quarto pages on *practical Education*, and not a word on God, Religion, Christianity'.[127]

It is clear, then, that male antijacobin writers could call upon a considerable cohort of female allies. It is clear also that by the end of the decade the voice of the Wollstonecraftian tendency had become muted. But this was not because all of the 'unsex'd' females had been terrorized into silence by

[127] *British Critic*, 15 (1800), 210.

antijacobin propaganda. Wollstonecraft died before the storm broke over her reputation. It was also the Grim Reaper who gave the quietus to Macaulay Graham and to Robinson, who continued to defend both the ideas and the life of Wollstonecraft to the end. Smith's last novel was as radical as *Desmond*, and she stopped writing because of illness, and because a partial settlement of her father-in-law's will removed the pressure of financial necessity. Hays adapted her rhetorical strategy so as to put radical ideas across in greater safety. More intriguingly, as has already been suggested, the female allies of the antijacobins, the approved, 'proper' female writers such as More, West, Hamilton and Edgeworth, continued to promote women's issues. For in spite of Polwhele's separation of sheep from goats, they shared much common ground with 'unsex'd' females on such matters as the intellectual capacities of women, their education and their social role.

2

Our narratives about them

The previous chapter was concerned with 1790s opinions about women writers. This chapter will survey the perspectives of recent academic writing. Over this territory there is considerable debate and disagreement. So first, in order to get a firm grip on the debate, it will help to begin by outlining the main narrative and theoretical frameworks which have explicitly or implicitly been invoked. Secondly, the central task of the chapter will be to introduce the questions and issues which modern scholarship has identified as the important ones when addressing the history of women at the end of the eighteenth century. This will set the scene for subsequent chapters, which will examine what the authors selected for this study had to say on these topics.

The frameworks

The narrative of the rise of feminism

An obvious narrative within which to marshal at least some of these writers is 'the rise of feminism'. But such a narrative could take more than one form. For example, the historian might single out those writers who most clearly anticipate modern feminism – Wollstonecraft and Hays, perhaps Robinson and Macaulay Graham. Such a selection would lend itself to a narrative of a steady rise of feminist ideas in the eighteenth century culminating in the revolutionary 1790s, followed by a sharp setback as a result of political reaction and the ideological campaign against 'jacobinism'.[1]

This narrow selection has not held the field, however; scholars have added more feminists, or precursors of feminism, to the list. For example, the Garland series of 1974, 'The feminist controversy in England, 1788–1810',

[1] Jane Rendall, *The Origins of Modern Feminism: Women in Britain, France and the United States, 1780–1860* (New York, Schocken Books, 1984), p. 66.

35

also included two 1790s women writers – Mary Ann Radcliffe and Priscilla Wakefield – who appear significant because at certain points their concerns coincide with those of modern feminism. Mary Ann Radcliffe was a minor novelist, sometimes confused with the more celebrated Ann Radcliffe. Her *The Female Advocate: Or, an Attempt to Recover the Rights of Women from Male Usurpation* of 1799 was a protest about the male invasion of occupations, such as millinery and shopwork, which formerly provided respectable employment for women; this invasion, Radcliffe insisted, was driving respectable but unfortunate women into prostitution. The quaker educational writer Priscilla Wakefield calls for better education for women in her *Reflections on the present Condition of the Female Sex* of 1798.

If the concerns in common with modern feminism are evident, then so are the differences. Radcliffe defends propriety and sets her remarks in a Christian frame. The conservative *British Critic* was clear that this work was not to be classed with that of Wollstonecraft and her followers, and that 'society at large may be much benefitted by the perusal of the labours of Mrs. Radcliffe'. But it did not entirely agree with her, thinking that many women 'fell' out of imprudence rather than economic hardship.[2] The review also welcomed Wakefield's little work, for Wakefield makes no mention of political rights and lays great emphasis upon moral purity and propriety.

Candidates who are even less obvious have been enlisted under the feminist banner. Burney was a conservative, politically, socially and morally. Nevertheless recent commentators, most notably Margaret Doody, have found feminist messages in her *oeuvre*.[3] Such an interpretation is possible only if a strategy of reading which looks for multiple meanings is adopted, or one like that of Gilbert and Gubar which unearths the indirect expression of complaint, of half-concealed female rage against confinement and injustice.[4] It is tempting to read Burney in this way, for the present-day reader cannot but feel indignation at the way Burney's heroines are treated by men, subjected to violence, sexual harassment and emotional cruelty. But in itself this is not sufficient to class Burney as a feminist; after all, we complain about the weather or about earthquakes, without supposing that anything can be done to put a stop to them. Surely Burney could only be labelled a feminist if there were evidence that she thought that the maltreatment of women by men was systematic and that the system could and should be reformed. There would be nothing feminist about thinking simply that the world was like that, and that it was incumbent upon Evelina, Cecilia and Camilla to adapt themselves to reality; that the heroine should change, not the world.

Martha Brown has argued that features of Burney's novels which some critics have traced to feminism were quite simply formal and traditional *topoi*

[2] *British Critic*, 14 (1799), 210.
[3] Margaret Anne Doody, *Frances Burney: the Life in the Work* (Cambridge, Cambridge University Press, 1988), pp. 206, 219–20.
[4] Gilbert & Gubar, *The Madwoman in the Attic*.

of the genre; for example, for a plot with suspense to get going, heroines (and heroes) need to be under threat – of violence, or poverty, of coercion into an unwanted marriage, or whatever. Moreover Burney's heroines are as often badly treated by women as by men.[5] Brown thinks that 'feminist' undertones are to be found only in Burney's last novel, *The Wanderer*. *Camilla* is a difficult book to interpret; one aspect of its greatness is the fact that its moral is not entirely obvious, that the situations it depicts, like real-life ones, are often morally ambiguous. It is not always clear which characters Burney would have us approve. Mrs Arlbery for example is an intelligent, wealthy older woman who speaks her mind without feminine reserve and defies convention while remaining chaste. Is she to be disapproved as improper, or approved as an eccentric but basically sensible woman? Does she represent transgression and indirection on Burney's part, a disguised, unavowed protest against the conventions which restrict women? Plausible arguments could be made for all three interpretations.

From one point of view, none of these writers, not even Wollstonecraft, was a feminist, because they did not identify themselves as such. The terms 'feminist' and 'feminism', used roughly as they are used today, did not make their appearance until the last decade of the nineteenth century.[6] Certainly the terms were not in use in the 1790s, and to denominate writers as such is arguably anachronistic. From another point of view, a writer might be identified as a feminist before that term had been coined, on the grounds that inclusion or exclusion under that label would simply depend on how 'feminism' was defined. For example, any writer who explicitly or implicitly complained about the lot of women as a class, or called for improvement in their lot, might be classified as feminist. In principle there is nothing objectionable about such a classification in accordance with a stipulated definition; but in practice there are dangers of anachronism and misinterpretation. It might lead us to overemphasize marginal aspects of their thought at the expense of central ones, or even to misread them altogether. So to say of Macaulay that she was a feminist who very largely anticipated Wollstonecraft and that her *Letters on Education* contained a 'well-developed critique of patriarchy' is surely exaggerated.[7] Furthermore, it is unlikely that any modern definition of feminism, however sensitively applied, would yield Polwhele's classification. The 1790s debate was not being conducted in our twenty-first-century terms.

Nevertheless an awareness that their debate was not ours has been a factor encouraging some scholars to add to the list of 1790s feminists rather than to

[5] Martha G. Brown, 'Fanny Burney's "feminism"; gender or genre?' in Mary Anne Schofield & Cecilia Macheski (eds), *Fetter'd or Free? British Women Novelists, 1670–1815* (Athens, Ohio, Ohio University Press, 1986), pp. 31, 33. Brown lists 'feminist' readings of Burney.

[6] See *OED*.

[7] Dale Spender, *Women of Ideas (And what Men Have Done to Them)* (London, Routledge & Kegan Paul, 1983), pp. 127–37.

diminish it. In effect they argue that 'unsex'd' and 'proper' female writers did not divide over many 'feminist' concerns. Mitzi Myers's work on Hannah More has been important in this respect. She insists upon the 'unexpected congruence of the ideals and programs expressed in such politically polar works as Wollstonecraft's *Rights of Woman* ... and More's *Strictures* ...'. 'In their different ways, they seek to endow woman's role with more competence, dignity, and consequence.'[8] More wrote in a distinctive female voice, she implicitly proposed the empowerment of women, and she played a key role in the development of a female ideology.[9] Kathryn Sutherland has written about More's 'counter-revolutionary feminism', calling for scholars to abandon a distorted left-wing reading of women's history which takes it for granted that feminists must be political radicals. She echoes Marilyn Butler's call for the recognition in this period of 'Tory feminism', a recognition which would link More back to the late seventeenth-century feminist (and Tory) Mary Astell.[10] If a conservative style of feminism is identified in this way, then at least Edgeworth and Hamilton,[11] and perhaps Wakefield and Mary Ann Radcliffe, would be contenders for inclusion under that heading.

Identification of a group of 'conservative' feminists who in fact shared a great deal of common ground with Wollstonecraft subtends a different narrative, more optimistic and progressive, than that of a 1790s flowering followed by repression and silence. Both Myers and Sutherland suggest that in the context of the time, More's was a more culturally realistic and practical way forward than Wollstonecraft's:

If the demands of such radicals as Wollstonecraft for equal political rights were premature, their demands for forceful social leverage and for freedom from sexual exploitation were not. ... [The doctrines of conservatives such as More] ... are more profitably viewed not as the unequivocal opposite of feminism in the nineties, but rather as a perhaps necessary precondition to, a stage of preparation for, nineteenth-century feminism.[12]

[8] Mitzi Myers, 'Reform or ruin: "A revolution in female manners"', *Studies in Eighteenth Century Culture*, 11 (1982), 203, 201.

[9] Mitzi Myers, 'Hannah More's Tracts for the Times: social fiction and female ideology', in Mary Anne Schofield & Cecilia Macheski (eds), *Fetter'd or Free? British Women Novelists, 1670–1815* (Athens, Ohio, Ohio University Press, 1986), pp. 265–6, 269, 274–6.

[10] Kathryn Sutherland, 'Hannah More's counter-revolutionary feminism', in Kelvin Everest (ed.), *Revolution in Writing: British Literary Responses to the French Revolution* (Ballmoor, Bucks, Open University Press, 1991), pp. 30, 33.

[11] Gary Kelly has a chapter heading 'Elizabeth Hamilton and counter-revolutionary feminism' in his *Women, Writing and Revolution*.

[12] Myers, 'Reform or ruin', p. 212.

Narratives of progress, decline and stasis

Narratives not only of feminism, but also of women writers in this decade, and indeed of women in general, can be divided into those of progress and those of decline, into the optimistic and the pessimistic. The chapter titles of Katharine Rogers's *Feminism in Eighteenth-Century England* reveal her narrative frame: 'The liberating effect of rationalism', 'The liberating effect of sentimentalism', 'Consolidation and moderate progress'.[13] Janet Todd's *The Sign of Angellica* also provides what is, on balance, an optimistic narrative. She identifies a number of positive developments. The prestige of sensibility, because it was conventionally regarded as a feminine quality, accrued also to women, giving them an extraordinary centrality in the culture as a whole. Narratives of female suffering and victimhood in prose fiction were psychologically satisfying, with their tragic closures; they depicted women whose lives were heroic and meaningful. Women were accorded enhanced cultural importance for their role in refining coarse male manners, and also, in the case of the bluestockings, for their learning. Women writers of the mid-century created *feminine* writing. While other commentators have thought that the antijacobin reaction at the end of the century marked a setback for women, Todd carries the narrative of progress across that watershed; the great novelists such as Burney and Austen had found a better way of elevating the status of women than the daring protests of Wollstonecraft and Hays, better because more adapted to the circumstances of the time.[14]

By way of contrast we might take a slightly earlier book, Mary Poovey's *The Proper Lady and the Woman Writer*.[15] Poovey is concerned with similar themes to Todd – the triumph of an ideal of sexual propriety, the growth of a conception of women as more moral than men, an enhanced emphasis on sensibility and romantic love. If woman is placed on a pedestal in the Victorian period, she ascended to that pedestal during the long eighteenth century. But ascent is a misleading metaphor; Poovey finds nothing positive in these developments. The ideal of the 'proper' lady, and the myth of romantic love, were quite simply patriarchal strategies for gulling women and repressing their sexuality; ultimately they had nothing to offer to women at all. In the manner of Simone de Beauvoir's *Deuxième Sexe*, Poovey insists that women were imprisoned in prescribed roles, as daughter, wife, mother, widow, virgin or whore which defined them in relation to men and to men's needs. Furthermore, these patriarchal strategies were immensely successful. For Poovey, it is not the case that Wollstonecraft went too far, was more radical than the time allowed: Wollstonecraft was not radical enough, she

[13] Katherine M. Rogers, *Feminism in Eighteenth-Century England* (Brighton, Harvester, 1982).
[14] Janet Todd, *The Sign of Angellica: Women, Writing and Fiction 1660–1800* (London, Virago, 1989).
[15] Poovey, *The Proper Lady and the Woman Writer*.

continued to buy the delusion of romantic love and took on the view of women as ideally asexual.

The commonest narrative of decline may be summed up in the saying 'from golden age to separate spheres'. This narrative may emphasize economic or cultural factors, or both. As an economic narrative it contends that economic changes associated with the rise of capitalism, or with the industrial revolution, banished women or at least middle-class women from money-earning work, or excluded lower-class women from more prestigious or highly paid work. Increasingly men earned outside the home while middle-class women were confined to unwaged domesticity, and the economic power and therefore independence of all women declined. As a cultural narrative it charts the rise of the ideology of the domestic woman, an ideology in its turn based upon an enhanced sense of gender difference.

Against narratives both of progress and decline, many historians have insisted that, for women, nothing much changed. Hence an article by Judith Bennett is entitled 'History that stands still'.[16] 'Much ... recent research seems to indicate that for the vast majority of women living between 1500 and 1800 the rhythms of everyday material life, of social obligation and expectation remained much the same.'[17] There was no decline, because there had been no golden age. There was no progress, because patriarchy continually adapted, conserving the dominance of men under varying circumstances. If the crude misogyny of early modern England abated, and women began their ascent to the Victorian pedestal, this was at considerable cost; women were desexualized and lost independence and assertiveness.[18]

Theoretical frameworks

Different narratives interweave with and are supported by differing theoretical, and perhaps political, stances. An important broad distinction is between what I shall call the 'liberal' and the 'radical'. I am not saying that the scholars I will discuss would use the terms in precisely the way I do, nor, as a consequence, would they necessarily choose these epithets as badges of self-identification.

By a 'liberal' stance I mean one which supposes that at any particular time there may be piecemeal improvements of a major or minor kind in the status and opportunities of women. What is essential about this approach is its underlying assumption about social and cultural structures; they are thought

16 Judith M. Bennett, '"History that stands still": Women's work in the European Past', *Feminist Studies*, 14:2 (1988), 269–83.

17 Richard Connors, 'Poor women, the parish and the politics of poverty', in Hannah Barker & Elaine Chalus (eds), *Gender in Eighteenth-Century England: Roles, Representations and Responsibilities* (London, Longman, 1997), pp. 127–8. Connors lists historians who have denied that there was a golden age for women.

18 Anthony Fletcher, *Gender, Sex and Subordination in England 1500–1800* (New Haven, Yale University Press, 1995), pp. 412–13.

of as sufficiently open-textured or loose-jointed or lacking in overall coherence to permit partial changes without transformation of the whole system. Such a liberal approach may be cautiously optimistic and progressive, proposing that the lot of women (at least in the 'first world' – an important qualification) has improved in a gradual way over a more or less long period of time as a result of economic, social, political and cultural changes and as a result of efforts by campaigning women and their male allies. This is obviously liberal in the sense that a representative liberal – and feminist – like John Stuart Mill, were he alive today, would presumably endorse it. Of course, because gains are possible, losses are possible too; a liberal approach as I am defining it is not necessarily committed to a narrative of progress.

By a 'radical' stance I mean one which supposes that structures are more total, cohesive and able to defend themselves than this. According to this stance the oppression of women has been, and to a considerable extent still is, deeply rooted in 'patriarchal' structures which are resistant to piecemeal reform and which require drastic resistance and subversion. As an illustration of a particularly uncompromising version of such radicalism we might cite Adrienne Rich's theory of compulsory heterosexuality, which argues that women, perhaps by nature erotically oriented towards other women, have been coerced and ideologically conditioned into the belief that they are by nature heterosexual; this 'compulsory heterosexuality' is in the interests of men and reproduction and is the core of the oppression of women.[19] Compulsory heterosexuality is held in place by the law, by economic and political power and by a massive endeavour of ideological conditioning. From this theory it follows that so far there has been very little progress for women, anywhere. Only a minority of self-styled radical feminists would agree wholly with Rich, but there are other theories which similarly cast doubt on the very possibility of piecemeal variation in the lot of women and which inform scholarly narratives. Radicalism in this sense does not endorse any overall account of progress; but it may sustain narratives of limited gains immediately followed by loss, as the patriarchal structure adapts to and neutralizes any threat to male dominance and control.

A number of influential theories which have informed recent work have tended to underpin or even imply a radical approach. Radicalism has been reinforced by the 'linguistic turn' of post-Saussurian linguistics and of post-structuralism and postmodernism. There is something puzzling about this; this reinforcement was not logically necessitated. Those who take the linguistic turn suppose that language is fundamental: we have no unmediated access to a 'reality' which is not constructed in language; there is no essential self apart from the 'subjectivity' which is constructed in discourse. But Derrida's post-Saussurian theory of language argues that meaning is endlessly deferred,

[19] Adrienne Rich, *Blood, Bread, and Poetry: Selected Prose 1979–1985* (London, Virago, 1987), p. 50.

never fixed; in itself this would seem to imply that the self and its reality are not determined in any rigid and irresistible fashion. For if I can endlessly reinterpret myself and my world, then that would seem to imply that I do not need to be imprisoned in any established, conventional discourse and in the reality it constructs. Such a theory would appear to be liberating, even 'liberal' in my sense of the word. A further important theme which feminist scholars take from postmodern philosophy is in principle neutral between liberal and radical stances. This is the claim that gender, as an aspect of subjectivity, is not a natural essence, rooted in the biological body, but culturally, or rather linguistically, constructed.[20] But this claim is not in itself new to feminist thought – it was voiced by Wollstonecraft, and she was not the first – nor is it specifically radical, for it was proposed, for example, by Mill. Postmodern linguistics in this case has simply offered a new way of theorizing an old position.

Postmodern philosophy and radicalism join hands in two ways. First, postmodernism is sceptical, not only about the self, and about final 'truth' and objective knowledge of 'reality'; famously, it is sceptical also about 'metanarratives'.[21] Grand historical narratives – Hegelian, Marxist and so on – are, as Hayden White for example argues, fictions, constructed by historians, not found in events.[22] Therefore any broad narrative of progress, such as liberals sometimes endorse, is utterly suspect. Once again, postmodernists are by no means the first to doubt narratives of progress; 'Whiggish' histories have long come under attack for reading and celebrating the past as if it were a prelude to whatever the historian wishes to commend about the present.[23] Second, it is possible to take from postmodernism (or more precisely from poststructuralism) an attitude which privileges structure and downplays agency. In a catchphrase, this is the notion of the 'death of the self', or the 'end of the individual'. If the essential or original or free authentic self of liberal humanism does not exist, if the self – or, in the preferred terminology, the 'subject' – is constructed by the discourses, it can then be supposed that the subject is a prisoner of those discourses, a prisoner moreover who is unaware or imperfectly aware of the bars and locks. The discursive structure is thought to be immensely powerful, the individual so helpless in the face of that structure that resistance is difficult to conceive. And if the discourse is thought of as patriarchal, the implications for women are dire.

Patriarchal discourse, and the difficulty of challenging it, is a central theme of post-Lacanian psychological theory. According to this theory, all

[20] Judith Butler, *Gender Trouble: Feminism and the Subversion of Identity* (New York, Routledge, 1990), p. 3.

[21] Alun Munslow, *Deconstructing History* (London, Routledge, 1997), pp. 14–15.

[22] Hayden White, *The Content of the Form: Narrative Discourse and Historical Representation* (Baltimore, Johns Hopkins University Press, 1987).

[23] Herbert Butterfield, *The Whig Interpretation of History* (London, G. Ball & Sons, 1931).

language – patriarchal language – is structured in accordance with a binary logic which has been erected upon a fundamental gender binary, namely the presence or absence of the phallus. When women speak this language – the only language presently available – they are imprisoned in patriarchal discourse. (Since discourse constructs reality, this of course means that women are imprisoned in a patriarchal reality.) It follows that there is no liberation for women in the terms of masculine language, no liberation by modifying and reforming the system men have created. A total repudiation of that system, of the language, and of the binary logic upon which it rests, is therefore called for: women need to draw upon the prelinguistic, the 'semiotic' of Kristeva, or, with Cixous and Irigaray, they need to find ways of speaking the female or maternal body by rejecting and undermining the coherence and clarity of 'phallogocentric discourse'. Some feminist critics have turned from here to Bakhtin's ideas about carnivalesque subversion of the rational order.[24]

It is immediately obvious that the 'linguistic turn' and postmodernism are forms of idealism; the fundamental object of study, the ultimate level of explanation, the only thing we can directly know or even know at all, is the discourse. This might seem utterly hostile to 'Marxist' perspectives on history and on texts, but in fact this has not been the case. Some 'new historicists' have attempted the difficult task of translating Marxist concepts into the postmodern world.[25] They suspect grand narratives, they doubt 'truth', they insist that historical narratives are constructed like literary ones, and they recognize that historians and critics of literature (including themselves) are not detached godlike observers but are determined by the society and culture in which they are situated. Nevertheless they propose to understand texts and contexts as parts of a single social and cultural whole, in particular to show how texts are involved with systems of class domination, reflecting, reinforcing, expressing, renegotiating, producing that domination. Feminists working within this paradigm are interested in the ways in which class and gender work together and shape each other. 'New historicism' too has a tendency towards radicalism as I have defined it when it is rooted in Marxism. For Marxism as a philosophy and a politics is hostile to liberal strategies; socioeconomic systems, such as the capitalist system, are theorized as interconnected wholes which can only be transformed as wholes; piecemeal tinkering is constantly subject to absorption and co-optation. The Marxist theory of ideology, the point at which Marxism and postmodernism most nearly approach one another, proposes a system of cultural conditioning which may be total or near-total in its effects.

24 For a discussion of these issues, see Kim L. Worthington, *Self as Narrative: Subjectivity and Community in Contemporary Fiction* (Oxford, Oxford University Press, 1996).
25 A good survey and discussion can be found in H. Aram Veeser (ed.), *The New Historicism* (London, Routledge, 1989).

Still, one cannot help feeling that postmodernists, with their theory of language as a constructed system whose relationship to any material reality is utterly problematic, ought to be more suspicious of key Marxist concepts – class, bourgeois, capitalism – because those concepts are so deeply rooted in a realist and materialist philosophy. The philosophy of Michel Foucault offers an alternative theory of domination more in tune with the linguistic turn. For he maintains that power is located and exercised in and through the discourses themselves. Discourses produce and shape subjects/selves; discourses are disciplinary practices which control and repress. Power is not located in any one place – the political or economic system, the capitalist class – but is diffused everywhere, wherever discourse is, and is exercised daily and in detail over bodies. Because discipline is exercised through discourse, it becomes internalized in those who use and are constructed by the discourse; they discipline themselves, and most do not need to be controlled by physical restraints.[26] It is not too difficult to combine this with a theory of an all-embracing, totally repressive patriarchy, exercising power in the home and over the most intimate aspects of life as well as in 'public' institutions.

Historical revisionism

Theories of the kind mentioned in the previous section have so far had a much greater impact upon literary than upon historical studies. Given that they all belong with the idealism of the linguistic turn, there is an obvious reason for this. Literary studies are exclusively or primarily concerned with texts, with expressions of ideas: most historians aspire to use texts in order to reconstruct the reality which they describe or represent. A further reason is that historians cannot but be suspicious of the ahistoricity of some of this theorizing. Neo-Freudian explanations never fully escape the charge of resting upon supposedly universal and ahistorical psychological or linguistic structures; the theory of patriarchy similarly privileges that which stands still over that which changes. Historians are likely to be sceptical about timeless structures of any kind. Still, they have been reproached for their less than wholehearted embrace of theory: as one writer has suggested, 'historical scholarship no longer [seems] the leading edge of feminist work, the source of energy and pressure for change'.[27]

In reply to this charge it may be said that historical investigation of eighteenth-century women has by no means stood still; on the contrary, a powerful tide of self-proclaimed 'revisionism' is reorienting the subject.[28] Four

[26] Zaczek, *Censored Sentiments*, pp. 39, 103, 176.
[27] Ann-Louise Shapiro, 'Introduction: history and feminist theory, or talking back to the beadle', *History and Theory*, Beiheft 31:4 (1992), 13.
[28] Hannah Barker & Elaine Chalus (eds), *Gender in Eighteenth-Century England: Roles, Representations and Responsibilities* (London, Longman, 1997), p. 3.

aspects of this may be mentioned. First, and here historians are at one with postmodernists, their suspicion of grand narratives has led them to play a leading role in subverting the narrative of 'from golden age to separate spheres'. Secondly, they have mounted a sustained challenge to the very idea of separate, gendered spheres and to the confinement of women in the private and domestic. This challenge has been supported, thirdly, by the insistence that the prescriptive texts – conduct books, prose fiction, sermons, etc. – studied by literary scholars, are precisely that: prescriptive, not descriptive of the lives women actually lived. There was a gap between ideology and lived reality. Fourthly, they have been unwilling to accept the view of women in the past as utter victims, permanently oppressed; they have argued that women were resourceful and not always powerless.[29]

From within literary studies, a view of women as something other than victims in a historical process driven by men has been proposed by for example Nancy Armstrong[30] and Mitzi Myers:

> Women's ways of ordering, of making significant their situation, must ... be carefully disinterred from the dominant structures which muffle them. Even though female models of reality and desire mostly follow the ground rules, their unique deviations from the norms make a woman's world of difference. Women's interpretations of their roles are not fully coincident with men's. ... [T]hey may ... invest women's roles with powerful, even subversive meanings quite different from conventional ascriptions of weakness and public insignificance.[31]

Within the ranks of historical studies, the most influential impetus to the adoption of these perspectives has been Linda Colley's *Britons* of 1992:

> I would still want to differ from those historians who have presented this period as one of unambiguous retreat and restriction for women, and from those who would go on to argue that 'in the nineteenth century women were restricted to the private sphere more than ever before'. ... If British women were being urged to remain at home more stridently in this period than ever before, it was largely because so many of them were finding an increasing amount to do outside the home. The literature of separate spheres was more didactic than descriptive.[32]

Bearing in mind these narrative and theoretical frameworks, and interpretative perspectives, we can now turn to the major issues which historians of women and their writing in this decade have addressed.

---

[29] In this sense they adopt the perspective of Mary Beard, *Woman as Force in History* (New York, Collier, 1946).

[30] Nancy Armstrong, *Desire and Domestic Fiction: A Political History of the Novel* (Oxford, Oxford University Press, 1987).

[31] Myers, 'Reform or ruin', p. 202.

[32] Linda Colley, *Britons: Forging the Nation 1707–1837* (New Haven, Yale University Press, 1992), pp. 262, 281.

The issues

I propose to consider the following themes in order, though as we shall see they overlap at many points and cannot easily be divided up: separate spheres, including access to political and economic life and to 'public reason'; romantic love and the companionate marriage; the topic of self-hood/subjectivity, which raises above all the issues of sensibility, and the evolution of concepts of gender; the ascent of women to the pedestal of alleged superior moral goodness and the related rise to cultural ascendency of the allegedly asexual nature of (most) women; the question of patriarchal discourse and, by contrast, the extent to which we can identify authentic women's voices; and finally, the issue of the relationship of gender to class.

Separate spheres

The issue of separate spheres – 'of that division as it appears in accounts of the relationship that pertains between that aspect of the public world deemed political and that contrasting dimension of social life called private, most often the household or the family'[33] – has been a core topic in feminist thought since the revival of feminism in the 1970s. The distinction has been used, so it is claimed, to exclude women from the domain designated public, thereby disempowering them; at the same time, the distinction conceals the fact that 'the personal is political', that power relationships, namely the power of men over women, inhabit the allegedly private realm. Here the principal narrative at issue for our period is the story of 'from golden age to separate spheres' already mentioned – the hypothesis that as the eighteenth century progressed, women lost opportunities they had previously enjoyed, as sharper definitions of gender, and a more rigid gendering of space, came into play.

Both students of literature[34] and historians[35] have argued this thesis. The rise of the domestic woman has been associated with the rise of the middle class, an issue to which a later section of this chapter will turn. It has also been linked to the tide of religious and moral revivalism, of evangelicalism, which flowed so strongly in the late eighteenth century and on into the nine-teenth.[36] Certainly the ideology of separate spheres is powerfully present in writings by evangelical women such as Hannah More. But here again we must remember that prescription is not the same as description. Wesleyan

[33] Jean Bethke Elshtain, *Public Man, Private Woman* (Princeton, Princeton University Press, 1981), p. 4.

[34] E.g., Shevelow, *Women and Print Culture*.

[35] E.g., Leonore Davidoff & Catherine Hall, *Family Fortunes: Men and Women of the English Middle Class 1780–1850* (London, Hutchinson, 1988).

[36] Catherine Hall, 'The early formation of Victorian domestic ideology', in *White, Male and Middle Class* (Cambridge, Polity Press, 1992).

methodism, though not the only form of evangelicalism, was central, and permitted women to preach between 1761 and 1803. Women continued to preach in radical evangelical sects, and preaching would have been thought of as a public role.[37]

Revisionist historians such as Colley have, as already noted, doubted that women were more restricted and confined at this time. Like Denise Riley they have thought that a sphere of philanthropic activity opened up for women between the political and the domestic, a sphere which Riley labels the social, in which for example women engaged in charitable work, visiting and managing schools, visiting and managing the poor.[38] In this way, Vickery thinks that evangelicalism brought a reorientation rather than a suppression of female public involvement. She also points out that if the historical literature is to be believed, like the ever-emerging middle class, 'it is hard to avoid the impression that the spheres definitively separated and the new domestic woman was born in virtually every century since the end of the Middle Ages'.[39] Vickery's own account does not sit 'comfortably with the accepted narratives and categories of English women's history, indeed, it is the very reverse of the accepted tale of progressive incarceration in a domestic, private sphere'.[40]

Discussions among feminist historians and literature specialists over the last ten to fifteen years have often taken as their starting point Habermas's theory of the creation and transformation of the 'bourgeois public sphere'.[41] This sphere, according to Habermas, was created in the early eighteenth century in England. It was a political sphere distinct from and an alternative to the other public sphere, the site of political power in the royal and aristocratic court. It was distinct also from the private spheres of economic life and domesticity (the intimate sphere). It was a sphere in which private individuals came together, in coffee houses and salons and through the medium of print, to deliberate about matters of common concern. It offered the possibility of criticizing, challenging and influencing aristocratic and court politics. Though it was a bourgeois sphere, and though it later became commercialized and ineffective, for Habermas it offered at its best a model of what democratic deliberation might ideally be like in a postbourgeois world. It was a moment of progress, even though that progress did not last.

37 Robert B. Shoemaker, *Gender in English Society 1650–1850: the Emergence of Separate Spheres?* (London, Longman, 1998), pp. 218–20.

38 Denise Riley, *'Am I that Name?' Feminism and the Category of 'Women' in History* (Basingstoke, Macmillan, 1989).

39 Amanda Vickery, *The Gentleman's Daughter: Women's Lives in Georgian England* (New Haven, Yale University Press, 1998), pp. 3, 288.

40 *Ibid.*, p. 288.

41 Jürgen Habermas, *The Structural Transformation of the Public Sphere: an Inquiry into a Category of Bourgeois Society* (Cambridge, Polity Press, 1989); Craig Calhoun (ed.), *Habermas and the Public Sphere* (Cambridge, Mass., MIT Press, 1992).

If one starts from Habermas, the question that is raised is, did women gain entry to the bourgeois public sphere in the eighteenth century?

An influential book by Joan Landes argues that the bourgeois public sphere was of no benefit to women, nor could it possibly be: 'I argue that the exclusion of women from the bourgeois public was not incidental but central to its incarnation ... I claim that the bourgeois public is essentially, not just contingently, masculinist.'[42] In this period, women were more rigidly excluded from citizenship. Landes's study is centrally concerned with France, with Rousseau's legacy to jacobinism and with the French revolution, but there is also a substantial discussion of Wollstonecraft. Her case is that even if the French revolution is regarded as a progressive moment for men, the birth of the modern democratic state, it was the opposite of progressive for women. The republican doctrine of equal and universal citizenship posed a threat to patriarchal dominance; this threat was neutralized by a sharper polarization of gender and a more emphatic gendering of separate spheres.

According to Landes, under the *ancien régime*, women of the court and aristocratic *salonnières* had political influence and were able to participate in public debate. By contrast women were excluded from the bourgeois public sphere, and were silenced. Women were thought to be irrational, driven by their emotions and particular preferences which, exercised through backstairs or bedroom influence, would corrupt the public sphere which should be impartial, concerned with the general good. The private sphere was the realm of emotion, particularism and the feminine; the public sphere should be characterized by reason, universality and masculinity. Moreover republican discourse downgraded the feminine, domestic sphere in that it elevated duty to the state over family loyalty. Even a woman as radical as Wollstonecraft failed to challenge this construction; she endorsed an essentially masculine conception of the public sphere, and offered women the opportunity to enter it, only by adopting masculine characteristics. She looked above all to men to take the initiative in opening the doors of the political arena for women. Others have endorsed Landes's assessment of the democratic revolution: 'It was impossible for women to speak as citizens without speaking *against* their womanhood.'[43]

Landes's argument draws its best sustenance from the indubitably misogynist politics of Rousseau and his jacobin followers; for the jacobins excluded women from the national assembly, closed down the women's

[42] Joan B. Landes, *Women and the Public Sphere in the Age of the French Revolution* (Ithaca, Cornell University Press, 1988), p. 7.
[43] Kate Soper quoting Barbara Taylor: Soper, 'Naked human nature and the draperie of custom: Wollstonecraft on equality and democracy', in Eileen Janes Yeo (ed.), *Mary Wollstonecraft and Two Hundred Years of Feminisms* (London, Rivers Oram Press, 1997), p. 213. See for a similar argument Dorinda Outram, *The Body and the French Revolution* (New Haven, Yale University Press, 1989).

groups and guillotined Olympe de Gouges, who most comprehensively had demanded civil and political rights for women. But this in itself is not enough to sustain her claim that the bourgeois public sphere was *essentially*, *neccessarily* and not just *contingently* antifeminist and masculinist. At crucial points her argument is not entirely transparent, but it appears to rest on an assumption that rationality and universality are essentially masculine, while authentically women's speech is wilful, disorderly, disruptive, chaotic. There are echoes here of post-Lacanian feminism's critique of 'phallogocentric' discourse, of its recourse to the prelinguistic energies of the female body as an alternative and its insistence that only total subversion of male logic will do. If this is Landes's stance, then her disappointment with Wollstonecraft is readily understandable, for Wollstonecraft thought that reason and the capacity for impartiality were wholly laudable, 'human' characteristics not masculine ones. Other scholars, by contrast, have thought that the bourgeois public sphere was only contingently masculine, that in itself it promises a democratic ideal and can be reformed to incorporate other classes, and women.[44]

There are empirical problems with Landes's argument, as well as conceptual and logical ones. Dena Goodman maintains that the distinction between an *ancien-régime* court which allowed women a political role, and a modern public sphere which rigidly excluded them, is false.[45] For the *salons* in which intellectual French women played a prominent part were distinct from the court and posed a challenge to it; they were in fact a part of the emerging public sphere. Nor is Landes's case any easier to sustain if the focus is shifted from France to England, and if we turn our eyes from ideological statements to actual practices. That there was a *rhetoric* of separate spheres is beyond doubt; but in spite of the linguistic turn, and the notion that 'reality' is discursively constructed, we cannot assume that rhetoric and reality correspond.[46]

Women discussed politics in coffee houses and in debating societies, mixed as well as single sex, though the debating societies declined in the 1790s in an atmosphere of political repression.[47] Elaine Chalus and Amanda Foreman have shown us how deeply aristocratic women were involved in politics right through into the nineteenth century, in canvassing, entertaining and addressing electors and organizing election campaigns. They helped to build political alliances, and sometimes even controlled seats and nominated

---

[44] Paula R. Backscheider & Timothy Dykstal (eds), *The Intersection of the Public and Private Spheres in Early Modern England* (*Prose Studies: History, Theory, Criticism*, 18:3, December 1995), 32–3.

[45] Dena Goodman, 'Public sphere and private life: toward a synthesis of current historiographical approaches to the old régime', *History and Theory*, 31:1 (1992), 15–16.

[46] Barker & Chalus, *Gender in Eighteenth-century England*, p. 2.

[47] Shoemaker, *Gender in English Society*, pp. 239–43.

MPs.[48] Jupp too gives instances of the very considerable political influence of royal and aristocratic women, some of whom took a deep interest in public affairs. They hosted political salons, and were the confidantes of leading statesmen. They were well read in current affairs – perhaps better read than the men – and they continued to listen to parliamentary debates after the gallery of the House of Commons was formally closed to women in 1778.[49]

In some boroughs the daughters of freemen were entitled to confer the right to vote on their husbands, who may have voted on their behalf; certainly the women were canvassed and entertained. Where the right to vote attached to property belonging to a woman, she might appoint a male relative to vote, and she might be paid for her vote. Women were formally involved in politics as witnesses in the House of Commons in cases of controverted elections.[50] Linda Colley has shown that the revolutionary and Napoleonic wars gave women opportunities for the public demonstration of their patriotism on an unprecedented scale.[51] Women petitioned and demonstrated over the Queen Caroline affair, and took a public role in charitable organizations. They played a crucial role in the campaign against slavery, already before the end of the eighteenth century abstaining from slave-grown produce and publishing antislavery poetry.[52] Some women activists moved from the last to political campaigns on behalf of women, including for the suffrage.[53]

One of the most valuable contributions to this discussion comes from Hilda Smith: she is concerned with the seventeenth century but her thoughts are important for eighteenth-century historians too.[54] She contends that a reason why women were not more demanding of political rights was that they did not see themselves as entirely excluded from a distinct 'public' realm of

[48] Barker & Chalus, *Gender in Eighteenth-century England,* pp. 151, 155, 164. A false impression of women's exclusion from electioneering has been derived from the lampooning of the Duchess of Devonshire's 'kisses for votes' in the 1784 Westminster election. But her offence was not electioneering, which was normal for aristocratic women; her offences were *how* she campaigned, and the fact that she campaigned for Fox rather than for a member of her own family.

[49] P. J. Jupp, 'The roles of royal and aristocratic women in British politics, c. 1782–1832', *Chattel, Servant or Citizen: Women's Status in Church, State and Society*, Institute of Irish Studies, Queens University Belfast, Historical Studies 19 (1995), 103–13.

[50] Elaine Chalus, 'Women, electoral privilege and practice in the eighteenth century', in Kathryn Gleadle & Sarah Richardson (eds.), *Women in British Politics, 1760–1860: the Power of the Petticoat* (Basingstoke, Macmillan, 2000), pp. 19–38.

[51] Colley, *Britons*, p. 260ff.

[52] For this see Clare Midgley, *Women against Slavery: the British Campaigns 1780–1870* (London, Routledge, 1992).

[53] Shoemaker, *Gender in English Society*, pp. 246–54.

[54] Hilda L. Smith, 'Introduction. Women, intellect, and politics: their intersection in seventeenth-century England', in Hilda L. Smith (ed.), *Women Writers and the Early Modern British Political Tradition* (Cambridge, Cambridge University Press, 1998), pp. 3–12.

politics. As the previous paragraphs have demonstrated, a range of political roles, both formal and informal, were open to women. To see them as totally excluded is to take back a more recent, and perhaps male, conception of politics, one which emphasizes the act of voting, political rights and agency within definable institutions – a conception which became dominant in the nineteenth century. Earlier periods operated with a broader understanding of politics in which patronage and family – and therefore women – played a part. Women may have lacked certain formal political *rights* (as did most men); this should not be taken to mean that they did not have a political *voice*. Women could not be *legislators*, but some of them could be *politicians*.[55]

Revisionist historians have made out a strong case to the effect that women were not entirely excluded from the political public sphere. Still, we must not forget that few women had any political rights, and that vital political rights were denied to all women. After demonstrating the enormous political influence of Mrs Arbuthnot in the early nineteenth century, Jupp tells how in her diary she wished she were a man so that she could speak in parliament or hold cabinet office.[56] Misogyny was not uncommon in political discourse; Colley and Wilson have shown that for much of the eighteenth century British propaganda gendered Britain as masculine, and the French as effeminate.[57]

Habermas thinks of the bourgeois public sphere as located not primarily in concrete spaces and in directly political action, but rather in the realm of printing and publishing. That women became increasingly active here is beyond dispute, and the fact that they were not rigidly confined to 'feminine' genres such as poetry and prose fiction was argued in Chapter 1.[58] Between three hundred and four hundred women published during the decade of the 1790s alone.[59] Some women were in this way able to exercise reason publicly, and sometimes about public affairs; before the 'feminists' of the 1790s there were the bluestockings, and before them, some remarkable learned women of the seventeenth century.[60] Many scholars have written

55 Kathryn Gleadle & Sarah Richardson (eds), *Women in British Politics, 1760-1860: the Power of the Petticoat* (Basingstoke, Macmillan, 2000), p. 7.

56 Jupp, 'The roles of royal and aristocratic women', 109.

57 Colley, *Britons*, p. 252; Kathleen Wilson, *The Sense of the People: Politics, Culture and Imperialism in England, 1715-1785* (Cambridge, Cambridge University Press, 1995), pp. 185-205, 212-18.

58 This is argued also by Stephen Howard, '"A bright pattern to all her sex"; representations of women in periodical and newspaper biography', in Hannah Barker & Elaine Chalus (eds.), *Gender in Eighteenth-century England* (London, Longman, 1997), pp. 241-4.

59 Shoemaker, *Gender in English Society*, p. 285; see his discussion of women in publishing pp. 285-90.

60 Ruth Perry, 'Radical doubt and the liberation of women', *Eighteenth-Century Studies*, 18:4 (1985), 472-93.

mildly progressive narratives about the incursion of women into public print, a development which the political reaction of the late 1790s did not arrest. The comet of militant feminism may have burnt itself out in the 1790s, but unitarian women – for example Barbauld, Edgeworth, Marcet, Aikin, Jebb – kept a gentler flame alight, linking eventually with Harriet Taylor and John Stuart Mill.[61] Of course a case can be made, and has been made, that most of these women writers wrote within discourses created by men, and did not succeed in mounting a serious challenge to patriarchy; but the alleged prison of patriarchal discourse is a topic for later in this chapter.

Let us turn next from politics to work. Whether the economic, the sphere of production and exchange, is to be deemed public or private is largely a matter of arbitrary choice. However the question is resolved, it has also been argued that women in this period were increasingly confined to a narrowly domestic realm cut off from productive activity. Historical classics by Alice Clark and Ivy Pinchbeck, as well as the more recent work of Bridget Hill, have told this story.[62] In the premodern economy, the place of production, whether it be farm or workshop, was not separate from the home, and women tended to play a full part in production, though often performing tasks differentiated from those of men. This gave them a status, and often money of their own; there was a rough-and-ready economic equality. But with the advance first of capitalism, then of industrialism, workplace and home were increasingly separate spaces; particularly above the poorest levels of society, men went out to work while women stayed at home and did not engage in paid employment. Occupations with a certain amount of status in the field of health care were closed to women: as they became professional-ized, men took them over. Separate spheres were thus reinforced, and women lost economic power and standing.

Literary scholars still tend to take this narrative for granted, but historians have increasingly abandoned it. Very few historians would now stand up for a lost golden age of the economy for women; they would be more likely to insist on an essential continuity in this area. In part this rests on an aware-ness that women were underprivileged economically before modernization; the highest-status and best-remunerated activities were reserved for men. In part also it is because of doubt about any sudden process of industrialization; present orthodoxy supposes a development which was geographically patchy, and much more gradual. The household continued to be the most common unit of production until after 1850.[63]

[61] See Watts, *Gender, Power and the Unitarians*.

[62] For a review of and challenge to the literature see Amanda Vickery, 'Golden age to separate spheres? A review of the categories and chronology of English women's history', *Historical Journal*, 36:2 (1993), 383–414.

[63] Hannah Barker, 'Women, work and the industrial revolution: female involve-ment in the English printing trades, c. 1700-1840', in Hannah Barker & Elaine Chalus (eds), *Gender in Eighteenth-Century England* (London, Longman, 1997), p. 83.

Detailed study of the evidence suggests that if employment opportunities for women reduced in some areas, such as brewing and medicine, they increased in others, such as tailoring, nursing and schoolteaching. Women came to dominate the making of women's clothing and accessories in the course of the eighteenth century. Of course all of these occupations can be viewed as extensions of normal domestic activity. The early industrial revolution and the putting-out system *increased* the amount of productive work for women in the home.[64] There was no diminution in the involvement of women in the printing trades during the eighteenth century.[65] Women continued to make and sell medicines, and if in genteel homes the male *accoucheur* took over from the female midwife, this was principally the choice of women themselves.[66] More and more women earned a living, or supplemented their incomes, by professional writing.[67]

It has also been argued that to place emphasis on income-earning work, or on productive work making household provender or saleable goods – what Adam Smith calls a 'vendible commodity'[68] – or on work outside the home, ignores the importance, responsibility and prestige of the work of running the home. Gentlewomen were groomed for the exercise of power and for the hiring and government of servants; female management skills were widely recognized as essential to the smooth running of the genteel household:

> In its staffing the household functioned like most eighteenth-century commercial enterprises. In the acquisition, co-ordination and direction of a range of different workers, the managerial effort of the genteel mistress-housekeeper was akin to that of a putting-out master or gentleman farmer.[69]

The status of the household manager reminds us that whether the story is of increasingly separate spheres, or of boundaries becoming more permeable, or of little or no change, is not the only question in dispute. The relative evaluation of those spheres is also an issue. If feminist historians in the 1960s thought that the problem, the oppression, was women's exclusion from the public sphere, some in the 1970s were ready to celebrate the private sphere as a women's sphere with its own distinctive ethic of care and solidarity.[70] Nor is it simply a matter of how we today might evaluate those spheres: how did women (and men) in the 1790s evaluate them? If Charles Taylor is

[64] Shoemaker, *Gender in English Society,* pp. 163–86.
[65] Barker, 'Women, work and the industrial revolution', p. 87.
[66] Vickery, *Gentleman's Daughter*, pp. 153–6, 94–6.
[67] Shoemaker, *Gender in English Society*, pp. 285–7; and see Cheryl Turner, *Living by the Pen: Women Writers in the Eighteenth Century* (London, Routledge, 1992).
[68] Adam Smith, *An Inquiry into the Nature and Causes of the Wealth of Nations* (1776) (London, Everyman, 1910), i, p. 295.
[69] Vickery, *Gentleman's Daughter*, p. 141.
[70] Linda K. Kerber, 'Separate spheres, female worlds, woman's place: the rhetoric of women's history', *Journal of American History*, 75:1 (June 1988), 11–14.

correct in supposing that a major aspect of the evolution of modern selfhood was a decline in the classical preference for political life and an enhanced valuation of ordinary life, then we cannot take it for granted that eighteenth-century ideology, in confining women to a private sphere, was thereby condemning them to essential inferiority.[71]

Indeed, Karen Offen has argued that nineteenth-century feminism was primarily a difference feminism, which celebrated the domestic virtues of women.[72] Central to this was an idealization of motherhood, perhaps even a shift in cultural emphasis from woman as sexual object to woman as mother.[73] Despite his misogyny, Rousseau had prepared the way for this, and perhaps this is one reason why he was so much admired by eighteenth-century women readers. For out of Rousseau it was possible to evolve the ideal of republican motherhood, of the mother who was the heart of the family, bringing up her sons to be patriots. Though confined to the domestic sphere, in this way she performed a function of the utmost public significance.[74]

Finally and more deeply, the concepts of separate spheres and of public and private are utterly problematic as tools of historical and textual analysis. To stress a point which has been well made by Linda Kerber, we have taken a set of concepts which were classically formulated, for example, by Aristotle, Rousseau, Hegel or Ruskin, and which enjoyed reasonably wide currency at certain times in the past, for example in Victorian Britain. We have then employed this ideology – for that is what it is – in our own historical reconstructions of the past.[75] But perhaps those concepts have hindered an accurate understanding of the past as much as they have helped it. Perhaps reality was different, and much more complicated. Gordon Schochet has argued that Habermas's terminology does not correspond to that used by those who allegedly created the bourgeois public sphere.[76] John Brewer has pointed to the many different meanings of 'private' in the eighteenth century:

---

[71] Charles Taylor, *Sources of the Self: the Making of the Modern Identity* (Cambridge, Cambridge University Press, 1989), pp. 211–47.

[72] Karen Offen, 'Defining feminism: a comparative historical approach', *Signs: Journal of Women in Culture and Society*, 14:1 (1988), pp. 119–57. See also Claire Goldberg Moses, '"Equality" and "difference" in historical perspective: a comparative examination of the feminisms of French revolutionaries and utopian socialists', in S. E. Melzer & L. W. Rabine (eds), *Rebel Daughters: Women and the French Revolution* (New York, Oxford University Press, 1992), pp. 238, 240, 242.

[73] Shoemaker, *Gender in English Society*, pp. 126–8; see Vickery's discussion of historical debates surrounding motherhood, *Gentleman's Daughter*, pp. 91–4.

[74] Rendall, *Origins of Modern Feminism*, p. 17.

[75] Kerber, 'Separate spheres, female worlds, woman's place', 10–11, 39.

[76] Gordon Schochet, 'Vices, benefits and civil society: Mandeville, Habermas, and the distinction between public and private', in Paula R. Backscheider & Timothy Dykstal, *The Intersection of the Public and Private Spheres in Early Modern England* (*Prose Studies: History, Theory, Criticism*, 18:3, December 1995), pp. 264–5.

Private tuition is contrasted with schools, private devotions and private Christians with the church, private beneficence with public charity, and private individuals with the family. . . . There is no fixed definition of private but many different definitions, some of which depend upon territories and spaces, others of which depend upon ends.[77]

Given a past of great social and cultural complexity (for example, England in the eighteenth century) it is unlikely that the historian will be able to find two enclosed and mutually exclusive spheres, one public to which only (some) men are admitted, the other private in which (most) women are confined. The historian of ideas will need to be on the lookout for complex mapping of space in texts, with associated evaluations and proposed exclusions and distributions of power.

Romantic love and companionate marriage

If one major narrative was 'from golden age to separate spheres', another is 'the rise of the companionate marriage'. This story became salient in the late 1970s, with the work of Stone and Trumbach.[78] According to this narrative, in some classes of society relationships between husband and wife became closer, more companionate, more important to both parties, increasingly based upon romantic love, and more egalitarian (even if, as Stone contended, that equality retreated in a more patriarchal Victorian age). Since the 1970s there has been a continuing historical debate between the theory of the rise of companionate equality, and the theory of enduring patriarchy.

Subsequent historians looking at actual marriages as revealed in letters and diaries have been highly sceptical about Stone's and Trumbach's narrative. For every period for which we have appropriate records we can find examples of intense affection and companionship between husband and wife, as well as the opposite; moreover it is contended that love and companionship do not necessarily imply equality. 'The overall patriarchal character of marriage is . . . a constant: whether one considers the property laws, wife beating, the double standard, or divorce and separation practices, men clearly retained the upper hand.'[79]

Perhaps the strongest evidence for enduring patriarchy comes from property and inheritance law. Susan Staves has shown how the law was developed and

---

[77] John Brewer, 'This, that and the other; public, social and private in the seventeenth and eighteenth centuries', in Dario Castiglione & Lesley Sharpe (eds.), *Shifting the Boundaries: Transformation of the Languages of Public and Private in the Eighteenth Century* (Exeter, University of Exeter Press, 1995), pp. 9, 10. See also the very interesting discussion in Vickery, *Gentleman's Daughter*, pp. 287–92.

[78] Lawrence Stone, *The Family, Sex and Marriage in England, 1500-1800* (London, Weidenfeld & Nicolson, 1977); Randolph Trumbach, *The Rise of the Egalitarian Family: Aristocratic Kinship and Domestic Relations in Eighteenth Century England* (London, Academic Press, 1978).

[79] Shoemaker, *Gender in English Society*, p. 112.

modified in the interests of men. For example, lawyers creatively found ways of reducing widows' portions below what the common law would have provided. Care was taken to ensure that gentlewomen would not starve, but the law restricted the amount of wealth, and their control over it, in such a way as to deny them economic agency.[80] Now it is true that the law reflects ideology as well as social realities; perhaps women were in practice better treated than the law would imply.[81] But it seems that where property was concerned, we cannot say that actual practice was more favourable to women than legal theory. Eileen Spring has powerfully demonstrated that the workings of property law ensured that, as far as demographic possibilities would allow, large concentrations of wealth were in the hands of men, preferably in the hands of eldest sons at the expense of younger sons as well as daughters.[82]

But this study is a history of ideas, and here there can be no doubt about the increasing salience in eighteenth-century texts of *ideals* of romantic love and married companionship, if only because of the massive expansion in the number of works of prose fiction which take this as a central theme. So if one focuses on the ideas, was this a positive development for women? Katherine Sobba Green thinks so; the 'courtship novel', in which, after many trials and tribulations, the heroine gets her man and his unstinting devotion, had much to offer women. She finds a feminist message in conduct books and novels, in that they are concerned with women's self-improvement, and with free choice in marriage.[83]

There has been widespread dissent from this optimism, nowhere expressed more clearly or in a grander narrative than by Susan Okin.[84] She starts with the abandonment of classical and medieval theories of a great chain of being, which readily legitimated gender hierarchy. They were replaced in political philosophy by a theory of natural rights which took as its starting point equal individuals, only to be subjected to the rule of another with their own consent. In principle, this was very threatening to male dominance, as the well-known difficulties in Hobbes and Locke on this question demonstrate.[85] 'By about 1700, it appears that the justification of women's political and legal inequality had worn very thin', as indeed Mary Astell was able to show. But 'a change was taking place in the sphere of family life that had catastrophic

---

[80] Susan Staves, *Married Women's Separate Property in England, 1660–1833* (Cambridge, Mass., Harvard University Press, 1990).

[81] Colley, *Britons*, p. 239.

[82] Eileen Spring, *Law, Land and Family: Aristocratic Inheritance in England, 1300–1800* (Chapel Hill, University of North Carolina Press, 1993), pp. 15, 87, 93.

[83] Katherine Sobba Green, *The Courtship Novel 1740–1820: a Feminized Genre* (Lexington, University of Kentucky Press, 1991), pp. 18–22, 161–2.

[84] S. M. Okin, 'Women and the making of the sentimental family', *Philosophy and Public Affairs*, 11:1 (1982), pp. 65–88.

[85] Classically exposed in Carole Pateman, *The Sexual Contract* (Cambridge, Polity Press, 1988).

implications for the future of women's rights and freedom'.[86] The ideology of romantic love and of the companionate marriage offered a new way of keeping women in their place, because it presented them as domestic beings, characterized by sentiment rather than by reason; and because it proposed that the interests of husband and wife were so intensely at one that he could represent her politically.

Others have echoed this thesis. The new ideology was simply new-style patriarchy, patriarchy in a softer, more insidious guise. Whereas previously the dominance of men over women appeared as naked and even brutal force, now that dominance, through the ideology of romantic love, became internalized in the psyches of women themselves. Men no longer needed to exercise control over women: women subjected themselves.[87] Joan Forbes writes of

> patriarchal ideologies of romance and romantic love ... the normalizing ideology of a patriarchal, heterosexual romance ... pivotal ... in securing women's subordination ... Affectional bonds and close emotional attachments to men, through which much of women's oppression is transacted, makes polarised opposition to men unthinkable for many women ... literary conventions like these [comprised] a textual tyranny over women.[88]

In a similar vein, Claudia Johnson celebrates Wollstonecraft for recognizing that 'heterosexual sentiment [is] corrupt beyond the point of recovery',[89] and because 'her novels not only resist the heterosexual plot, but displace it with protolesbian narratives wrested from sentimentality itself'. Johnson's references to 'compulsory heterosexuality' and her search in the novels she reads for attempts 'to establish a collective sense of identity inclusive of all women' suggest that her pessimistic narrative about romantic love is informed by a 'radical' theory akin to that of Adrienne Rich's 'Compulsory heterosexuality and lesbian existence'.

A theory closely related to Rich's, and which has had some impact on recent feminist readings of women's texts of this period, is the anthropological and psychological theory of the 'circulation of women'. This theory, by for example Gayle Rubin with debts to Lévi-Strauss, Freud and Lacan, explains marriages as originally transactions between men, designed to bond men together, in which gifts of women were exchanged. These exchanges

---

[86] Okin, 'Women and the sentimental family', 72.

[87] Elizabeth Kowaleski-Wallace, *Their Fathers' Daughters: Hannah More, Maria Edgeworth, and Patriarchal Complicity* (New York, Oxford University Press, 1991), pp. 12, 53, 110.

[88] Joan Forbes, 'Anti-romantic discourse as resistance: women's fiction 1775–1820', in Lynne Pearce & Jackie Stacey (eds.), *Romance Revisited* (New York, New York University Press, 1995), pp. 294–6.

[89] Claudia L. Johnson, *Equivocal Beings: Politics, Gender, and Sentimentality in the 1790s. Wollstonecraft, Radcliffe, Burney, Austen* (Chicago, University of Chicago Press, 1995), pp. 67, 48, 58, 66.

and the bonding which resulted were the origin of social organization and culture. So that women would not be kept, but exchanged, incest taboos and norms of heterosexuality concomitantly evolved.[90]

There is a prima-facie case for applying this theory to our period, because some marriages were arranged. But not all marriages were arranged; it was a cliché of the age that fathers were often as putty in their daughters' hands – 'The darling daughter was patriarchy's Achilles heel'. And when marriages *were* arranged, or when love matches led to negotiations preliminary to marriage, it was not men alone who did the negotiating. Marriages bound *families* together, and families included women. Vickery's study of the correspondence of genteel families shows that the approval of a wide range of family members, male and female alike, might be sought.[91] Rosemary O'Day has distinguished between the 'prescriptive' and the 'descriptive' family. Law and ideology may have prescribed patriarchal power, but the family was made up of, and needed, all its components. Harmonious relations were important to all members, including the head, and therefore roles and interests were subject to negotiation and compromise rather than to patriarchal fiat.[92]

Subjectivity

One of the grandest themes of recent scholarship on this period has been the evolution of the self (or of 'subjectivity' – the preferred term for some who wish to make it clear that they do not subscribe to a 'liberal humanist' theory of an authentic or essential self prior to or independent of cultural construction). Arguably too this is a theme of the utmost importance:

> Our subjective sense of self and our resources for self-representation are critical for empowering us to transcend present conventions about gender. How can women create personal and collective identities which expand our possibilities?[93]

> The question of self-representation is at the heart of feminist practice. Self-representation has to do not only with independence and agency, but with the

---

[90] Gayle Rubin, 'The traffic in women: notes on the "political economy" of sex', in Rayna R. Reiter (ed.), *Toward an Anthropology of Women* (New York, Monthly Review Press, 1975). For application of this theory to women's writing see Susan Fraiman, *Unbecoming Women: British Women Writers and the Novel of Development* (New York, Columbia University Press, 1993), pp. 42, 73 and Catherine Craft-Fairchild, *Masquerade and Gender: Disguise and Female Identity in Eighteenth-Century Fictions by Women* (Pennsylvania, Pennsylvania State University Press, 1993), p. 131.

[91] Vickery, *Gentleman's Daughter*, pp. 49, 54–5.

[92] Rosemary O'Day, *The Family and Family Relationships 1500–1900: England, France and the United States of America* (Basingstoke, Macmillan, 1994), p. xviii.

[93] Eileen Janes Yeo, 'Introduction', in Eileen Janes Yeo (ed.), *Mary Wollstonecraft and Two Hundred Years of Feminisms* (London, Rivers Oram Press, 1997), p. 2.

ways in which an individual gets access to those capacities. It is about subjectivity, as well as about voting.[94]

This is a vast, ramifying and fascinating topic. In order to make it manage-
able, I will first take notice of accounts which deal with selfhood in general,
both male and female, and will suggest how these perspectives have been
applied to women. Then I will turn to the all-important topic of sensibility.
Finally, I will look at the striking and ambitious stories that have been told
about the evolution of gender in this period.

Norbert Elias's account of the 'civilizing process'[95] is a rich and profound
meditation on the evolution of modern selfhood. He proposes that before the
civilizing process gets going, instincts and emotions are vented relatively
freely, directly and openly, and the conflicts which result are controlled by
external force. Beginning in the medieval court, the controls are progressively internalized; individual feeling and instinctual urges, and whatever is
thought of as 'animal', are increasingly repressed; reserved and refined
behaviour is cultivated so as to avoid embarrassing others. The culmination
of this process is the construction of an individual ego as it were in a locked
case, a detached self divided by an invisible wall of restraints from what goes
on outside, including from its own body; the body, and its engagement with
others, is rigidly controlled by this inner self. Elias thinks that this process
of restraint has benefited women; as men become more controlled, women
can behave more freely, to the point where a woman can appear on a beach
in a bikini without fear of rape.

Elias thinks that this process begins in court society, then becomes more
widely diffused, as bourgeois emulates aristocrat. But bourgeois circles, in
Germany and England for example, develop their own version so as to assert
the superiority of their class to the aristocracy. They contrast the insincere
and superficial ceremony, courtesy and formality, the concern with honour of
courtly *Zivilisation* with their own inwardness, depth of feeling, inner enrich-
ment and devotion to virtue; their *Kultur*, the result of *Bildung*, of moral,
intellectual and spiritual growth.[96] Students of English advice books have
correspondingly noticed the contrast between the courtly 'courtesy book' and
the middle-class 'conduct book'.[97]

Some have found a feminist message in conduct books, thinking that 'the
generally domestic, self-abnegatory spirit' of this genre 'was also well-suited

---

[94] Joan W. Scott, 'The imagination of Olympe de Gouges', in Eileen Janes Yeo
(ed.), *Mary Wollstonecraft and Two Hundred Years of Feminisms* (London, Rivers
Oram Press, 1997), p. 37.

[95] Norbert Elias, *The Civilizing Process: The History of Manners* (1939) (Oxford,
Blackwell, 1978).

[96] *Ibid.*, pp. 8–29.

[97] Marjorie Morgan, *Manners, Morals and Class in England, 1774–1858*
(Basingstoke, Macmillan, 1994).

to the situation of women'.[98] One might go further, and argue that an ideal of inwardness and virtue was one which women could achieve as easily as, perhaps more easily than men.[99] Charles Taylor's wide-ranging *Sources of the Self*, though it is not concerned with gender issues, can be invoked in support of this claim. When he turns to the 'care of the self' in the eighteenth century, he finds an enhanced evaluation of ordinary life, and the growing prestige of a kind of 'interiorized stoicism', which he associates with Shaftesbury.[100] This stoicism combines dignified self-control and restraint with benevolence, the 'negative utilitarianism' of the eighteenth century which thinks that suffering is an evil that should be removed; a 'feminist' ethic of care and concern, one might add, echoing Carol Gilligan.[101] This is an ideal of selfhood very different from that of the rather macho 'classical republican' citizen-soldier, an ideal much better suited to women. This is the perspective in which we might view the fact that the bluestocking Elizabeth Carter made and published a celebrated translation of the stoic Epictetus. In her preface and notes she recommended the combination of stoicism with sympathy and benevolence.[102]

So far I have been suggesting ways in which histories of subjectivity in the eighteenth century can be read as positive for women; but of course optimists have by no means had it all their own way. Elias thought that the civilizing process, though it meant a diminution of savage joys, of the direct release of emotion and the uninhibited satisfaction of pleasure, was nevertheless necessary. For as social life became more complex, as there was increasing interaction with strangers in a market society, so an internalization and intensifying of restraint became essential. Like Freud, Elias thought that a strong superego was essential to the survival of civilization itself.[103] A similar account of the internalization of discipline, but in a darker strain and without the optimistic teleology, is provided by Foucault, as we have seen, and a great deal of work by feminist scholars has agreed with him rather than with Elias.

Mary Poovey, for example, explores the self-control which the 'proper lady' learned from conduct books, and from novels which were often conduct books in disguise; she views it pejoratively, as self-denial in the interests of

---

[98] M. Curtin, 'A question of manners: status and gender in etiquette and courtesy', *Journal of Modern History*, 57:3 (1985), 407.

[99] William Stafford, 'Narratives of women: English feminists of the 1790s', *History*, 82:265 (1997), pp. 34–43.

[100] Taylor, *Sources of the Self*, pp. 251–9.

[101] Carol Gilligan, *In a Different Voice: Psychological Theory and Women's Development* (Cambridge, Mass., Harvard University Press, 1982), p. 160.

[102] Epictetus, *Moral Discourses* (trans. Elizabeth Carter, 1758; London, Everyman, 1910), pp. xv, xx, 320, 332.

[103] Norbert Elias, *The Civilizing Process: State Formation and Civilization* (1939) (Oxford, Blackwell, 1982), pp. 232–47.

men.[104] Susan Fraiman argues that the *Bildungsroman* – the novel of individual development, of the process which in Elias's terms produces the cultivated individual, with a rich interior life – provides a very different life-narrative when its subject is a woman. The goal of her education is to render her fit to be handed over by her male guardian to a husband, and her trajectory is downwards or circular, a blocked ascent; she loses her independence and agency, becoming confined, passive, doomed to eternal childhood.[105] Dorinda Outram argues with reference to French revolutionary ideology that Elias's *gebildete Mensch*, the self-controlled, self-enclosed individual, was thought of as indeed a *man*, and a bourgeois man at that, a reasoning mind set apart from and firmly in control of his body. He contrasted with and therefore was qualified to rule over more bodily beings – aristocrats who display their bodies, the carnivalesque, animal lower orders, and women, incapable of self-enclosed reason because they were governed by emotion and, as carers, continually involved with others.[106]

Sensibility

If reason, the principle of control, is at the heart of eighteenth-century speculation about the self, then sensibility stands right beside it. The salience of sensibility in writing of the second half of the eighteenth century – and not only in the obvious genres, poetry and the novel – immediately strikes the present-day reader. But what was the significance of sensibility for women? No simple answer can be given to this question, in part because 'sensibility' was not a simple or clear concept.[107] Sensibility is feeling; but what kind of feeling, and how evaluated?

Sensibility in eighteenth-century culture may be sympathetic feeling, a readiness to shed a tear over the suffering of humans or animals. The person of sensibility may be especially sensitive to the feelings of others, may exhibit 'delicacy'. It may be aesthetic feeling, aroused by works of art, especially poetry, or by contemplation of the beauties or sublimities of nature. It may simply be susceptibility to emotions of all kinds, including terror and despair. It may be romantic or sexual feeling. Sensibility may be active; as sympathy it will then be the cause of benevolence and beneficence. Or it may be passive; the person of extreme sensibility may be immobilized, rendered helpless by an excess of feeling. Sensibility may be a marker of superior

104 Poovey, *Proper Lady*, pp. 79, 110, 113, 242.

105 Fraiman, *Unbecoming Women*, pp. 5–6, 53.

106 Outram, *The Body and the French Revolution*, p. 16.

107 On sensibility and its complexities, see Janet Todd, *Sensibility: an Introduction* (London, Methuen, 1986); Chris Jones, *Radical Sensibility: Literature and Ideas in the 1790s* (London, Routledge, 1993); G. J. Barker-Benfield, *The Culture of Sensibility: Sex and Society in Eighteenth-Century Britain* (Chicago, University of Chicago Press, 1992).

humanity, refinement, cultivation, taste and genius. Or it may indicate a lack of self-control and judgement. Sensibility may be admirable when combined with reason and moral principle, deplorable when cut loose from those moorings. Sensibility may lead to melancholy, despair and the crime of suicide. Sensibility may be a mere fashion accessory, a show of modish feeling with no roots in the heart.

It is natural to suppose that sensibility was thought of as feminine: feminine feeling by contrast with masculine reason. Indeed, eighteenth-century commentators can be found saying just that.[108] From this it might be argued that when sensibility was viewed in a positive light, therefore this implied an enhanced respect for women and a validation of their point of view. In the main this is Katherine Rogers's opinion, though she insists that there was a downside: women of sensibility could all too easily be expected to devote themselves to caring for others, and sensibility glamorized dependency and self-sacrifice.[109] If sensibility sometimes valorized a form of subjectivity which women could readily adopt, it also tended to reinforce disabling stereotypes of women, as emotional therefore irrational, as passive, suffering and weak. Furthermore, as Marilyn Butler demonstrated in a classic study, in the aftermath of the French revolution the forces of conservatism in Britain succeeded in establishing a wide consensus that jacobinism, feminism, sensibility and sexual immorality went hand in hand.[110]

Sensibility, however, was not thought of as exclusively female: in literature men of feeling – Sir Charles Grandison, Yorick, Augustus Harley, Saint-Preux, Werther – were as prominent as Clarissa or Camilla. What was the meaning of this? One recent narrative tells of a 'feminization of culture'; the tendency of sensibility was to tame men, to reform them, to construct for them a subjectivity less macho and therefore more woman-friendly.[111] The man of sensibility would be less likely to do violence to women, more likely to make a refined, gentle and affectionate husband. This narrative is reinforced by the narrative of the growth of civility, of politeness. David Hume himself told this story in the mid-eighteenth century,[112] and associated the growth of civility with the influence of women; recent scholarship has echoed

[108] Jane Rendall, 'Virtue and commerce: women in the making of Adam Smith's political economy', in Ellen Kennedy & Susan Mendus (eds.), *Women in Western Political Philosophy* (Brighton, Wheatsheaf, 1987), pp. 58–9.

[109] Rogers, *Feminism in Eighteenth-Century England*, p. 125.

[110] Marilyn Butler, *Jane Austen and the War of Ideas* (Oxford, Oxford University Press, 1975), p. 33.

[111] Barker-Benfield, *Culture of Sensibility*, p. 239; Jones (ed.), *Women in the Eighteenth Century*, p. 11.

[112] David Hume, 'Of the rise and progress of the arts and sciences', *Essays* (1741) (Oxford, Oxford University Press, 1963), pp. 131–5. Hume also thought that sympathetic feeling was an essential basis or cause of moral sentiments. If sensibility = sympathy, this would imply that sensibility is not simply feminine, unless one thought that morality was feminine.

this: 'In a world that was being constructed around the touchstone of refined sociability or politeness, women had an assured place . . . [this was] a normative enhancement of the feminine'.[113]

This narrative has been roundly attacked by Claudia Johnson. She proposes instead that the 'feminization' of culture was not woman-friendly at all; rather it was yet another patriarchal strategy, a way of making the dominance of men appear acceptable. Furthermore it represented a hijacking of admirable feminine qualities by men which created a deep problem for female subjectivity, 'leaving women without a distinct gender site'. If men encroached upon conventionally feminine qualities, this drove women farther out; their sensibility, in order to distinguish itself from that of men, had to become extreme, 'saturated in turbulent and disfiguring excess':

> The sentiment celebrated in very different ways by Sterne, Goldsmith, Burke, and Rousseau validates male authority figures by representing them as men of feeling, but it also bars the women whose distress occasions their affective displays from enjoying any comparable moral authority by representing their affectivity as inferior, unconscious, unruly, or even criminal.[114]

Gendered bodies

A dramatic and ambitious narrative dominates scholarly thinking about gender in the eighteenth century, a narrative which has variously been proposed but perhaps best presented by Thomas Laqueur.[115] Early modern thinking about the body, it is widely recognized, was dominated by a cosmology and a medicine inherited from classical Greece. That cosmology was hierarchical, and took it for granted that men were better than women. Their gender superiority was conceived first and fundamentally as a matter of ontological and therefore social status expressed in behaviour; because men were higher on the great chain of being, therefore they did higher things, such as ruling and thinking. Biological, bodily differences as it were corresponded to this. Women's bodies were inferior because they were less perfect, secondary beings, rather than the other way round. Indeed, the medical theory inherited from classical antiquity proposed a 'single-sex body'; men's and women's bodies were thought to be fundamentally the same. It was just that men were better. But as the classical hierarchical cosmology came under attack, the prospect opened up that science would be

113 Lawrence E. Klein, 'Gender, conversation and the public sphere in early eighteenth-century England', in Judith Still & Michael Worton (eds), *Textuality and Sexuality* (Manchester, Manchester University Press, 1993), pp. 111, 107. See also Sylvana Tomaselli, 'The enlightenment debate on women', *History Workshop Journal*, 19 (1985), 101–24.

114 Johnson, *Equivocal Beings*, pp. 1, 11, 14.

115 Thomas Laqueur, *Making Sex: Body and Gender from the Greeks to Freud* (Cambridge, Mass., Harvard University Press, 1990).

forced to conclude that women, being essentially the same as men, were just as good as men.

Therefore according to Laqueur, and originally for ideological reasons in order to reaffirm male dominance, during the course of the seventeenth and eighteenth centuries a two-sex theory of the body gradually gained acceptance, eventually to be confirmed by observation; men's and women's bodies came to be understood as fundamentally different. In this way the gender difference came to be thought of as not primarily social, to do with status, role and behaviour, but rather as natural, rooted in the body, in biology.

If understandings of gender evolved in this way, then what did it imply for women? A hypothesis has been proposed by a number of scholars about a change in the way in which gender was experienced and lived. As for example Diane Dugaw has argued, when gender is thought of as a matter of social status expressed in behaviour, deportment and dress, rather than as a natural bodily characteristic, then gender is to some extent a matter of *acting* rather than of *being*.[116] The possibility therefore opens up for women to act masculine, to transgress the gender boundary. This possibility was realized by women like Charlotte Charke who cross-dressed, by women (the subject of a rich tradition of popular ballads) who dressed up as men and went off as soldiers, like Hannah Snell, by women who fought duels on stage and by actresses such as Peg Woffington, Dora Jordan and Mary Robinson who so often and to such acclaim took breeches parts. But the naturalization of gender by the end of the eighteenth century made such transgressions increasingly unacceptable.

On the face of it, this looks like another form of the 'from golden age to separate spheres' narrative. It has been said that the rise to cultural ascendency of a theory of incommensurable gender difference detracted from the Christian conception of the soul – the noblest part of each individual – as unsexed, equal to any other soul.[117] But *did* a notion of incommensurable gender difference achieve cultural ascendancy? And if it did, were there no counter-currents? From the theory that men's and women's *bodies* are fundamentally different, it does not necessarily follow that their *minds* are fundamentally different, or different at all. Now explorations of conceptions of gender in medical texts of the eighteenth century have certainly revealed the emergence of theories of mental and moral difference based in biology, developed for example by writers such as Roussel. This kind of theory takes as its data observed differences between men's and women's bodies, observed differences in their behaviour, and assumptions about their naturally differing roles – for example the female roles of childbearing and suckling. It then attempts to produce a coherent model or theory of the two sexes incorporating all of this data. So for example it is proposed that women's bodies are soft and delicate, whereas men's are hard and tough; women's brains are

[116] Dianne Dugaw, *Warrior Women and Popular Balladry, 1650–1850* (Cambridge, Cambridge University Press, 1989), pp. 121–3, 132, 138–40.

[117] Riley, *Am I that Name?* pp. 18–19.

smaller, and their nervous system more exquisitely developed. As a result women have a more intense sensibility, livelier feelings, stronger sympathies, but less rationality. And these differences, written on the body and the mind, are precisely such as fit women for a domestic and nurturing role, men for outgoing, competitive, acquisitive and dominant ones. Women feel and men think. Such theories depend to a high degree upon commonplace analogies and associations, for example of softness with feeling and hardness with reason. They also take as their normal woman not a tough peasant or working woman, but the leisured and inactive middle- or upper-class woman.[118]

We should not forget, however, that this was not the only theory of mind and character in play. There was a 'dualist' way of thinking stemming from Descartes which contended that body and mind were quite distinct; bodies were material, machines, whereas minds were souls and entirely immaterial. Bodies were sexed, but minds were not. The highest capacity of mind was reason, but women with minds like men's were just as capable of reason as men. But if a seventeenth-century Cartesian looked at people around him, he observed that in fact men and women were different in the way they thought, felt and behaved. How, if minds were fundamentally identical, were these differences to be explained? The answer was environment; different experiences, different educations, different cultural expectations, made men and women different. The differences did not arise from within, but from without. This Cartesian and environmentalist theory of women was proposed by the first French feminist, François Poulain de la Barre, in his *De l'égalité des deux sexes* of 1673, and in England in the writings of Mary Astell.

Even more influential in Britain was associationism, that theory of mind developed by Locke, Hume and Hartley. This theory contends that the original characteristics and powers of mind are very few. They are the ability to receive impressions from the five senses and from internal feelings such as hunger, pleasure and pain; the ability to recall these sensations in memory; and the ability to associate these simple sensations into more complex ideas, as for example certain sensations of colour, shape, feel and scent into the idea of a rose. All knowledge, all thought is built out of these simple capacities – capacities which, evidently, men and women share. Originally we start equal; if some become wiser than others, that is simply because they have had more valuable experiences. Differences in character too can be explained in terms of different experiences and associations. On the basis of this theory it could be argued that there were no natural mental or moral differences between men and women; and this was precisely what was argued by Helvétius and Condorcet in France, and by William Godwin in England. This theory was well known by the end

118 For different theories of gender in the seventeenth and eighteenth centuries, see Lieselotte Steinbrügge, *The Moral Sex: Woman's Nature in the French Enlightenment* (Oxford, Oxford University Press, 1992).

of the eighteenth century, and was especially influential in radical and dissenting circles.[119]

But to return to the narrative proposed by Okin, Laqueur and others, the difference of women was asserted in order to neutralize the threat to male dominance posed by a conception of biological similarity in an age of equal, human rights. But some, including Laqueur, have thought that women managed to draw an advantage out of this. Early modern culture, it is widely agreed, was not only patriarchal but also deeply misogynistic;[120] women were conventionally depicted as like men but worse, irrational, disorderly, lustful and lazy. The culture of sharp gender polarity which is said to have emerged during the eighteenth century came to be associated with the idea that women could be good in their own way, perhaps having qualities which men lacked. Thus the cultural status of woman was elevated; she was on her way to the Victorian pedestal.

This story is quite widely accepted; but scholars put different evaluative spins on it. If the story is true, then the question arises whether the improved moral and cultural status of women was worth the price paid for it in taking on a confining domestic ideal. From a liberal perspective, thinking in terms of gradualism and the pursuit of whatever gains are tactically feasible at a given time, the answer might be that it was. A radical perspective will see it as a more efficient and insidious way of securing patriarchal dominance.

The radical perspective has seemed most persuasive in relation to sexuality as an aspect of gender construction. For, it is generally argued, we are faced with the most astonishing transformation: in the sixteenth and seventeenth centuries, women were thought to have stronger sexual appetites than men, so strong that they were difficult to satisfy. By the nineteenth century, it was commonly thought that women were less sexually motivated, and perhaps that good women were not interested in sex at all. Most modern commentators have lamented this 'repression of female desire'. A qualified optimist like Katherine Rogers is nostalgic about the sexy women of the Restoration court, even though she recognizes that eighteenth-century women writers 'showed their feminine, properly conducted heroines triumphing over men through superior self-command. In this way the greater self-control imposed upon women became a source of strength and superiority rather than a mere deprivation'.[121] Mary Poovey finds little to admire in 'the Proper Lady, guardian and nemesis of the female self'.[122] And Cora Kaplan writes of Wollstonecraft that she 'sets up heart breaking conditions for women's liberation – a little death, the death of desire, the death of female pleas-

[119] Élie Halévy, *The Growth of Philosophic Radicalism* (1928) (London, Faber, 1972), pp. 5–9, 282, 437, 454.
[120] Fletcher, *Gender, Sex and Subordination*, pp. 70–2.
[121] Rogers, *Feminism in the Eighteenth Century*, p. 154.
[122] Poovey, *Proper Lady*, p. 47.

ure'.[123] But Nancy Cott has argued that we should not think of female passionlessness as pure loss and something imposed on women in the interests of men; women espoused the idea themselves, not only because it raised their moral status in an age of evangelical asceticism, not only because 'it routed women out of the cul-de-sac of education for attractiveness, thus allowing more intellectual breadth'; also it may have helped them to control their fertility in marriage.[124]

Masculine discourse, feminine writing

Janet Todd's *The Sign of Angellica* argues that the decade of the 1790s produces authors such as Wollstonecraft and Hays who are prepared to challenge respectability, asserting female desire and exposing the tyranny of patriarchal marriage. But their radical daring proves to be a dead end; antijacobin writers discredit them by associating their radicalism with sensibility read as sexual licence and with French revolutionary and terroristic politics. Other more conservative novelists choose a different strategy; Burney, Smith, Radcliffe, More, Edgeworth and Austen endorse chastity and respectability for women but at the same time forge a novel with a serious social message, a novel which with its overt moral purpose is more that mere entertainment. The standing of the genre is thereby enhanced, and with it the moral authority of the woman writer, who abandons the epistolary form to write a third-person narrative in her own voice.

But is this just too optimistic? Should our guiding thread rather be the narrative of women trapped within a discourse created by men?[125] Kathryn Shevelow's study of the eighteenth-century periodical argues that women writers were contained within 'the dominant patriarchal ideology'. In the eighteenth century, women became writers and readers on a hitherto unprecedented scale; but men wrote periodicals first, they wrote as and for women, and thereby they framed what women wrote and how they read. They represented women in a certain way, constructing for them a highly gendered and domestic subjectivity, a feminine ideal sharply differentiated from masculinity.[126] Nicola Watson's *Revolution and the Form of the British Novel* depicts women writers – Williams, Wollstonecraft, Hays, Smith, Fenwick – imprisoned in plots, in conventional narratives – in this case, in the sentimental plot of Rousseau's *Nouvelle Héloïse*. Rousseau's *Julie* briefly follows her desires,

[123] Cora Kaplan, 'Wild nights: pleasure/sexuality/feminism', in Nancy Armstrong & Leonard Tennenhouse (eds.), *The Ideology of Conduct: Essays on Literature and the History of Sexuality* (London, Methuen, 1987), p. 167.

[124] Nancy F. Cott, 'Passionlessness: an interpretation of Victorian sexual ideology, 1790–1850', *Signs: Journal of Women in Culture and Society*, 4:2 (1978), 219–36.

[125] Craft-Fairchild, *Masquerade and Gender*, p. 5.

[126] Shevelow, *Women and Print Culture*, pp. 2–3.

is defeated and dies; Watson contends that her 1790s authors fail to depict a desiring woman who wins through to happiness.[127] Barbara Zaczek's study of women's letters presents a related narrative in Foucaultian form. The expressive potential of letters for women was neutralized as disciplinary practices were created and embodied in the conventions of the letter genre itself, determining how a woman could write.[128]

Very often, narratives of this kind draw upon the legacy of Freud and his post-Lacanian successors in order to explain how women come to repress their authentic desires and to block off recognition of this repression. Elizabeth Kowaleski-Wallace's study of 'patriarchal complicity' in the writings of Hannah More and Maria Edgeworth is an example. She argues that her chosen authors – and indeed Wollstonecraft too – fail to mount a successful challenge to the law of the father. They accept its constitutive binaries of masculine/feminine, rational/irrational instead of deconstructing them. They are imprisoned by the process of psychological development which women undergo under patriarchy, a process which, because of male fear of the dangerous, explosive sexual energies of the female body, conditions women to turn to the father, in the process imbibing a persistent matrophobia.[129]

A similar case is argued by Catherine Craft-Fairchild in her analysis of women's writings.[130] Caroline Gonda too offers a Foucaultian account of the sentimental family as a more insidious because internalized form of patriarchal discipline. She notes the theme, common in women's novels of the period, of daughterly devotion to their fathers, a devotion which constricts the possibilities of female rebellion. Gonda finds a very dark side to this, in an overt or half-buried theme of father–daughter incest in so many novels.[131] The implication is that patriarchy and female internalization of patriarchal authority, compulsory heterosexuality, incest and the sexual abuse of daughters by their fathers form part of a single system.

Those scholars who have supposed that women writers in the late eighteenth century were imprisoned in patriarchal discourses have not denied that those writers, consciously, unconsciously or half-consciously, mounted some kind of a challenge and made some cracks in the walls of the prison. But they do insist that that challenge was muted or of limited effectiveness. Very often they think, with Gilbert and Gubar, that women's rage against their confinement was expressed and had to be expressed indirectly. So for example Susan Fraiman thinks that because 'no ideology is singular or seamless',[132] there is

---

[127] Nicola J. Watson, *Revolution and the Form of the British Novel 1790–1825: Intercepted Letters, Interrupted Seductions* (Oxford, Oxford University Press, 1994).

[128] Zaczek, *Censored Sentiments*.

[129] Kowaleski-Wallace, *Their Fathers' Daughters*.

[130] Craft-Fairchild, *Masquerade and Gender*.

[131] Caroline Gonda, *Reading Daughters' Fictions, 1709-1834: Novels and Society from Manley to Edgeworth* (Cambridge, Cambridge University Press, 1996), p. 34.

[132] Fraiman, *Unbecoming Women*, p. xiv.

always the possibility of exploiting its contradictions in order to suggest a dissentient point of view. Caroline Gonda invites us to distinguish between the 'moral' of the novel, the overt teaching – for example, in Inchbald's *Simple Story*, that disobedient, wilful women end up ruined – and the 'tendency' or hidden message – in this case, that the wayward Miss Milner is much more appealing than her repressed milksop of a daughter.[133]

These postmodern readings of texts with their emphasis upon the power of discursive, psychological and patriarchal structures have been much admired. Their originality and suggestiveness is valuable; but to a considerable degree their persuasiveness appears to rest upon a prior commitment to a radical stance as defined earlier in this chapter, and in some cases upon an acceptance of a preferred theory or theories, Lacanian, Foucaultian and so forth. Explaining what authors mean, and why they say what they say with the help of theories of this kind, can sometimes draw attention away from explaining in terms of the historical context. Women writers of the past are implicitly or explicitly criticized, because they do not think as present-day feminists do. Their failure is then explained with reference to a deep, half-hidden structure which modern theory has uncovered. But perhaps they think differently, because of a realistic sense of what was possible in the context of the time. The chapters that follow will give considerable attention to the question of whether and why 1790s women writers are discursively imprisoned, or whether they are able to break free by exploiting the contradictions and open-ended texture of discourses.

Against these narratives of discursive imprisonment may be pitted narratives which seek to trace the emergence of women's voices. Gary Kelly attempts to find a woman's voice in the writings of Wollstonecraft, Hays and Williams. He finds it, for example, in Williams's account of the French revolution from a woman's point of view, in which the revolution in all its stages is judged from the standpoint of a sympathetic sensibility, and for its impact upon domestic relations.[134] Meena Alexander reads Wollstonecraft as a writer who writes from the female body, therefore not like a male romantic, cut off in self-sufficient individuality, but always connected, maternal and nurturing.[135]

More ambitiously still, Anne Mellor has contended that there was a distinct female romanticism which came first; male writers colonized it, stealing feminine characteristics, and then obliterated from memory the female achievement when they constructed the canon. Masculine romanticism was Promethean, self-assertive and individualistic; feminine romantics laid greater emphasis upon care, co-operation and community.[136] Mellor also

[133] Gonda, *Reading Daughters' Fictions*, pp. 198–200.

[134] Kelly, *Women, Writing and Revolution*, pp. 60–5; see also Jones, *Radical Sensibility*, p. 147.

[135] Meena Alexander, *Women in Romanticism: Mary Wollstonecraft, Dorothy Wordsworth and Mary Shelley* (London, Macmillan, 1989).

[136] Anne K. Mellor, *Romanticism and Gender* (London, Routledge, 1993), pp. 3, 145.

points out that in her chosen period, 'there were over two hundred publishing women poets and at least as many novelists, as well as several playwrights, essayists, memoirists and journalists'.[137] This inevitably raises the question of why so very few women writers – perhaps, until very recently, no more than three women novelists – from this period made it into the canon, into twentieth-century publishers' lists and into university syllabuses and textbooks. This question has of late elicited some provocative but timely reappraisals.

According to Stuart Curran, in the 1790s the novel, poetry and theatre were all dominated by women writers.[138] Loraine Fletcher has argued that Charlotte Smith was developing a poetry of self-expression, and simplifying poetic diction, at the same time as Wordsworth, and that indeed he was influenced by her.[139] Jerome McGann has looked again at the poetry of the Della Cruscans who were ridiculed by Wordsworth, and among them particularly at Mary Robinson. In the 1790s she succeeded Southey as poetry editor for the *Morning Post*, to which Coleridge and Wordsworth also contributed. McGann argues that at that time her standing was higher than theirs; he insists upon the distinctiveness and skill of her poetry and suggests that the now better-known Lake Poets were happy to learn from her. Della Cruscan poetry represented a distinctive aesthetic, and according to McGann, Robinson, who wrote in a number of voices, was a poet of a feminized sensibility. But she was also a 'jacobin' poet, and other prominent women, such as Inchbald and Smith, were politically tainted too. So a critical effort was made to discredit them. A more significant factor in the long run was that Wordsworth's normative account of the nature of romantic poetry, the account which underlay *Lyrical Ballads*, came to be widely accepted by later critics. Poets were philosophers playing a public role, therefore male. The canon constructed around this aesthetic, the canon which held sway for two centuries, was therefore a male canon which ignored the contribution of women.[140]

Gender and class

It has become a cliché to insist that the chaste, domestic woman was a middle-class woman. More daringly, historians and critics of literature have laboured to implement the Joan Wallach Scott enterprise of demonstrating that gender is 'a useful category of historical analysis'[141] by arguing that this woman was central to the 'rise of the middle class'. In history the *locus*

137 *Ibid.*, p. 2.
138 Curran, 'Romantic poetry: the I altered', pp. 186–7.
139 Fletcher, *Charlotte Smith*, pp. 333–6.
140 Carol Shiner Wilson & Joel Haefner (eds), *Re-visioning Romanticism: British Women Writers, 1776–1837* (Philadelphia, University of Pennsylvania Press, 1994); McGann, *The Poetics of Sensibility*.
141 J. W. Scott, 'Gender: a useful category of historical analysis', *American Historical Review*, 91:4 (1986), pp. 1053–75.

classicus is Davidoff and Hall's *Family Fortunes*. This depicts a middle class establishing its cultural and moral distinctiveness from and superiority to both a dissipated aristocracy and the animalistic lower orders, by virtue of its observance of strict gender roles and separate spheres, focusing upon an idealized, woman-centred domesticity.[142] In this way women are accorded a star part in the making of the English middle class.

In literary studies, a parallel theme has been most powerfully argued in Nancy Armstrong's 'new historicist' *Desire and Domestic Fiction* and in *The Ideology of Conduct*, which show how a discursive construction of desire and gender was imbricated in the consolidation of bourgeois capitalist hegemony. According to Armstrong the middle class is made, that is to say given an identity and united in horizontal solidarity as a class strata, by common allegiance to an ideal, a shared desire for the domestic woman. This woman is utterly feminine, characterized by her rich emotional depths and moral values; she contrasts with the aristocratic woman who is all attractive surface, on public display outside woman's proper sphere. But the importance of women, in this view, is clear:

> Thus it was the new domestic woman rather than her counterpart, the new economic man, who first encroached upon aristocratic culture and seized authority from it. ... If there is any truth in this, then it is also reasonable to claim that the modern individual was first and foremost a female.[143]

Armstrong's narrative, which accords equal weight to class and gender, does not depict middle-class women as mere victims, always secondary to men. Their role in class consolidation was a primary one, they benefited from the rise of their class and the ideal domestic woman, though confined to her sphere, gained authority to regulate emotional relationships and the desires of men. Armstrong's is a history of class (and female) forms of power.[144]

The most trenchant attack upon this narrative has been launched by Amanda Vickery. She reminds us that the hypothesis of a class war between, on the one hand, a landed and court aristocracy, and on the other, a rising professional, commercial and industrial bourgeoisie, ignores the lesser gentry. Moderate landowners were a large class of people, overlapping with and connected to both aristocracy and the trades and professions, by ties of economic interest, sociability, kinship and marriage. They were not a new or a rising class, their disapproval of aristocratic dissipation did not preclude admiration and emulation, and they too were affected by the domestic ideal. Her study of Lancashire and Yorkshire families reveals social cohesion –

---

142 Davidoff and Hall, *Family Fortunes*.
143 *Ibid.*, pp. 96, 103.
144 *Ibid.*, p. 130; Armstrong, *Desire and Domestic Fiction*, pp. 4, 26, 96. Armstrong's argument has been criticized by Christopher Flint, *Family Fictions: Narrative and Domestic Relations in Britain, 1688–1798* (Stanford, Stanford University Press, 1998).

though with tensions – rather than cultural war.[145] If she is right then the theory of a connection between the rise of a new economic class and a transformation of gender – a theory which has had widespread currency[146] – looks decidedly shaky.

This survey of scholarship provides an agenda of questions to take to the texts in the following chapters. To ask whether the authors considered were feminists or not would perhaps be an anachronistic enterprise, or a play with words; but I shall ask whether they speak *for* women, with a view to advancing their interests and standing. To ask whether there was progress or decline for women invites answers varying according to the present-day commentator's political stance; but it is worth while asking whether 1790s women writers perceived progress or decline. The issue of whether there was a patriarchal structure imposing near-total domination upon women writers, or whether the 'historical revisionists' are nearer to the truth in their accounts of female resourcefulness, will inevitably haunt my discussion. A range of questions will be addressed about 'separate spheres': What did women writers have to say about women, work and politics and about their 'social' role? How did they use 'public', 'private' and related terms? Did they endorse a narrative of 'from golden age to separate spheres'? Did they gain entry to the 'bourgeois public sphere'? Did they think it necessary to abandon their womanliness in order to do so? How did they evaluate the public and the private? What use did they make of images of motherhood? To ask whether romantic love and companionate marriage were in the interests of women would once again run the risk of an anachronistic and political response. But what did women writers themselves think about romantic love and companionate marriage? Did they demand equality in marriage? Did any of them think that marriage was an inherently oppressive institution? Did they think that women were traded by men and in the exclusive interests of men, and did they challenge this 'political economy of sex'? Were there any calls for an alternative, female solidarity? What did they have to say about the relationships between fathers and daughters? Were women writers engaged in and advocates of the 'civilizing process'? Do they promote the 'self-enclosed self', and *Kultur* rather than *Zivilisation*? Is there any protest against the repressiveness of the civilizing process, and in particular against the sexual reserve of the 'proper' lady? Are expressions of female erotic desire to be found? Do they depict the process of development into womanhood as a movement to defeat, confinement and passivity? How do they conceive of, and evaluate, sensibility? Do they view it as a gendered attribute? Are they agents of a 'feminization of culture' and of men? What kind of

[145] Vickery, *Gentleman's Daughter*, pp. 13–37.
[146] See for example Tobin, *Superintending the Poor*, pp. 1–2, 5–6, 89; Myers, 'Reform or ruin', p. 203.

discourse do they construct about gender difference? Are they engaged in the enterprise of putting women on a pedestal? Do women writers find an authentically female voice in this decade? Or do they express themselves indirectly, covertly? How do gender and voice mesh with class? Do women writers promote a middle-class, domestic woman by contrast with a disapproved aristocratic, public one?

3

Female difficulties: women as victims

The previous chapter remarked upon the tension, in modern scholarly accounts, between pessimism and optimism, between often 'radical' studies which emphasize female victimhood, and 'liberal' and 'revisionist' accounts which stress the capacity of women to cope with and sometimes to triumph over the restrictions and disadvantages they faced. Which perspective did 1790s women writers themselves agree with? In this chapter I will explore the extent and the nature of their agreement with the dark, the gloomy and the pessimistic. I will look at the ways in which 'unsex'd females' voice a litany of complaints about 'female difficulties' – to quote the subtitle of Burney's *Camilla* – and about the oppression of women. I will also consider whether 'proper' females sometimes join their voices to the chorus. This will be a one-sided chapter, therefore: but it will in subsequent chapters be balanced by a consideration of the opposite stance. In particular Chapter 6 on 'Female opportunities: fashioning a self' will deal with the positive, constructive and optimistic in women's writings.

I shall consider both non-fiction and prose fiction texts; there are special and obvious difficulties in using the latter. Because they are professedly fictional, making inferences from them about 'reality' cannot but be problematic. Many of the situations described are at least in part prescribed by the exigencies of the type of narrative being constructed. A common aim of the narrator is to keep the reader in a state of suspense about the heroine, anxiously demanding 'So what happened next?', wondering whether she will escape from the calamities besetting her. This narrative requirement necessarily dictates 'female difficulties' of various kinds, dangers, oppression and maltreatment. But obedience to generic conventions does not confer complete freedom from the constraints of reality. For the thoughts, dilemmas, situations and actions of women as presented in works of prose fiction must have some resemblance to actuality, otherwise readers would have found them absurd or unintelligible. After all, none of these texts is in a utopian or dystopian genre. 'Romances', gothic tales with settings remote in place and time could obviously diverge more radically from women's experience than 'novels' set in the present day; but even romances would have to conform to what their readers could believe it possible for women to think and do. For novels to carry conviction, their accounts would have to have a familiarity about them at some level or other, if only at a symbolic level. They would have to be acceptable to their readers, as reminiscent or symbolically representative of common, or exceptional, or at the very least possible behaviour and situations.

Complaints are conveyed in a number of themes and stock narratives which occur and recur in both prose fiction and non-fictional writings. A strikingly common theme in the former is that of the imprisoned woman, occasionally in an actual prison, or madhouse, more often in a private dwelling. We can certainly read this as a reflection of reality, of what sometimes occurred; there were known examples of wives imprisoned by their husbands.[1] But perhaps it should also be understood as *symbolic* of the confinement of women, if not by actual locks and bolts, then by less concrete but equally disabling restrictions.

Examples could be found in almost every novel by an 'unsex'd female'. In Hays's *Victim of Prejudice*, Mary Raymond is kidnapped and held captive by Sir Peter Osborne in his London house as he attempts to force her to be his mistress; Lady Matilda suffers a similar imprisonment at the hands of Lord Margrave in Inchbald's *Simple Story*. Mary Raymond is also incarcerated in a debtor's prison, as is Gertrude in Robinson's *False Friend*. The heroine of Fenwick's *Secresy* is imprisoned by her uncle in his castle, behind moat and drawbridge; she fails in an attempt to escape by throwing herself into the moat. In Smith's *Young Philosopher*, Mrs Glenmorris is imprisoned in her mother's castle, then in Kilbrodie castle at the farthest edge of Scotland where her baby son's death is engineered; her daughter Medora is kidnapped and imprisoned twice by men who want to get their hands on either her person or her money. Sophia Clarendon is pursued and imprisoned by her father in Robinson's *Angelina*, because she will not agree to his marriage plans for her. Towards the end of the 1790s there was a minor outbreak of heroines imprisoned in madhouses even though not mad – first in Wollstonecraft's *Maria*, then in Robinson's *Natural Daughter* and Smith's *Young Philosopher*. But the greatest prevalence of wrongful imprisonment is to be found in the gothic romances of that 'proper' female, Ann Radcliffe. By the time that Adeline, heroine of *The Romance of the Forest*, is united with the hero, Theodore, she has spent most of her life and much of the novel in one kind of imprisonment or another, and has been threatened with veiling as a nun, with rape and death. Emily spends one-and-a-third of the three volumes of *The Mysteries of Udolpho* imprisoned in the castle of Udolpho, and Ellena in *The Italian* is imprisoned in a convent and almost forced to take the veil.

The imprisoned woman is the extreme case of the powerless woman,

1 Staves, *Married Women's Separate Property*, p. 214.

the woman held as a passive object in the hands of others. Powerlessness is thematized in other ways too. We do not usually get much of a sense of a process of *Bildung* in these novels, in which a young woman forms herself and grows in moral and intellectual stature as she confronts a series of difficulties and crises. Very often the heroine has been formed by others, frequently by men – fathers, lovers, uncles or other father-figures – or is static and undeveloping, her character apparently fixed. A clear example is in Smith's *The Old Manor House*. The heroine, Monimia, is a humble girl, little more than a servant with a rudimentary education. She is confined at night in her bedroom in a turret (imprisonment again). The hero Orlando comes to her by a hidden spiral staircase which opens behind her bed. Though she cuts the tapestry to let him in, their purpose is not explicitly sexual; he takes her to the library, there to form her mind with good books. There is an explicit reference to the myth of Pygmalion, who created a statue of a beautiful woman, fell in love with it and persuaded the gods to bring it to life; '[Orlando] had animated the lovely statue'.[2] Later we are told that Orlando has discovered in Monimia a hidden gem, which he intends to place in its proper setting.[3] This is the most striking and explicit example of the Pygmalion theme, but there are elements of it elsewhere, for example in both of the novels by Hays, in Wollstonecraft's *Maria*, Inchbald's *Simple Story*, Robinson's *Angelina* and *False Friend*, Helen Williams's *Julia*, and in Radcliffe's *Udolpho* and *Romance of the Forest*. In order to give a balanced account, it should be remarked that sometimes mothers or mother figures take on the role of Pygmalion to the young heroine, as for example in Smith's *Marchmont* or above all in West's *Advantages of Education*. George Delmont, Smith's *Young Philosopher*, was formed by his *mother*.[4]

It is unusual for heroines to be completely passive, acted upon rather than acting from cover to cover, never doing more than saying 'No!' when threatened with an unwanted marriage or sexual advance. Perhaps Monimia in Smith's *Old Manor House* and Ellena in Radcliffe's *The Italian* come closest to utter helplessness. Most heroines are more assertive and adventurous than these, but heroines who do not exhibit symptoms of feminine frailty at some point – fainting, bursting into tears, falling ill or going slightly mad because of anxiety or grief – are uncommon. Hannah More gives us strong women in her *Tracts*, most notably Mrs Jones, to whom we will return in a later

[2] Charlotte Smith, *The Old Manor House* (1793) (Oxford, Oxford University Press, 1969), p. 166.
[3] *Ibid.*, p. 309.
[4] And we do have examples of young women creating ideal young men in their imaginations, or rather recreating the object of their affections as they would have him to be, rather than as he is. This leads to the disastrous marriage of the heroine in Wollstonecraft's *Maria*, and the less than ideal marriage of Geraldine in West's *Tale of the Times*.

chapter;[5] but Mrs Jones is a childless widow, perhaps thereby in a sense unsexed (not in Polwhele's sense, of course). There is a heroine of uncompromised strength in Williams's *Julia*, but her femininity is not foregrounded either; she does not fall in love and remains unmarried. The same can be said of the secondary heroine, Caroline Ashburn, in Fenwick's *Secresy*. She is inclined to fall in love with Arthur Murden, but overcomes her feelings when she finds he loves Sibella; her strength, we feel, is at the expense of womanly desire.

Women as lovers, wives and mothers by contrast tend to exhibit vulnerability. Mrs Glenmorris in Smith's *Young Philosopher* has heroically surmounted the most appalling difficulties, including the kidnapping of her husband when pirates attacked their Scottish castle, but she goes temporarily insane when her daughter Medora is kidnapped. The eponymous heroine of Robinson's *Angelina* has 'a soul so sensible! intellects so illumined! taste so discriminating! genius so refined!',[6] but in fact she does nothing from beginning to end of the novel except wait, and sing, and sketch, and mourn. The heroine of Smith's *Montalbert*, though she has eloped, survived an earthquake and escaped from a remote Italian castle, almost dies when her child is taken from her. Even the strong-minded mother in West's *Advantages of Education* starts to waste away, having daily fainting fits and spending every night in tears as she witnesses her daughter's settled unhappiness when crossed in love. From all of this it appears that women writers found it difficult to construct a heroine who was wholly assertive and wholly powerful, without a trace of 'feminine' weakness. It was easier to depict unalloyed strength in a minor character or a villainess; the novels of Robinson and Smith furnish a catalogue of ostensibly disapproved female characters who are utterly ruthless and unconstrained. Perhaps it would be wrong to conclude that women writers did not wish to describe powerful women: it was rather that cultural conventions put obstacles in the way of doing so.

But it is not unreasonable to argue that the popularity of the 'courtship' novel was in part due to the fact that its concern was with a special moment of female power; poised between the authority of her father, and the authority of her husband, the heroine enjoyed a brief period of momentous choice, with her lover at her feet. Miss Milner in Inchbald's *Simple Story*, unusually poised because the man who sought her hand was also her guardian, her stand-in father, perceives this power: 'As my guardian, I certainly did obey him; and I could obey him as a husband; but as a lover, I will not'.[7] And in Robinson's *The Widow*, Mrs Vernon remarks, 'I know that husbands often

---

[5] Hannah More, 'A cure for melancholy: shewing the way to do much good with little money', in *The Works of Hannah More* (London, T. Cadell and W. Davies, 1818), vol. iv., and *The History of Hester Wilmot; or, the New Gown* (London, J. Marshall, 1796).

[6] Robinson, *Angelina*, ii, p. 92.

[7] Inchbald, *Simple Story*, p. 154.

make us poor women suffer, after marriage, for the impertinences of courtship.'[8]

A second major theme in woman-authored narratives of the period is sexual abuse or harassment. Very rarely does this culminate in actual rape. Jemima is raped by her employer in Wollstonecraft's last novel – this is a lower-class rape, a rape not involving gentlemen and gentlewomen. Mary Raymond is raped by Sir Peter Osborne in Hays's *Victim of Prejudice*. Geraldine Monteith is drugged, abducted and raped by Fitzosborne in West's *Tale of the Times*. The nun Ollivia in Radcliffe's *The Italian* had been forced into an unwanted second marriage by rape. Examples of physical violence against women are rare also. Sibella's uncle strikes her in Fenwick's *Secresy*, and Sir Edward Clarendon menaces violence against women more than once in Robinson's *Angelina*, raising his fist against his sister-in-law, and in a comic scene chasing the women round the room with a blunderbuss, causing Lady Selina Wantworth's feathered head-dress to catch fire when she gets too close to a candle. But Sir Edward Clarendon is presented as a savage, well beyond the pale of gentility. Hamilton's Hindoo Rajah observes the magistrates quickly dismiss a case so that they can get down to the more serious business of protecting the landlord's game: 'It was, indeed, only concerning a man who was said to have beaten his wife almost to death: a trifling crime, in the eyes of these Magistrates, when compared to the murder of seven partridges!'[9]

When one recalls what a major theme violence, including sexual violence, was later to be in Victorian polemics such as Mill's *Subjection of Women*, it is curious that the non-fiction texts of the 1790s concerned with the rights of women, by Wollstonecraft, Hays, Robinson and others, do not discuss rape and violence. Wollstonecraft is highly critical of Rousseau's *Emile*, but fails to point out that his insistence therein that women always say no, even when they mean yes, is a rapist's charter.[10] In her last novel, Wollstonecraft *does* consider male brutality towards women, but once again presents it as a lower-class phenomenon.

In prose fiction, the prospect if not the actuality of involuntary sexual intercourse secured by force, threats or confinement, or of voluntary but dishonourable sexual intercourse as a result of seduction and deception, regularly powers the plot. Few works of prose fiction do not contain examples, for this is the principal suspense-creating threat to the heroine; Ann Radcliffe is unusual in threatening her heroines with murder in *The Romance of the Forest* and *The Italian*. Examples are so common that a few will have to suffice. Forcing or tricking a heroine into a carriage is a common stratagem,

[8] Mary Robinson, *The Widow, or a Picture of Modern Times* (London, Hookham & Carpenter, 1794), i., p. 34.

[9] Hamilton, *Hindoo Rajah*, p. 120.

[10] Jean-Jacques Rousseau, *Émile ou de l'Éducation* (1762) (Paris, Garnier, 1964), pp. 448–9.

and Mary Robinson often uses this device in her novels; the crush and crowding when leaving the opera was apparently a particularly dangerous situation. In Burney's *Camilla*, Bellamy has a carriage constantly at the ready to whisk off the heiress Eugenia Tyrold; in the end he succeeds, and carries her away to a forced marriage at Gretna Green. Burney is acutely aware of sexual danger in all her novels. Camilla is trapped in a bathing hut at Southampton by two young men and a rakish old lord; she narrowly escapes abduction. Medora in Smith's *Young Philosopher* is inveigled into the mansion of Sir Harry Richmond in Yorkshire, a house of shame to which a succession of young women have been enticed to satisfy the owner's lust. Adeline in Radcliffe's *Romance of the Forest* is abducted and taken to the Marquis of Montalt's pleasure pavilion; he fails to persuade her into his bed, and she escapes in the nick of time, for it is clear that he intends to force her on the following day. Sir Henry Neville courts Maria Williams in West's *Advantages of Education*, offering marriage; but the reader has been let into the secret that his real plan is to enjoy her person without marriage, for she has no money. Attempting to blackmail women into bed is another occasional theme; in Smith's *Marchmont* the evil attorney Mohun offers to get Althea's husband out of debtor's prison in return for her person. In Robinson's *Hubert de Sevrac* a lawyer, Signor Lupo, tells Sabina, 'Your father's safety may be purchased by your smiles; think of it, and if you hold him dear, do not hesitate to snatch him from destruction'.[11] In the same novel, the Marquis de Briancour had committed the innocent de Fleury to the Bastille by *lettre de cachet*, so that he could blackmail de Fleury's daughter into his bed in return for her father's release.

A minor theme is the trading of women's bodies by men who ought to protect them. In Smith's *Desmond*, Geraldine Verney's husband attempts to give her to the Duc de Romagnecourt in order to clear his debts; Smith makes reference to this selling of wives' favours also in *The Young Philosopher*. And in a rare reference to domestic violence, Althea in Smith's *Marchmont* congratulates herself that she refused to marry Mohun: 'He might ... have beat me, or locked me up, or sold me if he could have met with a purchaser, to give course to his brutal humour, or contribute to his selfish indulgences. Such people have existed – do probably exist now.'[12] Maria in Wollstonecraft's last novel leaves her husband George Venables when she finds that he has struck a similar deal.

Lesser forms of sexual harassment are even more common. When in Smith's *Old Manor House* Sir John Berkeley Belgrave, MP, meets Monimia in the park accompanied only by a servant girl, he rudely demands an embrace and a kiss. Celestina in Smith's novel of that title lodges with the

11 Mary Robinson, *Hubert de Sevrac, a Romance, of the Eighteenth Century* (London, Hookham & Carpenter, 1796), ii, p. 269.
12 Smith, *Marchmont*, iv, pp. 279–80.

Rev. Thorold; his oldest son Captain Thorold pays her rude addresses. His youngest son Montague Thorold falls in love with her, and in spite of the fact that she has clearly refused him (she is already in love with someone else) he persists in his addresses while she lives in his father's house, and follows her when his conduct forces her to leave it, even as far as the Isle of Skye. Rosalie in Smith's *Montalbert* suffers from gross and persistent attention from Rev. Philibert Hughson; her 'father', who wants her off his hands, refuses to protect her (he turns out not to be her father after all). Repeatedly in novels men obtrude their attention by offering suggestive compliments to young women they hardly know, and by staring at young women they do not know.

Sexual threat is so prevalent in prose fiction, so taken for granted by authors and readers, that the language of *protection* is common currency, largely unremarked because unremarkable. A woman needs protection at all times. An unprotected woman in certain public places is in danger; a man who fails to protect his wife is failing in one of the first duties of a husband. There is never any suggestion that the law, or law-enforcement agencies, can be relied upon to protect a woman; sexual policing has to be done by family or friends, and the duel is the usual sanction against offenders. But we should note that it is not the case that women can only be protected by men, by fathers, brothers or husbands. They can also be protected by money, which will buy them safe lodging and carriage, or by other women who have the necessary money or safe lodging – as Smith's Celestina is protected by Lady Horatia Howard and by Mrs Elphinstone, or as Althea is protected by Mrs Marchmont. The issue of protection is explicitly raised in some non-fiction texts; Robinson complains angrily that men fail to protect women properly, but women are not allowed to protect their own honour by fighting duels. Of course she remarks upon the truism that women only require the protection of some men, because they are threatened by others: 'Man who *professes* himself her champion, her protector, is the most subtle and unrelenting enemy she has to encounter.'[13] And to take an example from a text by a 'proper' writer, Mary Ann Radcliffe insists that what women want, or should want, is not power, but men's protection in return for obedience; this is the real 'rights of women'.[14]

To actual confinement in prisons of various kinds, and effective confinement by the threat of sexual danger, we must add a third mode of disempowerment: lack of money. Women write obsessively about money in this period, as Copeland has so vividly demonstrated.[15] Everybody knows how

13 Robinson, *Thoughts*, p. 26.

14 Mary Ann Radcliffe, *The Female Advocate; or, an Attempt to Recover the Rights of Women from Male Usurpation* (1799; reprinted in *The Memoirs of Mrs. Mary Ann Radcliffe; in Familiar Letters to her Female Friend*, Edinburgh, Manners & Miller, 1810), pp. 397–8.

15 Edward Copeland, *Women Writing about Money: Women's Fiction in England, 1790–1820* (Cambridge, Cambridge University Press, 1995).

scrupulously Jane Austen specifies the capital and income of her male and female *dramatis personae*; novelists of the 1790s often go into finer detail than that. So for example we are told precisely how many guineas Althea has in Smith's *Marchmont*, and how they are progressively used up. A major theme of the novel is Althea's attempts to secure the money that is rightfully hers. In Burney's *Camilla* there is much detail about what the heroine receives, where it goes, and how she falls into debt; the crisis of the novel is brought on by her indebtedness. Depriving a heroine of money is an obvious way of plotting her into danger. The unrelenting series of disasters which overwhelms Mary Raymond in Hays's *Victim of Prejudice* could have been avoided if she had had money; Adeline in Radcliffe's *Romance of the Forest* is in the power of those who would destroy her, because she is penniless.

But depriving women of money is not merely a good plotting tactic in prose fiction; their lack of what it takes to get along is a preoccupation of non-fiction too. Wollstonecraft, Hays, Robinson, Mary Ann Radcliffe and Priscilla Wakefield all complain about the difficulties experienced by women without independent means and without a man to support them.[16] They know that most occupations are closed to genteel women, by custom, by prejudices about loss of caste and by lack of practical education. That trades formerly open to women have been taken over by men has become a cliché of the literature. 'Why does not the legislature tax such she-he gentry to the teeth? – Why are not men made ashamed of monopolizing trades' such as tailoring, hairdressing, millinery, mantua-making and stay-making? asks the author of the *Appeal to the Men of Great Britain*.[17] Wollstonecraft draws the devastating conclusion that women are forced to marry for support, and likens this to legal prostitution.[18] She was not alone in sounding this theme: Charlotte Smith wrote of her own unhappy marriage at the age of 15 that she had been 'sold, a legal prostitute' and that she was 'as a pearl that had been basely thrown away'.[19]

[16] Mary Wollstonecraft, *The Wrongs of Woman: or, Maria* (1798) (Oxford, Oxford University Press, 1980), p. 148; Mary Hays, 'Letter on female education', *Monthly Magazine* (March, 1797), pp. 194–5; Mary Robinson, *The False Friend: a Domestic Story* (London, T. N. Longman & G. Rees, 1799), i, p. 194; Radcliffe, *Female Advocate*, pp. 405, 410; Priscilla Wakefield, *Reflections on the Present Condition of the Female Sex; with Suggestions for its Improvement* (London, J. Johnson, 1798), pp. 51–3, 60, 65–73.

[17] *Appeal to the Men of Great Britain* (London, J. Johnson, 1798), pp. 200–1. (As remarked in Chapter 1, this anonymous work is almost certainly by Mary Hays.) The same thought is voiced by Robinson, Wakefield and Mary Ann Radcliffe.

[18] Mary Wollstonecraft, *A Vindication of the Rights of Woman: with Strictures on Political and Moral Subjects* (1792) (Cambridge, Cambridge University Press, 1995), pp. 135, 239.

[19] Fletcher, *Charlotte Smith*, pp. 25, 38. In fact the *Gentleman's Magazine* referred to marriages arranged for family advantage against the daughter's will as 'legal prostitutions' in 1794: Donna T. Andrew, '"Adultery à-la-Mode": privilege, the law and attitudes to adultery 1770–1809', *History*, 82:265 (January 1997), p. 15.

Nor is Wollstonecraft alone in recognizing that, when women lack independent property of their own and therefore become the property of men, their situation is not altogether different from that of negro slaves.[20] The parallel is drawn by Hays and Smith,[21] and frequently by Robinson; for example in *Hubert de Sevrac* the Marquis de Briancour, 60 years old, had married a woman young enough to be his granddaughter: 'She had been purchased, as the merchant buys the slave; and her lot was more terrible than even that of the ill-fated negro'.[22] Even the perfectly 'proper' Mary Ann Radcliffe compares the lot of women and slaves, suggesting that gentlewomen who fall from comfort and respectability may suffer more than the unfortunate African.[23]

The extreme narrative of women's oppression is the narrative of prostitution. Prostitution narratives are almost an eighteenth-century sub-genre, and their character evolves over the course of the century.[24] At the beginning of the century, the prostitute is often depicted as lusty, perhaps as a wicked and vicious predator. At mid-century, the campaign for the founding and funding of the Magdalen Hospital for penitent prostitutes produces a series of narratives in which the prostitute is described as a sinner but also as a victim, perhaps seduced and abandoned by an upper-class rake. The prostitute becomes an object of humanitarian sensibility, to be assisted, reformed and thereby controlled.

Women writers in the 1790s connect the prostitution narrative with the theme of women's deprivation of work opportunities; women who fall on hard times may find that they have no recourse other than to barter person for bread. They also lay the blame on society's unforgivingness of sexual lapses; a seduced and abandoned woman may be refused respectable employment. These complaints unite 'unsex'd' and some 'proper' female writers; they are developed or touched upon by Wakefield, Mary Ann Radcliffe,

---

20 Wollstonecraft, *Vindication of the Rights of Woman*, pp. 177, 184; Moira Ferguson, 'Mary Wollstonecraft and the problematic of slavery', in Eileen Janes Yeo (ed.), *Mary Wollstonecraft and Two Hundred Years of Feminisms* (London, Rivers Oram Press, 1997), p. 89.

21 Mary Hays, 'Letter on A. B.'s strictures on the talents of women', *Monthly Magazine* (July 1796), 470; Smith, *Desmond*, pp. 316, 319.

22 Robinson, *Hubert de Sevrac*, iii, 96.

23 Radcliffe, *Female Advocate*, p. 469. Both Radcliffe and Wollstonecraft have been accused of 'orientalism' for using black slaves in order to talk about women; Mary Nyquist, 'Wanting protection: fair ladies, sensibility and romance', in Eileen Janes Yeo (ed.), *Mary Wollstonecraft and Two Hundred Years of Feminisms* (London, Rivers Oram Press, 1997), pp. 81–4.

24 See Markman Ellis, *The Politics of Sensibility: Race, Gender and Commerce in the Sentimental Novel* (Cambridge, Cambridge University Press, 1996). See also Cindy McCreevy, 'Keeping up with the Bon Ton: the Tête-à-Tête series in the *Town and Country Magazine*', in Hannah Barker & Elaine Chalus (eds), *Gender in Eighteenth-Century England* (London, Longman, 1997), p. 219.

Wollstonecraft, Hays, Robinson and Inchbald.[25] The most accomplished dramatization of this narrative is Inchbald's story of Hannah Primrose in *Nature and Art*, which was noticed in Chapter 1. Inchbald's own sister had in fact become a prostitute.[26] The most forcible statement of the connection between prostitution and the economic disempowerment of women is made, in page after page, by Mary Ann Radcliffe.[27] Her illustrative narrative tells the story of a genteel middle-class woman, rendered destitute by the death of her husband, forced into prostitution in order to provide bread for her daughter, when attempts at begging and seeking for work have failed. She dies in agony of body and mind, afflicted by the diseases incident upon her trade and by remorse at the loss of her honour. The genteel, innocent woman forced into vice was a common myth; in fact prostitutes were overwhelmingly lower class, and their profession could offer an easier and more affluent lifestyle than other forms of working-class female employment.[28] But the narrative was entrenched in print culture, having been launched in the fund-raising propaganda of the Magdalen Hospital, and picked up in *The Times* in the 1780s.[29]

If the prostitute is woman *in extremis*, woman overwhelmed by 'female difficulties', some of our writers convey the impression that *all* women are near the edge. Mary Ann Radcliffe has a vivid sense of how easy it is for a woman to fall, because of the precariousness of her existence; at any time a father or a husband may die, or go bankrupt. Other women writers share this vision. Charlotte Smith declares that she will not write gothics, that she aims at realism;[30] yet her novels often have a gothic feel about them, as her impossibly virtuous heroes and heroines act against a background of almost unbelievable selfishness and wickedness on the part of villains and minor characters. Smith ratchets up the threats and misfortunes which assail her protagonists. By the end of *Montalbert* the heroine is destitute and apparently dying of grief because her husband, wrongly suspecting her of infidelity, has taken away her child and is about to fight a duel with the man who nobly rescued her from imprisonment in an Italian castle. At the same point in *Marchmont* the heroine is with her husband in a debtor's prison, suffering

[25] Wakefield, *Reflections,* pp. 66–7; Radcliffe, *Female Advocate,* pp. 405–17; Wollstonecraft, *Vindication of the Rights of Woman*, p. 149; *Appeal to the Men of Great Britain*, pp. 200–1, 278–81; Robinson, *Walsingham*, ii, 182–92; *The False Friend*, p. 194.

[26] Fletcher, *Charlotte Smith*, p. 321.

[27] Mary Ann Radcliffe, *Female Advocate*, p. 409.

[28] D. A. Coward, 'Eighteenth-century attitudes to prostitution' *Studies on Voltaire and the Eighteenth Century*, 189 (1980), 367–8; Shoemaker, *Gender in English Society*, p. 76.

[29] Vivien Jones, 'Placing Jemima: women writers of the 1790s and the eighteenth-century prostitution narrative', *Women's Writing*, 4:2 (1997), 206, 218; Ellis, *Politics of Sensibility*, pp. 170–3.

[30] Smith, *Banished Man*, ii, x–xi.

sexual harassment from another prisoner and from the attorney who is perse-
cuting them, while her mother-in-law who has protected her is dying of grief,
her financial resources exhausted.

Perhaps this sense of the precariousness of women's existence is most
dramatically conveyed by the 'proper' author of this chapter's title, Frances
Burney, in *Camilla*. Camilla is shockingly treated by her brother, who takes
her money and leads her into compromising situations which cause the breaking of the engagement with the man she loves. In the absence of the guidance
of her mother, who has to go abroad to nurse a sick brother, Camilla is
tricked into debt. Partly as a result her father goes to debtor's prison and her
beloved uncle moves from his mansion to a small house, so that he can econ-
omize and clear the family debts. So guilty does she feel that she dare not go
home. Her letters go astray and she ends up alone and penniless at a humble
inn, near to death and having feverish visions of her condemnation at the day
of judgement. The 'uncertainty of the female fate' had already been explained
to her by her father in a little sermon written for her benefit:

> The temporal destiny of woman is enwrapt in still more impenetrable obscurity
> than that of man. She begins her career by being involved in all the worldly
> accidents of a parent; she continues it by being associated in all that may
> environ a husband: and the difficulties arising from this doubly appendant state,
> are augmented by the next to impossibility, that the first dependance should
> pave the way for the ultimate. ... What, in this sublunary existence, is the state
> from which she shall neither rise nor fall?[31]

If this vision of the situation of women was widely shared by female writers,
then we may understand why so many heroines – for example
Wollstonecraft's, Hays's, Geraldine in Smith's *Desmond*, Gertrude in
Robinson's *False Friend* – fall half in love with easeful death, or contemplate
suicide.

But much (though not all) of this is fiction, it may be objected; and prose
fiction is likely to present the world in a dramatic, highly coloured, exaggerated aspect. In reply to this it must be noted that some of this fiction is
semi-autobiographical, and that there are explicitly autobiographical texts too
which paint a similar picture of 'female difficulties'. It has long been recognized that both of Wollstonecraft's novels draw heavily on her own life. In
addition, her *Letters Written During a Short Residence in Sweden, Norway
and Denmark* tell of her doings, her thoughts and her feelings at a critical
period for her. Hays's *Memoirs of Emma Courtney* is in part based upon her
unrequited love for William Frend; she draws upon her letters to him, and to
her confidant William Godwin in her text. Helen Williams's *Letters from
France* contain scattered information about her life in France as the revolution ran its course. Charlotte Smith recounts her troubles in prefaces to her

---

[31] Frances Burney (Madame d'Arblay), *Camilla: or, a Picture of Youth* (1796)
(Oxford, Oxford University Press, 1983), pp. 356–7.

novels and poems, and fictionalizes them in the persons of Mrs Elphinstone in *Celestina*, Mrs Denzil in *The Banished Man* and Mrs Marchmont in *Marchmont*. Mary Robinson comments on her own life in a number of her novels. There is also her autobiography, left uncompleted at her death. This is a text to be approached with caution; it reads all too like one of her racy novels, and raises the question of the extent to which art shapes the telling of life. It is also plain that in all of her autobiographical and semi-autobiographical writings, Robinson the ex-courtesan is concerned with self-justification.

What do these elements of autobiography have to say about 'female difficulties'? Wollstonecraft, Smith and Robinson all tell of betrayal by men. Robinson's father abandoned his family for a mistress and failed to support them; but he would not allow them to disgrace him by running a school so that they could support themselves. Her husband kept mistresses before and during their marriage; he even brought prostitutes into the debtor's prison where Mary Robinson had joined him with her baby girl. Later she was used then quickly dropped by the Prince of Wales, and her first novel, *Vancenza*, in which Prince Almanza seduces then abandons the heroine's mother, expresses her bitterness. *The False Friend* of 1799 may reflect her pain when Banastre Tarleton left her; she had supported him with her earnings and taken on debts for him, but when his mother died in 1797 he refused to share his inheritance with Robinson and married Susan Priscilla Bertie in December 1798.[32] The abandoned woman in *Vancenza* and the women whose love is unreturned in *The False Friend* all die, which was not true to life; Robinson survived betrayal.

Mrs Elphinstone in Smith's *Celestina* has a weak, good-natured husband who takes a mistress; this was not dissimilar to Smith's own situation.[33] Wollstonecraft's Scandinavian letters tell of her grief at the loss of the affection of Imlay, her 'husband' and the father of her daughter, who also consorted with mistresses; it hints at her longing for death:

> I cannot tell why – but death, under every form, appears to me like something getting free – to expand in I know not what element; nay I feel this conscious being must be as unfettered, have the wings of thought, before it can be happy. ... I stretched out my hand to eternity, bounding over the dark speck of life to come.[34]

She had attempted suicide both before and after her Scandinavian trip. The jottings which suggest the ways she was planning to finish *Maria* show that she was thinking of fictionalizing this seduction and betrayal.

[32] See Bass, *The Green Dragoon*.
[33] Elizabeth Kraft, 'Introduction' to Charlotte Smith, *The Young Philosopher* (1798) (Lexington, University of Kentucky Press, 1999), pp. xi–xiv.
[34] Wollstonecraft, *Letters Written During a Short Residence*, pp. 174–5.

Robinson's memoirs tell of frequent sexual harassment. When she was 14, on a night out at Drury Lane with her mother an officer stared at her until she was overwhelmed with confusion.[35] He persisted in his attentions and offered marriage; it turned out that he already had a wife and was pursuing 'some diabolical stratagem for the enthralment of my honour'. He continued to stalk her after he had been refused.[36] After her marriage, her husband's rakish associates Lord Lyttelton and George Robert Fitzgerald persistently attempted to seduce the 15-year-old girl, and on one occasion the latter almost managed to force her into his carriage.[37] On another occasion, George Brereton had her husband arrested for debt, and offered to cancel it if Mary Robinson would 'behave more kindly'.[38] Her problem was that she was outstandingly beautiful, but 'I was not properly protected by Mr. Robinson'[39] who was far too busy frequenting prostitutes and molesting the servants.[40] Writing her memoirs at the end of her life, Robinson declares that she has never known one year of happiness, and suggests that she has no desire to go on living.[41]

Both Robinson and Smith complain that their husbands failed to support them, and with reason. Robinson's husband was a rake and a gambler who associated with men way beyond his pocket; Smith's was recklessly extravagant, dissipating his wealth and descending into debt. Like Robinson, Smith joined her husband for a while in debtor's prison, and fled to France with him to escape his creditors.[42] Indeed Smith was a textbook case of a woman oppressed by a bad husband and by the inequities of property law in relation to women. Her husband left her to support their nine surviving children by her pen, and on occasion exercised his legal right to take her earnings. Robinson had to support herself and her daughter. Both women tell of their attempts at earning a living. In Smith's *Banished Man*, Mrs Denzil is a self-portrait. Her situation and many incidents in her story are copied from Smith's own experiences, and her oppressors have names similar to those of the men Smith identified as her persecutors. Mrs Denzil spends all of her time writing for bread, pestered by her publisher for more copy, her health undermined by unremitting toil and money worries:

> After a conference with Mr. Tough [a debt collector], she must write a tender
> dialogue between some damsel, whose perfections are even greater than those

35 Mary Robinson, *Memoirs of the Late Mrs. Robinson, Written by Herself* (1801) (published as *Perdita. The Memoirs of Mary Robinson*, London, Peter Owen, 1994), p. 35. She says she was 15, but she was not yet 15 when she married.
36 *Ibid.*, p. 36, 41.
37 *Ibid.*, p. 63.
38 *Ibid.*, p. 96.
39 *Ibid.*, p. 98.
40 *Ibid.*, p. 106.
41 *Ibid.*, p. 91.
42 For Smith's life see Fletcher, *Charlotte Smith*.

'Which youthful poets fancy when they love', and her hero, who, to the bravery and talents of Caesar, adds the gentleness of Sir Charles Grandison, and the wit of Lovelace.[43]

I endured it for my children, and perhaps because I felt a degree of self-approbation in stemming a tide of adversity under which the generality of women would have sunk.[44]

Of course, poverty is relative; Mrs Denzil has a maid, and laments that she must buy her wine by the dozen because she is not rich enough to buy a pipe [a small barrel].[45] Smith was born a gentlewoman, and, as she tells us, had in more prosperous days committed herself to raising her family as a gentleman's family (in this she succeeded).[46] In the preface to *Marchmont*, Smith defends herself against the charge of egotism for telling of her sorrows; she has completed thirty-two volumes in eight years.[47]

Martha in Robinson's *Natural Daughter*, estranged from her husband, struggles bravely to stand on her own feet. She works as a teacher, which Robinson herself had done, and as a lady's companion. She tries to live by her pen, like Robinson publishing poems, which are panned because she cannot afford to bribe the critics. She writes a two-volume novel in six weeks, for which the publisher pays her £10 and which he then brings out in several profitable editions. Exactly like Robinson, she writes a play, which is hooted off the stage by louts, hired by the society ladies whose gambling and dissipation it satirized. Like Smith, Robinson complains of the difficulty and the grind of earning a living by the pen:

> She had employed her pen, till her health was visibly declining ... All that her honourable, her incessant industry could procure, was insufficient for the purposes of attaining a permanent independence.[48]

> Reader ... you will perceive that of all the occupations which industry can pursue, those of literary toil are the most fatiguing. That which seems to the vacant eye a mere playful amusement, is in reality an Herculean labour.[49]

And for a while, Martha earns a good living as an actress; Robinson takes the opportunity to protest about the prejudice against acting as not consonant with female propriety. As she wrote in her memoirs about her acting career, 'I now felt that I could support myself honourably; and the consciousness of independence is the only true felicity in this world of humiliation'.[50]

[43] Smith, *Banished Man*, ii, p. 226.
[44] *Ibid.*, p. 232.
[45] Fletcher, *Charlotte Smith*, p. 106.
[46] Smith, *Banished Man*, i, p. vi.
[47] Smith, *Marchmont*, i, pp. vi–vii.
[48] Mary Robinson, *The Natural Daughter. With Portraits of the Leadenhead Family* (London, T. N. Longman & O. Rees, 1799), ii, pp. 69–70.
[49] *Ibid.*, ii, p. 114.
[50] Robinson, *Memoirs*, p. 94.

So far in this chapter, I have not considered differences between 'unsex'd' and 'proper' females on the topic of 'female difficulties'. We would not expect Polwhele's doyenne of 'proper' females, Hannah More, to complain about the oppression of women by men, and on the whole she does not. Difficulties and sufferings are sent by God as trials; they must be patiently borne, and the Christian woman must not allow herself to sink into despair. In her tract *'Tis all for the best*, Mrs Simpson actually welcomes a series of disasters, including the loss of her husband and his money, because they wean her from the world, and fix her hopes on heaven.[51] But barely suppressed anger is detectable in her *Strictures on Female Education* at the refusal of so many men to respect women's intellects, and to engage with them in conversation on serious subjects.[52]

The anger in Mary Ann Radcliffe's *Female Advocate* is overt; in return for women's submission, men should protect them, but often fail to do so, and 'When we look around us, nothing is more conspicuous in the eyes of the world, than the distresses of women'.[53] The most important 'female difficulty' in Burney's *Camilla* is a contradiction by which the heroine is trapped. Her father gives her conventional advice: do not let a man suspect that you love him, until he has first declared himself and made an honourable proposal. Meanwhile Edgar Mandelbert, the man she loves, has been advised by Dr Marchmont not to propose until he is certain that Camilla loves him with all her heart. It is all too easy in the twenty-first century to read the whole novel as a critique of the convention of feminine reserve; but as I contended in Chapter 2, it is by no means clear that that is Burney's meaning. It is just as likely that she thinks the convention a good one, and the difficulty inevitable.

The most interesting conservative narratives of female difficulties come from the pen of Jane West; she is quite consciously responding to the complaints of 'unsex'd females' and her aim is to show that if women crumple under difficulties, then they have only themselves to blame. I have already suggested that even would-be realistic novels such as Smith's have a touch of the gothic about them in that they plunge their heroines into situations of extreme danger and distress, threatened by unbelievably wicked villains. One of West's aims is to protest against these gothicisms and to present an alternative of the down-to-earth and the everyday. People do not come perfectly good or utterly evil; they come mixed. Unalloyed happiness, which in other novels suddenly breaks out for the heroine when she is finally united with the hero in a perfect romantic and companionate marriage, is unattainable in this sublunary sphere. Women must learn to content themselves with less, and to work at marriage, to build marital happiness by

---

[51] Hannah More, *'Tis All for the Best* (London, J. Evans & J. Hatchard, 1799).

[52] More, *Strictures*, ii, pp. 42, 45, 47, 51–2.

[53] Radcliffe, *Female Advocate*, p. 404.

self-control, self-sacrifice and forbearance.

These are themes of West's *Gossip's Story*, which may also be understood as a response to narratives of female victimization. The moral is that Marianne brings about her own unhappy ending in a marriage which goes sour by her own faults. She is characterized by excessive sensibility, weakness of mind, lack of self-control, and romantic delusions about love and friendship learnt from novels. She is guilty of imprudent behaviour when she criticizes her husband to a female friend in letters which she conceals from him, and when her conduct in fashionable society is naïve and unworldly. She thereby fails to win her husband's esteem. But it may be doubted whether the *tendency* of this novel accords with the *moral* West wishes to enforce. A twenty-first-century reader is likely to think Marianne a victim, and it is perfectly possible that a 1790s reader would have felt the same. An evil *woman*, her husband's mother, works to destroy her. But the husband is to blame too; Marianne is essentially virtuous and amiable, but he cannot come to terms with the fact that she is not perfect. When things go wrong, he fails to offer sympathy and understanding. And the message that women must learn to put up with something less than perfection is undermined by the fact that other heroes and heroines in this novel are quite faultless and enjoy utterly happy marriages.

The failure of the proposed moral clearly to emerge is even more apparent in West's antijacobin novel *par excellence*, her *Tale of the Times*. Once again the heroine, Geraldine Monteith, is partly blamed for her own misfortunes; she has not sufficiently cultivated her intellect, she lacks strength of mind, she has 'one fatal weakness', though it is by no means clear what it is.[54] She makes mistakes which contribute to putting her into the power of her ravisher, giving him her portrait, and her mother's jewels so that he may clear her husband's debts, thereby jeopardizing her chances of winning a rape accusation against him in court – 'a thousand fatal indiscretions rose to her remembrance'.[55]

But she is also motivated not to clear her name by the fear that her husband will challenge her rapist to a duel, and be killed. The reader, in fact, is likely to revolt against the author, and to think that West's determination to blame the woman is unfair. For Geraldine *had* worked at her marriage to a less than satisfactory man, she had influenced him for the good and resolved to be contented with her lot. 'She had laboured to subdue those more exquisite refinements of sensibility, which vainly look for consummate enjoyment in this world.'[56] She is amiable and virtuous, dutiful as a daughter, wife and mother.

She is raped by Fitzosborne, separated from her husband and children,

54 West, *Tale of the Times*, iii, p. 366.
55 *Ibid.*, iii, p. 280.
56 *Ibid.*, ii, p. 190.

and a reconciliation in the last pages cannot save her from death. Fitzosborne is a jacobin philosopher, who despises religion, chastity and the marriage vow; his plan is to seduce Geraldine and steal her from her husband by undermining her moral and religious principles. West has written a philosophical novel which aims to show how modern jacobin principles destroy a marriage, a wife's honour and her life. But in fact Fitzosborne totally fails to undermine Geraldine's principles, and he fails to seduce her. Her dishonouring and destruction are produced by perfectly old-fashioned, unphilosophical means: by the cunning entrapment of a husband into dissipation, adultery and debt; by the bribery and subornation of servants; by plotting and lying; by forged letters; and finally by contrived abduction and drug-facilitated rape. Geraldine is a victim, just as much as Mary Raymond in Hays's *Victim of Prejudice* – a victim of sexual abuse and of a man's lust for conquest. Moreover this novel is not a perfect antigothic, concerned only with 'the moral and the probable', as West claims;[57] for Fitzosborne in his remorseless and devious wickedness is a gothic, unbelievable villain. And he dies a gothic death in France, poisoning himself rather than face the guillotine; as he dies in agony, he hears too late that Robespierre has decided to reprieve and employ him. A review of both of these novels by West would appear to force us to the conclusion that it was not easy in the 1790s to write narratives of women which did not present them as victims.

So to sum up: who, or what, in the eyes of these authors, is to blame for 'female difficulties', and what, if anything, can be done about them? In these texts, fathers receive some blame, almost invariably for attempting to dictate marriage choices to their daughters; but fathers are just as likely to be depicted as loving friends of their daughters, their best protectors in a hostile world. Men are also criticized in their roles as lovers and husbands. The sexual predatoriness of men is a routine and a major complaint. Robinson, whose experience of maltreatment by partners was most extensive, is especially bitter. She insists that while women's love is mental or an affair of sentiment, men's love is sensual or corporeal; they are libertines and treat women as their prey: 'Man first degrades, and then deserts her'.[58] 'Man swears to love and cherish his wife, never to forsake her in sickness, or in health, in poverty or wealth, and to keep to her *alone* so long as they both shall live.'[59] But as he stands before the altar taking this oath, he fully intends to break it, knowing that his gallantries will be forgiven.[60] If women behaved as men do, all moral and religious order would be annihilated.[61] Husbands also bring their wives to ruin in the process of ruining themselves, by extravagance and by gambling; the gambling man is a stock theme for 'unsex'd'

57 *Ibid.*, i, p. 11.
58 Robinson, *Thoughts*, pp. 10, 26, 81.
59 *Ibid.*, p. 75.
60 *Ibid.*, p. 77.
61 *Ibid.*, p. 87.

and 'proper' females alike.[62] The implication of all this is the need for a reformation of male manners and morals.

So are these authors man-haters? Do they think that the root problem is the badness of men? It is not clear that women writers of the 1790s consistently think that one sex is inherently worse than the other. Individual women, they think, can be just as bad as individual men. Even in Robinson's novels we find the heroine done down just as often by wicked women as by wicked men. Her *False Friend* contains her blackest villain in the person of Treville, whose aim is to seduce or rape the heroine throughout the book; but he is matched by the equally villainous Miss Cecil, who at one point has the perfectly sane heroine imprisoned as a maniac. The same fate is inflicted upon her own mother by the bad sister Julia in Robinson's *Natural Daughter*. This epitome of wickedness – unchaste, ungrateful, dissipated, a liar and dishonest gambler – is guilty of ultimate evil: after murdering her own child she becomes the mistress of Robespierre and has her own sister condemned to the guillotine. Robinson is clear that the ostracism of unchaste women is as much the work of other women as of men, perhaps more their work; she blames the ending of her relationship with the Prince of Wales on the malicious gossiping of other women:

> I have never felt that affection for my own sex which perhaps some women feel: I have never taught my heart to cherish their friendship, or to depend on their attentions beyond the short perspective of a prosperous day. Indeed I have almost uniformly found my own sex my most inveterate enemies; I have experienced little kindness from them; though my bosom has often ached with the pang inflicted by their envy, slander, and malevolence.[63]

A stock theme of Smith's novels is the enmity towards the heroine of other women, jealous of her beauty and accomplishments. Even Wollstonecraft's Maria is betrayed into the madhouse by a woman, by a French maid she has hired.

It is not just men that 'unsex'd' females blame; their perception of the problem is more sophisticated than that. They home in upon cultural or systemic factors too. First, the harsh and unforgiving application of the rules of sexual propriety to women is a culprit, even for an ultra-'proper' female such as Mary Ann Radcliffe. This is the moral of Hays's *Victim of Prejudice*; the whole train of disasters which overwhelms Mary Raymond stems from the refusal of her mother's parents to take back their seduced and abandoned daughter. This too is the moral of the story of Hannah Primrose in Inchbald's *Nature and Art*, and of the story of Jemima in Wollstonecraft's *Maria*. Secondly, many of these writers are critical of the cultural assumptions which lead to an undervaluing of women, a refusal to recognize their genius, their strength of character and mind; this is the main theme of Robinson's *Thoughts on the Condition of Woman*.

[62] Radcliffe, *Female Advocate*, pp. 449–50.
[63] Robinson, *Memoirs*, p. 82.

Thirdly, custom and law, which put most of the property into the hands of men, and which close so many occupations to women, are blamed in the stories of men ruining their families by extravagance, and in the oft-repeated story of the prostitute. Sustained complaint about property law and the way the law is implemented is rare. Women writers of the 1790s do not express a coherent critique of property law in the manner of present-day commentators such as Staves and Spring. Passing critical remarks, however, are fairly common. Radcliffe laments that where formerly men used to endow their wives, in modern days women endow their husbands with large portions.[64] Wollstonecraft protests against the law which denies daughters their right to an equal share in the paternal inheritance.[65] In *Maria* she raises the issues of a husband's right to his wife's earnings, and the injustice to women of the laws of inheritance and the law which gives husbands the right to compensation in cases of adultery, but not wives.[66] The author of the *Appeal to the Men of Great Britain* hints that the laws of inheritance might be modified in favour of women.[67] Robinson complains about a woman's property passing to her husband on marriage, and contends that an able woman should have control of the family property, if she is married to a man of weak understanding.[68]

Finally, this list of the major perceived sources of 'female difficulties' must mention gender stereotyping, the construction of women for weakness and passivity, the main problem for Macaulay Graham and Wollstonecraft but an issue for other authors too, including Robinson and Hays. Even 'proper' females such as Hamilton, Edgeworth and More are concerned about this. Wollstonecraft's critique of gender stereotyping has at the very least an appearance of putting the blame for female difficulties upon women themselves. Her *Vindication of the Rights of Woman*, as a host of commentators have pointed out, takes a very low view of women. They are trivial-minded, immethodical, lazy, sensual flirts, obsessed with their appearance, passive and weak, unappreciative of higher aesthetic experiences and uninterested in public affairs. What is needed, therefore, is a revolution in female manners. Of course, Wollstonecraft blames these faults entirely upon bad education (cultural conditioning is how we would denominate it), holds men in great part responsible for this, and calls upon men to co-operate, or even take the lead, in elevating the female character. By the time of her last writings, her Scandinavian letters and *Maria*, the focus of her attack has turned away from women, and towards male power.[69]

'Proper' females such as More, West, Edgeworth and perhaps Burney are likely to blame 'female difficulties' on individual sinfulness or folly, whether

---

[64] Radcliffe, *Female Advocate*, p. 432.

[65] Wollstonecraft, *Vindication of the Rights of Woman*, p. 141.

[66] Wollstonecraft, *Wrongs of Woman*, p. 155.

[67] *Appeal to the Men of Great Britain*, pp. 201, 278.

[68] Robinson, *Thoughts*, pp. 3–4, 78.

[69] Wollstonecraft, *Letters Written during a Short Residence*, p. 27, 66.

on the part of the woman who suffers, or on the part of those who cause her to suffer. It follows that the only hope of removing 'female difficulties' – if indeed in this imperfect world hope is possible – lies in the moral reform of individuals. 'Unsex'd' females are more likely to target systemic factors, cultural, economic and legal, which cast so many women in the role of victims, and so many men in the role of oppressors. If these are the problems, what is to be done about them? In the chapters that follow, as we turn away from complaint and narratives of victimization, we shall see whether women writers have positive proposals for improving the lot of their sex.

4

Love, marriage
and the family

This chapter will pick up several of the issues, raised in Chapter 2, which have been contentious in recent scholarship: patriarchal authority in the family, the transacting of daughters between fathers and husbands, romantic love and companionate marriage, sexual propriety and sexual repression. It will look at women in different family and relationship roles: as daughters, as women in love, as wives, mothers, widows and spinsters. Throughout, the chapter will address the question of how women writers of the 1790s perceive sexual and family relationships. Do they reflect or describe or endorse a system of male dominance, or do they depict a society which is not perfectly dominated by men? Do they challenge the structures which privilege men, or seek to adapt them to women's needs?

Are daughters in revolt against patriarchal authority?

A major theme of texts authored by 'unsex'd females' and 'proper' ones too is choice in marriage. Since most works of prose fiction have courtship as their central theme, this is only to be expected in them; but it is an important topic in non-fictional texts also. This theme is explored by Smith, Wollstonecraft, Hays, Williams, Robinson, Inchbald, Fenwick, and also by Radcliffe, Burney, West and More. So salient is this issue in both fiction and non-fiction texts, that it is tempting to declare that they express an ideological conflict of the generations, an ideological revolt of daughters (and sons too, though that is not my concern) against parental authority. But, as we shall see, such a formulation would oversimplify what the texts are saying and exaggerate confrontation in their message. Though this book restricts its focus to the 1790s, it should be remembered that debates about choice in marriage and parental authority had been salient in men's and women's writings for a good part of the preceding century – the mid-century debate between Samuel Richardson, Hester Mulso and Mrs

94

Chapone is a particularly good example.[1]

One of the most striking and amusing dramatizations of intergenerational conflict is in Robinson's *Angelina*. Sir Edward Clarendon, a merchant who has made a fortune in the slave trade, wishes to marry his daughter Sophia to Lord Acreland. The marriage will benefit both men; Sir Edward will achieve a much-coveted alliance with nobility, and in return will pay Acreland's considerable debts. Sir Edward thinks of Sophia as private, disposable property, like his slaves:

> 'Profligate girl! What have you to do with independence? ... Are you not obliged to me for your daily subsistence?'
> Wasn't she my property? ... Havn't [*sic*] I a right to dispose of my own? Answer me that.[2]

But Sophia does not want her father 'to transfer me like a piece of rich merchandise'[3] to Acreland, for she is in love with Charles Belmont. On the eve of her wedding, she begs her father to call it off; he strikes her and throws her to the ground. She runs away, and after her recapture, eventually elopes with Belmont.

Every one of Smith's novels is critical of marriages arranged against the wishes of the children. In *Montalbert*, for example, the heroine Rosalie's mother was in love with Charles Ormsby. But the mother's father, Mr Montalbert, was 'the lord of many miles, where none, either in his house or around it, ever disputed his will'.[4] He was determined that his daughter would marry Mr Vyvian. The latter knew of her love for Ormsby, but he 'was indelicate and selfish enough to consider only the convenience of my fortune, and a person, which was then an object to a man, licentious and dissolute as he was'.[5] Mr. Montalbert raged against her: 'perseverance in a sort of conduct which *I will not understand*, lest the most terrible vengeance should follow ... I have said enough – go to your own room, and learn to obey.'[6] His vengeance *did* follow; he had Ormsby imprisoned, then sent abroad, and his daughter was forced into an unwanted marriage. But she had already given herself to Ormsby, thinking herself his wife in the sight of heaven, and Rosalie was the illegitimate result. Smith persistently uses the strongest language to characterize the disposal of young women in marriage: for example, Rosalie was 'Dragged to a scene [a ball], where she considered herself exposed as an animal in a market to the remarks and purchase of the best bidder'.[7] And in *Celestina* she writes of the heroine being 'consigned, like a bale of merchandize'.[8]

1 Gonda, *Reading Daughters' Fictions*, pp. 81–105.
2 Robinson, *Angelina*, i., p. 85; ii, p. 250.
3 *Ibid.*, i, p. 59.
4 Charlotte Smith, *Montalbert* (London, E. Booker, 1795), ii, p. 25.
5 *Ibid.*, ii, p. 10.
6 *Ibid.*, ii, p. 93.
7 *Ibid.*, i, p. 81.
8 Smith, *Celestina*, iii, p. 101.

So can we say that these women writers, like some present-day feminist anthropologists and literary critics, have an awareness of marriages as at bottom relationships between *men*, in which women are transacted by men (fathers and husbands) in order to bind the men together?[9] Some episodes would fit such a theory, such as Robinson's story of Sophia, Sir Edward Clarendon and Lord Acreland recounted above. Or in Smith's *Marchmont*, Althea's unloving and neglectful father Sir Audley Dacres commands her to marry Mohun, who is his lawyer and fellow-MP in a two-member borough. Mohun is a typically Smithian corrupt attorney, committed to masculine authority, contemptuous of women's intellects and surveying 'Althea with the sort of look that a sagacious jockey puts on when he is about to purchase a horse'.[10]

But the perception that these writers convey is not simply one of marriages as transactions of women by men. They also describe the role of fathers in forcing unwanted marriages upon their sons, and of mothers in arranging marriages for their sons and daughters, against their children's wishes. For example, in Smith's *Desmond* it is Mrs. Waverly, a rich and tyrannical widow, who arranges the unhappy marriages of her daughter and son, seeking only to unite them to riches and high birth. In the same novel Mrs. Fairfax, another widow, takes on the task of marrying off her daughters. In Smith's *Montalbert* the marriage of hero and heroine is obstructed because the hero's mother, again a rich widow, wishes to arrange a marriage of worldly advantage. In her *Celestina* it is Lady Castlenorth, not Lord Castlenorth, who plans the marriage of her daughter. In Radcliffe's *Italian* it is the Marchesa, not her husband, who is the driving force in keeping hero and heroine apart. In *Montalbert* we are given to understand that it is cruel and presumably unusual for a husband to arrange the marriage of a daughter without consulting his wife.[11] In her memoirs, Robinson recounts that she was forced into a disastrous marriage by her mother, even though her father was still alive (and living with his mistress).[12] If a revolt of the daughters is being described, it is a revolt against *parental*, not *paternal* authority; these writers depict a situation in which parents – mothers as well as fathers – exercised a contested power over the marital choices of their children both female and male.

'Who will dare to assert ... that obedience to parents should go one jot beyond the deference due to reason, enforced by affection?' demands Wollstonecraft. In this she applies to marriage the preference for reason over authority, whether political, priestly or parental, of the enlightened dissenting circle around the publisher Joseph Johnson, a preference which had found its characteristic expression in Godwin's *Political Justice*.[13] From the same

9 See the discussion in Chapter 2.
10 Smith, *Marchmont*, i, p. 134.
11 Smith, *Montalbert*, i, p. 182.
12 Robinson, *Memoirs*, pp. 39–41.
13 Mary Wollstonecraft, *An Historical and Moral View of the Origin and Progress of the French Revolution; and of the Effect it has Produced in Europe* (London, Joseph Johnson, 1794), p. 224.

circle, and in Godwinian language, Fenwick has a heroine declare, 'Wherever the commands of parents are contrary to the justice due from being to being, I hold obedience to be a vice', drawing parallels with marital and political tyranny.[14] If 'unsex'd' females like Wollstonecraft, Fenwick and Smith thought that tyrannical and wrongheaded parents ought to be disobeyed, 'proper' females like More thought that this was one of the worst and most dangerous aspects of jacobinical principles. More deprecates the 'revolutionary spirit in families'; 'Among the real improvements of modern times, and they are not a few, it is to be feared that the growth of filial obedience cannot be included'.[15] West laments the fashion in which 'Traits [i.e., tracts or treatises] on education subvert every principle of filial reverence'[16] and Hamilton doubts whether young women at liberty will consistently make wise marital choices.[17]

But the differences between 'unsex'd' and 'proper' females on filial obedience should not be exaggerated. More does *not* think that children should always obey their parents, even when their parents are wrong. Hester Wilmot refuses to work on Sunday; to placate her mother she works late on Saturday and gets up early on Monday. She refuses to go to the fair with her mother on Sunday, and refuses to read an improper book to her father. When her father takes the money she has saved for her new Sunday-school feast gown, to use as a gambling stake at The Bell, she secretly tells all to Mrs. Jones, the patroness of the Sunday school.[18] And when Black Giles the poacher steals Widow Brown's apples, and attempts to throw the blame on an innocent Sunday-school boy, his least bad son confesses the truth, thereby putting his father into the hands of the magistrate.[19] Perhaps More wishes to assert that duties to social superiors prevail over duties to parents. Certainly she is insisting that there is a higher moral authority than that of parents (including fathers) over children. That is not utterly different from what some 'unsex'd' females were claiming.

In fact More is no defender of marriages arranged by parents against their daughters' wishes, nor is West or Ann Radcliffe. Conservative writers walk a tightrope on the question of filial obedience. In West's *Gossip's Story*, the sensible, approved heroine Louisa is advised by her father to marry Sir William Milton; she falls on her knees and in tears begs to be excused marrying a man she cannot love. Her father insists that the final choice must be hers (he has already told Sir William this) and that he will not hold it against her if her decision goes against him. So good is Louisa, so committed to filial

---

14 Eliza Fenwick, *Secresy; or, the Ruin on the Rock* (1795) (Peterborough, Ontario, Broadview Press, 1994), p. 349.

15 More, *Strictures*, i, pp. 135, 134.

16 West, *Tale of the Times*, iii, p. 387.

17 Hamilton, *Hindoo Rajah*, p. 88.

18 More, *History of Hester Wilmot*.

19 Hannah More, *Black Giles the Poacher. Part II* (London, J. Marshall, 1796).

duty, that she resolves to do as her father wishes; fortunately she is saved from an unhappy fate by the revelation of a discreditable affair in Sir William's past. In West's *Tale of the Times*, Mrs. Evans married for love a man with no fortune, against her parents' wishes; in spite of this disobedience the Evanses are presented as a wholly virtuous couple living in an ideal companionate marriage. Conservative writers propose an ideal of filial duty on the one side, and on the other gentle parental authority, by which parents treat their children with respect. West's *Advantages of Education* depicts what we might call a 'softened matriarchy'; 'Some parents are apt, when they discover anything like a secret, to exert their authority, and insist upon an immediate disclosure'.[20] Mrs. Williams however, the model mother, declares to her teenage daughter Maria that she will not force her confidence, nor in a matter of marital choice will she give more than advice.[21]

This balancing act is abundantly clear in Burney's *Camilla*. Camilla and her sisters are perfectly dutiful daughters – dutiful equally to their mother and father – and their dutifulness is demonstrated in the most striking ways. They kiss their parents' hands, they prostrate themselves at their parents' knees. The climax of Camilla's misery comes at the end of the novel when she feels she has estranged herself from her parents by her misconduct, and her reconciliation with them is just as important a part of the dénouement as her reconciliation with her lover.

> More eloquent, as well as safer than any speech, was the pause of deep gratitude, the silence of humble praise, which ensued. Camilla, in each hand held one of each beloved Parent; alternately she pressed them with grateful reverence to her lips, alternately her eye sought each revered countenance, and received, in the beaming fondness they emitted, a benediction that was balm to every woe.
>   'I will see – or I will avoid whoever you please – I shall want no fortitude, I shall fear nothing – no one – not even myself – now again under your protection! I will scarcely even think, my beloved Mother, but by your guidance!'[22]

But the Tyrold parents too respect their daughters' individuality, refusing to force their confidence and being reluctant to deliver absolute commands and prohibitions.[23]

If 'proper' females are not defenders of absolute parental authority, neither are most 'unsex'd' females blithe advocates of filial resistance. Again Robinson's tale of Sophia and Sir Edward Clarendon tells it all. Though the father has been a tyrannical brute, when his business looks likely to fail his daughter feels a rush of affection: 'But should I ever behold that father

---

[20] Jane West, *The Advantages of Education, or, the History of Maria Williams, a Tale for Misses and their Mammas* (London, William Lane, 1793), i, p. 153.
[21] *Ibid.*, i, p. 201.
[22] Burney, *Camilla*, pp. 885, 895.
[23] *Ibid.*, pp. 219, 356.

reduced from affluence to indigence, should I see that overbearing mind shrinking under misfortunes, I should perhaps forget my own felicity, and consent to any honourable sacrifice that would snatch him from destruction.'[24]

When Charles Belmont becomes a rich heir, Sophia is happy in her father's consent to their marriage. And when it is revealed that Belmont is in fact Lord Acreland's long-lost son and heir, the wishes of Sir Edward for an alliance with the peerage, and of Sophia to marry the man she loves, are gratified and reconciled. Althea in Smith's *Marchmont* has been neglected by her father all her life, and she is to be banished from his sight for refusing to marry Mohun. Just like West, or Robinson, Smith walks a tightrope between filial obedience and independence. Althea tells her father:

> As long as my dear father lives, I shall never consider myself as exempted from his authority, even although the laws of my country may give me the liberty to act without consulting him. But though I never will offend him by quitting the place he assigns me, wherever that may be, I will never sell myself to a man I abhor.[25]

And Smith cannot leave it like that; father and daughter must be reunited. Eventually she is summoned to him, alone and very ill at Bath. He asks her to nurse him, and before he dies on the journey back to London, they are fully reconciled.

'Unsex'd' females in this decade find a way of managing the balancing act, endorsing choice in marriage without too blatantly condoning filial disobedience. They depict parental tyranny and intergenerational conflict as a thing of the past, a phenomenon of feudalism, of the *ancien régime*. The *locus classicus* is Helen Williams's tale of her friends the du Fossés in her *Letters from France*. M. du Fossé married the woman he loved, but she was poor and his father had planned a more distinguished match. The father imprisoned his son by *lettre de cachet*, his wife and child were forced to take refuge in England, and when the son escaped he was tricked into returning by false promises of reconciliation, and imprisoned again. The French revolution freed the son, reunited him with his wife and child, and the father having died restored them to their estate. In the most astonishing testimony to the balancing act discussed in the preceding paragraphs, Williams informs us that

> If the recollection of his evil deeds excites my indignation, it is far otherwise with Mons. and Madame du F——. Never did I hear their lips utter an expression of resentment or disrespect towards his memory; and never did I, with that warmth which belongs to my friendship for them, involuntarily pass a censure on his conduct, without being made sensible, by their behaviour, that I had done wrong.[26]

[24] Robinson, *Angelina*, iii, p. 318.
[25] Smith, *Marchmont*, i, p. 218.
[26] Helen Maria Williams, *Letters from France* (1790–6) (facsimile reprint, New York, Delmar, 1975), i, p. 194.

This story was sufficiently popular to be extracted and printed separately, and it spawned imitations, in Smith's *Celestina* and *Montalbert*, and Radcliffe's *Italian*.

Daughterly love

Neo-Freudian literary critics have had their say about the relationships between daughters and fathers in prose fiction of this decade, finding the theme of the daughter's incestuous desire for her father.[27] The clearest case for the incest theme is Robinson's *False Friend*. The heroine Gertrude is overwhelmed by her love for her guardian, Lord Denmore, and eventually hopes to marry him; unknown to her until the very end of the novel, he is her father (the reader suspects this almost from the very beginning). Explicit father–daughter incest was not absolutely unknown in eighteenth-century prose fiction[28] but was very rare; Robinson's novel may have been a shocker in 1799. Is it possible that readers thought Gertrude was *mistaken* about her feelings, that she was in fact feeling nothing more than daughterly love? Was the experience and the expression of daughterly love different then? 'When I behold him my cheek glows, my pulses beat more quickly, my heart throbs convulsively, all objects grow dim before my eyes, and I seem to lose the powers of discrimination'.[29] She kneels before his bust, presses the cold marble to her burning lips, and bathes it with tears; he has dominion over her senses.[30] The next best case is Inchbald's *Simple Story*; Miss Milner falls in love with her guardian, and marries him. Incest will be found here only if the reader begins by putting on Freudian spectacles in order to look for it.

More generally, daughters are regularly described as utterly devoted to their fathers, and perhaps it is this, rather than Robinson's *False Friend*, that really raises a problem of understanding and interpretation. Take for instance Julia's reaction to the death of her father, in Williams's novel. In a letter to her uncle, she writes:

'Oh my father! my ever-dearest father! how will your wretched child survive your loss!'

Julia was with difficulty persuaded to forsake the breathless remains of her father: she clung to his corpse in an agony of unutterable sorrow.

The last sigh of her father seemed to her the extinction of every earthly hope, and her aching heart refused that happiness which he could no longer participate.—Her father had always treated her as a friend, and her affection for him was unbounded.

27 Gonda, *Reading Daughters' Fictions*, p. 60.
28 *Ibid.*, pp. 34, 59,
29 Robinson, *False Friend*, iii, p. 75.
30 *Ibid.*, iii, pp. 204, 180.

She had lived in the constant habit of making every sacrifice to his comfort, that the quick sensibility of her own heart could suggest … sacrifices, which she carefully concealed from his knowledge, and of which she found the sole reward in her own bosom.[31]

Or take Lady Matilda's attitude to her father Lord Elmwood in Inchbald's *Simple Story*. Since her mother's infidelity when she was so small as barely to remember him, she has been banished from his sight. Though she will not be allowed to see him, she is overwhelmed by the thought of being under the same roof – 'I sleep in the same house with my father! Blessed spirit of my mother, look down and rejoice!'[32] She sighs and weeps before his portrait. She kisses the hand of her companion which her father has touched. She leans with filial piety over the seats in which he has sat; she takes up the pen with which he has been writing and holds a hat he has left behind with pious reverence. The emotional climax of the book, calculated to bring tears to the eyes of the gentle reader, comes when she is abducted by a dissolute lord who has concluded that her estranged father will not protect her. Lord Elmwood can no longer conceal from himself his repressed love for his daughter; he rides with pistols and armed retainers to her rescue and, 'Falling on her knees [she] clung round his legs, and bathed his feet with her tears.— These were the happiest moments she had ever known—perhaps the happiest *he* had ever known'.[33]

Devoted father–daughter relationships are to be found in West's *Gossip's Story* and *Tale of the Times* and in Radcliffe's *Udolpho*. In spite of the fact that he abandoned his family, Robinson in her *Memoirs* is indulgent towards her father, placing the blame on the 'young and artful woman' who seduced him from his domestic responsibilities.[34] When he died, she addressed an extravagantly worded poem to his memory.[35] Such language and situations strike twenty-first-century readers as odd, in need of explanation. The puzzle here at first sight lends colour to neo-Freudian explanations of such relationships as at bottom sexual, incestuous. In the *Spectator*, Sir Richard Steele wrote of the love of fathers for their daughters as 'the purest and most angelic affection'.[36] Caroline Gonda comments, 'For readers of our age, in which every year seems to bring an increasing incidence of father–daughter incest (itself, we now realize, often a euphemism for father–daughter rape), a passage such as the above cannot but be deeply disquieting'.[37]

Other ways of explaining the puzzle might be essayed. The very fact that the language and situations appear strange to us casts some doubt upon

31 Helen Maria Williams, *Julia* (London, T. Cadell, 1790), i, pp. 92, 94–6.
32 Inchbald, *Simple Story*, p. 226.
33 *Ibid.*, pp. 328–9.
34 Robinson, *Memoirs*, p. 28.
35 *Ibid.*, pp. 127–8.
36 *Spectator*, 449, 5 August 1712.
37 Gonda, *Reading Daughter's Fictions*, p. 1.

Freudian interpretations. For Freudianism purports to uncover relatively timeless structures of sexuality and feeling (though always mediated and expressed in ways appropriate to the time). But our sense here is of something utterly specific to its time, in need of a historical explanation. The expression and indeed the experience of love may not be atemporal phenomena. We need for the eighteenth century something like Jaeger's study of a particular structure of feeling in the middle ages.[38] Jaeger shows how men expressed intense love for social superiors in language closely akin to that of erotic passion, a language of longing for physical contact; but he also demonstrates that sexual intercourse was not at issue here. Part of the explanation is in terms of a historically specific relationship between friendship and configurations of power. Today power is diffused in formal and bureaucratic structures; then power was focused and concentrated in individuals. Friendship with powerful individuals will tend to have a character of its own. Power is charismatic, evoking reverence and devotion, and gratitude for favours received or expected. Something of the kind was surely going on in relations between fathers and daughters in the eighteenth century. Fathers were more powerful then than now. Not only did the law give them greater rights; daughters needed their protection in a more dangerous and less policed world. In a period of few employment opportunities, especially for upper- and middle-class women, fathers would often be the source of lifelong subsistence, providing financial settlements to enable daughters to marry well, and a home and an income to daughters who did not marry.

The books by 'unsex'd' and 'proper' females offer ample support to this view. The power of the father is vividly depicted in Lord Elmwood in Inchbald's *Simple Story*. Lady Matilda is utterly dependent upon him for home, income and future prospects, and also for protection. Emily is plunged into two-and-a-half volumes of peril in Radcliffe's *Udolpho* because her father dies, leaving her unprotected and rather short of money. The death of Mary Raymond's guardian leads to worse disasters in Hays's *Victim of Prejudice*. 'Alas! if my *father* forsakes me and casts me off, what other friend have I upon earth?' exclaims Althea in Smith's *Marchmont*.[39] Williams in her *Letters from France* tells of women who wished to die on the guillotine with their husbands or fathers, even bringing death upon themselves by the expedient of shouting 'Vive le Roi!'[40] These, surely, were women who not only did not wish to survive the ones they loved; they had no eligible life-prospects when the families which sustained them were destroyed.

Steele's opinions concerning the love of fathers for their daughters are endorsed by the author of the *Appeal to the Men of Great Britain*:

[38] C. Stephen Jaeger, *Ennobling Love: In Search of a Lost Sensibility* (Philadelphia, University of Pennsylvania University Press, 1999).

[39] Smith, *Marchmont*, i, p. 219.

[40] Williams, *Letters from France*, v, p. 217; vi, p. 65.

Men in the character of fathers too, are generally infinitely more amiable, and do more justice to the sex, than in any other character. . . . It is not often that the daughters of a family have cause to complain, of the father's partiality to his sons. . . . Most fathers of most countries, by their fond endearments, their engaging indulgence, their often partial and distinguished love to their daughters, leave impressions on their hearts more tender and lasting – more dear a thousand times to minds of sensibility – than all the wealth the mines of *Potosi* could bestow.[41]

Fathers rarely abuse their powers: husbands are much more inclined to tyranny.[42] In Burney's *Camilla*, Miss Dennel rushes into marriage to escape the authority of her father; but the reader is given to understand that she will be less free, and less indulged, as Mrs. Lissin.[43]

Are 'unsex'd' females in revolt against chastity?

Conservative writers were convinced that female chastity was in danger. More focuses her attack on Wollstonecraft:

A direct vindication of adultery was for the first time attempted by a *woman* . . . The Female Werter, as she is styled by her biographer, asserts in a work, intitled 'The Wrongs of Woman' that adultery is justifiable . . . corruptions seem to be pouring in upon us from every quarter . . . the crime above alluded to, the growth of which always exhibits the most irrefragable proof of the dissoluteness of public manners . . . this crime, which cuts up order and virtue by the roots, and violates the sanctity of vows, is awfully increasing . . . To restore a criminal to public society, is perhaps to tempt her to repeat her crime, or to deaden her repentance for having committed it.[44]

In Hamilton's *Hindoo Rajah*, the nephew of Dr Sceptic, converted to the New Philosophy, learns to contemn marriage, seduces his childhood sweetheart and makes her pregnant; she commits suicide, and so does he. Julia in Edgeworth's *Letters for Literary Ladies* is a victim of sensibility; she enters into a doomed marriage and, confused by modern philosophy, becomes an adulteress. Her sensible friend Caroline breaks off all relations with her, visiting her only at the end as she dies of remorse. The message is that there are only two possibilities for a woman: propriety or death. The admired heroines created by 'proper' female writers – Burney, Radcliffe, West – at all times observe the strictest propriety.

But exactly how much impropriety did 'unsex'd' female writers recommend or condone? Did they really offer a challenge to conventional sexual mores? Let us examine them one by one.

41 *Appeal to the Men of Great Britain*, pp. 260–1.
42 *Ibid.*, pp. 262–3.
43 Burney, *Camilla*, pp. 781–3.
44 More, *Strictures*, i, pp. 44–8.

Wollstonecraft only emerged as a scarlet woman at the end of her writing career. There is no hint of a call for erotic liberation in her feminist classic of 1792, which contains the (to us) astonishing passage:

> To such lengths, indeed, does an intemperate love of pleasure carry some prudent men, or worn out libertines, who marry to have a safe bed-fellow, that they seduce their own wives.—Hymen banishes modesty, and chaste love takes its flight.
>
> Love, considered as an animal appetite, cannot long feed on itself without expiring. And this extinction in its own flame, may be termed the violent death of love. But the wife who has thus been rendered licentious, will probably endeavour to fill the void left by the loss of her husband's attentions.[45]

In her reviews for the *Analytical*, written about this time or earlier, she objects to the indecencies of Sterne,[46] thinks Rousseau's *Confessions* too warm for youthful readers,[47] and contends that the moral tendency of Inchbald's *Simple Story* is dubious, because the author has made the adulterous Miss Milner too likeable.[48]

By 1794, in her *Historical and Moral View . . . of the French Revolution,* she was giving voice to the opinion which was to damn her in the eyes of the 'proper':

> Who will coolly maintain, that it is just to deprive a woman, not to insist on her being treated as an outcast of society, of all the rights of a citizen, because her revolting heart turns from the man, whom, a husband only in name, and by the tyrannical power he has over her person and property, she can neither love nor respect, to find comfort in a more congenial or humane bosom?[49]

Finally, in her posthumous, unfinished novel, she has her heroine stand up in court to defend her conduct in leaving a husband she (with good reason) despises and in giving herself to another man: 'I deemed, and ever shall deem, myself free'.[50] From their standpoint the defenders of propriety were absolutely right to concentrate their fire on this novel, for it repudiates conventional sexual morality, ushering in a new sexual morality whose time was not to come for another century or more. Wollstonecraft is arguing that whether a woman is chaste depends not on whether she is married to the man with whom she has sex, but on whether she loves him. So sex with a husband she has come to dislike is unchaste, immoral, disgusting:

> For a woman to live with a man, for whom she can cherish neither affection nor esteem, or even be of any use to him, excepting in the light of a house-

---

45 Wollstonecraft, *Vindication of the Rights of Woman*, p. 150.
46 *Analytical Review*, 9 (January 1791), 70.
47 *Ibid.*, 11 (December 1791), 528.
48 *Ibid.*, 10 (May 1791), 101.
49 Wollstonecraft, *Historical and Moral View,* pp. 224–5.
50 Wollstonecraft, *Wrongs of Woman*, p. 197.

keeper, is an abjectness of condition, the enduring of which no concurrence of circumstances can ever make a duty in the sight of God or just men.[51]

This is akin to the sexual morality of Godwin's *Political Justice*.

We find the same morality in the conduct and words of Sibella, the heroine of *Secresy* by Godwin's and Wollstonecraft's friend Eliza Fenwick. She insists that her premarital union with Clement is chaste, because they love each other and have exchanged secret vows:

> I heard Clement speak one day of some ceremonials which would be deemed necessary to the ratification of this covenant, when we should enter the world. [She is a 'child of nature' who has been secluded from society] – Methinks I shall be loath to submit to them. The vow of the heart is of sacred dignity. Forms and ceremonies seem too trifling for its nature.[52]

Other 'unsex'd' females, if they challenge propriety, do it more cautiously or indirectly than this. Mary Hays to be sure attracted a great deal of conservative venom, even for her *Victim of Prejudice* of 1799. It is a rewrite of *Clarissa*, and the open-minded reader will not find it more improper than Richardson's model. Clarissa was guilty of imprudence and filial disobedience; Mary Raymond in Hays's novel could not possibly be charged with doing anything to bring about her own rape. The only specific charge against the sexual morality of the novel (in the *Monthly Review*) was that it was not an unreasonable prejudice on the part of William Pelham's father to object to his son marrying the illegitimate daughter of a prostitute and murderer.[53]

Hays's real offences were her known association with Wollstonecraft, whose obituary she wrote, and her novel of 1796, *Memoirs of Emma Courtney*. As well as declaring her passion over and over again, in letters and by word of mouth, to a man who makes no return, the heroine offers, because of the inheritance conditions by which he is restricted, to give herself to him and live with him unmarried.[54] Her very correspondence with a man to whom she was not related or engaged was improper by the conventions of the time. Emma voices Godwinian arguments to the effect that existing moral rules are prejudices which would not stand the test of utility. Hays insisted in her preface to *Victim of Prejudice* that she had meant to *criticize* Emma Courtney's behaviour, not to praise it. Her *Letters and Essays* of 1793, and the *Appeal to the Men of Great Britain* of 1798 (assuming she was the author), would support her claim, for both works are quite proper. The latter does insist that to penitent women 'every encouragement should undoubtedly be given, that is consistent with delicacy and propriety, and particularly by

[51] *Ibid.*, p. 157; see the whole discussion, pp. 152–8.
[52] Fenwick, *Secresy*, p. 250.
[53] *Monthly Review*, 31 (1800), 82.
[54] Mary Hays, *Memoirs of Emma Courtney* (1796) (London, Routledge & Kegan Paul, 1987), pp. 125–6.

their own sex',[55] for profligate men are usually to blame for the seduction of innocent and unsuspecting females. Hannah More might object to that, but she could hardly object to the text's celebrations of chastity and modesty, and its un-Wollstonecraftian argument that divorce is contrary to the teachings of Christ and should only be permitted in cases of adultery, that crime 'most subversive of the peace and happiness of society'.[56] Still, one is left feeling that the moral of *Emma Courtney* is deeply ambiguous; it is easy to read it as an attack on propriety, or to wonder whether Hays at the time of its composition was absolutely clear where she herself stood.

In spite of the virulence of the anti-jacobin attack on Helen Williams, and in spite of her adulterous liaison with Hurford Stone, it would be difficult to find any hint of sexual impropriety in her writings. *Julia* indeed, a blue-stocking novel with a high religious tone, is a rewriting, a cleaning-up, of Goethe's *Werther* and perhaps of Rousseau's *Julie*. Both Werther and St Preux in Rousseau's novel make passionate overtures to women (Charlotte and Julie respectively) who return their love but cannot marry them; Julie surrenders to seduction. Williams's Julia by contrast remains virtuous. She tells Seymour, the Werther equivalent, 'I think there can be but one opinion of [Goethe's] book ... every one must acknowledge that it is well written, but few will justify its principles'.[57] Seymour is engaged to Julia's cousin and dearest friend Charlotte, but when he meets Julia he falls desperately in love with her. The present-day reader will think that he ought to break off his engagement and marry the woman he loves, but that does not appear to be Williams's view; for according to the conventions of the day, it would be unacceptably dishonourable to break such a promise. Seymour should rather have exerted his reason, and conquered his passion before it became irresistible – as Julia does, for she could have loved him if he had been free. Like Werther, Seymour dies, but without committing the sin of suicide: his frame weakened by sorrow and disappointed passion, he dies of a fever. Propriety at all times; Williams even endorses the conduct-book maxim that a display of sexual fondness by a woman excites disgust and aversion in a man of delicacy.[58]

Catharine Macaulay Graham had offended against propriety by marrying, when late in life and a widow, a man much younger and poorer than herself. No 'unsex'd' or 'proper' female is on record as approving of such conduct, which suggested an ungovernable and undignified sexual desire on the part of the woman. Similar behaviour is disapprovingly described in Smith's *Old Manor House*, Burney's *Camilla* and Fenwick's *Secrecy*; in all three cases the purchase of a younger man by a rich older woman ends in disaster. But

---

[55] *Appeal to the Men of Great Britain*, p. 237.
[56] *Ibid.*, p. 23; see the whole discussion pp. 18–25.
[57] Williams, *Julia*, ii, p. 202.
[58] *Ibid.*, i, p. 7.

in her writings Macaulay Graham like Williams is a defender of propriety. Like More or West she is critical of novels which give too vast an idea of the power of love, thinking Richardson's *Pamela* and *Clarissa*, with their 'warm' episodes, unfit for youth.[59] But she enters dangerous territory when she criticizes the double standard, which she thinks arose in the past from women being the property of men. She contends that it is very difficult to persuade a thinking girl that she should be chaste when men are not. Women are not utterly corrupted by one slip, and seldom become entirely abandoned until they are thrown into a state of desperation by the venomous rancour of their own sex. In a review in the *Analytical*, written when she was still in her anti-sex mood, Wollstonecraft wonders whether Macaulay Graham's remarks on female chastity are well timed, whether they might not tend to weaken the salutary prejudices which keep women chaste.[60] Of course Macaulay Graham is not recommending sexual licence; chastity is essential in order to preserve the purity and independence of the mind.[61] We ought to pay attention to Macaulay Graham's careful discussion here. It is all too easy *now* to think that codes of sexual propriety *then* simply controlled and repressed women and that they brought women no advantages. Macaulay Graham reminds us that, at least in the context of her own time, when a woman gave herself to a man, she thereby gave him a measure of power over her reputation, and diminished her own opportunities for independence and self-control. She also insists that women need to protect themselves by a code of chastity against the sexual aggressiveness of men.

As an actress and therefore suspect, Inchbald was very careful of her reputation. *Simple Story* is ostensibly a perfectly 'proper' novel – though when we come to look at what it intimates about female desire, we may conclude that covertly it is not so. At mid-point we learn that 'The beautiful, the beloved Miss Milner – she is no longer beautiful – no longer beloved – no longer – tremble while you read it! – no longer – virtuous'.[62] Having betrayed her husband in the arms of the Duke of Avon, she fled to a dreary retreat, there eventually to die in the manner approved for fallen penitents at the age of 35. *Nature and Art* was perhaps more offensive to conservatives. In itself the story of Hannah Primrose, the village beauty seduced by the squire's son and driven into prostitution and eventual hanging for forgery, did not give out a particularly new or subversive message. The fact that the blame for her downfall was placed mainly upon her seducer and his father, and upon social prejudice which denied her the chance of earning an honest living, would not greatly have offended. Such stories were familiar in the propaganda for the Magdalen Hospital for penitent prostitutes.[63] More

59 Macaulay Graham, *Letters on Education*, pp. 142–8.
60 *Analytical Review*, 8 (November 1790), p. 247.
61 Macaulay Graham, *Letters on Education*, p. 220.
62 Inchbald, *Simple Story*, p. 194.
63 Ellis, *Politics of Sensibility*, p. 172.

subversive was the charge of widespread hypocrisy. Poor girls are forced to make public penance in a white sheet in church; women of higher social standing get away with similar or worse sins.

> But this country rigour, in town, she could dispense withal; and like other ladies of virtue, she there visited and received into her house the acknowledged mistresses of a man in elevated life: it was not therefore the crime, but the rank which the criminal held in society, that drew down Lady Bendham's vengeance.[64]

We might call this the 'Robes and furr'd gowns hide all'[65] argument: 'For vice, Lord Bendham thought (with certain philosophers), might be most exquisitely pleasing, in a pleading garb. "But this youth sinned without elegance, without one particle of wit, or an atom of good breeding."'[66] The philosopher in parentheses is Edmund Burke; Inchbald is here guilty of a 'jacobin' response to his contention in *Reflections on the Revolution in France* that in court society, vice sheds half its evil by losing all its grossness.[67] The robes and furr'd gowns argument was taken up by other 'unsex'd' females such as Wollstonecraft and Robinson. So too was the charge that it was easier to get away with the greater crime of adultery, marital infidelity, than with the lesser crime of premarital sex, fornication, because the latter carried the danger of discovery through unmarried pregnancy. Society will overlook a woman's departures from chastity, provided that she is married and her husband tolerates them.[68]

Lorraine Fletcher has convincingly revealed the undercurrent of sexual subversion in Smith's novels, but it is all very carefully and indirectly done.[69] Smith herself was a perfectly virtuous wife and mother, and her heroines never indulge in sex outside of marriage. For example Geraldine, the heroine of *Desmond*, is as good as can be, dutiful towards her dissipated husband even after he offers her to a friend for money, even though she is loved devotedly by the heroic and handsome Desmond. Intriguingly, Geraldine is doubled in the novel by Josephine de Boisbelle, a Frenchwoman with whom Desmond *does* have a brief affair and who bears his illegitimate child. Geraldine and Desmond adopt the child after they marry. Is Smith nudging her readers to imagine that Desmond and Geraldine might have had

---

[64] Elizabeth Inchbald, *Nature and Art* (1796) (London, Pickering & Chatto, 1997), p. 42.
[65] Shakespeare, *King Lear*, Act IV, Scene vi:
Through tatter'd clothes small vices do appear;
Robes and furr'd gowns hide all. Plate sin with gold,
And the strong lance of justice hurtless breaks;
Arm it in rags, a pigmy's straw does pierce it.
[66] Inchbald, *Nature and Art*, p. 81.
[67] Burke, *Reflections*, p. 73.
[68] Robinson, *The Widow*, ii, pp. 85–6.
[69] Fletcher, *Charlotte Smith*, pp. 139, 151, 185.

an affair, at the same time making adultery less threatening by locating it in France? In *The Old Manor House* we are given to understand that Monimia does not have sex with Orlando before they marry, but the symbolism of Orlando entering her chamber at night by a passage which opens behind her bed, and of her cutting the tapestry to let him in, is very suggestive.

Though Smith's heroines are always chaste, they do not always behave with the strictest propriety, and the misbehaviour of some lesser characters is not always held up for complete disapproval. In *Celestina* for example there are three elopements, blamed on the obstructive parents, not the lovers. Worse still, we encounter a sympathetic courtesan, Emily, the sister of Mrs. Elphinstone (who is modelled on Smith herself). Emily had eloped (elopement number four) with a man who then refused to marry her, and had become a courtesan. Mrs. Elphinstone failed to persuade her 'to quit a manner of life, where she possessed boundless splendour and luxury, for such a precarious subsistence as women can earn in business'[70] (surely this remark in itself is half-way towards an encouragement of vice). Mrs. Elphinstone (like Smith) had been short of money; when her child was mortally ill, her respectable and affluent older brother refused assistance, and Emily the courtesan sent £40. We are not told that Mrs. Elphinstone refused this gift, drawn from the wages of sin. At the end of the novel however, propriety triumphs in the usual way for prose fiction plots, and Emily dies of consumption. Kept mistresses nobly assist the heroes of both *The Old Manor House* and *The Young Philosopher*. The message has been conveyed that fallen women are not necessarily bad women.

The second preface to *The Banished Man* contains a reply to the 'prudish' censurers who have criticized Smith's novels; she surmises that being no longer young, they have forgotten the power of love. One of her targets sounds like Hannah More: 'One was an authoress; one who is herself above all the weaknesses of humanity, and whose talents give to her character a peculiar hardness, which is all placed to the account of her understanding.'[71] In the novel itself, warm-hearted Captain Caverley judges 'prudes' to be 'illiberal-minded; selfish, odious cats'.[72] It was noted in a previous section that Rosalie, the heroine of *Montalbert*, was the bastard daughter of Mrs. Vyvian; the mother is presented as a saintly woman. Rosalie herself marries Montalbert clandestinely. In *The Old Manor House*, the naïve Monimia tells Orlando that she loves him before he has declared his love for her, and Orlando's sister Isabella sets her cap at Captain Warwick and elopes with him; two happy marriages are the eventual result. Smith is at the very least questioning the doctrine that women should not acknowledge their feelings for a man before he proposes. It is carefully done: she does not obviously

[70] Smith, *Celestina*, ii, p. 298.
[71] Smith, *Banished Man*, ii, pp. x–xi.
[72] *Ibid.*, ii, p. 177.

endorse 'forward' young women, but the narrative does not obviously condemn them either. Miss Goldthorpe falls in love with George Delmont, the young philosopher, more or less on sight, and effectively declares her feelings to his sisters in the expectation that they will tell him. Miss Goldthorpe is not an approved character, and George does not love her; but he admires and commends her honesty. Later she captures and marries his dissipated older brother. Miss Goldthorpe is not traded in marriage by men; she is rich and in control of her own money, and she transacts herself in defiance of her guardian, who had intended her for his son.

Robinson also has women proposing to men, though often disapproved women. In *Angelina*, Selina Wantworth proposes to Belmont; but the heroine Sophia also lets her feelings be known to him through an intermediary. In *Walsingham* the handsome young hero is propositioned by the dissipated gambler, Lady Amaranth, and pursued by the not disapproved Amelia Woodford. It has already been noted that the 'Robes and furr'd gowns hide all' argument is deployed by Robinson; it is an obsessive theme, and all of her works of prose fiction, and her *Memoirs* too, contain passages which must be read as defences of her career as a courtesan. She conducts an incessant guerrilla war against the conventions of sexual propriety. It was noticed in Chapter 1 that her *Natural Daughter* contains a lightly veiled defence of the sexual career of Wollstonecraft. Julia, the widow in her novel of that title, voices an extended plea for leniency to women who fall: 'The frailty of our sex depends on a thousand circumstances, and ought to claim the tenderest indulgence. A woman may be weak without being vicious; a variety of events may conspire to undermine the most powerful rectitude.'[73] When Julia, who is presented to the reader as a model of goodness, discovers that she is not a widow after all, and that her husband, thinking her dead, has remarried, she agrees to live with him ostensibly as his mistress, so that he may escape the charge of bigamy: 'I will ... suffer all the calamities that vulgar minds can heap upon me. I will convince the world, that the virtues of the heart, are not to be tarnished by the outward forms of life.'[74] All comes right when her husband's wicked second wife divorces him – right from Robinson's point of view, deeply shocking from the viewpoint of defenders of propriety.

In her *Angelina*, a kept mistress bravely assists the heroine at the cost of offending her noble patron and losing everything; she dies in the approved manner. But in *Walsingham*, Robinson does not bother to use this device in order to maintain propriety. Julie de Beaumont is a young gentlewoman who has been seduced and abandoned; her attempts to return to respectability are thwarted by women who make a parade of their propriety, and she is compelled to become a common prostitute. She rescues the hero from gaol;

[73] Robinson, *The Widow*, i, pp. 151–3.
[74] *Ibid.*, ii, p. 168.

he has compassion for her and assists her. Lord Heartwing takes a bet of 10,000 guineas that he will find a wife, and marry within a week; he marries Julie and wins his bet. He is a dissipated old roué, and they separate; she retires as a duchess on £600 per year. In the same novel, Amelia Woodford gives herself to Walsingham after a masked ball when they are both drunk; he decides he cannot marry her because he does not love her. The noble Colonel Aubrey, to whom she was engaged, insists on going ahead with the marriage: 'The world may condemn me; but I shall feel a more delightful gratification in snatching an amiable object from the insults of the world, than ever the libertine experienced in seducing innocence from the paths of virtue.'[75] Amelia dies, however, satisfying the demands either of propriety, or of the sentimental novel.

Heterosexual love and desire

If sexual morality is a matter of debate, so to a lesser extent is romantic 'love', whatever that may be. Getting the debate clear is a difficult matter, for the reader has a sense that these writers are talking about different kinds of love, some approved, some disapproved, without ever distinguishing them properly. Both some 'unsex'd' and some 'proper' females have doubts about love. Wollstonecraft in her *Vindication of the Rights of Woman* is determined to drive a wedge between love and the friendship of a companionate marriage, giving a clear preference to the latter. The *Appeal to the Men of Great Britain* declares that 'no reasonable woman, no woman with a spark of common sense, dreams that a husband is to continue a lover, in the romantic sense of the word'.[76] This sentiment is not uncommon in the literature of the age, but exactly what it means is intriguing and by no means obvious. More writes of the danger of loving too much, thereby becoming too much attached to this world rather than the world to come. Of course this is a standard Christian theme, an echo of Christ's call to his disciples to leave their families and follow him. West, like Wollstonecraft, is critical of what she sees as the romantic illusion of love in her *Gossip's Story*, also like Wollstonecraft giving preference to marital companionship. It is tempting to say that much of the prose fiction of the age presents a female fantasy of romantic love, of impossibly perfect happiness with an adoring man,[77] and that some writers – Wollstonecraft, More, West – see through the fantasy. But maybe this is anachronistic; perhaps we should not expect 1790s writers to share present-day feminist judgements of romantic love. When we survey their writings as a whole, it is to be doubted whether *anyone* is consistent in dismissing it as a fantasy.

Doubts are expressed about love; on the other hand, all of these writers,

75 Robinson, *Walsingham*, iii, pp. 143–4.
76 *Appeal to the Men of Great Britain*, p. 85.
77 Todd, *Sign of Angellica*, p. 186.

all of our 'unsex'd' and 'proper' females except perhaps Macaulay, can be caught idealizing love, explicitly or implicitly. None of these writers is in favour of merely prudential or worldly marriages, marriages without love. West has the wise mother in her *Advantages of Education* object to marriages between partners very unequal in wealth and status, but this is precisely because generosity and gratitude are a poor substitute for 'free and uncon- strained tenderness'.[78] In the same novel she has Mrs. Herbert, on her husband's death, marry the man she originally loved even though she has to give up her fortune to do it. More's animadversions against love, and against romantic novels which make too much of it, are belied by other passages. Ideal men, such as the shepherd of Salisbury Plain in the tract of that title, love their wives with an aching adoration, and she commonly exemplifies the bliss of heaven by everlasting companionship with a loved husband or wife. Is there an implicit distinction here between romantic love (suspect) and marital love (approved)? Wollstonecraft stopped disparaging love when she fell in love with Imlay, and for a brief time had her love returned: 'For years I have endeavoured to calm an impetuous tide—labouring to make my feel- ings take an orderly course.—It was striving against the stream.—I must love and admire with warmth, or I sink into sadness.'[79]

If Hays thinks in her *Appeal to the Men of Great Britain* that *romantic* love is not found in the married state, her *Letters and Essays* idealize marital love. Williams writes love into the heart of an epic history in her *Letters from France*, elevating it to heroic grandeur as husbands and wives die together, or kill themselves when their partner is guillotined. Smith's heroes invariably worship the women they love, and so do Radcliffe's. In her *Romance of the Forest*, Adeline is adored not only by Theodore, whom she will eventually marry, but also by Louis la Motte, an impossibly perfect man who loves her so much that he is ready nobly to give her up, and do everything in his power to save Theodore from execution. In the same novel La Luc is devoted to the memory of his long-dead wife, visiting her memorial and looking forward to being reunited with her in heaven. Heroes and heroines die of unrequited love – Sibella and Murden in Fenwick's *Secresy*, Frederick in Williams's *Julia*. The overt *moral* in these cases may be that passion should be controlled by reason, but the *tendency* is to celebrate love's power. Now unless we are to dismiss this near-universal idealization of love as a mere literary convention, having very little meaning, there is a problem in recon- ciling it with those remarks in criticism of romantic love noted above.

One very simple point may be offered in explanation. Objections to romantic love are frequently suspicions of a stylized gallantry, an affected devotion – 'a maze of tender and unmeaning rhetoric'[80] – which the author

[78] West, *Advantages of Education*, i, pp. 206–7.
[79] Wollstonecraft, *Letters Written during a Short Residence*, p. 95.
[80] West, *Advantages of Education*, ii, p. 220.

wishes to distinguish from true love. Marianne in West's *Gossip's Story* cannot realize that a show of sensibility is not the same as genuine feeling, and so she refuses the admirable Pelham because 'he fell far short of that kneeling ecstatic tenderness, that restless solicitude, that profound venera- tion' which her reading of romantic novels had led her to expect.[81] Her father advises her:

> Have you observed so little of real life as not to perceive, that the kind of address you talk of, is chiefly practised by the designing part of mankind, upon the woman whose person or fortune is the object of their desire?
>   Whether your lover was a sentimental sniveller, or an artful designer, the mock majesty with which you were invested could not continue in the married state.[82]

If we are fully to understand the issues here, it is necessary to explore what women writers have to say about female desire. Sensibility, briefly characterized in Chapter 2, will be discussed in a later chapter, but here it is necessary to remark that the discourse of sensibility bears no simple rela- tionship to a discourse of sexual desire. The *Anti-Jacobin*, à propos Wollstonecraft, certainly equates an excess of sensibility with a proneness to sexual immorality;[83] and Wollstonecraft herself, in her *Vindication of the Rights of Woman*, at times equates sensibility with sex, and implies that an overheated sensibility leads to promiscuity.[84] But a simple equation of sensi- bility with sexual immorality or even with sexual desire is not common in woman-authored texts of this decade. Promiscuous women in Robinson's novels, for example, characteristically *lack* sensibility, or merely affect it. Even Marianne, West's exemplar of a destructive sensibility in *A Gossip's Story,* is never tempted into immorality, and indeed her extreme delicacy and refinement of feeling make her something of a prude.[85]

Women writers of this period are very reserved about desire, more so than was the case at the beginning of the eighteenth century. There is scarcely ever a hint of frankly lusty females like Moll Flanders or Fanny Hill. Mary Raymond in Hays's *Victim of Prejudice* has a nightmare vision of her mother 'in the arms of her seducer, revelling in licentious pleasure'.[86] In Radcliffe's *Udolpho* we encounter Signora Laurentini, who gives herself to the Marquis de Villeroi, follows him to France and poisons his wife so that she may take her place. She was 'a dreadful victim to unresisted passion', but her overt sexuality is distanced and rendered unthreatening to English readers by her foreignness; she was possessed by 'all the delirium of Italian love'.[87] The

[81] Jane West, *A Gossip's Story* (London, Longman, 1797), i, p. 46.
[82] *Ibid.*, pp. 95–6.
[83] *Anti-Jacobin Review* (April 1799), 40.
[84] Wollstonecraft, *Vindication of the Rights of Woman*, p. 141.
[85] West, *Gossip's Story*, i, p. 203; ii, p. 148.
[86] Hays, *Victim of Prejudice*, p. 123.
[87] Ann Radcliffe, *The Mysteries of Udolpho* (1794) (Oxford, Oxford University Press, 1980), pp. 659, 656.

same can be said of Janetta Laundy, the abandoned, promiscuous Frenchwoman who offers 'all the delights [of her] love' to Clement Montgomery in Fenwick's *Secresy*.[88] Such intimations that women might have desires as aggressive and assertive as men's are rare indeed.

We may interpret this, with Poovey, Todd and Shevelow, as a sign of the rise of the 'proper' lady, increasingly controlled by a narrow and restrictive cultural construction of femininity, for whom any confession of sexual desire was unthinkable. If we take this view, we will regard the rare expressions of female desire in woman-authored texts as doomed protests against this repression. Alternatively, we may with Nancy Cott argue that passionlessness had advantages for women, and was not simply imposed on them in the interests of men, for it gave them some control over sexual intercourse and pregnancy, and played a part in elevating their moral standing.[89] Both of these perspectives have some validity; but in addition the texts under consideration here suggest that something else was going on. Moll Flanders and Fanny Hill were created by men, and the lusty heroines of Aphra Behn and Delarivier Manley in the first half of the century behave like men. Some women writers of the 1790s are working out their own view of the appropriate way of describing sexual desire and expression.

Overt discussions of female desire are not too numerous, but we can find them scattered through the writings of Robinson, in Hays's *Memoirs of Emma Courtney*, in Inchbald's *Simple Story* and in Wollstonecraft's last, unfinished novel. Even when she wrote the *Vindication of the Rights of Woman*, Wollstonecraft insisted that it was wrong for women to feign frigidity: 'Women as well as men ought to have the common appetites and passions of their nature.'[90] In 1798 Wollstonecraft was not advocating passionlessness:

> When novelists or moralists praise as a virtue, a woman's coldness of constitution, and want of passion; and make her yield to the ardour of her lover out of sheer compassion, or to promote a frigid plan of future comfort, I am disgusted.
>
> Nay it is ... indelicate, when she is indifferent, unless she be constitutionally insensible; then indeed it is a mere affair of barter; and I have nothing to do with the secrets of trade.
>
> We cannot, without depraving our minds, endeavour to please a lover or husband, but in proportion as he pleases us.[91]

Wollstonecraft here argues that it is wrong for a woman to have sexual intercourse with a man, even her husband, not only if she does not love him but also if she does not desire him. In her *Scandinavian Letters* of 1796 there are

88 Fenwick, *Secresy*, p. 318.
89 See references and discussion in Chapter 2.
90 Wollstonecraft, *Vindication of the Rights of Woman*, p. 217.
91 Wollstonecraft, *Wrongs of Woman*, p. 153.

hints of the sexual pleasure she enjoyed with Imlay: 'My bosom still glows.— ... still nature will prevail—and if I blush at recollecting past enjoyment, it is the rosy hue of pleasure heightened by modesty.'[92]

In Inchbald's *Simple Story*, Miss Milner falls in love with Dorriforth, and confesses: 'I love him with all the passion of a mistress, and with all the tenderness of a wife.'[93] And it is a passion of the body; when he praises her, every fibre feels a secret transport, and when her jealousy is aroused, every limb aches with agonizing torment.[94] Her passion is constantly and explicitly contrasted with the passionlessness of Miss Fenton, to whom Dorriforth is betrothed: '"Their passions for each other just the same—pure—white as snow."' "And I dare say, not warmer," replied Miss Milner.'[95] Dorriforth realizes he cannot be happy with such a woman, and breaks off the engagement; Miss Fenton is happy to become a nun. Inchbald's disapproval of her 'insipid smile of approbation' and 'cold indifference at the heart' is perfectly plain.[96]

In Wollstonecraft and Inchbald, then, we have veiled but nonetheless unmistakable endorsements of female desire; passionlessness is definitely not recommended. Mention has already been made, with reference to Robinson's *False Friend*, of the very physical symptoms of Gertrude's love for Lord Denmore (who shockingly turns out to be her father). In Hays's *Memoirs of Emma Courtney*, Emma declares of Harley that she *loved his person*[97]- an expression almost invariably used in the literature of the decade about men's feelings for women, to denote a purely sexual desire.[98] She describes the 'glowing effervescence' of her feelings and declares, 'at length, I loved you, not only rationally and tenderly – *but passionately* – it became a pervading and a devouring fire!'[99] After Harley has persistently failed to return her love, Emma marries Montague, and the marriage is described as a perfect companionate friendship, at first. But in the end the marriage falls apart, driving Montague into the arms of a servant girl, because Emma cannot passionately love him, and he cannot accept this. The examples of women who declare their love without waiting for the man's proposal, and who pursue men and elope, are further acknowledgements of female desire. If we postulate that there is a veiled discourse of desire in women-authored texts, then the interesting question will be, how is this desire characterized? Unveiling the lineaments of female desire will be a difficult and delicate process. Characterization of it is very largely indirect. If we wish to explore it, we have to pay attention to what is said about *men* – implicitly, about the kind of

---

92 Wollstonecraft, *Letters Written During a Short Residence,* p. 95.
93 Inchbald, *Simple Story*, p. 72.
94 *Ibid.*, pp. 84, 119.
95 *Ibid.*, p. 124.
96 *Ibid.*, p. 137.
97 Hays, *Emma Courtney*, p. 78.
98 See, for example, the next quotation from Wollstonecraft, below.
99 Hays, *Emma Courtney*, pp. 131, 130.

man who is desirable, and the kind of man who is not. A pattern of female desire is also implied by what these writers have to say about acceptable and unacceptable expressions of *men's* desire. The nature of the desirable man, and the manner of his desire, provides a recipe for woman-pleasing romantic and erotic relationships.

These writers are unanimous in demanding that men shall not regard the women they claim to love as mere physical objects, as occasional means to the relief of the tension of lust. Desire must go hand-in-hand with affection and must therefore be unselfish; the man's concern should be with what the woman wants, as well as with what he wants. Thus Macaulay Graham insists on regarding her sex 'in a higher light than as the mere objects of sense'.[100] In a review of Jerningham's *Abelard to Eloisa*, Wollstonecraft contends that justice has not been done to Eloisa's love; but above all,

> the vain and frigid Abelard has been misrepresented still more violently, and the selfish author metamorphosed into a lover, contrary to all historical evidence; for there is little reason from his letters to suppose, that he ever loved anyone but himself. The person of Eloisa was desirable, and it raised desire in Abelard – that once quenched she could only gratify his pride.[101]

And Robinson declares that 'The fact is simply this: the passions of men originate in sensuality; those of women, in sentiment: man loves corporeally, woman mentally: which is the nobler creature?'[102] In her *Walsingham*, Amelia argues that the extravagant professions of courtship are a show, put on like garments; in true affection, the object 'becomes a part of our existence. We find it as closely united with vitality, as the air we breathe; it is a sort of second self'.[103] The great theme of her *False Friend* is the intensity and the constancy of the love women feel, a love which men all too often fail to return because they are selfish and merely sensual in their desires.[104] Desire, then, is not for instant gratification but for an enduring, complex, rich union, at once physical and emotional.

Closely connected with this is the demand that love should be of mind and character, not merely of physical beauty. To a considerable extent this is true even of Smith and Radcliffe, whose heroes typically and tritely fall in love with their heroines at first sight. Smith does not escape presenting her heroine as an object, captivating the hero by her invariable beauty and sexual allure; but then, just as invariably, the hero notices that her expression of countenance promises animation, intelligence and an excellent understanding, and further acquaintance reveals the sweetness of her temper and the excellence of her heart.[105] Other authors are more firm in their rejection of objec-

[100] Macaulay Graham, *Letters on Education*, p. 62.
[101] *Analytical Review*, 13 (May 1792), 60.
[102] Robinson, *Thoughts*, p. 10.
[103] Robinson, *Walsingham*, iii, p. 330.
[104] Robinson, *False Friend*, ii, p. 93.
[105] Smith, *Old Manor House*, pp. 28, 517.

tification. Macaulay Graham notes that women fall in love with qualities of mind, even if housed in a homely form.[106] Why should men not do the same? Edgeworth goes so far as to contend that beauty is in great part a quality of the soul, that shines in the face.[107] In Inchbald's *Nature and Art*, Henry falls in love with Rebecca for her mind and character – she is in fact rather plain, compared with her showy sisters. His desire to find his father – and the parallel structure of the plot – take him abroad for twenty years; when he returns, he finds that he loves his now middle-aged sweetheart just as much as ever. In Burney's *Camilla*, the heroine's sister Eugenia is outstandingly learned and cultivated, a model of unselfishness and good principles. But she had suffered an injury and smallpox as a child, leaving her as an adult disfigured, stunted, hump-backed and lame, an object of ridicule to the unfeeling. When her sense of her own ugliness strikes home, she is devastated. In order to bring her into a right frame of mind, her father takes her to see, through a gate, an exquisitely beautiful young woman. As they watch, the woman suddenly flings herself about, wildly laughs and cries, slavers and speaks incoherently. In this rather bizarre way, Burney enforces her opinion that mind is more important than beauty; the point is rammed home by Eugenia's eventual marriage to the cultivated and handsome Melmond. At first, Melmond had fallen in love (on sight) with Eugenia's beautiful cousin Indiana; but Indiana is a vain, trivial-minded doll, an automaton.

Nancy Armstrong has written penetratingly about the refashioning of male desire, by means of conduct books and novels, into a desire for inner depths rather than for a glittering, adorned surface.[108] She has interpreted this as desire for the private, domestic, feminine woman, and has contended that the rising prestige of such a woman was integral to the forging of a middle-class identity. Without doubt our 'unsex'd' and 'proper' female writers are all without exception deeply engaged in the enterprise of privileging depth over surface, mind over the merely physical. The class and gender dimensions of this will be explored in subsequent chapters. But it is important to recognize that these woman-authored texts not only refashion *male* desire; they at the same time propose a form of *female* desire.

The desirable man desires the woman he loves with respect. In Smith's *Celestina*, Montague Thorold displays 'that sort of respectful idolatry by which few women can help being gratified however they may wish to repress it'.[109] A word which is very often used in this context, which does a great deal of work and whose richness requires considerable unpicking, is 'delicacy'. Delicacy implies respect for a woman's modesty, a care to avoid raising her blushes. It also means a wider sensitivity towards her feelings,

[106] Macaulay Graham, *Letters on Education*, p. 179.
[107] Edgeworth, *Letters for Literary Ladies*, p. 3.
[108] Armstrong, *Desire and Domestic Fiction*; Armstrong & Tennenhouse, *The Ideology of Conduct* (discussed above in Chapter 2).
[109] Smith, *Celestina*, iii, p. 267.

and an unselfish determination to avoid giving her offence; delicacy is about tact and gentleness. Delicacy describes an ethos, at once aesthetic and moral, basing refined good manners upon a genuine concern for others. Montague's brother Captain Thorold fails to show it; he stares so as to make Celestina uncomfortable, and obtrudes 'gallant', flirtatious remarks. Vavasour too loves her in the wrong way, for he is 'incapable of feeling for her distress, or of listening to anything but his passionate impetuosity'.[110]

The contrast between respectful and disrespectful love is formally drawn in the parallel careers of William and Henry in Inchbald's *Nature and Art*:

> William owned to Henry, that he loved Hannah ... and hoped to make her his mistress.
>
> Henry felt that his tender regard for Rebecca ... did not inspire him even with the boldness to acquaint her with his sentiments, much less to meditate one design that might tend to her dishonour.
>
> William, he saw, took delight in the agitation of mind, in the strong apprehension mixed with the love of Hannah; this convinced Henry that either he, or himself, was not in love: for his heart told him he would not have beheld such emotions of tenderness mingled with such marks of sorrow, upon the countenance of Rebecca, for the wealth of the universe.[111]

In *Simple Story* she contrasts the proper, respectful and delicate love of Dorriforth with the improper, impudent, flirtatious love of Lord Frederick Lawnley, and the brutal love of Lord Margrave. When Lord Frederick follows Miss Milner against her will, seizes her hand and devours it with kisses, Dorriforth, momentarily carried away with anger, leaps forward and strikes him. Miss Milner is terrified beyond description, and once they are safely indoors, Dorriforth drops on his knees to entreat her forgiveness for the indelicacy he has been guilty of in her presence, for alarming her and for losing sight of the respect which was her due.[112]

The respectful man, the man of delicacy, makes himself desirable to women; the indelicate man is repellent. To return to Smith's *Celestina*, Vavasour, who is courting Celestina, looks at her with eyes inflamed and fierce from his late hours and free use of wine; he debauches all night and sets off on the following day 'with a very little alteration of his dress'.[113] In her *Montalbert*, the Rev. Philibert Hughson persecutes the heroine with flirtatious speeches, gets drunk and sits gasping and staring with open mouth and watery eyes.[114] There are more vivid descriptions of undesirable men in *Desmond*. Geraldine Verney's husband appears in front of his wife and children with the disgusting appearance of a debauch of liquor not slept off, and

110 *Ibid.*, iii, p. 152.
111 Inchbald, *Nature and Art*, pp. 45, 50–1.
112 Inchbald, *Simple Story*, p. 61.
113 Smith, *Celestina*, iii, pp. 148, 167.
114 Smith, *Montalbert*, i, pp. 33, 51.

clothes not since changed. His friend Lord Newminster lounges on a sofa with his riding boots on in front of the ladies, yawns in their faces and addresses his dog: 'Oh! thou dear bitchy—thou beautiful bitchy— damme, if I don't love thee better than my mother or my sisters.'[115]

Wollstonecraft is perfectly explicit about the impossibility of desiring men like this. In *Maria*, the heroine describes how her husband became repellent to her. His affection for women was of the grossest kind. Women are expected to take care to make themselves attractive; why should they be expected to endure a slovenly man? She tells of the disgust she has felt when confronted by the squalid appearance of her husband at the breakfast table, 'lolling in an arm-chair, in a dirty powdering gown, soiled linen, ungartered stockings, and tangled hair, yawning and stretching himself'.[116] In Williams's *Julia*, the elegant and refined Mrs. Meynell is married to Captain Meynell, who is good-hearted and genuinely loves her; but his manners are coarse, his person is dirty, he is rude and vulgar, and his wife is 'disgusted by his fondness'.[117]

These texts demonstrate an unmistakable connection between female desire and that 'civilizing process' described by Norbert Elias.[118] The advance of civility in this sense means an increasing control and discipline of behaviour, so as to avoid giving any discomfort or uneasiness to others which might lead to conflict or social breakdown. We witness here an attempt by spokeswomen for the generally less powerful sex, wielding the might of the pen and manipulating the conventions of desire and its expression, to reform men and their behaviour towards women. There is no need to suppose that most women writers in this decade were self-conscious about it, that they sat down before their writing-desks saying, 'Now how can we make men more woman-friendly?' For any courtship novel will inevitably present and contrast men to be understood as desirable and undesirable. Women readers will learn what they ought to desire; men readers will learn how to behave, in order to be desirable.

Some women writers, such as Wollstonecraft, Hays and Robinson, were fully conscious of this process: 'The women seem to take the lead in polishing the manners every where, that being the only way to better their condition.'[119] This quotation is from Wollstonecraft's *Scandinavian Letters* of 1796, a work whose view of the 'civilizing process' is significantly different from that of her *Vindication of the Rights of Woman* of 1792, or even of her *Historical and Moral View of the Origin and Progress of the French*

115 Smith, *Desmond*, pp. 32, 142.
116 Wollstonecraft, *Wrongs of Woman*, p. 147. Though Todd reads this as an expression of sexual fascination; *Mary Wollstonecraft*, p. 430.
117 Williams, *Julia*, ii, p. 91.
118 An issue which has been explored by Barker-Benfield in his *Culture of Sensibility*; see the discussion above in Chapter 2.
119 Wollstonecraft, *Letters Written During a Short Residence*, p. 243.

Revolution of 1794. Elias's distinction between *Kultur* and *Zivilisation* fits the *Vindication* very well. As he sees it, advocates of *Kultur*, speaking for the middle classes, are critical of *Zivilisation*, of a surface veneer of polished manners and refined behaviour having little or no moral content, which they associate with the public sphere of court society and aristocracy. Instead they propose deeper, more solid virtues, acquired in private through reading and reflection.[120]

This was very much Wollstonecraft's opinion in 1792, and it informs her hostility to the court society of the French *ancien régime* in her work of 1794. But by 1796 she is prepared to say that she has much more respect for polish and refinement, which she sees as leading towards more important qualities: 'Improving manners will introduce finer moral feelings.'[121] She confesses that she was previously too harsh in her judgement of French civilization.[122] She contrasts the good breeding of the gentleman with the coarseness of those who are not genteel.[123] This change of emphasis is partly to be explained by her experience of travelling around the provinces of what she perceived as more 'backward' countries. In part also it is a deeply personal thing, an expression of her resentment of her unfaithful lover, whom she accuses of a lack of refinement and delicacy, the result of his devotion to commerce and money-getting. But it can also be interpreted as a shift in the focus of her feminism. In 1792 her main concern was to change *women*, to persuade them to become virtuous and rational human beings rather than beautiful dolls, adorned surfaces with nothing underneath. By 1796 – perhaps in part because of her unhappy experiences with Imlay – she is much more concerned with reforming *men*, with making them less coarse, sensual and tyrannical.[124] In general, we may say that 'unsex'd' and 'proper' females have a high regard for refinement and polish in men: the rough diamond, the rugged exterior concealing the heart of gold, is very rarely promoted.[125] Chesterfield's *Letters to his Son* were notorious for recommending amoral or even immoral good manners, but none of these writers despise manners if coupled with morality. In Williams's *Julia* indeed we meet Mr. Chartres, who might have come from the pages of Chesterfield as a warning. Though educated and cultivated, he is gauche and tactless, unable to dance, walk across a room or offer a plate of cakes without making an exhibition of himself. He is no object of female desire.

Can this endeavour to reform men be understood as an attempt to make then less masculine? There is a prima-facie sense in this interpretation. The

[120] Elias, *Civilizing Process*, pp. 4–29.
[121] Wollstonecraft, *Letters Written During a Short Residence*, p. 138.
[122] *Ibid.*, pp. 213–18.
[123] *Ibid.*, p. 251.
[124] *Ibid.*, pp. 213–15, 219.
[125] See, perhaps, M. Barreaux in Radcliffe's *Udolpho*; or Captain Caverly in Smith's *Banished Man*; but neither of these would count as coarse.

ideal man in all of the texts under consideration here is not without sensibility, and occasionally sheds a tear. He is gentle, tender and considerate,
capable of loving with devotion. His tastes are domestic and he is not
homosocial: 'When dinner was ended, and the desert gave place to wine,
Josepha and Miss —— retired to the drawing-room. Clermont allured by the
sound of the harpsichord, and preferring the company of the ladies to the
noisy toast, and bacchanalian song, soon followed them.'[126] In Smith's *Old
Manor House*, the boisterous manners of his uncle, his licentious and vulgar
mirth, are disgusting to the hero Orlando, 'who had lately been accustomed
to associate only with women, or with his father and the General; the conversation of the former of whom was pensively mild, and that of the latter so
extremely courtly that he seemed always to fancy himself in the drawing-
room'.[127]

On balance, however, this would be a misleading characterization. It
would run the risk of implying a gender essentialism, the notion that certain
characteristics are eternally feminine or masculine. Even if this were
avoided, even if 'less masculine' were taken to mean by contrast with the
standards of masculinity of the 1790s, the characterization would be inaccurate. For the hero, though gentle and a man of sentiment, may be contrasted
with effeminate men, as Orlando, when he goes as a lieutenant to America,
is contrasted with an effeminate and cowardly young Cornet. There are
effeminate men in Robinson's novels, like Lord Powderwood in *Walsingham*,
who puts a small patch on his face, retouches his rouge and parades in front
of a mirror. Clermont Lynmere, the utterly effeminate man in Burney's
Camilla, is another mirror-stalker, and in fact not a man of sensibility at all.
Of course, 'effeminate' in the usage of the day is not the precise opposite of
'masculine'; women too may be criticized for effeminacy, without any
suggestion that they ought to be masculine rather than feminine.[128] But tender
heroes normally exhibit conventionally masculine characteristics. Orlando is
a brave hero as a soldier in America, and is only just dissuaded from fighting a duel in England. The ideal man – such as Charles Belmont in
Robinson's *Angelina*, or Theodore in Radcliffe's *Romance of the Forest* –
combines sensibility with fiery courage and a strong sense of manly honour.
It will therefore be more accurate to say that these writers are exploring
different styles of masculinity, than that they are recommending that males
should be less masculine.

Many of the texts under consideration have interesting material on this;
Hays, Robinson, Smith, Radcliffe, Burney and Inchbald are quite consciously
depicting different kinds of masculinity. Radcliffe's gothic villain Montoni in
Udolpho is presented as a mode of manhood of a past era, utterly unsenti-

[126] Hays, *Letters and Essays*, p. 144 (this essay is by Hays's sister Eliza).
[127] Smith, *Old Manor House*, p. 291.
[128] Wakefield, *Reflections*, p. 17.

mental, reserved, forceful, his violent passions barely contained. He is contrasted with modern men of refinement and sensibility: the hero Valancourt, the heroine's father St Aubert. It is tempting to speculate, as some commentators have done, that Montoni is an object of half-repressed female fantasy, but quite certain that this was not Radcliffe's intention. Dorriforth/Lord Elmwood in Inchbald's *Simple Story* is an object of desire who has some of Montoni's qualities – strong, reserved, obstinate, a powerful man who arouses fear. He fights two duels with Lord Frederick Lawnley, in the second as good as castrating the man who has seduced his wife.

In all of her novels Smith presents the reader with a stylized contrast between what it is difficult not to see as 'old' and 'new' men. The profile of the 'new' man comes into sharper focus when contrasted with the 'old'. The old man is homosocial, addicted to 'manly' pursuits such as drinking, gambling and hunting. He is an excellent judge of horseflesh and a connoisseur of carriages. He runs into debt; he swears and embarrasses women with his suggestive remarks. He abuses women: the Rev. Philibert Hughson in *Montalbert* boasts that he and his friends threw an old woman into the river for fun. But for all his machismo, he is invariably a coward, and backs down when the 'new' man stands up to him. True manliness is exhibited in protecting women, not in harassing them: the sentimental Theodore nearly brings about his own death in defending Adeline against rape in Radcliffe's *Romance of the Forest*. The two kinds of masculinity are systematically placed side by side in the persons of Smith's *Young Philosopher*, George Delmont, and his older brother Major Delmont. George thinks his brother *unmanly* for sexually harassing and failing to protect Medora, when he meets her alone and a fugitive at the inn. Inchbald provides a similar contrast in Henry and William in *Nature and Art*.

In Burney's *Camilla*, wholly approved men such as Mr Tyrold and Edgar Mandelbert, thoughtful, gentle, considerate yet resolutely principled, or Hal Westwyn, who combines these qualities with a fiery bravery, are opposed by wholly disapproved men such as the effeminate Clermont Lynmere, the sexual predator Lord Valhurst or the ruthless fortune-hunting Bellamy. In between we encounter a veritable catalogue of styles of masculinity which are more or less imperfect: the benevolence and sensibility of Sir Hugh, which is not balanced by any strength of mind; the sensibility and refinement of Melmond, which goes just too far to be wholly admirable; the high camp foppery – but real sense, courage and kindness – of Sir Sedley Clarendel; the young buck masculinity of Lionel Tyrold and Lieutenant Macdersey, spirited, aggressive, thoughtless and selfish; the pedantic bookishness of Dr Orkborne, who in his failure to engage with the world is a manifestly inadequate man; the selfish, insensitive vulgarity of Mr Dubster.

Is there any difference between 'unsex'd' and 'proper' females on this issue of reforming men? West's *Gossip's Story* has all the appearance of a critique of it. Marianne, the heroine of too much sensibility, has hysterics when her new husband, Clermont, loses his temper with his dog. When some of his college friends come to stay, she is offended that he stays up drinking with them, and she persuades him not to join them in cruel sports. West wants the reader to see this as a symptom of the lack of judgement and unrealistic expectations which eventually ruin the marriage. Marianne should have shown forbearance, and accepted her husband with his faults. In the same novel, when Pelham bursts into tears at the sight of Mr Dudley on his deathbed, the latter tells him to check his unmanly sorrow.[129] But Pelham is otherwise presented as an ideal man and he would not be out of place as a hero in the pages of Smith, Robinson or Inchbald. Edmund Herbert, the hero of *The Advantages of Education*, is the standard 'new' man of delicacy and refinement. So is the gentle Henry Powerscourt in *A Tale of the Times*; he is permitted to shed tears without reproof. Sir William Powerscourt in that novel is a delightful Sir Roger de Coverley figure, benevolent and down-to-earth, but because of his lack of polish he is hardly the ideal object of desire, lacking as he is in 'those nicer touches of the heart'.[130]

Powerscourt's daughter Geraldine marries Lord Monteith, who has a good heart but lacks intellectual culture and sensitivity. His is explicitly a rough, boisterous type of masculinity. When she first meets him, Geraldine recreates him as the ideal object of female desire in her own mind, and like Pygmalion becomes deeply enamoured with the creature of her own imagination.[131] When reality breaks in, she is commended by West for resolving not to be unhappy with this less than perfect being, but he is clearly no model for Geraldine or for West, and indeed Geraldine has some temporary success in reforming him. West parades her dissent from 'jacobin' and 'sentimental' novels, but in the end her depiction of the desirable man is little different from theirs; a more determined emphasis upon the Christian basis of his principles is all it amounts to. She also makes a determined and conscious break with the cliché of love at first sight, presenting it as invariably disastrous. In all three of her 1790s novels, the approved hero and heroine are not initially mutually attracted; love grows as they become better acquainted with one another's qualities of mind and character. For example, Pelham had first loved the fascinating loveliness of Marianne, in the end he falls for 'the superior loveliness of intellectual beauty' in Louisa.[132] But this is simply the logical outcome of that insistence upon desiring a person, rather than a beautiful object, which 'unsex'd' and 'proper' females share.

Hannah More is to a considerable extent in agreement with 'unsex'd' females in insisting that many men need reform. To be sure, her approved man is cast also in a Christian image, but he has much in common with the

129 West, *Gossip's Story*, ii, p. 194.
130 West, *Tale of the Times*, i, p. 144.
131 *Ibid.*, i, pp. 112–15.
132 West, *Gossip's Story*, ii, p. 193.

'new' man of Smith or Inchbald. He is certainly a man of sensibility, ready to shed a tear, as the good shoemaker in *The Two Shoemakers* does when he finds the bad shoemaker dying in misery and repentance in prison.[133] He is kind and humane to animals. Of course he is well-mannered, in a Christian way; humble, meek, long-suffering, ready to turn the other cheek, in control of his temper, gently spoken, never swearing, domestic and deeply in love with his wife, whom he has married not for her beauty or wealth but for her mind and her virtues. If a man is not quite perfect in these ways, it is the duty of his wife to inspire him with higher ideals. This Christian masculinity is contrasted in the tract mentioned above with the rough masculinity of the ungodly, of homosocial men who prefer the alehouse to the home and who refer to themselves as bucks, blades, bloods or jackboots, drinking and gambling, roaring and rioting.[134] In her tracts More does not write about the aristocracy and gentry who are the familiar denizens of three-decker novels; she writes *de haut en bas*, addressing the lower and lower middle classes. But her models of good and bad masculinity were more widely applicable.

It is appropriate to conclude this discussion of women in love by returning to Burney's *Camilla*, perhaps the most thoughtful reflection on this subject. Burney has a clear perception of the lot of women in the 1790s. She knows, and accepts, that most women lack economic independence, that their fate in life to a large extent depends on men and what men do, and that for most women marriage is the most eligible option. She recognizes that those few women who have independent means, or women with wealthy parents, will be courted for their wealth rather than for themselves. She recognizes also that women are regarded, to use our language, as sex objects. She is indeed in protest against this, and wants men to esteem women for inner qualities. While accepting many of the conventions, Burney is determined that a woman shall not be an object to be transacted.

Given these constraints, how can a woman preserve her dignity and self-respect? How can she retain her pride and her delicacy? Not if she pursues a mercenary marriage; not if she entraps a man by her beauty into making an offer which honour then obliges him to fulfil; not if she herself makes advances to a man, which he then rejects; not if she enters into marriage with a man who is after her fortune. Negotiating a relationship which assures her self-respect is incredibly difficult. It is possible that Burney herself achieved this; her blissfully happy marriage was to a French emigré who had no money to give her, and to whom she could give little money, when she was well past the bloom of youth. The ideal therefore is a marriage of free mutual choice, with parental consent, based upon love, similarity and mutual esteem focused upon qualities of mind and character. This is Camilla's aim. She will

---

[133] Hannah More, *The Two Shoemakers* (London, J. Evans & J. Hatchard, 1795), p. 44.
[134] *Ibid.*, pp. 31, 41.

not show her love until she is sure of a return. The situation of Hays's Emma Courtney would be intolerable to her. After their engagement, she is anxious to prove that her attachment to Edgar has nothing mercenary about it. She does not want him to marry her, unless he both loves and respects her. Therefore the crucial turning point in the novel is when Camilla releases him from his engagement, because she perceives that he is no longer sure she is worthy, but is determined to marry her because he has given his word. She is too proud to be united to him on such terms.

Marriage

Since most works of prose fiction in this decade are about courtship, ending when, after all the misunderstandings and obstacles, the hero and heroine finally come together, they have rather less to say about marriage. Even Smith's *Montalbert*, in which the heroine is married in the first of the three volumes, is a courtship novel in disguise, for she is secretly married as a minor without her guardian's consent by the Roman Catholic rite. Her marriage is not legally binding, and for most of the remaining two volumes she is separated from her husband, who has unjustified doubts of her fidelity. The goal of the narrative, therefore, is the final reconciliation of the lovers.[135] There are further narratives of married heroines in Robinson's *Natural Daughter*, Smith's *Desmond*, Wollstonecraft's *Maria*, and West's *Gossip's Story* and *Tale of the Times*. All of these are unhappy or doomed marriages and one is tempted to say that these authors, having hymned romantic love to the skies, find themselves unable to carry the ideal through into descriptions of the married state.

In fact the evidence will not bear this conclusion. *Desmond* and *The Natural Daughter* are courtship narratives with a difference too, in which the heroine's dreadful husband functions as the obstacle, destined to die so that she can in the last pages marry Mr Right. Does Wollstonecraft mean to suggest in *Maria* that heterosexual marriage has little to offer women? Some feminist critics think so,[136] but at the time of writing, she married, and her friend Mary Hays wrote in her obituary that she had at last found the happiness she sought in marriage and motherhood, before she was tragically cut off.[137] West of course does not mean to suggest that marriages cannot be happy, and minor characters instantiate blissful ones, as they do in the novels of Robinson, Smith, Burney and Radcliffe. There are happy and unhappy marriages in More's tracts.

---

[135] Note that Fletcher reads this novel as an account of an unhappy, unsuitable marriage; the heroine, she thinks, has obviously married the wrong man; *Charlotte Smith*, p. 245.

[136] Johnson, *Equivocal Beings*, pp. 61, 67, 69.

[137] Mary Hays, 'Obituary of Mrs. Godwin, late Mary Woolstonecraft' (*sic*), *Monthly Magazine*, 4 (September 1797), 233.

As we saw in Chapter 2, it has been argued that the idealization of the 'sentimental family' of the eighteenth century, of the companionate marriage, provided a new rationale for the subordination of women, the old ones having broken down. The myth of a family totally united in its interests and based on love legitimated male rule within the household, and the right of husbands and fathers to represent their families in the political realm.[138] Others have referred to the companionate marriage as 'new style patriarchy'.[139] Historians of property law have demonstrated the extent to which economic power was kept in the hands of men.[140] So what did women writers think about the companionate ideal? Did they view it as a stratagem, a trick, a false illusion of female happiness?

In spite of the pessimism of her novels and of the *Vindication of the Rights of Woman*, not even Wollstonecraft consistently took this view. Her well-known remark that 'an unhappy marriage is often very advantageous to a family, and ... the neglected wife is, in general, the best mother'[141] does not imply that *companionate* marriage is bad for the family. Nor does her claim that marriage is often legal prostitution imply that it always is.[142] Her assertion that in heaven there will be no marrying or giving in marriage is a biblical quotation and part of an argument for better education, rather than an argument against marriage as such.[143] She frequently refers to the tyranny of men being 'softened' (that is the word she uses), but what she is complaining about is condescending gallantry, the exaggerated flattery of women which treats them as children of a larger growth – 'the lullaby strains of condescending endearment'. She quite clearly distinguishes this from the rational companionship which is her ideal.[144]

The unhappy marriages of Smith's *Desmond* and Wollstonecraft's *Maria* are unhappy precisely because they are not companionate. Geraldine Verney's husband is homosocial and never at home; his and his wife's pleasures, tastes and views of life are utterly different.[145] Verney has a low view of the understandings of women, will not converse with them on serious subjects, and thinks that they 'are good for nothing but to make a show while [they] are young, and to become nurses when [they] are old'. He shouts, 'Away with ye all ... there, get ye along to the nursery, that's the proper place for women and children'.[146] In *The Young Philosopher*, Major Delmont scorns the 'sweet, pretty ideas of connubial felicity, taken from novels',

---

[138] Okin, 'Women and the sentimental family', pp. 65, 72, 74.

[139] Kowaleski-Wallace, *Their Fathers' Daughters*, p. 110.

[140] Staves, *Married Women's Separate Property*; Spring, *Law, Land and Family*. See the discussion above in Chapter 2.

[141] Wollstonecraft, *Vindication of the Rights of Woman*, p. 100.

[142] *Ibid.*, p. 135.

[143] *Ibid.*, p. 103.

[144] *Ibid.*, pp. 104, 105, 131, 132, 139, 175.

[145] Smith, *Desmond*, pp. 130–1.

[146] *Ibid.*, pp. 142–3.

where the hero and heroine find their happiness in one another's company. He marries for her money a woman who lacks sweetness and understanding, and as a result becomes thoroughly unhappy.[147] Wollstonecraft's Maria tries to improve her husband's taste, but finds they have few subjects in common; he has little relish for her society, she endeavours to establish social converse at their fireside in vain, and she concludes that she cannot become the friend or confidante of her husband.[148] There is a parallel in her depiction of Rousseau's uncompanionate marriage with Thérèse Levasseur.[149]

This is a subject on which 'unsex'd' and 'proper' females are united. In a series of discussions and little stories which systematically contrast companionate and uncompanionate marriages, Hays writes of 'the refined pleasure of living with a rational and equal companion[.] In such an intercourse, when enlivened by love, if happiness resides on earth, surely it is to be found!'[150] This is a sad remark, for Hays never married. Williams's M. du Fossé likewise found that 'domestic happiness was the first good of life. He had already found by experience, the insufficiency of rank and fortune to confer enjoyment, and he determined to seek it in the bosom of conjugal felicity'.[151] The moral of Smith's *Young Philosopher* is that there is nothing better than a happy marriage and tranquil family life, free from want but not necessarily opulent, in which husband and wife share in 'literary leisure and love',[152] gardening, botanizing and enjoying the beauties of nature. And from the other side of the political divide, West heads a chapter with a quotation from Thomson's 'Spring':

> An elegant sufficiency, content,
> Retirement, rural quiet, friendship, books,
> Ease and alternate labour, useful life,
> Progressive virtue, and approving heaven;
> These are the matchless joys of virtuous love.[153]

As the reference to books in the quotation implies, companionship is invariably *cultivated* companionship, whose components are literary leisure, serious conversation and an appreciation of nature involving a developed aesthetic taste and philosophic reflection. In one of Hays's essays, Melville marries Serena, hoping for 'elegant and domestic tenderness'. He soon finds that though pretty she is insipid, that the settled vacuity of her features announces the blank within. She would rather play with her lapdog than contemplate the sublime and beautiful in nature, or listen to Melville's

[147] Smith, *Young Philosopher*, pp. 257, 351.
[148] Wollstonecraft, *Wrongs of Woman*, p. 145.
[149] *Analytical Review*, 6 (April 1790), 389.
[150] Hays, *Letters and Essays*, p. 22.
[151] Williams, *Letters from France*, i, p. 129.
[152] Smith, *Young Philosopher*, p. 172.
[153] West, *Tale of the Times*, iii, p. 64.

readings of Hamlet. He realizes that 'the mere varnish of a fair complexion could make no amends for a weak and empty mind'.[154]

What about the issue of the companionate ideal and equality? It has almost become a consensus among present-day historians that companionship in marriage does not imply equality.[155] That may or may not have been the opinion of men in the 1790s; it was not the view of 'unsex'd' female writers at the time. When Catharine Macaulay Graham connects marital companionship with better education for women – and thereby their elevation towards mental equality with men – she simply states a commonplace, echoed by Wollstonecraft.[156] 'Women, then, I must take it upon me to say, ought to be considered as the companions and equals, not as the inferiors,—much less as they virtually are,— as the slaves of men,'[157] writes the author of the *Appeal to the Men of Great Britain*. In her *Letters and Essays* Hays explicitly calls for rational *and equal* companionship in marriage, and she tells the little story of the happy and equal marriage of Hortensius and Hortensia.[158] 'To be the companion, I must be equal – To be the friend, I must have comprehension and judgment', proclaims Sibella in Fenwick's *Secresy*.[159] Wollstonecraft declares quite bluntly that women should not obey men.[160] The failed marriage in Robinson's *Natural Daughter* is with a man who 'was rigidly tenacious of an husband's authority ... one of those prejudiced mortals who consider women as beings created for the conveniencies of domestic life' and assumed that his wife would be 'passive when he asserted the authority of an husband'.[161] The heroine will not put up with marital slavery. In her *Thoughts on the Condition of Woman* Robinson repudiates husbandly authority and calls for wives to be partners and equal associates; companionship is possible on no other terms.[162] In Smith's *Young Philosopher*, the villainy of the attorneys, Brownjohn and Sir Appulby Gorges, is marked by their sexual tyranny and contempt for the understandings of women.

The thesis that the ideal of companionate marriage is in fact a strategy, an ideology calculated to keep women in subjection, therefore fails when applied to 'unsex'd' females. They employ it as an ideology with an opposite tendency, as a way of claiming equality. If, as some historians have argued against Stone and Trumbach, there was no rise of the egalitarian family in this period, then the significance of prose fiction and non-fiction texts of the

154 Hays, *Letters and Essays*, pp. 38–41.
155 Fletcher, *Gender, Sex and Subordination*, p. 411.
156 Macaulay Graham, *Letters on Education*, p. 49.
157 *Appeal to the Men of Great Britain*, p. 127.
158 Hays, *Letters and Essays*, pp. 22, 117ff.
159 Fenwick, *Secresy*, p. 157.
160 Wollstonecraft, *Vindication of the Rights of Woman*, p. 107.
161 Robinson, *Natural Daughter*, i, pp. 71–3.
162 Robinson, *Thoughts*, pp. 69–70.

1790s which portray egalitarian companionship will be that they are not reflecting reality, but are campaigning for change. Nevertheless the frequency of dominant wives in prose fiction is witness of a perception that marriages were not necessarily or invariably patriarchal, and we can glean clues about some circumstances in which they were not. In Smith's *Marchmont* the wicked stepmother, Lady Dacres, dominates her husband Sir Audley Dacres because she brought the money into the marriage. In *The Young Philosopher* the utterly evil Lady Mary has power over her husband because she came from a higher social rank. In West's *Advantages of Education*, Charlotte expects especial deference from her husband, because she brought him a fortune (she does not get it). In Robinson's *False Friend*, Lady Melcomb, vulgar, sprung from trade, provided the money to a destitute peer and wears the trousers. In prose fiction however women who wear the trousers are often disapproved women, or downright villainous, which implies a cultural expectation so strong that even 'unsex'd' females cannot feel at ease with dominant wives.

But what about 'proper' women writers? Does the thesis of the companionate ideal as a patriarchal strategy work in their case? 'Proper' females such as Wakefield and Radcliffe can certainly be found paying lip-service to the authority of husbands or to the inferiority and dependence of women.[163] In More's tracts, bad women regularly dominate their husbands, implying that good women are subservient. In West's *Tale of the Times* Geraldine's tragedy is partly attributed to the fact that her husband is too uncultivated to guide her. She needs that guidance, however, not because she is a woman and a wife, but because of the deficiencies of her own education; and given that she is less defective than him, she rules and manages as long as the marriage is a success. In the same novel, the ideal marriage of Henry and Lucy is companionate, and hymned in the following terms: 'How bright the radiance of love purified by esteem! How mild the lustre of equal minds, humble but not contracted fortunes, similar tastes, and moderate desires!'[164]

Even 'proper' females can contemplate with equanimity the leadership of wives in the domains of religion and morality:

> From the superior purity of the morals of women, and the exquisite tenderness of mothers for their offspring, as well as from the timidity of the female character, there is great reason to believe, that many families might have been rescued from ruin, had the boldness of speculation, or the imprudence of adventure in the husband, been restrained by the temperate views of the wife.

So alarmed is Wakefield at her own boldness here, that she promptly disclaims any desire to challenge the headship of the husband.[165] An

[163] Wakefield, *Reflections*, pp. 75, 108; Radcliffe, *Female Advocate*, pp. 398, 404, 463.

[164] West, *Tale of the Times*, iii, pp. 64, 90.

[165] Wakefield, *Reflections*, pp. 107–9.

'unsex'd' female such as Hays can be far more confident and assertive: 'In the reformation of manners so loudly called for, let us catch the glorious enthusiasm, and take the lead!'[166] Hays, if she was the author of the anonymous *Appeal to the Men of Great Britain*, declares that everybody knows of strong and virtuous women who have ruled and reclaimed weak men.[167] In Robinson's *Natural Daughter*, Lady Louisa Franklin marries and reforms the scatter-brained but good-hearted coxcomb Sir Lionel Beacon, presumably in the process curing him of his failure to appreciate mind in women. But it is not only 'unsex'd' females who can be bold in asserting the moral leadership of women. In spite of the fact that she has Will Chip the carpenter say 'For the woman is below her husband'[168] no one is more insistent upon the role of wives in moral leadership than the doyenne of 'proper' females, Hannah More herself. In her *Strictures*, the ideal wife is by no means a weak dependant; she is to counsel her husband, to reason and reflect, to judge, discourse and discriminate, and to strengthen him in his principles.[169] In her tracts we encounter wives who rescue their husbands from drunkenness and turn them to God.

Motherhood

The first section of this chapter, about the revolt of daughters, showed women writers depicting a parental authority in which mothers shared. Camilla reveres her mother as much as her father. Conversely, just as there could be tyrannical fathers against whom resistance was justified, so there could be tyrannical mothers. But can we go further than this, and say with some recent neo-Freudian commentators that 'unsex'd' and 'proper' females unwittingly reveal repressed matrophobia?[170] In her *Vindication of the Rights of Woman* Wollstonecraft condemns mothers because of their brutish affection for their children, an affection which blinds them to the claims of justice and the public good – implicitly because they are not rational and impartial as fathers are supposed to be.[171] This is unusual:[172] when mothers are criticized, it is normally for a *lack* of maternal affection, for not being womanly enough. There are certainly very bad and unloving mothers in prose fiction of the 1790s – for example Lady Mary in Smith's *Young Philosopher*, Lady

166 Hays, *Letters and Essays*, p. 157.

167 *Appeal to the Men of Great Britain*, p. 142.

168 Hannah More, *Village Politics. Addressed to all the Mechanics, Journeymen, and Day Labourers, in Great Britain. By Will Chip, a Country Carpenter* (London, F. & C. Rivington, 1792), p. 11.

169 More, *Strictures*, i, p. 98.

170 Kowaleski-Wallace, *Their Fathers' Daughters*, pp. 29, 39–40, 53.

171 Wollstonecraft, *Vindication of the Rights of Woman*, pp. 242–3.

172 Though it is echoed in the *Appeal to the Men of Great Britain*, p. 166.

Clermont in West's *Gossip's Story*, Mrs Bradford in Robinson's *Natural Daughter* and Mrs Ashburn in Fenwick's *Secresy*. But most authors provide balancing examples of model mothers. More intriguing is the very frequent *absence* of the mothers of heroines, dead before the story begins. Even if we do not count cases where the mother dies early in the course of the work, or cases where the heroine has or finds a substitute mother in an aunt or older woman, still in over half of the full-length works of prose fiction surveyed here, the mother is absent. Is an unconscious repression of the maternal going on? Without doubt there is something here to provoke thought; this cannot be a mere coincidence.

But perhaps we do not need to resort to imaginative hypotheses. Quite simply, in the real world it was not uncommon for mothers to be absent, for every pregnancy brought the danger of death in childbirth.[173] More prosaically, the absence of the mother was an obvious narrative tactic. If the heroine's mother were present, protecting and guiding her, then nail-biting crises could not easily occur. Camilla's mother does not die, but she is fortuitously absent in Portugal for seven of the ten books. The plot can only work because Camilla is left without her guidance, and the reviewer in the *British Critic* saw this quite clearly:

> The characters of Mr. and Mrs. Tyrold are finely drawn, but the latter is too much removed from sight ... It is evident, indeed, that under her prudent superintendance, the errors and misfortunes of Camilla could not easily have arisen. It was therefore necessary to remove her, to produce the distress of the plot.[174]

Mrs Tyrold is an impressive mother, and so is Mrs Williams in West's *The Advantages of Education*. She is devoted to her daughter yet solicitous gently and tactfully to correct her faults, strong, cultivated, intelligent, with firm principles and judgement. Her wisdom and perception save her daughter from seduction and rape, but so competent is she that the reader is never in any doubt as to the outcome. With so excellent a mother watching over the heroine, there can be little suspense.

In her preface West tells that one of her chief designs is 'to place the maternal character in a dignified and pleasing point of view', and that she certainly does.[175] Mrs Williams is a perfect educator for her daughter, and the role of mothers as educators is a frequent theme in woman-authored texts of the 1790s. From Macaulay Graham through Wollstonecraft and Hays to More they are unanimous too in using the nurturing responsibilities of mothers and their role as educators of their children as a basis for a claim to better education for women, including scientific education.[176] The political

173 Vickery, *Gentleman's Daughter*, pp. 97–8.
174 *British Critic*, 8 (1796), 535.
175 West, *Advantages of Education*, i, p. ii.
176 Wollstonecraft, *Letters Written During a Short Residence*, p. 37.

importance of women as childrearers and educators – what has been called 'republican motherhood' – will be considered further in the next chapter.

Motherhood can be a very sturdy and reliable pedestal for women to stand on. Women writers can call upon it to assert and defend their own worth. No one had a more demanding task in salvaging her own reputation than the ex-courtesan Mary Robinson; motherhood served her purposes very well. Her *Vancenza* ends with a celebration of the mother–daughter bond worthy of Hollywood:

> Elvira groaned deeply ... 'Hark!' said she, 'I hear the sound of ten thousand harps, they are borne by troops of angels! See! they throng about a glittering vision! It is my mother – she beckons me to her embrace – I come.'
> She made an effort to rise – her strength failed – *she sunk into the arms of* DEATH![177]

Vancenza is reputed to be a *roman à clef*; if so the obvious unlocking is that the dead mother, abandoned by Prince Almanza, is Mary Robinson, abandoned by the Prince of Wales. She assumes the mantle of devoted motherhood in several passages in her memoirs too:

> I cannot describe the sensations of my soul at the moment when I pressed the little darling to my bosom, my maternal bosom; when I kissed its hands, its cheeks, its forehead, as it nestled closely to my heart, and seemed to claim that affection which has never failed to warm it.

In a very short book she tells us twice that she breast-fed her own child; she continued to do so after the normal time.[178] In fairness to Robinson, her daughter lays equal emphasis on her maternal tenderness in her completion of the memoirs: the daughter refused adoption by Robinson's wealthy brother, because it was conditional upon her renouncing her mother.[179]

Wollstonecraft's agreement with Rousseau in the *Vindication of the Rights of Woman* that mothers should suckle their own children instead of consigning them to wet nurses is quite widely shared. Given the ancient and widespread view that sexual intercourse was harmful while nursing,[180] this implied periods of sexual abstinence.[181] Macaulay Graham however doubts whether upper-class women should be encouraged to suckle; they will not give up their luxuries and midnight revels, which overheat the milk, and their perfumes may throw their infants into convulsions. An active young wench as a wet nurse whose tongue never stands still will bring a child on better than a wise matron.[182] In this we hear Macaulay Graham's decidedly upper-

---

[177] Mary Robinson, *Vancenza; or, the Dangers of Credulity* (London, 1792), ii, p. 149.

[178] Robinson, *Memoirs*, pp. 63, 70, 74–5, 79–80, 87.

[179] *Ibid.*, pp. 131–2, 142, 152, 155.

[180] Valerie Fildes, *Wet Nursing: A History from Antiquity to the Present* (Oxford, Blackwell, 1988), pp. 16, 83, 104, 162.

[181] Wollstonecraft, *Vindication of the Rights of Woman*, p. 151.

[182] Macaulay Graham, *Letters on Education*, pp. 33–4.

class voice. Wakefield, who speaks from much lower down the social ladder, thinks that all mothers should perform the 'first maternal office', and is unusual in speaking up for the deserted children of the wet nurses. If this requires women of fashion to give up their luxuries and dissipations for a while, then so be it.[183]

Wollstonecraft's lyrical descriptions of her maternal feelings in her *Scandinavian Letters* help to establish her moral superiority to her correspondent, the man who has abandoned her.[184] Smith, worried about the loss of genteel status in becoming a professional writer, justifies her decision by describing, in prefaces and in fictionalizations of herself, her devotion to her many children and her health-destroying labours to support them and launch them in life.[185] Meanwhile the father dissipates his fortune and falls into debt; it is clear who has secured the moral victory.

Women without men

In her novels of the 1790s West, herself married and a mother, assumes the authorial voice of a spinster, 'Prudentia Homespun'. In *Advantages of Education* she has Mrs Williams declare that 'Many of the fraternity of old maids discover, by their good humour and cheerfulness, (Mrs Williams and I are acquainted) that their situation by no means deserves the ridicule and odium generally affixed to it', that she is far from thinking that female happiness is of necessity connected with marriage and that preparing her daughter to catch a man has not been her chief view in her education.[186] Rousseau contended that women did not need political rights, because they had power over their husbands through sexual allure: the witty author of the *Appeal to the Men of Great Britain* reminds her readers that there are ugly women and old women whose interests need to be considered too.[187] Edgeworth thinks that a good education is essential to women whose lot it is not to marry; it gives them other interests and makes them less likely to be burthensome to their friends or to society.[188] In Smith's *Marchmont* the heroine Althea has received an excellent and loving upbringing in the hands of her unmarried aunt, a woman remarkable for goodness, good manners and elegance. At one point Althea resigns herself to a single life, 'and when she recollected all her aunt was, she thought of this rather with complacency than regret'.[189] Miss Woodley is a likeable spinster in Inchbald's *Simple Story*, a sheet-anchor for

[183] Wakefield, *Reflections*, pp. 14–17.
[184] Wollstonecraft, *Letters Written During a Short Residence*, pp. 66, 127, 187–8.
[185] Smith, *Banished Man*, i, pp. v–vi, ii, pp. 214–15, 226, 231–2.
[186] West, *Advantages of Education*, ii, pp. 224–7.
[187] *Appeal to the Men of Great Britain*, p. 119.
[188] Edgeworth, *Letters to Literary Ladies*, p. 17.
[189] Smith, *Marchmont*, ii, p. 24.

both Miss Milner and Lady Matilda. One of Robinson's most delightful characters is Miss Juliana Pengwynn in *Angelina*, an outspoken and formidable, though comical, *femme savante*. She stands up to Sir Edward Clarendon, who might have appeared on a *commedia del' arte* cast list as 'a tyrannical father' and who declares 'I hate old maids—and I hate learning'.[190] But his daughter, thinking of her learned aunt, praises the character of a spinster.[191]

There are, then, positive images of women who do not marry, and as we would expect unmarried authors such as Hays, Edgeworth and More do not express any prejudice against older unmarried women. Other authors do not entirely avoid negative images or indeed vulgar prejudices. Perhaps this was inevitable, in a culture which took it for granted that the destiny, the career-goal of women was marriage and that any woman who did not marry was either a failure or a misfit. Mrs Mittin declares that she calls herself Mrs so as to be taken for a young widow, which everybody likes; she will not call herself Miss for fear of being identified as an old maid.[192] Even Mrs Williams insists that all women ought to marry if an eligible opportunity offers, and advises her daughter against any girlish determination not to marry.[193] In West's *Gossip's Story*, Marianne's foolish friend rejects two unexceptionable offers and resolves to stay single out of hatred of men.[194]

Considerable hostility to spinsters comes to the surface in Smith's novels: their bitterness and malice is frequently attributed to their failure to attract a husband. In *Desmond*, much trouble is caused by a 'canting prude', a 'gossiping tabby', Miss Elford. We are given to understand that her malice stems from jealousy of married women, and that her virtue has never been tried, because she has never had any offers.[195] There are malevolent, prudish, evangelical bluestocking spinsters in *The Young Philosopher*, Mrs Crewkherne and Mrs Grinsted (unmarried women past a certain age were regularly referred to as Mrs, not Miss). The suspicion arises that Smith has Hannah More in her sights, as perhaps does Robinson in her satire on a prudish old maid in *The False Friend*.[196] Mrs Grinstead treats Mrs Glenmorris with unbelievable wickedness, and her hatred is explained as a consequence of her disappointment that Glenmorris did not marry her instead.[197] In *The Old Manor House*, Mrs Rayland has stayed unmarried out of antique pride, because no offers were received from any man with a lineage as old as hers. She treats her nearby relatives the Somerives with contempt, because one of them, who *would* have been an acceptable suitor, had fallen in love with and married her companion instead.

190 Robinson, *Angelina*, i, p. 81.
191 *Ibid.*, i, p. 278.
192 Burney, *Camilla*, p. 469.
193 West, *Advantages of Education*, ii, pp. 224, 228.
194 West, *Gossip's Story*, ii, p. 221.
195 Smith, *Desmond*, pp. 171–2, 191–3, 196, 304.
196 Robinson, *False Friend*, ii, p. 42.
197 Smith, *Young Philosopher*, p. 211.

We might note, however, that Mrs Rayland, the unmarried heiress, is thereby her own mistress, independent and powerful. Widows who inherit can be independent and powerful too, such as Lady Mary in *The Young Philosopher*, Lady Aubrey in Robinson's *Walsingham* or Mrs Arlbery in *Camilla*. But widows, when they appear, are rarely rich and powerful in these texts; more often they have a modest competence, like the good mother in West's *Advantages of Education*. No doubt in reality they were often lonely and vulnerable; historians of property law have shown how men and their lawyers pared away their portions. Their plight is dramatized in those stories such as Mary Ann Radcliffe's of destitute widows, forced into prostitution. The good-hearted Ellesmere in Smith's *The Banished Man* inherits the family estate but will not live there: 'It has always appeared to me particularly cruel, that at a late period of life, the mother of a family should be driven from her home by one of the children she has raised, and be compelled to seek other connections in some remote and inferior residence.'[198] The author who has most to say about widowhood is Hannah More. In her tracts we encounter useful widows, above all Mrs Jones, who though she has little money is blessed with independence and time, which she can devote to community service.

What about relationships alternative to conventional family and heterosexual ones? What about non-family relationships between women? Do we find celebrations of female solidarity? Is there even, as some scholars have suggested, a repressed lesbian subtext seeking indirect expression?[199] In her *Letters from France*, Williams is thankful for the true spirit of fraternity (should that be sorority?) which prevailed among the forty female prisoners plus nuns who were confined together in the Luxembourg prison. Mutual forbearance and amity like that could transform a world.[200] But in her novel, though Julia and Charlotte are mutually devoted, and though Julia comes to the rescue of Mrs Meynell, other women are malign, and the tragic dénouement is brought about by the malevolent jealousy and gossiping of Miss Tomkins. There is an ideal and indeed romantic friendship between Sibella and Caroline Ashburn in Fenwick's *Secresy*, and Caroline insists that 'Men, my dear Sibella, have not that enthusiasm and vigour in their friendships that we possess'.[201] Robinson describes noble female solidarity in her *False Friend*; Martha thinks that Lord Francis Sherville has had an affair with Mrs Sedgley and that he is the father of her natural daughter. Though Martha is herself in love with Sherville, she pleads with him to forgive and, implicitly, to marry her friend. In *Angelina*, several women act together to defeat the patriarchal plans of Sir Edward Clarendon – Sophia, Mrs Horton, Mrs

198 Smith, *Banished Man*, iv, p. 230.
199 The argument of Johnson, *Equivocal Beings*.
200 Williams, *Letters from France*, v, p. 185.
201 Fenwick, *Secresy*, p. 114.

Delmore, Mrs Chudleigh, Miss Juliana Pengwynn. But examples such as these, accidents of the plot as it were, cannot be interpreted as proof that Robinson was a herald of female solidarity, and indeed, as noted in the previous chapter, she explicitly declared that she was not. [202] In all of her novels, heroines are just as much persecuted by other women as by men.

In fact it would be very difficult to make a case for a celebration of female solidarity in these texts. Wollstonecraft's *Vindication of the Rights of Woman* is packed with unsisterly remarks. Radcliffe takes her heroines to convents, and in *Udolpho* the convent near the Chateau Le Blanc, with its admirable, maternal abbess, is a haven where the heroine thinks of seeking sanctuary. This is balanced, however, by the convent in *The Italian*, ruled by a wicked abbess, in which Ellena is imprisoned. Radcliffe discusses the conventual life and her verdict is against it, not only because of its lack of freedom but also because of the selfishness of women who seclude themselves from the normal duties of a woman. West is fairly hostile to intense female solidarity; the heroine Marianne's marriage in *Gossip's Story* is destroyed above all by her imprudent and romantic friendship with Eliza.

Nor is there any clear evidence of repressed lesbianism in any of these texts; such evidence could only be found, or created, by imaginative readings beneath their surface or against their grain. The relationship between Maria and Jemima in Wollstonecraft's last novel has been read in this way. Jemima helps Maria to escape from the madhouse, and one of the author's sketches for the book's completion has Jemima restoring her child to her and living with her; but Jemima also assisted her into the arms of Darnford, and she lives with Maria as her housekeeper. The friendship of Caroline and Sibella in *Secresy* finds expression in romantic language – '*I love you: – I love you, Sibella, with all my soul*'[203] – but to love with the soul is not to love with the body, and it is anachronistic to read the eighteenth-century language of sensibility as a twenty-first-century language of sex. Caroline does everything in her power to unite Sibella with a man. Anna Seward, that 'proper' lady who lived in Lichfield cathedral close, is hardly even hinting at lesbianism in her poem addressed to the ladies of Llangollen; is she taking precautions against such an interpretation when she writes of 'FRIENDSHIP, permanent as pure' and of 'pure Friendship's spotless palm'?[204] The only reference to lesbianism in all of these texts of which I am fairly confident is a disapproving one; Wollstonecraft adds to her catalogue of charges against Marie Antoinette that her 'strange predilection for handsome women blighted the reputation of every one, whom she distinguished'.[205]

---

[202] Robinson, *Memoirs*, p. 82.
[203] Fenwick, *Secresy*, p. 46.
[204] Anna Seward, *Llangollen Vale, with Other Poems* (London, G. Sael, 1796).
[205] Wollstonecraft, *Historical and Moral View*, p. 253.

Conclusion

Has this chapter revealed women writers as helpless prisoners of patriarchal discourses? All women writers to a certain extent and some more than others worked within the prevailing norms, whether unquestioningly or because they had a clear perception of what was possible and realistic. There was little challenge to heterosexual marriage and motherhood as a woman's destiny. All women writers subscribed to the idea that women are, or should be, sexually modest, though some thought that the extent of that modesty should be open to negotiation and that sexual reticence need not mean an absence of sexual desire. Reverence for parents, especially for fathers, is usually endorsed, with the caveat that their authority should be exercised reasonably and with due respect for the daughter.

But is this to be *imprisoned* in patriarchal discourse? If one thinks that any acceptance of conventions of romantic love, or of some form of the institution of marriage, or of heterosexuality as a norm, is to be so imprisoned, then the answer will be yes. Even Wollstonecraft accepts these conventions, most of the time. If one thinks that late eighteenth-century English society was patriarchal through and through, then the answer will again be yes, for women writers do not describe women as always subordinated to the interests of men in the family. But if one does not start with those assumptions, then the answer will be that they were not complete discursive prisoners. Some writers directly and defiantly challenge the authority of tyrannical fathers and husbands. They criticize the more unjust and oppressive aspects of the canons of sexual propriety. Others – the majority, even including 'proper', conservative females – find ways of adapting and developing discursive conventions in order to enhance the status or advance the interests of women. They endorse marriage, but insist that it should be companionate and even egalitarian. They idealize romantic love, and mobilize that ideal in order to demand freedom of marital choice for women. They accept norms of female sexual modesty, but build out from them to demand that men treat women with delicacy and respect. They embrace the discourse of civility, and on it they build a model of a new, more woman-friendly, more desirable male. They construct an ideal of moral motherhood and thereby enhance the status of women. It is arguable that in the context of the time, given the possibilities and limitations they inherited, these were real achievements.

5

Separate spheres?

If we are to find women writing within a discourse whose meaning is their disempowerment and confinement, then we will naturally turn to the vocabulary of space. We will look for a doctrine of separate gendered spheres, occupied by 'public' man and 'private' woman. These concepts, however, must be approached with great caution. 'Public' and 'private' are relational concepts, like 'big' and 'small'. Whether something is big or small depends on what it is being compared with, and nothing is absolutely big or small. Much the same is true of 'public' and 'private'. Perhaps only the innermost and uncommunicated thoughts and feelings of the individual are absolutely private,[1] and perhaps only political institutions like parliament are absolutely public. Therefore the meaning of these concepts can never be taken for granted; it must always be elucidated in specific contexts. Other words may stand in for these concepts; in 1790s texts we will have to be on the lookout for 'world', 'social', 'domestic', 'retirement', 'rural' and even 'reason' and 'religion'. Having identified how these words are used in the 1790s, we can then ask the questions raised by present-day feminism and political philosophy: how are the public and the private evaluated? and do they demarcate gendered separate spheres? Would these concepts, if translated into reality, imply the disempowerment of women? In the section that follows, on the use of language, I have taken care when describing an author's opinion only to use the words she herself employs to refer to spheres or spaces.

Language

What might be called the 'classic' doctrine of separate spheres, of public man and private woman, can certainly on occasion be found, most often in the

---

[1] From one point of view not even these are private, if they are shaped and constructed by public discourse.

writings of 'proper' females, but occasionally slipping from the pens of 'unsex'd' ones also – as in Wollstonecraft: 'Boys may be reckoned the pillars of the house without doors, girls are often the only comfort within.'[2] The orthodoxy of propriety is firmly stated by Wakefield: it is inadmissible for women to mix in the public haunts of men, for them to risk their delicacy, reserve and moral purity. Modesty is the reason for the confinement of women to the domestic; it is not that they lack abilities. Domestic privacy is the only safe place for young women, and even the grave matron cannot step far beyond that boundary with propriety.[3] Frequent attendance at places of public diversion is wholly incompatible with that purity of character which is the essence of female perfection; reason and decorum debar women from the public service of their country.[4] Their responsibilities are domestic, supervising consumption, the domestic staff and the education of their children.[5]

Edgeworth insists that the field of women is private, performing the duties of domestic retirement, whereas men are occupied with the necessity of pursuing a profession, the ambition to shine in parliament, or to rise in public life.[6] In a chapter on dissipation and the habits of modern life, a chapter whose theme is the superiority of home delights to public amusements, More asserts that domestic life is to woman the appropriate sphere.[7] In her tracts we encounter good women who are never seen outside the home, except in church (though church was certainly thought of as a public space). West has a good father declare to his daughter that his sex is formed to fill an ampler space in the world than hers, which is formed to fulfil the retired duties of life.[8] Edgar Mandelbert in *Camilla* worries lest public distinction will spoil Camilla for private life, depriving her of the taste for conjugal and maternal duties which is the essence of the true female character.[9]

Just as there are statements of the 'classic' doctrine, so there are explicit challenges to it which are at the same time and *ipso facto* recognitions of its power. The author who above all confronts the gendering of space is Hays. Her heroine Emma Courtney writes of the magic circle, of insulation, of being hemmed in on every side, of being pent up and of lacking a sufficiently wide field – and incidentally deplores the barbarous and odious custom of women withdrawing after dinner, leaving the men to talk and drink.[10] In the *Appeal to the Men of Great Britain* Hays writes of women's exclusion, of their enclosure (again) in a kind of magic circle, of the little sphere in which

2 Wollstonecraft, *Wrongs of Woman*, p. 135.
3 Wakefield, *Reflections*, p. 9.
4 *Ibid.*, pp. 94–5.
5 *Ibid.*, pp. 81–2.
6 Edgeworth, *Letters for Literary Ladies*, pp. 27, 31.
7 More, *Strictures*, ii, p. 149.
8 West, *Gossip's Story*, ii, p. 25.
9 Burney, *Camilla*, p. 444.
10 Hays, *Emma Courtney*, pp. 86, 116.

a wife is permitted to move, of the public influence of men and the private influence of women.[11] The language of separate spheres is present here, and is contested, as it is by Wollstonecraft when she deplores the situation of women 'immured in their families groping in the dark'.[12]

These 'classic' deployments of a language of separate gendered spaces are not however the most frequent or the most important uses of public and private and of related words. The single most salient binary is between, on the one hand, the public or the 'world', and on the other, the private, or 'retired' or 'domestic', or 'social'. This binary is not a gendered one. Taking examples from *Camilla*, public in this sense might refer to a public breakfast, that is to say a breakfast gathering in a public building open to all genteel people who choose to come; or a public water-party or picnic, events to which many guests have been invited; or public theatricals or balls, open to all who buy a ticket as opposed to private theatricals or balls where attendance is by invitation only. 'Public' is used a great deal in *Camilla*, but never to refer to the economic or the political, spheres which never appear centre stage. Or to take examples from Smith's *Celestina*, the public in this sense includes assemblies, balls, the opera, and London pleasure gardens open to all such as Ranelagh. West refers to 'places of publick resort' in London, the equivalent of church in the country as meeting-places for the young and unmarried.[13] In all of these uses, 'public' refers to spaces of heterosociality. Now 'proper' females may think that it is especially bad for women to become 'worldly', to devote too much of their time to such places, but their complaints are swimming against the tide. For it is not just the case that women are permitted in these public spaces; the whole point is that men and women shall meet and mingle there – that is what most of them are designed for.

In all texts by 'unsex'd' and 'proper' females without exception there is a clichéd piety which is critical of the 'world', of the dissipation of public places. The opposite of the world is the better place. This opposite is the domestic or the retired; it is regularly the rural as opposed to the urban. This theme is very much in evidence in Wollstonecraft's *Vindication of the Rights of Woman*. It is the form in which the language of public and private appears in Hays's earlier work, her *Letters and Essays*. In her later *Appeal to the Men of Great Britain* she contends that 'Every virtue, every acquirement, every branch of knowledge which is either useful or ornamental ... may ... be cultivated ... in the private, the domestic, in the rural scenes of life.'[14] Now an incidental or implicit effect of this evaluation *might* be to encourage women to occupy a separate sphere in the home, but this is not the explicit message. The critique of the world and the praise of retirement are directed

11 Hays, *Appeal*, pp. 40, 53, 89, 111.
12 Wollstonecraft, *Vindication of the Rights of Woman*, p. 69.
13 West, *Gossip's Story*, i, p. 22.
14 *Appeal to the Men of Great Britain*, p. 250.

at men too; this is not apparently an enforcement of gendered spheres.

This then is the principal use of the language of public and private, but the terms are complex, entering into a number of different binary oppositions and having varying implications for gender. Macaulay Graham uses these terms a great deal, referring for example to public charity, in which both fine gentlemen and ladies engage,[15] and contrasting the public, worldly voice, by which she means conventional prejudices, with reason. She refers to public acts of devotion, implicitly by contrast with private prayer.[16] Very often by 'public' she means the state, and accordingly 'private' means everything else, implicitly economy and society as well as the domestic. She contrasts being at court with a private station.[17] In a discussion of public and private education, public is education after the manner of Plato, provided and controlled by the state in order to manufacture good citizens.[18] She distinguishes state morality and private obligations,[19] contrasts private enjoyments and private life with public service,[20] general with private good,[21] public counsels with private manners.[22] Her language here is clearly influenced by classical republicanism, with its contrast between private interest and public virtue. This language has often been gendered; public virtue is exhibited in political and military service requiring manly courage, and the word virtue itself has as its root the Latin *vir*, man. But it is not obvious that Macaulay Graham's use of the language is gendered in precisely this way, for she can contrast domestic *virtue* with national happiness,[23] political with moral virtues.[24]

A brief survey of other uses in other authors is in order. In Inchbald's view, referring here to a man, William, private charity is better than public, that is to say the unostentatious and the face-to-face is better than the showy – as in the words of the Gospel, 'Let not your left hand know what your right hand doeth'. Wollstonecraft discusses public or national and private or domestic education. In a chapter devoted to this question, private education means education in the home, public in a school; but in an earlier chapter, private education is contrasted with the education imparted by the opinions and manners prevalent in the society.[25] Neither of these uses is gendered: the discussion of public and private schooling begins with boys, and a major theme of the *Vindication* is the way in which public education, in the sense of public culture, forms women for the worse.

15 Macaulay Graham, *Letters on Education*, p. 289.
16 *Ibid.*, p. 95.
17 *Ibid.*, p. 230.
18 *Ibid.*, pp. 15–22.
19 *Ibid.*, p. 225.
20 *Ibid.*, p. 232.
21 *Ibid.*, p. 246.
22 *Ibid.*, p. 260.
23 *Ibid.*, p. 247.
24 *Ibid.*, p. 266.
25 Wollstonecraft, *Vindication of the Rights of Woman*, p. 89.

Robinson refers, conventionally enough, to her public situation as an actress; she also refers to the public protection of the Prince of Wales.[26] In other words, official recognition as his mistress would enable her to appear in the world without shame or danger. For an unprotected woman was in danger in certain public places.[27] This was a truism of the age; but it is not being said that a sensible, respectable young woman must at all times be in the home, or in the company of a male or older female escort. Apparently she was not necessarily so confined. In Radcliffe's *Udolpho*, Emily often goes for walks in the twilight by herself, and in *The Romance of the Forest*, Adeline walks alone in the forest and on the beach.[28] Smith's *Celestina* too walks alone and unharmed in the country; but when she is separated from her friends at Ranelagh, she is taken for a prostitute and suffers harassment. Public foyers in theatres and opera houses were similarly dangerous for unescorted women, precisely because prostitutes sought custom there. So for example in Robinson's *False Friend*, when Gertrude was separated from her party in the theatre lobby she was 'exposed to a variety of insults from the profligate of both sexes'.[29] Different spaces were governed by different codes. In this sense, the wide open spaces of the countryside, though not private or domestic, were not public spaces. Fletcher tells us that Smith and her daughters were not particularly concerned about travelling unescorted.[30]

For More a principal binary is religion and world, a binary which is not equivalent to, but which nevertheless is related to the binary of private and world which was in such common use. More's evangelical, 'heart' religion implies intense private devotion as well as public worship, and for an evangelical Christian the world means the arenas of politics, economic life and public sociability. Public dissipation in the world leaves too little time for the private self-examination that religion requires. The most important domain, for a man and for a woman, is the sphere of religion; but both men and women, as good Christian soldiers, must be prepared to go out into the world, there to fight the good fight. They should be *in* the world, but not *of* it.

The opposite of the world, of places of public resort and dissipation, may also include the 'social'; 'domestic' and 'social' are regularly paired. Social in this sense may mean the face-to-face society of friends and of the locality, and it too is preferred; as More puts it, sociability is better than gregariousness.[31] If women are being urged to forsake the public, therefore, the sphere

26 Robinson, *Memoirs*, pp. 35, 115.
27 *Ibid.*, p. 35.
28 There is no reason to suppose that Radcliffe means something like the passage in Austen's *Sense and Sensibility*, where Elinor and Marianne see in the distance 'a man on horseback riding towards them'; half a page later, 'He dismounted, and giving his horse to his servant . . .'.
29 Robinson, *False Friend*, ii, p. 254.
30 Fletcher, *Charlotte Smith*, p. 78; Vickery, *Gentleman's Daughter*, pp. 269–70.
31 More, *Strictures*, ii, p. 137.

they are being encouraged to move in has at least two departments, and the social may be an extensive sphere. In West's *Advantages of Education*, social life embraces service to the poor and the sick in the local community, and is a business for women.[32] The social in this sense is perhaps thought of as continuous with the private and the domestic, given that the establishments of the gentry played an important role in the rural community. But in the *Appeal to the Men of Great Britain* we are told that 'true happiness, like true virtue ... [is attained] by that mixture of home joys and social intercourse with the world; which, as most congenial to human nature, is not only most conducive to present enjoyment; but to future and progressive improvement'.[33] In this passage not only is the 'social' recommended to women: it is distinguished from the domestic and assimilated to the world, to the public. 'Social' is an unstable word at this time; it can indicate spaces outside the home, but also a quality of relationships to be found within the home, friendly, intimate and non-hierarchical.[34]

Income-earning work

Was the space of economic activity seen as divided by the gender binary? Any investigation of the gendering of work in 1790s texts must be sensitive also to the dimension of class. Intimations that it might be better for a woman not to engage in a certain economic activity may have everything to do with the latter rather than with the former. For example, in Smith's *Marchmont*, the Marchmont ladies and Althea, desperately short of money, open a shop, but give it up as soon as a windfall comes their way. It is not that it is improper for *women* to run a shop. Mrs Marchmont is concerned that it will humble her daughters' prospects in life: 'Who would marry girls from a shop?'[35] In *The Old Manor House*, Monimia quietly takes in sewing work, against the wishes of her husband Orlando, who thinks that all the world ought to be at her feet. The issue is whether his genteel family will be disgraced.[36] Orlando himself has refused a career in trade, and in the end Smith rewards him with a country estate. As remarked in an earlier chapter, Smith went to great lengths to explain why she, a gentlewoman, felt justified in working as a professional author.

Wollstonecraft remarks that the professions of milliner and mantua-maker are degrading to a gentlewoman, and governessing can be humiliating.[37] So

---

[32] West, *Advantages of Education*, i, p. 69.
[33] *Appeal to the Men of Great Britain*, pp. 171–2.
[34] Williams, *Letters from France*, i, p. 123; Burney, *Camilla*, p. 811.
[35] Smith, *Marchmont*, iii, p. 264.
[36] Smith, *Old Manor House*, pp. 493–4.
[37] Wollstonecraft, *Wrongs of Woman*, p. 148; *Vindication of the Rights of Woman*, p. 239.

when reading these texts, the question needs to be borne in mind whether it is being said that opportunities for income-earning work are limited for *women*, or for *genteel women*, who wish to earn money in a way which does not compromise their gentility. In fact much of the complaining is about the latter; few of these authors write about the poor, other than as servants or as objects of charity. Hays however notes that many poor hard-labouring women support large families, because their husbands are profligate.[38] Robinson insists that lower-class women do heavy manual work;[39] her point is to question the alleged superior strength of the male sex. More's tracts, because they are addressed to a lower- and a lower-middle-class audience, bring humble working women on stage; for example we hear the story of Betty Brown the St Giles orange girl, who improves herself by going to church and ends up keeping a handsome sausage shop near the Seven Dials.

It should not be assumed that income-earning work was a major topic for women writers of the 1790s; Wollstonecraft devotes only a few paragraphs to it in her *Vindication of the Rights of Woman*, and there is little more than a passing reference in Hays's *Letters and Essays*. Two 'proper' females, Wakefield and Mary Ann Radcliffe, and the anonymous author, probably Hays, of the *Appeal to the Men of Great Britain*, provide the fullest discussions. But Wollstonecraft, Hays, Robinson, Smith, Wakefield and Mary Ann Radcliffe devote a little space to complaining about the difficulty of earning a living for genteel women who lack a father, a private income, a husband or a husband competent to provide. Most of them knew about this by personal experience. Most ink was spilt on the narrative, recounted in an earlier chapter, of the desperate woman of good birth and breeding driven by lack of work opportunities into prostitution.

As was explained in Chapter 2, historians have recently debated the 'golden age to separate spheres' hypothesis. Was the latter part of the eighteenth century a period in which women were increasingly excluded from income-earning work, as that work moved out of the home into workshops and factories? An older generation of historians thought that this was the case; the younger generation has doubts. If earlier historians were mistaken about this, then the mistake was also made in the1790s. Mary Ann Radcliffe remarks that 'In those days, when manufactures and commerce were not so extensive ... while the father and the brother were employed in trade, the mother and daughters were employed in the domestic concerns of the household. In fact, they were then the manufacturers also.'[40] Williams remarks that French women were equally employed in agriculture and manufacturing with the men. She commends the practice under the old regime in France of educating French girls intended as merchants' wives in arithmetic, so that

38 Hays, 'Letter on female education', p. 195.
39 Robinson, *Thoughts*, p. 18.
40 Radcliffe, *Female Advocate*, p. 431.

they can act as their husbands' first clerk. If the husband dies they can carry on the business, whereas the wives of English merchants are frequently ruined.[41] Are 1790s women inventing their own myth of a lost golden age? Wakefield repeats the clichés about women withdrawing from productive labour, and about men moving in on what ought to be female trades. But she also remarks that new work opportunities are opening for women, on account of their better education and the commercial expansion of the nation.[42]

So why, according to this 1790s story, are English women excluded from income-generating work? Two explanations are offered: first, that men have taken over, pushing women out of trades such as mantua-making, millinery and midwifery which were formerly theirs; second, that tradesmen aspiring to gentility have withdrawn their wives and daughters from the shop, the workshop and the counting-house, and have had their daughters educated in ornamental rather than in useful skills. These are not good as explanations; if these changes were ocurring, why at this time?

However that may be, and whether this exclusion from productive activity is new or not, it is widely deplored. For most women, it is contended, practical usefulness is better and a more secure route to a respectable life than airs and graces and the hope of marrying upwards. 'Unsex'd' females like Robinson long for the independence of men which earning a living would bring.[43] Wollstonecraft thinks that economic independence would give women the option of not marrying; as Hays puts it, an economically independent woman would 'be freed from the disgraceful necessity of bartering her person to procure a maintenance' – whether she is referring to commercial prostitution or marital prostitution is not entirely clear.[44] 'Proper' females like More or Wakefield think that all women below the higher ranks ought to be able to assist their husbands in trade or on the farm, and that the economic well-being of the family may require it.

What more or less approved income-generating work do we hear of women actually undertaking in texts by 'unsex'd' and 'proper' females? They sew and embroider, they make clothing, they draw (for example botanical drawing) and paint and colour engravings. They act as governesses and ladies' companions. Lower-class women may be servants or laundrywomen. Robinson reminds us that they follow the plough, brew, bake, carry heavy loads and work in manufactories.[45] They keep shop. They help their husbands in their businesses, especially in the counting-house; as widows they may run the business. They may perform healthcare services, and not only as midwives. There is a residual awareness that women may have

41 Williams, *Letters from France*, iv, p. 123; ii, pp. 63–4.
42 Wakefield, *Reflections*, pp. 171–4.
43 Robinson, *Vancenza*, ii, pp. 75-6; *False Friend*, ii, p. 237.
44 Hays, 'Letter on female education', p. 195.
45 Robinson, *Thoughts*, p. 19.

medical expertise, though it is evidently becoming rare, a matter for remark and even mockery. Emma Courtney helps her husband in his medical profession, and cares not only as a nurse but also as a surgeon for Harley when he is thrown from his horse. La Luc's maiden sister in Radcliffe's *Romance of the Forest* prepares and administers medicines to guests and villagers. In Smith's *Celestina*, a disapproved character, Mrs Calder, is an expert in medicine and has written a book on the goitres of the Alpine peasant. Wakefield lists apothecary work as an occupation suited to women. Of course women write for a living – novels, poetry, plays.

This is a substantial catalogue of economic activities; is there any call for other occupations to be opened up to women or monopolized by women? To start at the 'proper' end, Wakefield is most concerned with the defensive activity of warding off men's encroachment upon women's trades. She is quite clear that many occupations are unsuited to women. This has nothing to do with any innate lack of mental ability. Lack of physical strength rules out some occupations; but above all, female modesty dictates a gendered separation of spheres in the world of work. Having said this, she *does* list a wide range of occupations differentially suitable for women of different classes, among them teaching and running schools (she calls for a teacher-training college for women), sculpture, confectionary, turning and toy-making. She tells approvingly of the Spencer sisters who ran a farm, filling dung carts one day and entertaining the highest society the next.[46] Delicacy dictates that some jobs should be done by women rather than by men: staymaking, dealing with women's commodities in shops, teaching girls music and dancing, laying out female corpses. Jobs that bring women into public, such as acting, are not suitable. Lower-class women should not work in the fields or in manufactories alongside men; domestic manufacturing is preferable. She does contend, however, that women's wages should be the same as men's for the same work.

Turning to 'unsex'd' females, we do not find very much more. Wollstonecraft rather unspecifically thinks that women might pursue 'business of various kinds'. A woman might practise as a physician as well as be a nurse. Decency dictates that midwifery should be the province of women.[47] In spite of her fiery insistence upon the equality of women, even in courage and physical strength, Robinson says little about new employment opportunities. Her main concern is to assert the genius of women, their mental and aesthetic abilities. This leads her to call for a university for women, eventually to be staffed by an entirely female faculty.[48] As a former actress, she insists that acting is an honourable and respectable occupation for a woman.

The fullest discussion of female employment probably by an 'unsex'd'

[46] Wakefield, *Reflections*, pp. 171–3.
[47] Wollstonecraft, *Vindication of the Rights of Woman*, pp. 238–9.
[48] Robinson, *Thoughts*, p. 93.

female is in the *Appeal to the Men of Great Britain*. As already remarked, this is a difficult work to interpret. If it is by Hays writing in the aftermath of the scandal of Godwin's biography of Wollstonecraft, then this confirms the impression of a calculated rhetorical strategy, with irony and indirection and some care to insinuate radical opinions without shocking too many susceptibilities. Minds are unsexed, the author asserts; education could therefore equip women to do anything men do. It follows that in principle women have the capacity for politics, not only the science of politics but also the art of governing. The talents and perseverance of many a woman if possessed by a man would suffice to place him on the woolsack, or put a mitre on his head. But the author does not actually say that women should enter these professions. What she says is that if women's talents were fully developed, they might become 'what is tantamount, to a Chancellor, a Bishop, a Judge, or a General – An useful, an amiable, and an interesting woman'.[49]

In a later discussion, she admits that nature has denied to women the bodily strength, the abilities and the inclination for being, for example, masons, carpenters, blacksmiths and farriers. Common sense and propriety exclude women from the professions of law and divinity, from taking part in public assemblies as these professions would require. Here it is far from easy to be sure of the author's real opinion. Why common sense and propriety exclude women is not further elaborated; on the contrary we are assured that 'The natural flow of eloquence, and command of language, – the glow and warmth of imagination, – the nice discrimination with which they are so generally gifted ... [and] their greater purity of morals' would make most women exemplary divines, and still better lawyers.[50] Women certainly have the abilities and the inclinations in a very peculiar degree for the professions of physic and surgery, 'Yet we must confess, that modern delicacy and propriety of manners, are, in this respect so decidedly against them, that no arguments that can be used, are sufficient to counterbalance them'.[51] If there were any doubt before, it is now clear that irony is intended here. That she writes tongue in cheek is evidenced by her argument that though delicacy and propriety prescribe that women should be physicians to their own sex,

> prejudice is so inveterate, that things will never be as they should be. I judge by myself, for I would do any thing but die, rather than have a *woman* physician. I never knew but one, and the very sight of her acted upon me like an emetic; and she had nearly the same effect, upon most of her female acquaintance. I fancy her patients were mostly men, as she was tolerably handsome; though I really don't know.[52]

By twenty-first-century standards, this all seems rather unambitious.

49 *Appeal to the Men of Great Britain*, pp. 38, 79–80.
50 *Ibid.*, pp. 194–5.
51 *Ibid.*, pp. 198–9.
52 *Ibid.*, p. 199.

Should we conclude that women writers, the 'unsex'd' as well as the 'proper', either out of timidity or because they are indoctrinated with an ideology of female modesty, have endorsed or failed to challenge separate spheres where work is concerned? It might look as if the remunerated employment being recommended for women is all in some way related to the domestic – work on the farm or estate, or in the family business probably based in the home, manufacturing and creative activities which would be carried on in the home, keeping the shop which would usually be located under the living quarters, educational and medical services so closely related to the caring and nurturing responsibilities of daughters, wives and mothers. But much productive work still *was* domestic in these senses. Perhaps we should see this as a wide field, rather than a narrow one. Some professions obviously involved public performance, notably the church, the law and acting. Perhaps the first two were special cases, on which no general conclusion should be built: there were theological arguments to debar women from the ministry, and most women authors have a very low opinion of the legal profession. Some 'unsex'd' females such as Robinson and Williams wrote in defence of actresses, and some women writers, for example Robinson and Inchbald, had been public workers on the stage.

Finally, as Vickery has reminded us, we should not allow present-day preoccupations with waged work and access for women to 'public' employments to blind us to the importance and status of the genteel household manager in an age of large households and many servants, some of whom were still engaged in productive activities.[53] Both 'unsex'd' and 'proper' females emphasize this. In Robinson's *Walsingham*, Frances the bad daughter devotes her time to fashionable female accomplishments, while it was the task of Penelope the good daughter 'to superintend the household, ... to preside over the dairy, ... to regulate the book of family accounts' and to distribute the family's alms to the poor.[54] Hays is careful to distinguish between household drudgery, which should be performed by servants, and the elevated business of management:

> She enters into all the domestic duties of her station with the most consummate skill and prudence; her economical deportment is calm and steady; and she presides over her family like the intelligence of some planetary orb, conducting it in all its proper directions without violence, or disturbed effort.[55]

She is critical of husbands who interfere in this domain of female authority.[56] Wakefield too discusses this role for the gentlewoman, employing a vocabulary of inspection, management and government: 'Every domestic

[53] Vickery, *Gentleman's Daughter*, p. 127ff.
[54] Robinson, *Walsingham*, i, p. 25.
[55] Hays, *Letters and Essays*, p. 28 (quoting Fitzosborne), see also *Appeal to the Men of Great Britain*, pp. 239–47.
[56] *Ibid.*, p. 132.

department should be regulated by her orders, and be conducted under her inspection: The eye of a judicious manager pervades every object, and at a glance regulates the whole.'[57] Women should be responsible for judicious, well-planned, economical consumption, neither extravagant nor too mean for the status of the family.[58] In her tracts More constantly praises *notable* women. Notable is an adjective we have lost in the sense in which More uses it; it signifies a woman who is a distinguished household manager. Good farmers' wives and daughters should keep the books and *manage* the dairy (i.e., not do the heavy work).[59] In her *Strictures* she writes that

> Oeconomy, such as a woman of fortune is called on to practise, is not merely the petty detail of small daily expences, the shabby curtailments and stinted parsimony of a little mind operating on little concerns; but it is an exercise of sound judgement exerted in the comprehensive outline of order, of arrangement, of distribution; of regulations by which alone well governed societies, great and small, subsist.[60]

These writers do not think that domestic management in a genteel household is a diminished or ignoble sphere. Hamilton, in a eulogy of Lady Grey, whose husband was chronically ill, evinces no difficulty in writing of her managing both 'the affairs of her family, and the concerns of his estate'.[61]

Roles in religion and the community

As we have seen, a classic separation of spheres is firmly asserted by Wakefield. But then she goes on to bestow a considerable range of activities, or rather duties, on women outside the home. The sphere of domestic retirement turns out not to be woman's sole province after all. She has divided society into four classes: the nobility and landed gentry; professionals and merchants in easy circumstances; tradesmen and artisans lifted above want; and the labouring poor. Women of the first class should not frequently attend places of public diversion, for that would be incompatible with the purity of character which is the essence of female perfection.[62] Nevertheless, theirs is a *public* station – that is the term Wakefield uses – and they should be concerned for the public welfare; the most admirable of them will devote their time, their talents and their fortunes to the improvement of public morals and the increase of public happiness.[63] They should devote their money and their time to the supervision and assistance of the female poor in

57 Wakefield, *Reflections*, p. 105.
58 *Ibid.*, pp. 32, 34, 81–2, 100–2.
59 More, *Two Wealthy Farmers*, pp. 5, 13.
60 More, *Strictures*, ii, p. 5.
61 Hamilton, *Hindoo Rajah*, p. 279.
62 Wakefield, *Reflections*, p. 94.
63 *Ibid.*, pp. 81, 97, 99.

their neighbourhood. They should patronize and manage useful institutions for the improvement of the morals of the poor, and the increase of their happiness. They should regularly inspect workhouses, schools of industry and cottages, and pay special attention to the rearing of the children of the poor and the preservation of the morals of female parish apprentices. This might be done on a formal basis, with female visitors officially appointed and making weekly or monthly reports. Each girl apprenticed by a parish might be placed under the inspection of one or two of the most respectable female inhabitants.[64]

Women of the second class have less money, but they can devote time and personal exertion to the poor. They can give religious and moral instruction, sympathy and consolation, and advice on how to manage money, cut out clothes, prepare better meals, keep cottages clean and apply simple medicines to the sick.[65] Like those founders of Sunday schools Mrs Trimmer and Hannah More, they can contribute very considerably to the civilization of the poor. They should concern themselves with religious instruction as well as with physical welfare. These activities in the community are to be combined, as already noted, with the regulation of the household; and when attention is paid to what Wakefield says about that, it appears that the gendered public/private divide has been blurred in two ways. First, the qualities of character a woman needs to be effective in the domestic sphere are ones which might be associated with the public – reason, judgement, self-control, courage, application and attention to principles. Second, the public sphere is to be reformed by women taking out into it their special qualities, fostered in domesticity: caring, nurturing and purity of morals. Women have a special role in the reformation of morals, without which the nation cannot be preserved from decay.[66] The reformation of manners/morals was promoted as an agenda for women by Wollstonecraft, Hays and Mary Ann Radcliffe too.

Similar roles were recommended to a much wider readership in the highly successful publications of Hannah More; as Myers puts it, she was in effect replacing a decaying social paternalism with maternalism, a proto-Victorian ethic of responsibility and nurturance.[67] The first chapter of her *Strictures* is addressed 'to women of rank and fortune, on the effects of their influence on society'. She calls upon them to contribute to saving their country by raising the depressed tone of public morals and awakening the drowsy spirit of reli-

[64] *Ibid.*, pp. 82–7.
[65] *Ibid.*, pp. 110–11.
[66] *Ibid.*, pp. 69–70.
[67] Mitzi Myers, 'A peculiar protection: Hannah More and the cultural politics of the Blagdon controversy', in Beth Fowkes Tobin (ed.), *History, Gender & Eighteenth-Century Literature* (Athens, University of Georgia Press, 1994), p.232. Myers argues that the 'ideational corset' of evangelicalism empowered women and 'braced no less than it bound' (p. 245).

gious principle.[68] What women can do is most vividly portrayed in those tracts addressed to the middling ranks, which give the history of Mrs Jones: *A Cure for Melancholy*, *The Sunday School* and *The History of Hester Wilmot*.

Mrs Jones is a widow, living in a village on a narrow income. She is melancholy and inactive, and one day the vicar, who has just preached a sermon on the good samaritan, finds her in tears because she does not have enough money to help the poor. He advises her to cure her melancholy by going about and doing good. She resolves to spend two or three days a week in the parish, with a few good little books in her pocket to give away, looking for opportunities. The baker is giving short weight; she persuades the black-smith and the squire to take action against him. She gets the squire to enforce the law prohibiting Sunday trading against Mr Wills, and encourages villagers to shop with Mrs Sparks, who gives less credit but charges lower prices. She urges the rich men of the village not to buy the coarse cuts of meat for soup and gravy, so that there will be cheap meat for the poor. She prevails upon the squire to take away the licences of the Bell and the Chequers. The villagers turn to brewing their own beer, which the men drink at home, and the by-product yeast enables the women to bake their own bread, in a parish oven built by Sir John and the squire at her request. She secures a supply of milk, takes over the management of the girls' school in the parish and arranges work experience in the houses of the local gentry. She establishes a Sunday school, cajoling the local notables and farmers to fund it. Because she is concerned with the religious instruction of the poor, hers is a religious as well as a social-welfare role; she is the vicar's right-hand woman in the parish. And Hannah More, that 'bishop in petticoats', effectively has Mrs Jones preach a sermon when she delivers an exhortation to the assembled mothers of the village, encouraging them to send their children to Sunday school.

A final example may be taken from West's *Tale of the Times*. Geraldine Monteith goes with her husband to his Scottish castle, and resolves to estab-lish a model village for his idle and impoverished tenants, with neat white houses and gardens. 'I will frequently visit them; I will be their legislator, their instructor, their physician and their friend.'[69] She endows a school, enhances the pastor's stipend so as to increase his influence, and establishes a carpet manufactory and spinning room to provide work. She also performs her role as the social leader of the district.[70] She calls her village Jamestown after her husband, and is careful to attribute every improvement to his liber-ality; but she is the directing soul. Are we to interpret this activity on her estate as activity in the private sphere, an extension of the domestic? Her

[68] More, *Strictures*, i, p. 4.
[69] West, *Tale of the Times*, ii, p. 10.
[70] *Ibid.*, ii, p. 28.

husband meanwhile devotes himself entirely to leisure: 'I shall hunt one day, fish another, go to the bowling green a third.'[71] Surely this apportioning of activities does not make him a more public figure than she is?

I have given examples in this section from the writings of 'proper' females; I could equally well have cited Edgeworth and Burney. I chose these examples because they are the most vivid and fully worked, but also because it is fascinating to see how these writers with one voice propose a separation of spheres, and then with another undermine it. In this way women are depicted as empowered as well as, perhaps more than, confined. There is no divide between 'unsex'd' and 'proper' females on the role of women in the community; descriptions of women undertaking welfare work of this kind, though more lightly sketched, and encouragements of them to do so, are to be found in writings by Macaulay Graham, Hays, Smith and Williams.

Politics: representations of female activity

Women were not entirely excluded from politics in Britain at the end of the eighteenth century, as recent work, discussed in Chapter 2 has made abundantly clear. But active involvement is very rarely reflected by 'unsex'd' or 'proper' females, and given that a high proportion of their published output is in the form of prose fiction concerned above all with courtship, or conduct literature concerned with manners, morality and personal development, perhaps this is only to be expected. Some of the men in Williams's *Julia* are politicians, and a separation of spheres is manifest: the gentlemen air the politics of the day, while the ladies discuss the subject of the opera.[72] Williams is mockingly aware that the involvement of most men, even gentlemen, in the sphere of politics is nominal. Mr Clifford devotes all of his time to piety, benevolence and the society of his friends, enjoying a rubber of whist every evening; he has 'no subject of anxiety except the affairs of the state. He felt, indeed, the most watchful solicitude to preserve the balance of power in Europe, and was sometimes in low spirits on account of the national debt'.[73] Conversely, Williams gives glimpses of women engaging in politics: Julia negotiates patronage to help out Mrs Meynell's husband, and Mr Seymour secures additional emoluments for himself by paying court to the wife of a powerful man. In Smith's *Marchmont*, Sir Audley Dacres has the use of two parliamentary boroughs which his wife has inherited.[74]

Descriptions of female political involvement on any scale are only to be encountered in Williams's *Letters from France*, wherein it goes without

[71] *Ibid.*, ii, p. 14.
[72] Williams, *Julia*, i, p. 38.
[73] *Ibid.*, ii, p. 178.
[74] Smith, *Marchmont*, i, p. 229.

saying the activists are French women. 'The women have certainly had a considerable share in the French revolution.'[75] She tells of them engaging in bread riots, taking victuals to their sons and husbands who were beseiging the Bastille, donating their jewels ('le don patriotique') at the shrine of Liberty, attending the national assembly, attacking the convention on behalf of the jacobins in 1793, and holding deliberative assemblies and presenting their views to the convention. She celebrates Madame Roland's political engagement. She paints the heroism of Charlotte Corday, the murderer of Marat, in glowing colours; at her trial she asserted 'that it was a duty she owed her country and mankind to rid the world of a monster whose sanguinary doctrines were framed to involve the country in anarchy and civil war, and asserted her right to put Marat to death as a convict already condemned by public opinion'.[76] Williams makes no explicit claim for political rights for women, and as a Girondist and a moderate she does not approve of the activities of jacobin women and the 'furies of the guillotine'. The message of her book, however, is in principle to commend rather than to condemn political intervention by women.

Politics: claims for formal rights

As remarked in Chapter 2, the lack of formal political rights is not the same as exclusion from the political sphere; but to what extent do 'unsex'd' females demand such rights? Some of them clearly wanted this, but their writings devote surprisingly little space to explicit demands. Macaulay Graham remarks that women lack political and civil rights, and hints, without being at all specific, that in future they may secure them.[77] In more than one place in the *Vindication of the Rights of Woman*, Wollstonecraft complains that women are denied a political existence, but her demands are never more concrete and precise than when she writes that 'I may excite laughter, by dropping an hint, which I mean to pursue, some future time, for I really think that women ought to have representatives, instead of being arbitrarily governed without having any direct share allowed them in the deliberations of government'.[78] In *Maria* she devotes a few pages to women's lack of civil rights, the consequence of 'partial laws enacted by men'.[79]

The *Appeal to the Men of Great Britain* insists that 'The laws with regard to the sex, ought, undoubtedly, to be revised and corrected',[80] but does not

---

75 Williams, *Letters from France*, i, p. 37.
76 *Ibid.*, v, p. 131.
77 Macaulay Graham, *Letters on Education*, pp. 210, 215.
78 Wollstonecraft, *Vindication of the Rights of Woman*, p. 237.
79 Wollstonecraft, *Wrongs of Woman*, pp. 154–6.
80 *Appeal to the Men of Great Britain*, p. 277.

explain how. The author briefly intimates 'that a greater degree, a greater proportion of happiness might be the lot of women, if they were allowed as men are, some vote, some right of judgement in a matter which concerns them so nearly, as that of the laws and opinions by which they are to be governed'.[81] The same work appears to be suggesting that women should not serve as MPs; but this may simply be a tactical retreat on Hays's part. Robinson is vehement against unjust man-made laws, especially those which give husbands control of the marital property, and remarks in a footnote that women have been admitted into the public councils of American tribes and ancient Britons, but demands no more than that women be admitted to 'the auditory part of the British senate' – to the gallery, from which they were excluded.[82]

Though the abstract rights of women are *mentioned* often enough by British female writers, an agenda of *specific demands* is nowhere proposed; there are no lists of the political and civil rights of women to compare with that drafted by Olympe de Gouges.[83] It goes without saying, therefore, that no British woman pens an analysis of the concept of rights and its application to women, not even Wollstonecraft in her celebrated work with the word in its title. Indeed the sole right which receives an extended discussion in that book is the right to a good education. The radical potential of the language of rights was not fully exploited by 'unsex'd' females. Perhaps this was simply realism: unlike France Britain was not having a revolution. At a time when no success had been achieved in extending the male franchise, the prospect of political and more equal civil rights for women may have seemed too remote to merit extended discussion. Or perhaps formal rights loomed less large in general consciousness than they have done since the reform agitation of the 1830s and Chartism. Perhaps they were just as concerned with asserting their rights to take an *interest* in politics, and to a political voice in the 'bourgeois public sphere' of informal discussion and printed publication.

Nevertheless it appears that 'proper' females suspected that more was meant than had been put down in writing, and perhaps with good reason. For if political and civil rights are grounded on natural rights, and if it is insisted that natural rights are human rights, universal and not confined to particular classes of person, then it is difficult to see how those rights can be denied to women. It is by no means obvious how a convincing argument can be constructed to deny them equal rights. In her dedication Wollstonecraft quotes Talleyrand-Périgord to the effect that according to abstract principles, it was impossible to explain how one half of the human race could exclude the other from all participation in government; nevertheless he thought that women should not have political rights.

81 *Ibid.*, p. 150.
82 Robinson, *Thoughts*, pp. 78–9, 89.
83 Rendall, *Origins of Modern Feminism*, p. 50.

Wollstonecraft introduces her book as a reply to Talleyrand, and goes on in her introduction to speculate whether, when the French constitution is revised, the rights of woman will be respected. Perhaps it was enough to say this, to plant the seed and leave it to germinate in the mind of the reader. Towards the end of the book she writes, 'When therefore I call women slaves, I mean in a political and civil sense; for indirectly they obtain too much power ... [let them] share the advantages of education and government with man'.[84] This surely *implies* that women should have direct political power. 'Unsex'd' females had not yet laid on the table explicit and precise demands for reform of the law, for the vote and for seats in parliament, but this did not prevent 'proper' ones from engaging in pre-emptive strikes.

West dismisses female politicians and philosophers as a 'fashionable infection'.[85] Hamilton mocks the female politician who would drive the chariot of state in the person of Miss Ardent.[86] More finds the female politician a disgusting and unnatural character.[87] In Edgeworth's *Letters for Literary Ladies*, two men debate the education of daughters. The Edgeworth-approved voice in this debate argues for the education of women, but declares, 'Do not, my dear Sir, call me a champion for the rights of woman; I am too much their friend to be their partisan, and I am more anxious for their happiness than intent upon a metaphysical discussion of their rights'.[88] This voice does not even approve of women performing local administrative roles, such as overseeing the poor of a parish. As a utilitarian, Edgeworth could no more appeal to natural rights than Bentham, who thought them nonsense; but Edgeworth's repudiation of them is more than a technical philosophical issue. She is committed to separate spheres; moreover she refuses to recognize that men and women might have opposed interests. The *ideal* of the companionate family here obscures the *realities* of marital conflict.

Politics: a gendered and exclusionary discourse?

Present-day scholarship identifies a number of political discourses in this period through which descriptive and normative claims were made. Alongside the natural rights discourse noted above, there was an important 'republican' discourse influenced by the philosophy and history of classical Greece and Rome.[89] I have already remarked the masculine overtones of this

---

84 Wollstonecraft, *Vindication of the Rights of Woman*, pp. 262–3.
85 West, *Advantages of Education*, ii, p. 203.
86 Hamilton, *Hindoo Rajah*, p. 262.
87 More, *Strictures*, i, p. 6.
88 Edgeworth, *Letters for Literary Ladies*, pp. 29–31.
89 Wollstonecraft's engagement with this discourse is explored in Virginia Sapiro, *A Vindication of Political Virtue: the Political Theory of Mary Wollstonecraft* (Chicago, University of Chicago Press, 1992).

discourse, emphasizing as it does civic and military virtue, having as its ideal a man who is a citizen and a soldier. As was explained in Chapter 2, it has been contended by for example Landes and Outram that this discourse played a major part in the political defeat of women in this period.[90] Its model political actor, it has been argued, corresponded to what Norbert Elias has described as the modern *homo clausus*, a man whose conduct is governed by an abstract reason uncontaminated by emotion and the drives of the body, a man whose reason is in firm control of his affections and passions.[91] Such a man would be capable of the cool, detached, impartial consideration required by justice and by political affairs. Men could think of the universal; women were too interested in the particular. Women, emotional, irrational, connected by their fruitful bodies to their families, were incapable of impartiality and therefore unfit for politics. Rousseau was the modern prophet of this classical discourse about the political incompetence of women, and the jacobins were Rousseauists. Marie Antoinette was projected as a symbol of this unfitness; they guillotined her and also the prominent 'feminist' woman Olympe de Gouges, they closed down women's political clubs and excluded women from the assembly.

Landes has contended that this discourse was so powerful that women failed properly to contest it. Even Wollstonecraft took it on board, and consequently the only way she could create a political space for women was by *degendering* them, by calling in her *Vindication* for women to give up feminine characteristics and adopt masculine ones – to conform, to use Elias's term, to the model of *homo clausus*. But we have to ask ourselves whether Landes is right in thinking that women writers of the period failed to mount an effective challenge to this discourse, in the process looking at a wider range of woman-authored texts than she did. Certainly some of them *sometimes* spoke it (but not always), for example Charlotte Smith in *Desmond*, and Macaulay, who was a classicist and a republican. She criticizes Burke for addressing the passions rather than reason, and erects the fabric of her political discourse upon an antithesis of personal or partial interest or private ambition with the welfare of the community or the public good.[92]

The Landes thesis certainly works best for Wollstonecraft up to and including her *Historical and Moral View*; though even here her texts only

[90] See also Wendy Gunther-Canada, 'The politics of sense and sensibility: Mary Wollstonecraft and Catharine Macaulay Graham on Edmund Burke's *Reflections on the Revolution in France*', in Hilda L. Smith (ed.), *Women Writers and the Early Modern British Political Tradition* (Cambridge, Cambridge University Press, 1998), pp. 146–7.

[91] Elias, *Civilizing Process*, pp. 257–60.

[92] Catharine Macaulay Graham, *Observations on the Reflections of the Right Hon. Edmund Burke, on the Revolution in France* (London, C. Dilly, 1790), pp. 39, 47, 51, 61, 72, 75–6, 89, 90.

support it if they are read selectively, as we shall see later. In the *Vindication of the Rights of Woman* she charges her sex with being trivial-minded and sensual, irrational slaves to their bodies, sacrificing justice and humanity to their narrow affections for husbands and children, excessively swayed by passion and sensibility.[93] These charges, indeed, are levelled against women *as they are*, and her call is for women to reform; but on occasion this call for reform is worded as a call to become more *masculine*.[94]

Her *Historical and Moral View of the Origin and Progress of the French Revolution* is a book not without elements of misogyny, expressing a strongly gendered discourse about politics. For this book is evidently written from within a classical republican paradigm,[95] which narrates history in terms of a conflict between virtue and corruption. In this paradigm, virtue, associated with courage, patriotism and simple living, is masculine; corruption, associated with selfishness, luxury, voluptuousness, commerce and court society, is effeminate or feminine. The corruption which brought down the *ancien régime* in France is symbolized by the queen, Marie Antoinette, of whom Wollstonecraft paints an unremittingly hostile portrait. She was a harlot, who used her sexual allure to manipulate the king on behalf of her favourites and contrary to the interests of France; she plundered the public so that she could send money to her brother Joseph II of Austria.

> Is it then surprizing ... that an empty mind should be employed only to vary the pleasures, which emasculated her circean court? And, added to this, the histories of the Julias and Messalinas of antiquity, convincingly prove, that there is no end to the vagaries of the imagination, when power is unlimited, and reputation set at defiance.
>
> Lost then in the most luxurious pleasures, or managing court intrigues, the queen became a profound dissembler; and her heart hardened by sensual enjoyments.[96]

Parallel sentiments are to be found in her review of the Letters of Mme du Barry in the *Analytical*.[97] Here the patriots of the national assembly are contrasted with the luxury and oppression of the latter days of Louis XV, manipulated by his mistress working on his fear and lust. Wollstonecraft has very little that is good to say about French women and their role in the revolution. Her portrait of the women who went out to Versailles to force the king and queen back to Paris is as hostile as Burke's; they were 'the lowest refuse of the streets, women who had thrown off the virtues of one sex

---

93 Wollstonecraft, *Vindication of the Rights of Woman*, pp. 242–3.

94 *Ibid.*, pp. 74–5.

95 See for example J. G. A. Pocock, *Virtue, Commerce, and History: Essays on Political Thought and History* (Cambridge, Cambridge University Press, 1985).

96 Wollstonecraft, *Historical and Moral View*, pp. 133–4; see also pp. 33–47, 160–1, 253, 338.

97 *Analytical Review*, 12 (January 1792), p. 102.

without having power to assume more than the vices of the other'.[98] She cannot accept that this was a female political initiative; they were put up to it by the men, who hid behind their skirts: 'That a body of women should put themselves in motion to demand relief of the king, or to remonstrate with the assembly respecting their tardy manner of forming the constitution, is scarcely probable.'[99] She even sneers at the women who, in a celebrated gesture, donated their jewellery for the good of their country; this was one vanity taking the place of another.[100] Finally, the evils which afflicted the *ancien régime*, and the excesses of the revolution, are associated with the gendered character of the French, their feminine volatility and emotionalism, their lack of reason and steady judgement: 'A variety of causes have so effeminated reason, that the French may be considered as a nation of women.'[101] Much of this could have come from the pen of Rousseau, and his conclusion would seem to follow: that women, or at least the feminine, should be kept out of politics altogether.

A selective reading of Wollstonecraft, therefore, can present her as a misogynist imprisoned, as Landes argues, in a language hostile to women's political incorporation. No other 'unsex'd' female was much caught in the toils of classical republicanism; and it is debatable whether Wollstonecraft and Macaulay were, if their writings are considered whole. Wollstonecraft's language, in referring to *masculine* virtues of courage, justice and rationality may simply be unfortunate; arguably her better thought is to call these *human* virtues, and she is not obviously wrong in setting up an ideal of human excellence which transcends gender. If gender differences are thought of as historical and contingent rather than timeless and essential, then the gendered aspects of classical republican discourse will be separable from its political ideals. Rousseau argues that *because* women have such and such faults, *therefore* they should be excluded from politics. *Because* their influence is exercised in private, *therefore* it is immune to public scrutiny, and liable to be corrupt, selfish and dangerous to the state. Wollstonecraft by contrast argues that *because* 'women cannot, by force, be confined to domestic concerns; for they will, however ignorant, intermeddle with more weighty affairs, neglecting private duties only to disturb, by cunning tricks, the orderly plans of reason which rise above their comprehension',[102] *therefore* they should be better educated so as to understand reason's plans. *Because* history is filled with examples of vice and oppression which the private intrigues of female favourites have produced; *because* weak women, under the influence of childish passions and selfish vanity, lead statesmen astray,

98 Wollstonecraft, *Historical and Moral View*, p. 426.
99 *Ibid.*, p. 453.
100 *Ibid.*, p. 361.
101 *Ibid.*, p. 247; see also pp. 468, 496, 509.
102 *Ibid.*, p. 69.

therefore their influence should be brought into the public domain and they should be freed 'from all restraint by allowing them to participate the inherent rights of mankind'. Make them free, and they will learn to be wise and virtuous.[103] This is to make creative and radical use of the discourse of classical republicanism, rather than to be imprisoned by it, and Macaulay Graham argues in similar vein.[104]

No other 'unsex'd' and 'proper' females are as misogynist as Wollstonecraft in her *Historical and Moral View*. Smith, Robinson and Williams write more favourably about Marie Antoinette, in the end celebrating her as a heroic victim, praising her for her devotion to her husband and children.[105] None is so concerned to arrive at an accommodation with republican discourse as Wollstonecraft and Macaulay Graham. Robinson simply refuses the terms of debate as proposed for example by Rousseau. In France, women were admitted into the councils of statesmen and the cabinets of princes, and Robinson commends this.[106] Edgeworth thinks that the influence of women on political men is inevitable, necessary and important and in principle not harmful if women are sufficiently enlightened.[107] More, an essentially Christian thinker, does not deploy the pagan language of classical republicanism at all. She draws no contrast between civic virtue and private, female interests. On the contrary she expects women to exercise a vital and beneficial influence on public morality. She does not with classical republicanism idealize independence; Christianity teaches connectedness, mutual dependence.[108] These defences of female influence, exercised in private, do nothing to advance the cause of women's formal involvement in public politics, but they do suggest that the power of a misogynist republican discourse was limited.

The presuppositions of republican discourse are contested in more fundamental ways. Burke, in his great commentary on the fall of Marie Antoinette, had condemned the revolution in France as a work of abstract reason, disowned by the feeling heart. Both Wollstonecraft and Macaulay Graham took issue with this, preferring reason to emotion in politics. Was this a tactical mistake on their part from the point of view of the cause of women's citizenship? They vindicated the French revolution; but Burke had vindicated the place of sensibility in politics. Women might be thought deficient in reason; no one doubted their sensibility. Burke had opened the way for other

103 *Ibid.*, p. 272.

104 Macaulay Graham, *Letters on Education*, pp. 213–15.

105 Smith, *Banished Man*, iv, p. 77; Robinson, *Thoughts*, p. 27; Williams, *Letters from France*, iv, p. 40, v, pp. 153–6. Robinson commemorated her as a martyr in *Monody to the Memory of the Late Queen of France* (London, T. Spilsbury & Son, 1793).

106 Robinson, *Thoughts*, pp. 61–2.

107 Edgeworth, *Letters to Literary Ladies*, pp. 31–2.

108 More, *Strictures*, ii, p. 170.

'unsex'd' and 'proper' females to deny that different, gendered faculties are appropriate to separate spheres – masculine reason to the public, and feminine sensibility to the domestic realm.

We need to remind ourselves that British moral philosophers in the eighteenth century were *not* unanimous in thinking that the basis of morality was reason. They did not even agree among themselves that the public morality of justice was founded upon reason, some of them appealing to a moral sense or to moral sentiments as the basis of morality.[109] Burke in fact draws upon a strand in moral thinking, developed by David Hume and the source of classic utilitarianism, which contends that reason is incapable of discovering moral truths. Moral ideas are grounded in sympathy or fellow-feeling. If this is the case, it might be thought that women, if their sympathetic feelings are stronger, are therefore more likely to act virtuously. Another strand, particularly associated with dissenting culture and found in the writings of for example Price, Priestley and Godwin, synthesizes reason and sympathetic feeling in a moral ideal of general benevolence. Invocations of these ideas are to be found in the writings of 1790s women. For example, Macaulay Graham appeals to 'unconfined benevolence', and maintains that sympathy is the source of all the virtues including equity (i.e., justice).[110] Williams writes of her heroine Julia that 'in a mind where the principles of religion and integrity are firmly established, sensibility is not merely the ally of weakness, or the slave of guilt, but serves to give a stronger impulse to virtue'.[111]

Repudiation of the political primacy of reason is the most striking theme to emerge from Williams's *Letters from France* and because of this no other woman-authored text of the decade is more important on the subject of women and politics. Williams's eight volumes are an extended and developing commentary on the place of feeling in politics, constantly and specifically applied to women.[112] In the first volume, written before the rise of jacobinism and the terror, while she was still a wholehearted friend of the revolution, Williams sounds the theme that the heart has its part to play in politics as well as the head, inspiring patriotic fervour and a willingness to make sacrifices for the nation. The leaders of the French revolution have not trusted merely to the force of reason: the processions and ceremonies which mobilize the people of Paris are addressed at once to the imagination, the understanding and the heart.[113] She finds her own heart catching with enthusiasm the general sympathy, and her eyes filling with tears.[114]

In this first volume, some of her remarks might lend comfort to those who would argue the incompetence of women for public affairs. Her own commit-

[109] D. D. Raphael, *The Moral Sense* (Oxford, Oxford University Press, 1947).
[110] Macaulay Graham, *Letters on Education*, pp. 105, 275.
[111] Williams, *Julia*, i, p. 178.
[112] Gary Kelly argues this in his *Women, Writing and Revolution*, p. 32ff.
[113] Williams, *Letters from France*, i, pp. 6, 62.
[114] *Ibid.*, i, p.14.

ment to the revolution, she declares, did not result from reasoning about principles of justice: 'I have not been so absurd as to consult my head upon matters of which it is so incapable of judging'.[115] Her wandering thoughts would have broken the fine-spun threads of reason; but when a proposition was addressed to her heart, her perception was quick.[116] She was engaged by her feelings for individuals, for example by her friendship with the du Fossés, imprisoned and separated under the *ancien régime*, reunited and restored to happiness by the revolution. The feelings of private friendship led her to sympathize with public blessings.[117] Williams's tone is not apologetic, but defiant: when a proposition is addressed to her heart, she can decide in a moment points upon which philosophers and legislators have differed in all ages.[118] In her second volume she tells the story of Madeleine and Auguste, a parallel to that of the du Fossés. Madelaine has not much meditated upon politics, she has not studied the declaration of rights made by the constituent assembly; but she thinks that 'obtaining liberty of choice in marriage was alone well worth the trouble of a revolution'.[119]

If by this point the reader is inclined to feel that she has done the women's cause little good, subsequent volumes exhibit the evil of reason divorced from feeling, and the failure, in practice, of a separation of spheres. The fury of the jacobins, unconstrained by the ordinary feelings of human nature, immolates its victims in the name of great principles.[120] Not only is their political reason untempered by sensibility; it invades and obscenely violates the domestic. Husbands were torn from wives, parents from children. She tells no more memorable story than that of the peasant woman of Arras, selling her butter in town, suckling a three-month-old infant. On seeing a cart of victims going to execution, she commented that they were dying for very little reason. For this treasonous remark she was guillotined, and 'when she received the fatal stroke, the streams of maternal nourishment issued rapidly from her bosom, and, mingled with her blood, bathed her executioner'.[121] In Nantes, young women were publicly stripped naked, tied to young men in a 'republican marriage', sabred and thrown into the river.[122] Amée Cecile Renaud, a girl of 19 who insulted Robespierre, was stripped of her own clothes and forced to appear at her trial in squalid and disgusting rags.[123]

Conversely, sensibility inspired the victims of tyranny with heroism, and because of their superior sensibility, women were peculiarly distinguished for

[115] *Ibid.*, i, p. 66.
[116] *Ibid.*, i, pp. 195–6.
[117] *Ibid.*, i, p. 72.
[118] *Ibid.*, i., p. 196.
[119] *Ibid.*, ii, pp. 174–5.
[120] *Ibid.*, iv, pp. 1–2.
[121] *Ibid.*, vii, pp. 121–2.
[122] *Ibid.*, vii, pp. 42–3.
[123] *Ibid.*, vi, pp. 66–9.

their admirable firmness in death – like the 24-year-old wife who shouted 'Vive le roi!' at her husband's trial so that she could die with him.[124] Williams presents the moderates with whom she sympathizes and who were soon to be executed by the jacobins as people in whom head and heart were combined and balanced. So for example La Source was a man of acute sensibility who detested the crimes by which the revolution had been sullied; in his soul liberty was less a principle than a passion.[125] Madame Roland united extraordinary endowments of mind with all the warmth of a feeling heart. When Williams visited her in prison shortly before her execution, she found her resigned to death, and prepared to meet it with a firmness worthy of her exalted character. But when Williams asked about her daughter, she burst into tears; the courage of the victim of liberty was lost in the feelings of the wife and the mother.[126]

In effect Williams has suggested with great power that a sharp separation of reason and sensibility, of public and domestic concerns, will ultimately be destructive of both. Nor was she the only woman writer to make such a case. Smith's hero d'Alonville in *The Banished Man* has a jacobin elder brother, who has repudiated his father (the Viscount de Fayolles) and his family name. Smith explicitly associates his crimes with a Roman disregard of the ties of nature. D'Alonville exclaims, 'accursed be the infamous maxims that tend to break the ties of blood and friendship, and leave us nothing in their place, but the empty bonds of stoicism, which the heart denies'.[127] This calls to mind Burke's remark, 'But that sort of reason which banishes the affections is incapable of filling their place', and his appeal to the sentiments 'which the heart owns, and the understanding ratifies'.[128]

Other 'unsex'd' females question the notion that women are less fitted for politics by their nature or situation than men. The *Appeal to the Men of Great Britain* insists that women have perhaps as much reason and certainly more sensibility.[129] 'Women in general possess even fortitude, that first of masculine virtues, in a much greater degree, and of a much superior kind, to that possessed by the men.'[130] In her *Letters and Essays* Hays agrees with Dyer that women are more principled than men; they are less prejudiced by the possession of pensions and places, and because they have more experience of oppression, they are more firm advocates of liberty.[131] Robinson too proclaims the superior altruism and indeed heroism of women; men are more likely to be motivated by sensuality, interest or ambition.[132] It is difficult to

124 *Ibid.*, v, pp. 213–14.
125 *Ibid.*, iv, p. 423.
126 *Ibid.*, v, pp. 196–7.
127 Smith, *Banished Man*, iii, pp. 164–5.
128 Burke, *Reflections*, pp. 74–5.
129 *Appeal to the Men of Great Britain*, p. 148.
130 *Ibid.*, p. 175.
131 Hays, *Letters and Essays*, pp. 11–12.
132 Robinson, *Thoughts*, pp. 9–10, 43–4.

believe that the Landes thesis works for these writers, and to judge them imprisoned in a masculine discourse about politics.

More generally, women writers, 'proper' ones as well as 'unsex'd', enter the political debate from the standpoint of humanitarian sensibility. They proclaim and express womanly feeling, caring and compassion, a ground on which female political action was to be based in the nineteenth century. An extensive agenda of humanitarian causes is in evidence. Macaulay Graham attacks slavery and cruel punishments; she is appalled by the maltreatment of animals, is opposed to hunting and even feels compassion for the worm on the fisherman's hook.[133] Hays and Robinson echo her sentiments, and indeed the campaign against slavery is a perennial theme of Robinson's novels and poems. In *The False Friend* she criticizes the use of slave-grown sugar.[134] Radcliffe's polemic against the denial of work opportunities to women, a denial which drives some unfortunates into prostitution, is saturated through and through with the discourse of sensibility and humanitarianism. In several of her novels Smith launches an attack on cruel prison conditions; in *Desmond* for example she also criticizes severe punishments under the law, especially executions, the slave trade, the neglect of the poor and inhuman punishments in the armed forces. The heroine of that novel teaches her little boy not to hurt lizards. More's humanitarian and Christian stand against the slave trade is well known. Hamilton in her *Letters of a Hindoo Rajah* advocates a whole catalogue of humanitarian reforms: she commends Howard's prison work, condemns the slave trade, hunting, the game laws, debtor's prisons, press gangs, the failure of the rich to care for the poor, cruel punishments in the army and the lack of a system for notifying poor families of their war dead.

In effect this is to say that womanly sensibility is a qualification rather than a disqualification for having opinions on political matters. It undermines a separation of spheres on the grounds of alleged gender characteristics. Not only do women writers make a case for feeling in politics; from Wollstonecraft through Edgeworth to Wakefield they proclaim that women must exercise reason in the domestic sphere. Edgeworth as we have seen is a classic advocate of separate spheres, but her argument in no way rests upon the view that men are rational and women emotional. Her aim is through education to make women rational, so that they can perform enlightened household management, take long views, calculate and regulate the expenses of a family.[135]

Politics: the interconnectedness of the domestic and the political

Women writers present the interconnectedness of the political and the domestic in other ways too. 'Unsex'd' females constantly draw parallels between

[133] Macaulay Graham, *Letters on Education*, p. 122.
[134] Robinson, *False Friend*, ii, p. 8.
[135] Edgeworth, *Letters for Literary Ladies*, p. 21.

political oppression and domestic tyranny and imply that the two stand or fall together. They propose a continuum of power not divided by a public/private binary. Both 'unsex'd' and 'proper' females insist upon the political importance of what happens in the home. We have already seen how Williams epitomizes the evils of the *ancien régime* in the control of fathers over the marital choices of their children, bastilling their sons for marrying commoners. Smith repeats this theme in *Celestina*, and finds an English parallel in a powerful, feudal father in *Montalbert*. In *Angelina*, Robinson presents a brutal, autocratic father in Sir Edward Clarendon, who is also a slave trader; he regards his daughter as disposable property too. His daughter voices her rebellion not only against her father's will, but also against aristocracies of birth. In *The Widow*, the villainous rake Lord Woodley declares his contempt for the common people, and regrets that the law and the constitution will not allow him to treat them as he pleases:

> Thus am I obliged to check the ardour of my soul, compelled to restrain my power over mankind by the gothic rules of freedom and humanity, and forced to curb my heart which pants for the exercise of unlimited subjection; since I cannot tyrannise over my vassals, I will over the *women*; they shall at least feel my dominion, and be subservient to my pleasures.[136]

Lord Arcot in *The False Friend* deplores both political and domestic democracy, which he is convinced go hand in hand: 'If a wife breaks the fetters of matrimonial restraint, though we all know that women were born to be slaves, why, forsooth, she is only called a lover of Liberty.' Gertrude replies to him, speaking up for political equality and the rights of women.[137] Fenwick's Caroline Ashburn repudiates unlimited unexamined obedience, whether it be to a sovereign, a parent or a husband.[138]

The *Appeal to the Men of Great Britain* throughout uses the language of politics and power to talk about domestic relations. Subservience of a wife to an unworthy husband is a degrading 'system of politics in morals'.[139] In a discussion of relations between husband and wife the author criticizes tyrannical husbands and insists that 'sound politicks' require men to allow women privileges and a degree of liberty. Injustice and impolicy on the part of men will result in feigned submission, mean subterfuge and petty treacheries.[140] By this point it has ceased to be clear whether the author is discussing the public or the private, for to all intents and purposes the distinction has been blurred. In other places she writes of 'social and domestic politics', absolute and unlimited power in domestic life, domestic tyranny incompatible with natural justice, of women as subjected to the authority and superiority of

136 Robinson, *The Widow*, ii, pp. 90–1.
137 Robinson, *False Friend*, iv, pp. 98–101.
138 Fenwick, *Secresy*, p. 349.
139 *Appeal to the Men of Great Britain*, p. 56.
140 *Ibid.*, pp. 86, 91.

men.[141] She marvels that principles of private and domestic justice have not kept pace with those of a public and political nature.[142] In this important and thoughtful text, Hays, if she is the author, systematically refuses the concept of separate spheres working according to different principles.

The impact of the domestic upon the political is, if anything, a yet more laboured theme. The ideal of republican motherhood in Wollstonecraft's *Vindication of the Rights of Woman* and elsewhere is a major component. Paradoxically Rousseau was an important influence here, allocating to women the task of binding together the family, and by precept and example teaching children to love something greater than self. Wollstonecraft takes this ideal and refashions it. In *Emile* Rousseau proposed that Sophie, the ideal wife for his hero, needed no strenuous intellectual training, no cultivation of her reason. Wollstonecraft replies that if women are to train up their children to be patriots, they must be patriots themselves; and since patriotism requires an understanding of principles, and a large-minded ability to rise above petty, selfish concerns, therefore women need trained, rational minds just as much as men do. They even need scientific education, if they are to care properly for the health of their children.[143] The wife who manages her family, educates her children and assists her neighbours while her husband is employed in any of the departments of civil life is also an active citizen.[144] Whereas classical republicanism counterposed public virtue and private interest, Wollstonecraft declares that public spirit must be nurtured by private virtue, that 'public virtue is only an aggregate of private' and that few have had much affection for mankind who did not first love their parents, their brothers and sisters.[145]

Wollstonecraft's republican motherhood is the radical end of a spectrum of views about the public importance of the home. Nearest to her stands Macaulay Graham, who also has a strong sense of the interconnectedness of public and private virtue and happiness. No woman author, however, 'unsex'd' or 'proper', is in any real disagreement with this. According to Mary Ann Radcliffe, political and private happiness are invariably connected, and the sexual immorality which results from the failure to protect women, from driving them destitute into prostitution, is a threat to national happiness and the public good.[146] No one is more insistent upon the importance of female patriotism than More in her *Strictures*. The general state of civilized society, she declares, depends to a high degree on the sentiments and habits of women, and on the nature and degree of estimation in which they are held.[147]

[141] *Ibid.*, pp. 96, 263–4, 274–5.
[142] *Ibid.*, p. 288.
[143] Wollstonecraft, *Vindication of the Rights of Woman*, p. 274.
[144] *Ibid.*, p. 236.
[145] *Ibid.*, pp. 229, 291, 256.
[146] Radcliffe, *Female Advocate*, p. 421.
[147] More, *Strictures*, i, pp. 1–6.

Now to write about women in a way which undermines or refuses a discourse of gendered separate spheres is an achievement. So too is challenging the assumptions that the domestic can be secluded from structures of political power and that female nature is unsuited to political life. But these discursive triumphs do not in themselves give women access to political spaces. Evidently practical organization and action is required too. But even before that, further argumentative work needs to be done, as was remarked when the absence of an analysis and an agenda of women's rights was noted above. Furthermore, to say that what women do in the home is crucial to the quality and even the survival of the nation, is a two-edged sword; a possible inference is that since women have so much power there, since they have so much domestic work of public importance to do, therefore rights to vote and to be elected are unnecessary and undesirable. A cynic might regard the attribution of informal influence to women as a consolation prize, awarded by designing men to women, and by gullible women to themselves.

Evaluations of spheres

It is at least plausible to suggest that the failure to attack the citadel of formal political power was encouraged by a further dimension of dissent from republican discourse. From Plato and Aristotle onwards, this discourse proposed that the private was of less value than the public. The public realm of civic engagement was the arena of the human in its highest sense, the space of free and virtuous activity where individuals devoted themselves, ideally, to a more universal good. There the virtuous man performed his part with resolution, courage and dignity in the full view of his equals. The private by contrast catered for the lower needs of mere physical survival which humans shared with animals; hidden from the public gaze its moving principles were appetite and self-interest, its characteristics necessity and particularity.

Now it is not the case that this ranking and this location of virtue were accepted by female authors in the 1790s. There was a widespread view that fulfilment, happiness and morality were to be found in retirement from the great world, and a widespread suspicion of the ethics and the motivation of politicians. The hero and heroine of *Camilla* listen with rapt attention while Melmond reads the closing lines of Thompson's 'Spring', 'An elegant sufficiency, content . . .', quoted in the previous chapter. In *A Tale of the Times*, West quotes Cowper's 'domestic happiness, the only "bliss of paradise which has survived the fall"'.[148] Now we might expect, not just a celebration of the domestic, but also a polemic against the republican patriotism which inspired French revolutionaries from the pen of a *conservative* writer. West provides

[148] West, *Tale of the Times*, iii, p. 366; Cowper, *The Task*, iii, lines 41–2.

166

just that, briefly in *A Gossip's Story*[149] and more extensively in *The Advantages of Education*.[150]

> Those actions that pass before the world's eye, are equivocal: they may proceed from the sublimest motives, or they may be the offspring of vanity. We all act and speak well, when in the presence of those, whose esteem we are anxious to acquire.
>
> But I would follow the man who thus speaks and acts, to his family. I would see him, when, free from the restraint of observation, his character assumes its natural aspect. Is he still the kind benevolent philanthropist?[151]

West's values are fundamentally at odds with a pagan philosophy which esteems bold and courageous action on the public stage; as a protestant Christian she cares more about the inner motivations revealed more clearly in private life. It comes as no surprise to find More uttering similar sentiments: it is better to be an obscure Christian in a village than a hoary courtier or wily politician,[152] virtue brings happiness but not glory.[153] It is absolutely clear that she thinks the best life to be a retired rural and domestic one, clear too that she thinks it the best life for men as well as women. Other 'proper' females – Edgeworth, Burney, Hamilton – think the same.[154] In Radcliffe's *Romance of the Forest*, the domestic idyll, reminiscent of Rousseau's Clarens in *La Nouvelle Héloïse*, is represented by La Luc's mountain retreat at Leloncourt, where he devotes himself to 'the luxury of doing good' to his poorer neighbours, to the contemplation of nature and to philosophic researches. At the end of the novel, Adeline and Theodore, though they have the wealth and the estates to figure splendidly at court, retire also to a modest country house nearby.

None of this is surprising from the pens of 'proper' females; but 'unsex'd' ones are just as convinced of the pre-eminence of retired, domestic joys. This is the case even with Macaulay Graham and Wollstonecraft, who come nearest to republicanism. In this respect they are in fundamental dissent from any masculinist republican discourse. Macaulay Graham in her *Letters on Education* appears as more of a 'softened', humanized stoic than a classical republican. Stoics thought that men should perform their public duties, but their principal recommendation was a quest for freedom and contentment independent of ambition and public success. So she is critical of pride and restless ambition,[155] and finds her leisured, sociable ideal in 'the soft and tranquil pleasures that an elegant retreat affords', a life of moderate, every-

---

149 West, *Gossip's Story*, i, p. 221.
150 West, *Advantages of Education*, ii, pp. 200–3.
151 *Ibid.*, pp. 201–2.
152 More, *Strictures*, i, p. 132.
153 *Ibid.*, i, p. 184.
154 Edgeworth, *Letters for Literary Ladies*, p. 36; Hamilton, *Hindoo Rajah*, pp. 90–1, 278, 293, 306.
155 Macaulay Graham, *Letters on Education*, pp. 107–8.

day joys.[156] She thought that Cicero's character was tarnished because he was not a complete stoic, because he had too high a regard for public glory;[157] and, significantly, she condemns Brutus for allowing his desire for the glory of a reputation for justice to triumph over parental affection. The Brutus in question was a consul of the Roman republic; his two sons conspired against the state, and he condemned them to be stretched on the ground, beaten by the lictors and beheaded in his presence. One of the grimmest republican images of the French revolution is David's painting of Brutus sitting at home, sternly impassive as the corpses of his sons are carried in: meanwhile the women of the family give way to shrieks and tears.

Towards the end of Wollstonecraft's first *Vindication*, there is a lightly sketched rural ideal, with prosperous peasants and moderately wealthy middle-class gentry to guide them. Friendship replaces master–servant relationships, modest egalitarian comfort is preferred to aristocratic grandeur. 'Domestic comfort, the civilizing relations of husband, brother, and father, would soften labour, and render life contented.'[158] In this ideal, any distinction between the public and the private disappears, largely by virtue of the extinction or forgetting of the public, and the expansion of the domestic to cover everything. Similarly in her second *Vindication*, demands for political participation are not foregrounded. She quotes Mme de Staël commending Rousseau: though Rousseau would exclude women from public affairs, he recognizes and endorses the power they exercise over men by virtue of their feminine charms. It is surely significant that Wollstonecraft's reply takes issue with Rousseau's celebration of women as sexual objects, but totally ignores the reference in the quotation to women's exclusion from public affairs and the theatre of politics.[159] Wollstonecraft's main demand is for better education for women, and one justification for this is to make them better mothers. But also, and perhaps to an even greater extent, one of the goals she is proposing for women is private in the extreme sense of that word, an ideal of personal development which will be explored more extensively in the next chapter.

Wollstonecraft is not a model republican in that she does not have a particularly high regard for civic engagements. She does not think that there is much that is ennobling about British politics,[160] nor does she think that the private is necessarily corrupting and inimical to virtue. On the contrary, public affections and virtues must ever grow out of the private character;

---

[156] *Ibid.*, p. 291.
[157] *Ibid.*, p. 450.
[158] Mary Wollstonecraft, *A Vindication of the Rights of Men, in a Letter to the Right Honourable Edmund Burke; Occasioned by his Reflections on the Revolution in France* (1790) (Cambridge, Cambridge University Press, 1995), pp. 59–62.
[159] Wollstonecraft, *Vindication of the Rights of Woman*, pp. 185–6.
[160] *Ibid.*, p. 233.

public virtue is only an aggregate of private.[161] Of course a good republican can recognize that civil society is in a corrupt condition, while still holding on to a vision of a republic of virtue which might be attained in better times; but this is not really Wollstonecraft's stance. Instead of saying that a better civil society would produce more virtue and heroism, she contends that if society were more reasonably organized, there would be less need of great abilities or heroic virtues.[162] The best life, for women *and* for men, is a happy family life with 'a taste for literature, to throw a little variety and interest into social converse, and some superfluous money to give to the needy and to buy books'.[163]

The model man of classical republicanism was the citizen-soldier. A revealing indication of Wollstonecraft's distance from this tradition is her lack of respect for the military. She does not think that in her own day the armed camp is a school of heroic virtue. In her case this is not simply a lament about the corruption of modern times in a Rousseauist or classical republican style after the manner of Ferguson,[164] and a call to return to the heroism of the past; Wollstonecraft is inclined to think that war, and therefore the profession of the soldier, are relics of barbarism.[165] Soldiers she thinks, spending much of their time idle and useless about the camp, strutting in their uniforms and devoting themselves to gallantry, display similar faults to conventionally stereotyped women.[166] Nor is Wollstonecraft alone in charging soldiers, in effect, with effeminacy; the charge is repeated by Robinson and Hamilton, and we encounter vain and slightly effeminate soldiers in the pages of Smith's novels.[167]

The retired ideal is not merely shared but heartily endorsed by 'unsex'd' and 'proper' females alike. It is conspicuous in Hays's *Letters and Essays*. Just to give one example, the model man Hortensius, though a citizen of the world possessed of social and patriotic affections, nevertheless declines the path of public honours, for which his virtues and abilities eminently qualified him, to live a life of retirement and community sociability.[168] It is a commonplace in all of Smith's novels. The wicked and worldly Lady Molyneux thinks that Celestina 'would make a good quiet wife for her brother, and be well adapted to that insipid domestic life, his turn for which she had always pitied and despised'.[169] Willoughby indeed longs for a 'life

[161] *Ibid.*, pp. 256, 291.

[162] *Ibid.*, p. 140.

[163] *Ibid.*, p. 233.

[164] Adam Ferguson, *An Essay on the History of Civil Society* (1767) (Edinburgh, Edinburgh University Press, 1966), pp. 228–31.

[165] Wollstonecraft, *Vindication of the Rights of Woman*, pp. 235–6.

[166] *Ibid.*, pp. 92–3.

[167] Robinson, *Thoughts*, p. 18; Hamilton, *Hindoo Rajah*, p. 225; Smith, *Banished Man*, i, pp. 178–9; *Old Manor House*, p. 121.

[168] Hays, *Letters and Essays*, pp. 117–19.

[169] Smith, *Celestina*, i, p. 239.

of elegant and literary retirement' with Celestina.[170] (Praise of the pleasures of good books is so frequent that the reader begins half to wonder whether publishers of novels required it.) The young philosopher, George Delmont, aspires to avoid 'those fettering connections and professions, by which men of family usually make what is called their way in the world', to devote himself to a life of philosophizing, gardening, botanizing, poetizing and enjoying the beauties of nature, to 'literary leisure and love'.[171] Smith heads a chapter with three lines from Cowper's *Task*:

> O friendly to the best pursuits of man,
> Friendly to thought, to virtue, and to peace,
> Domestic life in rural quiet pass'd.

Even Robinson, who in her glory days had been at the centre of the great world, mistress and friend of courtiers and politicians, subscribes to the retired ideal in her novels. There are lively and witty passages of satire in *The Widow*, in which depraved and dissipated women of the *haut ton* express their boredom with country life; the heroes and heroines of course love rural retreat, domestic life and reading. Her first novel, *Vancenza*, condemns the 'follies of public life' with a peculiar bitterness and intensity, and the castle of Vancenza is a rural and domestic idyll.[172]

What are we to make of this retired ideal? Is it merely a cliché, a stock piece of literary padding? We might be tempted to think this when we remember the very long history of debates over country versus town, suspecting an unthinking repetition of an entrenched theme.[173] But the retired ideal is far too conscious, far too prevalent both in works of prose fiction and in carefully considered non-fiction arguments for that. Though it is presented as an ideal for both women and men, it is obviously an appropriate because attainable ideal for the former. Is it therefore a symptom of resignation and defeat, of making the best of a bad job, of sour grapes? Perhaps this plays a part; but it is also a manifestation of that idealization of ordinary life which has been so central to Christian culture, marking it off so sharply, as Nietzsche recognized in his *Genealogy of Morals*, from the pagan politics of classical Greece and Rome. As Williams puts it.

> The precious essence of content can be more easily extracted from the simple materials of the poor, than from the various preparations of the rich. Its pure and fine spirit rises from a few plain ingredients, brighter and clearer than from that magical cup of dissipation, where the powerful, and the wealthy, pour their costly infusions.[174]

[170] *Ibid.*, iv, p. 8.
[171] Smith, *Young Philosopher*, pp. 69, 172.
[172] Robinson, *Vancenza*, i, p. 81.
[173] Raymond Williams, *The Country and the City* (London, Chatto & Windus, 1973).
[174] Williams, *Julia*, i, p. 219.

Conclusion

However tentative women writers may have been in requesting access to formal, institutional politics, this modesty did not extend to what Habermas calls the 'bourgeois public sphere' – the public discussion of public affairs through the medium of print, if not in other public meeting places. Here women writers boldly claimed their right to a voice. The replies to Burke's *Reflections* by Macaulay Graham and Wollstonecraft are both successful polemics, though in different ways. Williams's *Letters from France* were a powerful and important intervention in the debate on the unfolding events in France. Smith's political stance was Foxite Whiggish with 'Girondist' sympathies; her *Desmond* and *The Young Philosopher* have extended political discussions and are in effect 'jacobin' novels, but in fact all of her novels contain political reflections. In her preface to *Desmond* she rejects the view that women have no business with politics,[175] and in *The Banished Man* Lady Ellesmere is criticized for taking no interest in the French revolution.[176] French affairs are discussed in Robinson's novels, and democratic and feminist sentiments aired. She dares to be antigovernment; an utterly wicked character in *The False Friend*, Mrs Ferret, is a government spy and informer. Her *Hubert de Sevrac*, a sustained critique of the *ancien régime*, is a 'jacobin' gothic romance. Inchbald's *Nature and Art* and Fenwick's *Secresy* are 'jacobin' novels.

In spite of occasional animadversions against female politicians, 'proper' females too intervene in the political debate. There are no politics in *Camilla*, but in 1793 Burney published a pamphlet entitled *Brief Reflections relative to the Emigrant French Clergy*. Hamilton's *Hindoo Rajah* criticizes political corruption, taxes and war, defends toleration of dissenters while criticizing methodism, and defends Warren Hastings against Burke's charges. West's *Tale of the Times* is an attack on jacobin politics and morality. More was closely associated with Wilberforce's political programme,[177] she wrote antislavery poetry and political tracts, and in a chapter on conversation in her *Strictures* she insisted that it was right and proper for women to discuss religion and politics.

So was there in the 1790s a discourse of separate spheres which, if it is assumed that discourses are socially and politically powerful, could have contributed to the disempowering of women and their presentation as inferior to men? I hope that I have succeeded in this chapter in demonstrating that women writers were not imprisoned in a disempowering discourse. There are

[175] Smith, *Desmond*, p. 6.
[176] Smith, *Banished Man*, ii, p. 111.
[177] Anne Stott, 'Patriotism and providence: the politics of Hannah More', in Kathryn Gleadle & Sarah Richardson (eds), *Women in British Politics, 1760–1860: the Power of the Petticoat* (Basingstoke, Macmillan, 2000), pp. 40–5.

certainly the components, the fragments of one, but they do not cohere into a coercive structure of language. 'Unsex'd' and 'proper' women exploit the gaps, the contradictions, the ambiguities and the open texture of discourse in order to create a space for female action. 'Public' and 'private' and related terms are not used with a single, coherent set of meanings. They do not construct one map, but rather maps which overlap and disagree. Nor are 'public' and 'private' regularly constructed as discrete, separate spaces; they interconnect and interpenetrate. In 1790s Britain there were physical spaces from which women were excluded, but woman-authored writings recognize no *spheres* from which they were totally debarred. Women could not be priests, but the church belonged to them as much as to men, and More has them performing religious roles. They could not be members of the houses of parliament, but women writers refused to accept complete exclusion from politics. They could not be lawyers, and most women writers thought that they should not be soldiers or blacksmiths; but they write approvingly of female involvement in farming, manufacturing, commerce, shopkeeping, medicine and the arts.

No 'unsex'd' female agrees that women have mental or moral characteristics or limitations which of necessity debar them from spheres suited only to men. 'Proper' females such as More, Hamilton and Edgeworth do not recognize any mental or moral inferiority. Even if they accept that sensibility is peculiarly feminine, they think that there is a place for sensibility in politics; and in any case, men are not alone capable of reason and self-control. The only characteristic which women writers see as a limit to women's activity is female modesty. Female modesty principally means female sexual vulnerability, vulnerability to the assaults and rudeness of men; in effect, therefore, females are disempowered and confined by a fault which is not in them but in the males, and women writers were already deep into the project of reforming men. Finally, no woman writer accepts that the domestic is an inferior space. It is the best space, best for men as well as for women. It can be the best in this way, because it undergoes considerable expansion at their hands, into the 'social', into activity and usefulness in the community.

6

Female opportunities:
fashioning a self

We would expect the female self to be called to find at least a part of her fulfilment in performing the social roles of wife and mother, and this is just as much the case with 'unsex'd' females such as Wollstonecraft and Hays as it is with 'proper' ones like Edgeworth and Wakefield. When she sums up the excellencies of Wollstonecraft at the end of her obituary, Hays begins with 'mother, wife, beloved companion' and puts her public role as a writer second. Elsewhere she refers to the title of mother as a 'sacred name'.[1] It is important to recognize that intelligent women and women by no means prisoners of convention could think that partial if not complete fulfilment was possible in socially sanctioned roles. For Wakefield, social duties emphatically come first, and the improvement of a woman's own mind holds the second place.[2] To be socially useful is the thing. More explicitly advocates this in preference to living for oneself. In 'Bear ye one another's burdens' More describes a vision of good Christians in this vale of tears: 'there was no such thing as what we call *independence* in the whole Valley'.[3]

But this chapter will be concerned with the woman considered in herself, for her own sake, not as ancillary to man or as the location of a role. It will ask whether texts by 'unsex'd' and 'proper' females depict women creating and asserting themselves, having their own independent worth and dignity. Its topic is women writers' 'subjective sense of self' and their 'resources for self-representation' which are 'critical for empowering' them 'to transcend present conventions about gender' and for expanding their possibilities.[4]

We would expect this point of view to be more openly asserted by 'unsex'd' females than by 'proper' ones. Macaulay Graham praises inde-

[1] *Appeal to the Men of Great Britain*, p. 214.
[2] Wakefield, *Reflections*, p. 89.
[3] Hannah More, *Sunday Reading. Bear Ye one another's Burdens, or the Valley of Tears: a Vision* (London, J. Marshall, 1795), p. 3.
[4] Yeo, *Wollstonecraft and Two Hundred Years of Feminisms*, p. 2.

pendence, and denies that the end of the education of a woman is to make her agreeable to a husband.[5] The *Appeal to the Men of Great Britain*, in spite of its emphasis upon the social duties of women, finds the idea of breeding up women merely with a view of catching a husband very degrading;[6] a woman's duties are first to God, *then to herself*, in considering her own happiness, and only after that to men.[7] In spite of her promotion of 'republican motherhood', Wollstonecraft's *Vindication of the Rights of Woman* proposes above all a woman's self-development, the cultivation of her reason and her virtue (though of course virtue opens out into duties to others). 'The being who discharges the duties of its station is independent; and speaking of women at large, their first duty is to themselves as rational creatures, and the next, in point of importance, as citizens, is that, which includes so many, of a mother.'[8] In fact in Wollstonecraft's classic a woman's primary orientation appears to be not towards social roles but towards herself and God. 'Every individual is ... a world in itself.' Women have duties as daughters, wives and mothers, but 'the end, the grand end of their exertions should be to unfold their own faculties and acquire the dignity of conscious virtue'.[9] The ideal for a woman is to some extent therefore a solitary one, in which she finds herself in relation to God, imitating, as far as she can, his perfections. As the quoted passage reveals, Wollstonecraft wants women to be *independent*. Sometimes she appears to give that word the meaning we would expect, i.e., legal and financial independence. But this cannot be her goal for all women, as she accepts that most of them will be supported by a husband. Therefore independence also means being governed by one's own reason, rather than by the will of another; or it means dependence only on God, 'Whose service is perfect freedom'.[10] The radicalism of this detachment of women from a merely social, ancillary status should not be underestimated. In spite of their avowed aim of preserving women's social embeddedness, even 'proper' females, as we shall see, also propose this care and cultivation of the self.

The appearance of the body

A discussion of the care of the self needs to pay some attention to what 'unsex'd' and 'proper' females have to say about the care and presentation of the physical body. Though automatic and perhaps unthinking tribute is paid to conventions of womanly weakness in prose fiction – women faint and fall

[5] Macaulay Graham, *Letters on Education*, pp. 67, 208.
[6] *Appeal to the Men of Great Britain*, p. 227.
[7] *Ibid.*, pp. 145–50.
[8] *Ibid.*, p. 235.
[9] *Ibid.*, pp. 95, 127.
[10] Wollstonecraft, *Vindication of the Rights of Woman*, pp. 106–7, 140, 206, 232.

desperately ill when under stress – no woman writer, when she consciously confronts this issue, thinks that weakness of body is at all desirable, and there are calls for women to become more robust. Macaulay Graham is scathing about women who 'lisp with their tongues, ... totter in their walk, and ... counterfeit more weakness and sickness than they really have, in order to attract the notice of the male'.[11] Mental and moral qualities are favoured by strength and health, and so girls should be encouraged to be physically active. She commends Spartan women, who endeavoured to improve their natural strength, so that they might be fit to breed heroes. Cold baths are favoured, and down beds disapproved.[12] Wollstonecraft has much to say along the same lines; she would allow young girls to run wild just like boys, and instead of 'relaxed beauty ... or the graces of helplessness' prefers bodily strength 'such as appears to make us respect the human body as a majestic pile fit to receive a noble inhabitant, in the relics of antiquity'.[13] Robinson would have women swim, race and play ball games: 'We should then see British Atalantas, as well as female Nimrods.'[14] Nor is this only an issue for 'unsex'd' females; Wakefield calls for strong mothers too, and thinks that girls should exercise in the open air just as boys do, rise early, eat moderately and take cold baths.[15]

The classical references in Macaulay Graham and Wollstonecraft are significant, for we find in many texts a neoclassical aesthetic of the female body.[16] Elaborate adornment is universally condemned; simplicity of attire, even plainness, is commended. The image that comes to mind is of a woman with her hair simply done up, in a white empire-line gown with no jewellery, sitting in a bare neoclassical room. In Williams's *Julia*, the heroines appear at dinner dressed with the most graceful simplicity, while the dissipated Mrs Seymour is very fantastically arrayed.[17] Later Mrs Seymour sings a duet with a friend, 'so tricked out with ornament, and performed with such affected distortions of the lips, and apparent labour' that nobody admires it except her blindly doting mother.[18] Williams is advocating an aesthetic of honesty, of being true to the body rather than attempting to present it as what it is not. In a discussion of bodily appearance Wollstonecraft connects simplicity and sincerity.[19] In a veritable epitome of the neoclassical ideal, she commends the sober satisfaction which arises from the calm contemplation of proportion, simplicity and truth.[20] Women should not ornament, or rather disfigure

11 Macaulay Graham, *Letters on Education*, p. 48.
12 *Ibid.*, pp. 24–5, 26, 41–2.
13 Wollstonecraft, *Vindication of the Rights of Woman*, p. 267.
14 Robinson, *Thoughts*, p. 88.
15 Wakefield, *Reflections*, pp. 13–15, 19–23.
16 Hugh Honour, *Neo-Classicism* (Harmondsworth, Penguin, 1968), pp. 114–22.
17 Williams, *Julia*, i, pp. 145–6.
18 *Ibid.*, ii, p. 141.
19 Wollstonecraft, *Vindication of the Rights of Woman*, p. 174.
20 Wollstonecraft, *Vindication of the Rights of Men*, pp. 57–8.

their persons; the best dress is the simple garb that fits close to the shape.[21] In Holstein she was amused by the grotesque and unwieldy garb of the women, which distorted and concealed the human form.[22] It is entirely in keeping that both Wakefield and Hays should be glad that corsets – a 'vile and unnatural mode of dress' – had gone out of fashion.[23]

It is also an aesthetic of grandeur and dignity, the successor to and antithesis of a rococo aesthetic of frothy prettiness. It is almost a commonplace remark in these texts that true beauty is the result of mental and moral qualities shining in the face. Macaulay Graham quotes the stoic maxim that the wise man alone is beautiful.[24] She also hopes that

> The inventive faculties, which are now pressed into the service of milliners and hair dressers, would be better employed; and the motley shew which society at present sets forth, would give place to a gravity and a dignity of appearance more conformable to the high ideas we have conceived of a rational nature.[25]

Likewise Wollstonecraft distinguishes between pretty women and fine women, and prefers the latter.[26] She commends the beauty of older women, in whom 'vivacity gives place to reason, and to that majestic seriousness of character, which marks maturity'.[27] Miss Milner is admired in *Simple Story* when she dresses with 'dignified simplicity' and her daughter Lady Matilda is dignified too.[28]

'Proper' females can be found endorsing this aesthetic. Hamilton's Hindoo Rajah goes to a ball, and comments on the disfiguring deformity of female dress: 'their robes, instead of falling in easy and graceful folds around their limbs, are extended on huge frames, made of bamboo'.[29] West is not untouched by it when she has the modest Geraldine, tastefully dressed, make a better impression in London than the showy, overdecorated Lady Arabella. We are meant to agree with Sir William Powerscourt, who refuses to allow his wife to wear fantastic headdresses of feathers and flowers. But West also has her doubts about 'classical' attire; evidently she thought that simple gowns which followed the contours of the female body could be too revealing, and Prudentia Homespun reproaches 'the sensual copyists of a Cleopatra or an Aspasia', clad in 'the loose drapery of Grecian Bacchanals'.[30]

[21] *Ibid.*, p. 216.
[22] Wollstonecraft, *Letters Written During a Short Residence*, pp. 242–3.
[23] *Appeal to the Men of Great Britain*, pp. 200–1.
[24] Macaulay Graham, *Letters on Education*, p. 178.
[25] *Ibid.*, pp. 299–300.
[26] Wollstonecraft, *Vindication of the Rights of Woman*, p. 119.
[27] *Ibid.*, p. 147.
[28] Inchbald, *Simple Story*, p. 14.
[29] Hamilton, *Hindoo Rajah*, pp. 164, 175.
[30] West, *Tale of the Times*, i, pp. 4–5.

Surface and inner depths

The neoclassical aesthetic, emphasizing fundamental qualities rather than surface adornment, the serious rather than the showy, the honest rather than the artificial, can be related to Elias's distinction between *Kultur* and *Zivilisation*. In Elias's view, the distinction serves the interests of a middle class seeking to define and assert itself against aristocratic, courtly society. *Zivilisation* is proposed as the mode of behaviour of the latter; it values the surface show of polish, refinement and good manners, the *savoir-faire* which enables social life to go on smoothly and harmoniously. Chesterfield's *Letters to his Son* classically propose this courtly ideal. *Kultur* is thought of as something more; it goes deeper, and the cultivated person in this sense has developed inner qualities that the merely civilized may lack. A civilized self-presentation, as Chesterfield's letters betray, may superficially be agreeable and appealing, without having any basis in moral qualities – 'They [Chesterfield's letters] teach the morals of a whore, and the manners of a dancing master', as Dr Johnson remarked. The middle-class person of *Kultur* is superior to the courtier by virtue of deeply internalized moral, intellectual and aesthetic qualities. Elias's contrast is evident in the generic shift in the latter part of the eighteenth century from the courtesy book, a manual of polished, courtly manners, of externals, to the conduct book, more concerned with moral qualities and the development of the inner self.[31] Nancy Armstrong pays attention to these in her development of Elias's theory. She contends also that the first assertion of middle-class worth and identity was through women.[32] The inner qualities that marked middle-class women off from aristocratic women were the characteristics of domestic femininity and sensibility.

If a sociologist were to draw up cast lists for novels of the 1790s, many could have 'Lady X, villain, a woman of *Zivilisation*', and 'Miss Y, heroine, a woman of *Kultur*'. These clichéd *personae* move through the pages of Robinson, Smith, Williams, Inchbald and West. Perfect examples are to be found in Robinson's *The Widow*. Lady Seymour, Lady Allford and Mrs Vernon are women of fashion, in the circle of the *haut ton*, 'adorned by rank, [and] glittering amidst the luxuries of splendour'. Though Lady Seymour is only a parson's daughter, she is puffed up with aristocratic pride and thinks that birth is more important than talent. These women have a contempt for literature and rural life; they long for the bright lights of the metropolis, for the social whirl, the masked ball, the gambling table. Their self-presentation is confident and forward. They make great show of sexual respectability and

---

[31] Morgan, *Manners, Morals and Class*, pp. 10–13.

[32] Nancy Armstrong, 'The rise of the domestic woman', in Armstrong, Nancy & Tennenhouse, Leonard (eds.), *The Ideology of Conduct: Essays in Literature and the History of Sexuality* (London, Methuen, 1987), pp. 96–7.

will have nothing to do with women whose reputations are dubious; but they coquette and plan adulterous affairs. They despise sensibility, and are immoral and heartless. In a *Don Giovanni*-like scene, Mrs Vernon goes with her friends to laugh at a rural wedding; she flirts with the rustic bridegroom until the bride is driven to try to drown herself in the lake. She writes, 'Pray secure me a box at the opera, at *any price*. I shall strike my name out of the list of annual subscribers to the lying-in hospital; 'tis throwing money away, and encouraging folly'.[33]

Julia, the widow in Robinson's novel, is by contrast distinguished for mental perfections. She is modest and retiring, and of unblemished chastity in thought and deed. She loves rural solitude, domestic quiet and good books. When Mrs Vernon compels a young woman with two small children to leave the shelter of a tree, so that the quality may be protected from the storm without rubbing shoulders with the peasantry, Julia gives the young woman her purse. Julia is a woman of sensibility, though it is well controlled by principle. For both Robinson and Smith, the merely civilized persons who are all surface lack true sensibility; either they exhibit fashionable, 'tonnish' apathy, or their sensibility is affected, a fashion accessory. So in Robinson's *Natural Daughter* the Bad Sister Julia acts sensibility to perfection, cannot eat after meeting a wounded discharged soldier, and is too distressed to help him. The Good Sister Martha whose sensibility is real helps him to turkey and a large glass of madeira, and finds him lodging for the night.

One more quotation from Robinson is in order, from her 'gothic', *Hubert de Sevrac*:

Mlle. de Sevrac, having always lived in a circle, where to *seem*, and not to *be*, was the task of universal labour, fancied that the art of pleasing was more useful than the toil of thinking; and the smile of an approving multitude more gratifying, than the sober commendation of conscious integrity! but when the tongue of flattery was silenced by her changed situation, the voice of Truth began to fascinate her ear, and as the colour of her fortune assumed a darker shade, the light of intellect expanded![34]

This theme runs through the novel. Robinson could be writing about herself in this passage; lame and abandoned, she had fallen from the heights of fashionable sociability to the struggle of literary hackwork. She had certainly begun to think. As a former actress, she was well placed to reflect upon the difference between *seeming* and *being*. So, for the same reason, was Inchbald. In *Nature and Art* there are reflections on being a self of a kind which might occur to an actress and dramatist. Inchbald describes vain or proud selves, who always wish to appear well in the eyes of others; they take their hue, like the chameleon, from surrounding objects and therefore have no integrity or consistency. Always aware of being looked at, their attention

33 Robinson, *The Widow*, i, p. 159.
34 Robinson, *Hubert de Sevrac*, ii, pp. 142–3.

is focused upon themselves; others are to them merely lookers, of no further interest. These are contrasted with authentic selves, of whom the two Henrys, father and son, are examples. The latter are governed by genuine feelings and principles; they think of others and forget the self. The young Henry meets his proud relations, and surveys them, 'not as demanding "what they thought of him," but expressing, almost as plainly as in direct words, "what he thought of them." . . . and as to *himself*, he did not appear to know there was such a person existing: his whole faculties were absorbed in *others'*.35

This is in part a contrast between self-conscious and naïve subjectivities. In Schiller's classic discussion, the naïve person, in a sense more 'primitive' but also more direct and honest, is immersed in what he or she is doing, relatively unreflecting.36 By contrast the more 'advanced' rational or self-conscious person can rarely escape from self-reflection, from an inner division into a self that does and a self that looks on. Many distinguished male thinkers, particularly Hegel and his followers, have attributed a timeless *naïveté* to the feminine self, self-consciousness to the modern masculine self.37 It is interesting that many 1790s female writers take a contrary view, thinking that women, objects of the male gaze and thereby culturally conditioned constantly to appraise themselves, cannot easily escape from a self-consciousness which makes authentic self-expression and genuine relationships with others difficult.38 In Williams's *Julia* we meet Mrs Seymour, vain and selfish, always aware of how she looks, always preparing herself as a sight: 'She spoke to her visitors as if she were interested in what she said, but she scarcely knew what it was. She was not thinking of the persons who had just entered: her concern was that her manner of receiving them might be thought graceful by the spectators.'39

Something resembling the *Kultur/Zivilisation* antithesis is at the heart of Wollstonecraft's *Vindication of the Rights of Woman*, and it is a theme in many of her other writings. She calls on women to cultivate their minds, and lavishes scorn on those dolls whose sole concern is to adorn and prettify their persons. The *Vindication* is as it were an extended commentary on Macaulay Graham's injunction to 'look for something more solid in women, than a mere outside'.40 As her other *Vindication* makes plain – and here her

35 Inchbald, *Nature and Art*, p. 22; see also pp. 13, 21, 25, 41.

36 Friedrich Schiller, *On the Naïve and Sentimental in Literature* (*Über naïve und sentimentalische Dichtung*, 1795) (Manchester, Carcanet, 1981), pp. 29–30, 38–9, 42.

37 G. W. F. Hegel, *Philosophy of Right* (*Naturrecht und Staatswissenschaft im Grundrisse: Grundlinien der Philosophie des Rechts,* 1821) (Oxford, Oxford University Press, 1952), pp. 114–15.

38 Cf. John Berger, *Ways of Seeing* (Harmondsworth, Penguin, 1972), p. 47.

39 Williams, *Julia*, i, pp. 31–2; see also pp. 35–6, 44.

40 Macaulay Graham, *Letters on Education*, p. 50.

neoclassicizing seriousness connects with that idealization of plain-speaking honesty so strong in dissenting culture[41] – she is hostile to all show and sham. She has a strong sense of the voice with which she wishes to speak. She believes in sincerity and authenticity, directness and plainness, in uttering her innermost thoughts and feelings without reserve or concealment, disdaining all tricks of rhetoric – in explicit contrast to the voice of the arch-rhetorician, Edmund Burke. Burke was moved to tears by the thought of the starry glitter of Marie Antoinette and her court, now fallen from their high estate. Wollstonecraft rather perceives 'depravity of morals under the specious mask of refined manners'.[42] She does not believe that Burke's tears are genuine; they are show too. He is a cold romantic character, and romantic to her means 'false, or rather artificial, feelings'. His passion is not real, and therefore he has been forced to ransack his head for 'stale tropes and cold rodomontade'.[43]

All of Wollstonecraft's writings are pervaded by these contrasted models of subjectivity, and by a language of surface display versus inner depth, appearance versus reality, artificial sentiments versus genuine feelings. In a review of Williams's *Julia* which runs the gamut of this language, she praises the author because 'the reader of taste will never be disgusted with theatrical attitudes, artificial feelings, or a display of studied unimpassioned false grace. . . . [E]very sentiment is uttered in an original way, which proves that it comes directly from the heart with the artless energy of feeling, that rather wishes to be understood than admired'.[44] She criticizes the French nobility on the grounds that 'Insincere in their manners, their taste for the arts, eloquence, etc. was artificial; in short, their politeness and finesse undermined the energy naturally fostered by truth'.[45] In another review, she laments that 'the world is filled with people who feel by rule, and only see what others have seen'.[46] Elsewhere she contrasts 'imitations of nature' with 'servile copies of models'.[47] These were to become stock themes of romantic aesthetics too; from neoclassicism to romanticism was but a short step. This was Wollstonecraft's *Weltanschauung*, and from its point of view she was urging women to slough off conventional ways of looking at themselves and the world, to view themselves with their own eyes rather than as it were with men's eyes as objects for men, and to enter into themselves in order to discover and to express their own authentic feelings.

'Proper' female writers make use of this discourse too, but sometimes

[41] William Stafford, 'Dissenting religion translated into politics: Godwin's *Political Justice*', *History of Political Thought*, 1:2 (1980), 296.

[42] Wollstonecraft, *Vindication of the Rights of Man*, p. 39.

[43] *Ibid.*, pp. 28–9.

[44] *Analytical Review*, 7 (May 1790), 98.

[45] *Ibid.*, 12 (February 1792), 219.

[46] *Ibid.*, 8 (October 1790), 175.

[47] *Ibid.*, 9 (January 1791), 44.

with different emphases. More in her *Strictures* came closer to Wollstonecraft than she would have liked to think. She developed the contrast between mere manners and morals, and just like Wollstonecraft deplored the cultivation of surface, of beauty, of weakness and excessive sensibility. Sometimes the similarity of language and example is quite striking. Still, she was not like Wollstonecraft concerned with authentic female self-expression; such an idea would have struck her as excessively individualistic, even selfish. West too criticizes women who prefer external accomplishments to mental treasures.[48] She mocks the impertinence and frippery which passes for taste and elegance, 'the refinement which banished serious discussion from polished circles ... the vanity of universal acquaintance [and] those restraints upon the emotions of a genuine nature which fashion prescribes and insipidity adopts'.[49] But we cannot imagine Prudentia Homespun engaged in the exploration and expression of her authentic inner self; she is too down-to-earth and old-fashioned for that.

Wollstonecraft's ideal of *Kultur* does not square readily with Armstrong's account of it as an ideal of middle-class domestic *femininity*. Certainly it repudiates one kind of femininity, a kind which Armstrong would label as aristocratic. But it is not obvious that Wollstonecraft's cultivated, feeling, rational, authentic woman is *ipso facto* feminine. She may be a good wife and mother as a result, but that is not the point; she is proposed as an admirable *human*, and the model would do equally well for her husband. Wakefield fits the Armstrong thesis a little better. She is a critic of female education devoted to 'the attainment of attractive qualities, shewy superficial accomplishments, polished manners, and in one word, the whole science of pleasing',[50] and thinks that 'purity of sentiment ... is as much superior to its substitute, external manners, as is a real gem to one that is artificial'.[51] Too much exhibiting the person in public places is subversive of domestic happiness,[52] even for women in high life; she calls the female nobility to mental cultivation so that they may better perform their domestic duties and engage in the noble enterprise of the reformation of vice.[53]

Gender

To what extent, then, are the subjectivities proposed and explored by 'unsex'd' and 'proper' females gendered subjectivities? Are the selves that 'unsex'd' and 'proper' females would nurture *feminine* selves? Do they endorse a sharp gender

[48] West, *Tale of the Times*, i, p. 74.
[49] *Ibid.*, i, pp. 50–1.
[50] Wakefield, *Reflections*, p. 30.
[51] *Ibid.*, p. 22.
[52] *Ibid.*, p. 77.
[53] *Ibid.*, pp. 88, 97.

polarity, and if so, how do they conceptualize it? Where do they think the gender differences lie? Do they think of gender as natural or artificial, inescapable or escapable? Do any of them think of it as a matter of choice, as an enacted or chosen mode of self-presentation? Is there any celebration of cross-dressing? Do any of them aim at androgyny, at a self detached from gender, a *human* self? And if they do, how is that androgyny conceived? As a balance of 'masculine' and 'feminine' characteristics, or as leaning towards one or the other pole? Do any of them wish to emulate masculine characteristics, or conversely celebrate femininity?

There has recently been considerable emphasis upon a sharpening of the gender polarity at the end of the eighteenth and the beginning of the nineteenth centuries.[54] It has been argued that gender differences were increasingly conceptualized as *natural*, rooted in the biological body; men's and women's bodies and minds were physiologically different. But awareness of this way of thinking about gender should not lead us to ignore the fact that there was a rival tradition, growing out of associationist psychology, which contended that men's and women's minds were essentially identical, and that differences of mind and character were entirely the result of education and circumstance. It has been claimed that Catharine Macaulay Graham 'was unique in her categorical denial of innate sexual differences';[55] but this is quite wrong, as Macaulay's own insistence that 'the doctrine of innate ideas ... [is] in a great measure exploded among the learned' implies;[56] 'philosophic radicals' and their precursors in England and France such as Helvétius, Condorcet, Hartley and Godwin were explicit environmentalists. The 'sociological' approach pioneered, for example, by Montesquieu and the Scottish historical school also tended to explain differences contextually. At the very least Wollstonecraft, Hays and Fenwick were environmentalists too.

Environmentalism sustains what we might call an extreme position, advanced by Macaulay Graham and Wollstonecraft. Macaulay Graham declares herself to be an associationist, in the tradition of Locke and Hartley. She thinks with them that the mind of the newly born child has no characters written upon it, and that therefore character results from experience and education putting their stamp upon the mind. She clearly believes this to be true of the sexes, and that therefore sexual character is artificial. She also has a clear conception of 'femininity' as a culturally encouraged affectation of weakness, helplessness and irrationality and an obsession with appearance. These characteristics function to render women sexually attractive to licentious men, while depriving women of virtue, reason and dignity.[57] Macaulay

54 Drohr Wahrmann, '*Percy*'s prologue: from gender play to gender panic in eighteenth-century England', *Past & Present*, 159 (1998), 113–60.

55 Florence S. Boos, 'Catherine [*sic*] Macaulay's Letters on Education', *University of Michigan Papers in Women's Studies*, 2:2 (1976), 65.

56 Macaulay Graham, *Letters on Education*, p. 203.

57 *Ibid.*, pp. 213, 220.

Graham wants men and women to have exactly the same education of the mind, and roughly speaking her ideal, outlined in the following passage, is an androgynous one: 'I know not what you may think of my method, Hortensia, which I must acknowledge to carry the stamp of singularity; but for my part, I am sanguine enough to expect to turn out of my hands a careless, modest beauty, grave, manly, noble, full of strength and majesty.'[58] But only roughly; there are equivocations and problems here. Macaulay Graham still feels it necessary to mention beauty in this very short list of excellences, and it is difficult not to think of 'modest' as a gender marker. At the very least it means a sexual reticence especially recommended to women; and 'modest' carries a further connotation of gentle unassertiveness. These are dangerous notions, potentially very disempowering for women. 'Manly' is a slippery word, capable of meaning 'humanly'; but though Macaulay Graham is recommending *human* excellences to both men and women, nevertheless that word is testimony to her belief that these excellences have been associated hitherto with the character of a man rather than with that of a woman.

Wollstonecraft was influenced by Macaulay Graham's *Letters on Education*, and at the time of her *Vindication of the Rights of Woman* was to a large extent adopting her position. She bases herself upon the theory of associationism and malleability of character and calls upon women to become rational and strong-minded. Even more than Macaulay Graham, she excoriates any affectation of 'feminine' frailty and light-mindedness. Like Macaulay Graham she has a tendency to slip into referring to her ideal of character for women as a *manly* character. In the *Vindication* she says of Macaulay Graham that 'In her style of writing, indeed, no sex appears,'[59] but in her review of Macaulay's *Letters on Education* she refers to her as 'this masculine and fervid writer'.[60] I do not think there is any confusion or contradiction here, for she explains what she means in the *Vindication*, calling upon women to imitate 'the manly virtues, or, more properly speaking, the attainment of those talents and virtues, the exercise of which ennobles the human character, and which raises females in the scale of animal being, when they are comprehensively termed mankind'.[61] The reference in the quotation to the scale of animal being is an important clue to the way Wollstonecraft thinks; looking at the two *Vindications* we find a tendency to define 'man' (and also 'woman') by contrast with 'animal' or 'brute',[62] and an unwillingness to define 'man' by contrast with 'woman'. Wollstonecraft really does wish to demote one binary and privilege another. But if Wollstonecraft is not confused or contradictory, we have to say that her

---

58 *Ibid.*, p. 221.

59 Wollstonecraft, *Vindication of the Rights of Woman*, p. 188.

60 *Analytical Review*, 8 (November 1790), 241.

61 Wollstonecraft, *Vindication of the Rights of Woman*, p. 75.

62 E.g., Wollstonecraft, *Vindication of the Rights of Man*, pp. 12, 41; *Vindication of the Rights of Woman*, pp. 75, 77, 79, 242.

version of androgyny in the *Vindication* leans towards the conventionally masculine. Her praise of 'manly' virtues goes with her sense that the human virtues have hitherto been more exhibited by men than by women, and this implies a derogation of the 'feminine'.

Wollstonecraft does in one place criticize overbearing women, recommending modesty instead.[63] But her chapter devoted to modesty sets out to explicate the ideal in such a form that it will no longer be a marker of gender. She distinguishes its two senses, of sexual reserve and avoidance of over-assertiveness. She defines the second sense as 'a just opinion of ourselves'. The modest man or woman will not think more highly of him or herself than he or she merits, but on the other hand will not be merely humble, irresolute and diffident; on the contrary, such a person will be capable, at the right time, of determination and assertion.[64] In the sexual sense, Wollstonecraft denies that modesty should be a peculiarly feminine trait. Her account of modesty in this sense broadens it out from the merely sexual. Obscene and sexually suggestive talk should be avoided by both sexes, but so should most explicit reference to bodily functions. More generally, obtruding one's corporeality upon others is to be avoided; girls should not sleep in the same room, or wash together. If I am interpreting Wollstonecraft's rather coy language correctly, women should not use the commode in front of their maids, even if they take care to cover their legs.[65] We should not offend members of our domestic circle by appearing before them dirty and dishevelled in the morning. The value of modesty, as defined here, is to do with self-respect and dignity, and a concern not to cause the slightest embarrassment or discomfiture to others. It is in fact that scrupulous care to avoid obtruding the fluids and processes of the body upon the attention of others, whose evolution Elias has tracked in *The Civilizing Process*: 'There is one rule relative to behaviour that, I think, ought to regulate every other: and it is simply to cherish such an habitual respect for mankind as may prevent us from disgusting a fellow-creature for the sake of a present indulgence.'[66] As such, it is not a gendered pattern of behaviour.

Though Wollstonecraft's *Vindication of the Rights of Woman* proposes an androgynous ideal, it also conveys a strongly delineated picture of existing, disapproved, gender difference – virtually all the disapproval falling upon females. Degraded femininity is characterized by cultivated frailty, weakness, helplessness, trivial-mindedness, but also by excessive sensibility. Sensibility in itself is identified as a feminine characteristic; she quotes the conventional view (which she does not share) 'that the sexes ought not to be compared; man was made to reason, woman to feel: and that together, flesh

63 *Ibid.*, p. 272.
64 *Ibid.*, pp. 207–8.
65 *Ibid.*, p. 214.
66 *Ibid.*, p. 226.

and spirit, they make the most perfect whole, by blending happily reason and sensibility into one character'.[67] So she describes Williams's *Letters from France* as 'truly feminine', the work of a writer with a heart 'accustomed to the melting mood', 'true to every soft emotion'.[68] In the *Vindication* she has very little good to say of sensibility, indeed no antijacobin writer could be more harsh: it is a polished instinct, more animal than human; when not enlarged by reason into benevolence, it is selfish; it is a disabling badge of weakness, and it opens women up to sexual seduction.

Here then we have a forthright doctrine about gender. There is a clear gender binary; it is artificial not natural; it is wholly bad and should be done away with. The ideal for men and women is a masculine-leaning androgyny, and women should only be women in bed: 'This desire of being always women, is the very consciousness that degrades the sex. Excepting with a lover, I must repeat with emphasis, a former observation, – it would be well if they were only agreeable or rational companions.'[69]

How widely was this 'extreme' doctrine shared, by 'unsex'd' and 'proper' females? Eliza Fenwick, a member of the Godwin circle, writes this Wollstonecraftian doctrine into *Secresy*. The heroine Sibella is a kind of child of nature, brought up in seclusion from the world and from the corruptions of society. As a consequence she is to some extent free of what we would call sexual stereotyping. She has received a 'masculine' education, she has no feminine fears of darkness, ghosts or other irrational terrors and is sufficiently lacking in sexual reserve to declare her passion for Clement Montgomery and to give herself to him. The other heroine, Caroline Ashburn, is strong-minded and assertive, the monitress to whom men and women turn for advice; she has sufficient courage to confront the stern patriarch, George Valmont, in his castle and demand that he release Sibella. But there are hints that Fenwick does not wish to abolish gender difference altogether: Caroline Ashburn insists that educated women need not lack softness.[70]

No other 'unsex'd' or 'proper' female subscribes entirely to Macaulay Graham's and Wollstonecraft's masculine-leaning androgynous ideal. Amused or hostile mockery of 'masculine' women is widespread, for example in More's sketch of the latest fashions in female dress and deportment: 'the bold and independent beauty, the intrepid female, the hoyden, the huntress, and the archer; the swinging arms, the confident address, the regimental, and the four-in-hand'.[71] None of the writers being considered here has a good word to say for women who don male attire, nor for the masquerade which occasionally licenses them to do so. Those who would annihilate gender distinctions fail to understand where the

---

[67] *Ibid.*, p. 139.
[68] *Analytical Review*, 8 (December 1790), 431–2.
[69] Wollstonecraft, *Vindication of the Rights of Woman*, p. 181.
[70] Fenwick, *Secresy*, p. 295.
[71] More, *Strictures*, i, p. 68.

true happiness of women lies: 'Each sex has its proper excellencies, which would be lost were they melted down into the common character by the fusion of the new philosophy.'[72] West too has a fling at 'dashers' who drive four-in-hand and lay wagers,[73] and Hamilton pokes fun at the Amazonian Miss Ardent who looks forward to the day when women, at last acknowledged as the superior sex, will seize the reins of government and guide the steeds of war.[74] In 'proper' females this is only to be expected, but 'unsex'd' ones line up against the Amazons too.

Hays, in her obituary of Wollstonecraft, commemorates her for her combination of masculine and feminine qualities: she was 'no less distinguished by admirable talents and a masculine tone of understanding, than by active humanity, exquisite sensibility, and endearing qualities of heart'; hers was 'impassioned reasoning'.[75] If this is an androgynous ideal, because of its praise of the conventionally feminine it is not quite the same androgyny as in Wollstonecraft's own *Vindication of the Rights of Woman*. In her *Letters and Essays*, written shortly after the *Vindication*, Hays notes that 'some men of real good sense and candour' have thought that Wollstonecraft carried the idea of there being no sexual character too far,[76] and the impression is left that Hays thinks them not altogether wrong. By 1798, the *Appeal to the Men of Great Britain* is declaring that the manners of the two sexes must be somewhat different so as to render them completely pleasing to each other, and is lightly disapproving of the fashion for military attire and deportment for women, rather in the style of Hannah More.[77] Women have much greater delicacy than men; a bold and overbearing character is more disagreeable in them; nature blends vivacity and tenderness in the female character and women have more sensibility than men.[78]

In the novels of Smith and Robinson we find similar endorsements of gender difference, and criticisms of 'masculine' women. For example Geraldine, the ideal woman in *Desmond*, has strength of understanding but unlike many intellectual women 'no presumption; none of that anxiety to be heard, or that dictatorial tone of conversation that has so often disgusted and repulsed me'.[79] Orlando's 'manly tenderness' is contrasted with the 'lively sensibility' of his sisters, and Miss Roker, one of the villainesses of the plot, wears a riding habit, carries a cane in one hand, puts the other on her hip and speaks in a loud and masculine voice.[80] Lady Llancarrick, an obtrusive and harmful gossip, wears masculine attire, fancies herself a genius and immod-

72 *Ibid.*, ii, p. 21.
73 West, *Tale of the Times*, ii, p. 89.
74 Hamilton, *Hindoo Rajah*, p. 262.
75 *Monthly Magazine*, 4 (September 1797), 232–3.
76 Hays, *Letters and Essays*, p. 21.
77 *Appeal to the Men of Great Britain*, pp. 187–91.
78 *Ibid.*, pp. 32–3, 121, 127, 148.
79 Smith, *Desmond*, p. 142.
80 Smith, *Old Manor House*, p. 459.

estly likes to draw attention to herself.[81] Disapproved characters in *The Young Philosopher* include effeminate men and masculine women; Smith does not favour an ungendered self-presentation, and all her heroines are conventionally beautiful and modest in both senses. Robinson demands that women get the same education as men, but insists that 'education cannot *unsex* a woman ... tenderness of soul, and a love of social intercourse, will still be her's [sic]; even though she become a rational friend, and an intellectual companion'.[82] In *Walsingham*, Mr Hanbury thinks that masculine lessons of improvement for women will not degender them: 'The art of pleasing will be the natural inmate of her bosom; she will, by instinct, cultivate the softer graces.'[83] In the same novel the hero is shocked to meet depraved women in high society who gamble, swear and proposition him, and who toss off large goblets of champagne at a gulp.[84]

There is little support, then, for an androgyny after the manner of Wollstonecraft and Macaulay Graham, either from 'proper' or 'unsex'd' females. But now we come up against something curious; when we question more carefully what these authors say about gender boundaries, they begin to look rather unstable and insubstantial, feeble barriers that would not resist much pushing. The gender difference looks somewhat ephemeral under scrutiny, and even 'proper' females turn out not to be strict enforcers. This is most apparent if we examine what they have to say about mental power, intellect, rationality, genius.

Gender and genius

Wollstonecraft abstains from claiming complete mental equality of the sexes. In part this stems from a judicious sense that until men and women are educated equally, a definitive decision will be premature. But also she thinks that strength of body and strength of mind are not unconnected; perhaps from the constitution of their bodies, 'men seem to be designed by Providence to attain a greater degree of virtue', and, implicitly, of mental power as well.[85] Of course Wollstonecraft disputes any *fundamental* difference and inequality of mind, and calls for equal education.

More proposes that women are both different and inferior. Men have superior strength of body and a firmer texture of mind, more suited to the deep and daring scenes of government and war, to science and commerce and to those professions which demand a higher reach and a wider range of powers. Women by contrast have more softness and refinement, delicacy and

81 Smith, *Montalbert*, iii, pp. 118, 173-4.
82 Robinson, *Thoughts*, pp. 55-6.
83 Robinson, *Walsingham*, i, p. 232.
84 *Ibid.*, ii, pp. 97-9, 118-19.
85 Wollstonecraft, *Vindication of the Rights of Woman*, pp. 95, 109-10.

quickness of perception, nice discernment, acute observation and intuitive penetration. Superior women may equal superior men in single faculties, but the mind of the superior man will be better as a whole.[86] To a present-day reader this is a rehash of the worst stereotypes, as bad as Rousseau. But then More proceeds to undermine her own conventional view of gender. Of course, weak and silly men are inferior to first-rate women.[87] It will be impossible to decide on the degree of difference between male and female intellects before women are given proper education.[88] And how should women be educated? Not exactly the same as men – there are too many indecent passages in Greek and Latin texts, for example. But what More recommends is an education designed to *counteract* what she has identified as the gender characteristics of women's minds.[89] They should engage in serious study designed to harden the mind, including not only geography and natural history but also logic and philosophy.[90] They should learn the art of close reasoning.[91] More may have thought that she was a foe of the masculinization of women; others were not so sure. Myers contends that men saw her as subversive of gender. Cobbett referred to her as an 'old Bishop in petticoats', and Mary Russell Mitford found her 'masculine not in a good sense ... she writes like a man in petticoats, or a woman in breeches. All her books have a loud voice, and a stern frown, and a long stride'.[92] By the standards of some of their contemporaries, however, the position of More and even of Wollstonecraft on female intellect is decidedly timid.

In spite of her hints to the effect that Wollstonecraft went too far in denying differences of sexual character, Hays authored an uncompromising assertion of intellectual equality in 1796. Her argument is based on associationist philosophy in Godwin's version. The inequality that exists took its rise in a very small degree of superior bodily strength on the part of the men. This enabled them, in barbarous times, to subjugate women and subsequently to prevent them from fully realizing their bodily and mental powers (this narrative was a cliché of enlightenment history).[93] Despite these disadvantages there have been outstanding women – for example Semiramis, Zenobia, Boadicea, Sappho, Hypatia, the Queen Catherines of the north, Elizabeth I, Mesdames de Chatelet and Dacier, Mrs Macaulay – who have vindicated female mental power.[94] There is a similar list in the *Appeal to the Men of Great Britain*. In the same work, the author declares that mind is of no sex,

---

86 More, *Strictures*, ii, pp. 21–6.
87 *Ibid.*, ii, p. 27n.
88 *Ibid.*, ii, pp. 28–9.
89 *Ibid.*, i, p. 163.
90 *Ibid.*, i, pp. 164–5.
91 *Ibid.*, i, p. 166.
92 Myers, 'A peculiar protection', pp. 241, 227.
93 See Tomaselli, 'The enlightenment debate on women'.
94 Hays, 'Letter on A. B.'s strictures', 469–70.

and offers arguments like those Mill would later put forward in his *Subjection of Women*. We will not be in a position to assess the relative abilities of men and women until we have studied both sexes in all the different situations, circumstances and varieties of human existence; it cannot be proved that men are better fitted to govern women than women are to govern themselves, because female self-government has never had a fair trial. The fact that women have always been subordinated does not prove that women are naturally inferior; it merely proves that they have never been given their chance.[95]

Robinson's *Thoughts on the Condition of Women* demands that women be permitted 'to assert a majesty of mind', and to receive exactly the same classical education as men.[96] She disagrees with More that the classics are unsuitable for women because of their explicitness about sex, as well she might; Robinson knew too much to be easily embarrassed, and More knew very little.[97] She furnishes a six-page list of British female literary characters living in the eighteenth century. 'In what is woman inferior to man? In some instances, but not always, in corporal strength: in activity of mind, she is his equal.'[98] There is nothing tentative or modest about Robinson's stance: 'I argue thus, and my assertions are incontrovertible.'[99] Why do men ridicule masculine women? (For 'a masculine woman' read 'a woman of enlightened understanding.) Because men are afraid to compete with them on equal terms.[100] These views are carried into her novels. The Marchioness de Vallorie in *Vancenza* is beautiful but also studious, an adept at classical learning. Walsingham's mother was 'studious', and in the same novel Isabella's dying father wants her instructed 'in the more solid and masculine lessons of improvement, such as form the scholar and dignify the attributes of reason'.[101] Gertrude in *The False Friend* is characterized by 'mental splendour'. In Robinson's *Angelina* we meet Miss Juliana Pengwynn, learned in the European languages both ancient and modern, whose conversation erupts with quotations and historical allusions. None of the men can match her for learning. She is a comic character, but heroic and likeable too; a transgressive assertion of female intellect.

It must be insisted that mental equality is not the opinion of 'unsex'd' females only. 'That men are naturally stronger than women is evident; but strength of mind has no necessary connexion with strength of body,' declares Edgeworth.[102] She would develop the intellects of women, teach them

95 *Appeal to the Men of Great Britain*, pp. 34, 103–4, 108–9.
96 Robinson, *Thoughts*, p. 83.
97 *Ibid.*, p. 68n.
98 *Ibid.*, p. 17.
99 *Ibid.*, p. 3.
100 *Ibid.*, pp. 72–3.
101 Robinson, *Walsingham*, i, p. 232.
102 Edgeworth, *Letters for Literary Ladies*, p. 29.

chemistry and mathematics, and above all cultivate their reasoning faculty. Like Wollstonecraft she is highly critical of sensibility, and effectively denies the gender contrast, as far as the fundamental qualities of mind are concerned. The reader is left wondering whether she has left any secure basis for her endorsement of separate spheres. West's model mother Mrs Williams had her mind strengthened by her widower father, who initiated her into the severer studies, commonly confined to male pupils. She learnt classics, to think justly and to reason correctly. Her deficiencies in feminine attainments – specified as 'graceful polish' and 'delicacy' – were remedied by a fortunate female friendship.[103] Hamilton praises the Scots of the recent past for educating their daughters as well as their sons: Christianity teaches that men and women have equal souls, which means that they are rational beings occupying a station of equal dignity in the intelligent creation.[104] Burney gives us Eugenia in *Camilla*, who as a result of a chapter of accidents receives a scholarly classical education such as a boy might get at public school and university. Others laugh at her for this, but Burney's authorial voice disapproves of the laughter, not the learning; she is implicitly saying that girls have as much talent for it as boys and Eugenia is presented as heroic and noble-minded. In fact, no 'unsex'd' or 'proper' female dissents from the view that (middle-class) women are capable of and should receive an education based on a tough curriculum, designed to strengthen their reasoning powers, identical to or very little different from that which (middle-class) men receive. More and others add that there is no danger that learning will distract women from domestic duties; if anything it will substitute for and discourage worldly dissipation, the round of luxurious sociability.[105]

Though Rousseau had said that the achievements of genius were beyond the reach of women,[106] the attribution of genius to women by 'unsex'd' and 'proper' females is not uncommon. At this time, the word had not yet settled into the meaning privileged by romantic aesthetics, i.e. an absolutely outstanding, inexplicable, unteachable giftedness and originality possessed by very few men.[107] In the 1790s it is more likely to mean a more widely diffused but nevertheless high degree of ability, a kind of flair distinguishable from learned skills, perhaps especially in the creative arts. Wollstonecraft finds the spell of genius in Radcliffe's *Italian*.[108] Robinson attributes genius of the first order to Wollstonecraft and Macaulay.[109] In *The Advantages of Education*, Maria loves the enthusiasm of genius which she finds in poetry,

[103] West, *Advantages of Education*, pp. 96–7, 101.
[104] Hamilton, *Hindoo Rajah*, pp. 87–8, 130–1.
[105] More, *Strictures*, ii, pp. 148–51.
[106] Rousseau, *Émile*, p. 488.
[107] Penelope Murray (ed.), *Genius: the History of an Idea* (Oxford, Blackwell, 1989), pp. 2–4.
[108] *Analytical Review*, 25 (May 1797), 516.
[109] Robinson, *Thoughts*, p. 12.

and chooses as her favourite an 'Ode to the Imagination'. Since the ode is supplied by the author, is West claiming genius for herself?[110] Radcliffe's Adeline in *The Romance of the Forest* writes poetry and has natural genius. Emily in *Udolpho* not only learns Latin and English to go with her native French; she also has 'native genius' revealed by her proficiency in the elegant arts.[111] Rosalie in Smith's *Montalbert* is a woman of high intelligence and genius. In order to appreciate these attributions we should call to mind that they were uttered at a time when the best English novelists were women and when there were a number of distinguished female artists and several celebrated female poets. The genius of women, according to the definition of the time, was salient then; genius could not easily be used as a gender marker to distinguish between male and female minds, and to downgrade the latter.

Gender and sensibility

Do 'unsex'd' and 'proper' females cite sensibility as a gender marker? Do their accounts of female subjectivity recommend or disapprove of it? As remarked in Chapter 2,[112] 'sensibility' was used without definite boundaries, overlapping with and sometimes including sentiment, passion, sympathy and imagination. In this way sensibility is 'not reason', and perhaps this should be thought of as a Lacanian binary based upon the gender binary. If so, gender will not correlate with sex, for it will scarcely be contended that men do not or should not exhibit passion, sympathy and imagination.

We have already seen that Wollstonecraft thought that sensibility *was* a gender marker, and that her call for females to become humans rather than women implied a repression of sensibility, or at least its subordination to reason. That was her view at the time of the *Vindication of the Rights of Woman*, and in her *Historical and Moral View of the Origin and Progress of the French Revolution* she adopts the same opinion. But in her *Scandinavian Letters* of 1796 she wrote in a very different voice; readers admired the work for her self-revelation in it as a woman of sensibility. Had Wollstonecraft regendered herself, returned to the feminine?

It would not be difficult to make a collection of remarks by 'unsex'd' and 'proper' females associating sensibility especially with women. But when their texts are read whole, it becomes increasingly difficult to find in them a clear gender map drawn in terms of sensibility. Sensibility is associated with women and is celebrated in Robinson's novels, some of which are obviously liable to the charges levelled by the antijacobins. Julia, the heroine of *The*

110 West, *Advantages of Education*, ii, p. 83.
111 Radcliffe, *Udolpho*, p. 3.
112 Readers may wish to remind themselves of the dimensions and evaluations of sensibility, briefly outlined on pp. 61–2.

Widow, has 'the soft, the irresistible *sensibility* so peculiar to the females of Britain'.[113] *Angelina* is a sentimental novel, with all the clichés and no criticism of sensibility in women or men, nor any suggestion of any need to control it. There is a perfect sentimental hero in Sir George Fairford. The reader encounters characters who weep, faint and almost die of grief. Sensibility is expressed in romantic effusions which More and West would surely have found ridiculous and offensive: lovers worship and adore the celestial, perfect objects of their love. By the late 1790s, perhaps as a result of attacks by conservative critics, Robinson's attitude to sensibility revealed more ambiguity. Walsingham, who is presented as a man of sensibility, ends up seducing Amelia Woodford, whom he has mistaken, at a masquerade, for Isabella, the woman he loves; Amelia yields because she is passionately in love with him. In her letters in *The False Friend* Gertrude expresses her aching longing for her guardian, Lord Denmore; no seduction occurs because, though she does not know it, he is her father. But she dies of grief when Denmore is killed in a duel, and the truth revealed. Ostensibly both *Walsingham* and *The False Friend* are meant as critiques of excessive sensibility, but arguably the moral is subverted by the tendency, which is to reveal the power of sensibility and to a certain extent to praise it. Robinson was not willing to give up sensibility in the face of conservative assaults. In her last novel, *The Natural Daughter*, ambiguity is resolved by drawing a contrast between the false, showy, depraved sensibility of Julia and the true, active, benevolent and even heroic sensibility of Martha.

If we set on one side Wollstonecraft's early 1790s denunciations of sensibility, and the novels by Hays and Robinson which can be read as dangerous celebrations of it, we find that other texts by 'unsex'd' and 'proper' females are not so far apart in their evaluations of sensibility – though this is partly because the meaning they give to the word is fluid and variable. There is a unanimity – and this embraces Hays and Robinson – in denouncing affected sensibility, sensibility as an accessory, a fashionable style of self-presentation. There is unanimity too in opposing sensibility so excessive that it becomes destructive. Destruction in this context is more likely to mean a self-destroying yielding to grief, a lack of firmness in facing up to the disappointments and realities of life, than sexual lapses.

A common move is to contrast sensibility with stoic apathy, which inevitably results in a favourable evaluation of the former. This is a stock theme in Smith's novels, for example. In her preface to her well-known translation of Epictetus, Elizabeth Carter had found much to commend in stoicism, but not its cultivation of apathy; for Christianity teaches that we must care, that we must love one another. Sensibility meaning sympathy for others *of the right kind* is universally commended. It must be active sympathy, helping others in distress, rather than a passive collapse into floods of

---

[113] Robinson, *The Widow*, i, pp. 176–7.

tears. Commonly too it is argued that sympathy must be generalized, its individual, personal feeling combined as it were with the universality of reason. Wollstonecraft judges that sensibility directed only at those near to us is merely an extended selfishness; Macaulay Graham praises 'that tenderness of feeling which produces the most valuable of all excellencies, an unconfined benevolence'.[114] To recommend *general* as opposed to *partial* benevolence, general benevolence which emulates God's love of all creation, is a cliché of the religious thought of the eighteenth century.[115]

The character of More's religious beliefs prevented her from being an out-and-out foe of sensibility. For she was an evangelical, and evangelicalism was a religion of the heart. Conversion is a turning of the heart towards God; but to say this implies the need for a feeling heart.[116] More draws a distinction between the amiable sensibility of the *heart*, and the sensibility of the *nerves*; the latter 'was easily found or feigned; till a false and excessive display of feeling became so predominant, as to bring in question that true tenderness, without which, though a woman may be worthy, she can never be amiable'.[117] More pens the most trenchant criticism in her later chapter 'On the danger of an ill-directed sensibility'; but it is by no means a simple repudiation of sensibility. More begins by recognizing that a person may have too little sensibility, with feelings starved of native energy, deadened affections and a cold, dull, selfish spirit.[118] The sensibility of the heart impels women to do good to others, and to love God. Though it can and should motivate men too, women have an advantage here, because of the vividness of their sensibility. She goes so far as to imply that their tender and lively feelings make it easier for women to be good Christians.[119] The religious value of sensibility is advanced by other female authors, 'unsex'd' and 'proper': 'Sensibility of heart, if not quenched by sensual indulgence, ever leads to piety, and guides us to the source of all loveliness and excellence: the precepts and duties of religion are all included in benevolence – for "God is love."'[120]

Both Hays and Radcliffe maintain that the sensibility aroused by contemplation of the grandeur and beauty of nature leads to a sense of God's greatness and goodness. And though *sensibility* may sometimes be a target of criticism, *heart* never is – even though no clear and consistent distinction between sensibility and heart is to be found in any of the texts. Even Wollstonecraft in her two Vindications commends heart. Sometimes she equates it with conscience, but its connection with feeling is never lost.

114 Macaulay Graham, *Letters on Education*, p. 105.
115 Stafford, 'Dissenting religion', 290–1.
116 More, *Strictures*, ii, p. 244.
117 *Ibid.*, i, p. 67.
118 *Ibid.*, ii, pp. 95–6.
119 *Ibid.*, ii, p. 31.
120 Hays, *Letters and Essays*, p. 200.

Some 'unsex'd' females also contend that sensibility is a condition of, or at least may contribute to, great achievements, agreeing as it were with Pope's couplet, 'On life's vast ocean diversely we sail; / Reason the card, but passion is the gale'.[121] Reason's map will get us nowhere without the driving forces of passion, of which sensibility is a part; but those forces are threatening if we do not steer well. So Macaulay thinks that persons of quick and lively parts, great activity of mind and lively sensibility may be original geniuses and rise to the highest fame; but if their passions are not under sufficient control, they may act a mad and ridiculous part in the world.[122] This came to be Wollstonecraft's view also; in her 1797 essay on poetry, she equated extreme sensibility with genius.[123] By the time of her last novel she had come to think that 'True sensibility . . . is the auxiliary of virtue, and the soul of genius'.[124] But when she wrote of her heroine, 'What a creative power has an affectionate heart! There are beings who cannot live without loving, as poets love; and who feel the electric spark of genius',[125] the message is two-edged. Maria's sensibility is a high quality, but it leads her to fall in love with a man who does not live up to the image of him created by her passionate imagination. Hays promotes sensibility on these grounds with some enthusiasm. She quotes Rousseau: 'Common men know nothing of violent sorrows, nor do great passions ever break out in weak minds. Energy of sentiment is the characteristic of a noble soul.'[126] The very antithesis of reason and sensibility is questioned by Hays; reason is the auxiliary of passion, or rather, passion is the generative principle of reason, passion arouses the energy of mind.[127] These are the opinions of Emma Courtney, who is criticized for excessive sensibility; but they are echoed in part by Mr. Raymond, who is not. He tells Mary Raymond that 'vivid sensations, exquisite sensibilities, powerful energies, and imperious passions . . . necessarily accompany superior mental excellence', but goes on to say that they have all too frequently brought their possessors to destruction, 'when habits of self-government and independence of mind have not been early and assiduously cultivated'.[128]

Here is almost universal common ground for 'unsex'd' and 'proper' females; sensibility is good, indeed a source of much moral, religious and artistic excellence, provided that free rein is not given to feeling at the expense of moral principle, provided that sensibility is regulated by reason.

---

[121] Pope, *Essay on Man*, ii, line 107.

[122] Macaulay Graham, *Letters on Education*, pp. 157–9.

[123] *Works of Mary Wollstonecraft*, ed. J. Todd & M. Butler (London, William Pickering, 1989), vol. 7, pp. 7–11.

[124] Wollstonecraft, *Wrongs of Woman*, p. 176.

[125] *Ibid.*, p. 86.

[126] Hays, *Emma Courtney*, p. 158.

[127] *Ibid.*, p. 145.

[128] Hays, *Victim of Prejudice*, p. 28.

If the line is drawn around the camp of sensibility in this way, most 'unsex'd' and 'proper' females come within it; a few arms and legs overhang the boundary here and there. Take Williams as an example. Wollstonecraft thought that there was 'such feminine sweetness in her style', and her *Letters from France* are a sentimental history of the French revolution.[129] Her novel, written just before sensibility became a hot political issue, borrows heavily from the sentimental tradition. There are affecting death-bed scenes, and weeping over animals – birds get rescued twice, flies are rescued, there is a noble dog. Sensibility, she maintains, can be the ally of virtue, and can lead to general benevolence. But the core of the novel is the contrast between the uncontrolled, Wertherish sensibility of Frederick Seymour, which destroys him, and the disciplined sensibility of Julia, which saves her. The difference between authors comes down to whether they place most weight upon the dangers of unregulated sensibility – More, West, Edgeworth – or with Robinson, Smith and Hays upon the potential good in a well-regulated sensibility:

> That the passions, under proper regulation, form the whole of our enjoyment through life; cannot for one moment be doubted ... Religion itself, were but a cold and selfish principle, if not influenced and animated in some degree, by the heart,—the seat of the passions. They all therefore tend to good, though they may all be perverted ... But for them life would be one dead calm, without ebb or flow, without hopes or fears.[130]

The dividing line is one of emphasis rather than of essence, and it does not run neatly between 'unsex'd' and 'proper' females. No one is more aware of the dangers than Wollstonecraft in her Vindications; celebrations of (regulated) sensibility are in the pages of Radcliffe and Hamilton.

Now sensibility, defined, promoted and limited in this way, is not a gender marker. The critique of sensibility, the insistence by 'unsex'd' and 'proper' females alike that it must be balanced by reason, largely rules out the possibility of identifying it as a mark of femininity. In any case, excessive sensibility is a failing of which men may be guilty as well as women. Sensibility controlled by reason is an ideal of character for men and women alike. A passage from More's *Strictures* is especially interesting here. She is writing about what today we would call fashions in subjectivity – what she calls fantastic codes of artificial manners. She begins by satirizing exaggerated sensibility and feminine weakness and triviality in words which could have come straight out of Wollstonecraft; and then 'Fashion ... by one of her sudden and rapid turns, instantaneously struck out sensibility and affectation from the standing list of female perfections; and by a quick touch of her magic wand, shifted the scene' and brought in the masculine female, the Amazon. More goes on to remark on the errors of the two extremes, and to

---

[129] *Analytical Review*, 7 (May 1790), 98.
[130] *Appeal to the Men of Great Britain*, pp. 208–9.

recommend the middle path, equally remote from each excess.[131] She has in effect called in question a sharp gender polarity, and in the process hinted that gender has something theatrical about it. Despite her avowals that she writes in favour of maintaining the differences between the sexes, throughout her *Strictures* and her tracts this process of subverting the gender polarity goes quietly and no doubt unwittingly on. Good Christian men should be gentle, meek, humble and domestic, ready to turn the other cheek and to shed a tear for the sufferings of others, good Christian women should be strong-minded, educated, rational and active, useful, never merely ornamental.

Gender, modesty and assertiveness

We have failed to find a strong and sharp construction of gender polarity in texts by 'unsex'd' and 'proper' females around reason, intellectual power, genius or sensibility. Is it to be found in terms of a contrast between feminine modesty and masculine assertiveness? This looks more promising. Few examples can be found even of 'unsex'd' females openly proclaiming that women should *not* be modest, that they should be as assertive as men. Wollstonecraft's discussion of modesty, and Fenwick's creation of assertive females, was noted earlier.

Hays's Emma Courtney looks like a self-conscious essay in describing a female who is not modest, neither in the sexual sense nor by virtue of any retiring deference. There is a remarkable passage where Emma describes her verbal joustings with the family of her uncle, in whose house she briefly lives after her father's death. She has been encouraged by her mentor, Mr Francis, to be spirited, not plaintive and feminine,[132] and indeed she speaks her mind, aggressively and assertively. At a family dinner she interrupts a man, insults her cousin, ignores her aunt and intimates that most of the company are 'fools and coxcombs'.[133] Here is a woman who refuses to accept that men have precedence in speech, and that women should be diffident of their opinions. This is a challenge to male superiority at a very fundamental level, another reason why conservatives found the book so deeply offensive. Hays's commendation of modesty in the *Appeal to the Men of Great Britain* commends it in the sexual sense only. Hays's other heroine, Mary Raymond, claims for herself 'generous heroism', and resolves not to be 'weak and womanish'.

The assertiveness of Emma Courtney is highly unusual among approved women characters in prose fiction by 'unsex'd' and 'proper' females alike. It is much more usual for women authors not to violate in the persons of their

131 More, *Strictures*, i, pp. 66–9.
132 Hays, *Emma Courtney*, p. 35.
133 *Ibid.*, pp. 42–4.

heroines the convention enforced in More's *Strictures* that women should not take the lead, that the modesty of their sex ought never to allow them even to be as shining as they are able, that very often it is best for them to listen intelligently while the men talk.[134] So for example in Robinson's *Angelina*, the forthrightness of Juliana Pengwynne is neutralized and made acceptable by her status as a comic character. Aggressive women are more usually disapproved characters – like Mrs Crewkherne in Smith's *Young Philosopher*. Overt challenge to women's position as the sex which speaks second is rare.

If overt challenge is rare, covert subversion is to be found. 1790s women writers in effect pull the rug from under any justification of female modesty. The most obvious justification has been undermined by all 'unsex'd' and 'proper' females insisting that women are scarcely, if at all, inferior to men intellectually and are just as capable of rationality. So is a justification offered in terms of a natural timidity, a lack of courage and initiative, on the part of women? Feminine timidity was explicitly criticized by Macaulay Graham, and savagely scorned by Wollstonecraft:

> Fragile in every sense of the word, they are obliged to look up to man for every comfort. In the most trifling dangers they cling to their support, with parasitical tenacity, piteously demanding succour; and their *natural* protector extends his arm, or lifts up his voice, to guard the lovely trembler – from what? Perhaps the frown of an old cow, or the jump of a mouse; a rat, would be a serious danger.[135]

This passage is typical of Wollstonecraft's contempt for a large part of her own sex in the *Vindication*. Other 'unsex'd' and 'proper' females undermine the notion of female timidity in a more positive way. They offer the reader examples of women who are quietly assertive, courageous and even heroic, women who are not passive but whose actions direct the course of events. Williams's *Letters from France* contain many inspiring examples: Charlotte Corday, anonymous women who save their lovers from death, a woman who stabs the judge who condemned her father, above all Madame Roland, who is described as if she were a heroine out of Plutarch:

> She had provided herself with a few books, and I found her reading Plutarch. She told me she expected to die; and the look of placid resignation with which she spoke it, convinced me that she was prepared to meet death with a firmness worthy of her exalted character.
>
> When more than one person is led at the same time to execution, since they can suffer only in succession, those who are reserved to the last are condemned to feel multiplied deaths at the sound of the falling instrument, and the sight of the bloody scaffold. To be the first victim was therefore considered as a privilege, and had been allowed to Madame Roland as a woman. But when she

134 More, *Strictures*, ii, pp. 46, 65.
135 Wollstonecraft, *Vindication of the Rights of Woman*, p. 138.

observed the dismay of her companion, she said to him, 'Go first: let me at least spare you the pain of seeing my blood shed.'[136]

Wollstonecraft herself is not always critical of her sex; she lists heroic women, women of courage and resolution – Sappho, Eloisa, Mrs Macaulay, the Empress of Russia, Madame d'Eon.[137] The last was in fact a man who liked to dress in women's clothes; Robinson makes the same mistake about him when she commemorates him alongside courageous women, like Hannah Snell and Lady Harriet Ackland, who went to war with their husbands or lovers.[138]

Smith's *Banished Man* opens as the invading French army approaches a castle in Germany. The Baroness de Rosenheim and her daughter Madame D'Alberg have been left in charge. In the night they hear a royalist nobleman and his son groaning in the fossé; the men in the castle are too cowardly to go to their aid, and so the women lead the way. In *Marchmont* Smith creates the 'exalted heroism' of Althea, a young woman of remarkable strength of mind and courage who explores an apparently haunted house, stands up to brutal bailiffs and accompanies her husband to all the perils of a debtor's prison. Smith gives her greater resolution and presence of mind than the hero, Marchmont, who reflects

> I believe that women, whom we have proudly called but children of larger growth, have, when they possess good understandings, more fortitude than men. Not to recall to observation the heroines of Antiquity, I feel ashamed of my impatience, when I contemplate the most illustrious woman of modern times, [Madame Roland] sitting in her dungeon amidst the most degraded of the human species ... such was her firmness of mind ... [139]

Robinson gives her readers a thoroughly assertive heroine in Martha: 'giddy, wild, buxom, good-natured, and bluntly sincere ... gay, robust, and noisy'.[140] She contradicts her father, and gives as good as she gets. When he has an apoplectic fit, and her sister swoons tastefully on the carpet, Martha shakes him up and brings him round. She earns her own living, at one point as a companion to a young heiress, Miss Gerard. There is a kidnap attempt, and when four masked villains ambush their chaise, demanding to know which is Miss Gerard, Martha bravely replies that she is the person, and is promptly whisked off to imprisonment in a madhouse.

It is not only 'unsex'd' females who give us courageous and assertive heroines. Adeline in Radcliffe's *Romance of the Forest* braves many dangers, but is outshone by Emily in *Udolpho*. Emily is a courageous and active heroine. She constantly exhibits more self-command than the hero,

---

136 Williams, *Letters from France*, v, pp. 196–7, 200.
137 Wollstonecraft, *Vindication of the Rights of Woman*, p. 155.
138 Robinson, *Thoughts*, pp. 44–54.
139 Smith, *Marchmont*, iv, p. 342.
140 Robinson, *Natural Daughter*, i, p. 6.

Valancourt. She goes off on her own through a frightening wood at night, to seek help for her dying father. As a prisoner at Udolpho she stands up to the terrifying gothic villain, Montoni, in defence of her aunt. She advises her aunt to avoid punishment at Montoni's hands by signing over her estates, even though, she believes, this will mean the loss of her own inheritance. After her aunt's death (she accompanies the corpse at night to its interment in a gloomy crypt) she refuses to sign her inheritance over to Montoni, so as to preserve it for Valancourt. She yields in the end, but only to avoid rape at the hands of Verezzi.

Real-life opportunities for women to be as romantically brave as Emily cannot have come along very often in late eighteenth-century England – though Emily is not an unbelievable character. 'Proper' females – and 'unsex'd' ones too – draw attention to the courage and strong-mindedness, even heroism, which may be required of women in ordinary and domestic life. On occasion the imagery More uses to describe the life of the Christian woman is drawn from warfare; life is a battle, against sin and against trials sent by God. Onward, Christian soldiers, with women often in the lead, saving their husbands and fathers from drink and dissipation, turning them towards God.[141] West remarks that 'it is but seldom that [women] will be called forth to perform high acts of heroic excellence' but for all that their life is 'continual warfare' and so they must not neglect the 'highly important preparatory duties, [which] may be compared to the military exercises which are practised in times of peace'.[142] Mrs Williams in her *Advantages of Education* is a truly impressive character, very rarely showing signs of feminine weakness; she is in control, saving her husband from ruin and foiling the plans of the man who would seduce her daughter. Though he is socially her superior, and 'master of every form of graceful address, he felt uneasy, disconcerted, and anxious to avoid the penetrating composed look of Mrs. Williams, which seemed to search into every secret of his soul'.[143] She prevails upon another man not to challenge the seducer to a duel.

The most insidious and pervasive challenges to feminine deference and unassertiveness are located in the women's voices which find utterance in the authorship of texts. Some 'proper' females are careful to avoid offending in this way; for example Mary Ann Radcliffe declares:

> The writer of this volume being a female, with only a female's education, is sufficiently aware of her inadequacy to the undertaking ... [she] at length has so far surmounted her timidity, as to submit the following sheets, with all their imperfections, to the inspection of a generous public ... so feeble an advocate ... my poor abilities ... it will be my utmost ambition to be the humble means ...[144]

141 More, *Strictures*, i, pp. xvi–xvii, 2–5.
142 West, *Advantages of Education*, i, p. i; ii, pp. 49–50.
143 *Ibid.*, i, p. 149.
144 Radcliffe, *Female Advocate*, pp. 394, 396, 400.

This should probably be understood as the deployment of a typical and long-standing modesty topos, traditionally a rhetorical strategy for insinuating rather bold suggestions. Other 'proper' writers do not even bother to use this defensive strategy. More and Edgeworth write in voices which could not be identified as female by a reader ignorant of the author's name. There is never anything apologetic about More's *Strictures*, written with authority and confidence; the book resembles a sermon as much as anything else. Edgeworth's *Letters for Literary Ladies* speak the voice of reason, indeed of close, logical reasoning; she enforces distinctions and exposes inconsistencies. West writes as a homely, down-to-earth and unpretentious spinster; but 'Prudentia Homespun' is quietly and wittily assertive. Wollstonecraft presents herself as a philosopher and a superior person, as good as any man. As a *male* author she would be thought loud and aggressive. Above all Macaulay Graham's voice merits the epithet magisterial; confident, assertive, learned in history and philosophy. In her reply to Burke she provides close reasoning and presents herself as manly – a 'plain thinking man'[145] – rational and dispassionate by contrast with his passion, prejudice, imagination and poetry. He attempts to rouse the timid mind; she stays candid and cool.[146] She has inverted the gender binary, presenting herself as masculine and him as feminine.

After examining the writings of 'unsex'd' and 'proper' females, one is left with the sense that the gender binary has been undermined or hollowed out; everything of solid substance has been extracted. Any basis for femininity in a lack of intellect, or reason, or genius, or courage, or strength of mind, or in a natural and irremediable excess of sensibility not to be found in men, has been subverted or challenged. All that is left is the outer surface, the appearance of gender difference, manifested in womanly softness, tenderness, delicacy, refinement; a stylistics of the body, an aesthetic difference no longer grounded in fundamental natural characteristics. Feminine modesty remains the most substantial marker, and an important one, because it implies confinement and secondariness. But it too has been deprived of any essential basis. Modesty in the sexual sense is necessary because of the sexual predatoriness of men; it is not grounded in any essential female characteristic, and perhaps men could be reformed. Modesty as deference and diffidence is undermined when the mental equality of women and their capacities for courage and heroism are recognized.

Gender transgression and variation

There has always been an awareness in Western culture that maleness does not necessarily go with manliness, nor femaleness with womanliness. The

[145] Macaulay Graham, *On Burke's Reflections*, p. 10.
[146] *Ibid.*, p. 44.

effeminate man and the masculine woman put in appearances in the pages of 1790s prose fiction, as in earlier and later texts. But if such people are thought of as exceptional, and disapproved, the gender binary is not challenged and it remains possible to claim that masculinity is natural or appropriate to men, femininity to women. Some texts however convey the impression that the sex–gender link is looser than that and perhaps more optional; that genders overlap rather than observe a strict boundary, and that the variety of human character this enables is not necessarily to be deplored.

In Burney's *Camilla* the effeminacy of Clermont Lynmere is ridiculed. But the attitude of the author to the unmasculine foppery of Sir Sedley Clarendel appears to be less disapproving. It is an act, an assumed mask; underneath there is good sense, courage and decency. Sir Hugh Tyrold, with his extreme sensibility and weak-mindedness, is no model of masculinity in the sense of strength and resolution, but his self-doubt and benevolence render him loveable rather than despicable. Like Sir Sedley he is part of the rich tapestry of humanity, and 'What, at last, so diversified as man? what so little to be judged by his fellow?'[147] Even more striking is the pairing of Rev. and Mrs Tyrold:

> In their tempers there was a contrast which had scarce the gradation of a single shade to smooth off its abrupt dissimilitude. Mr Tyrold, gentle in wisdom, and benign in virtue, saw with compassion all imperfections but his own ... the mildness that urged him to pity ...
>
> His partner had a firmness of mind which nothing could shake: calamity found her resolute; even prosperity was powerless to lull her duties asleep.
>
> Mr Tyrold revered while he softened the rigid virtues of his wife, who adored while she fortified the melting humanity of her husband.[148]

Here is an explicit gender reversal; yet no reader could imagine that Burney thinks this unfortunate, that it would be better if the Tyrolds corresponded more closely to stereotypes.

In spite of her defensive assertions that educating women will not unsex them, and in spite of the fact that she does not with Wollstonecraft disapprove of femininity, no author conveys a stronger sense of the artificiality and optionality of gender than Robinson. In real life she was an actress who invented and reinvented herself, carefully taking control of her own image; we can see this in her many portraits which scarcely seem to depict the same woman, in the range of voices she adopted in her poetry, and in her memoirs.[149] I do not think it is going too far

---

[147] Burney, *Camilla*, p. 913.

[148] *Ibid.*, pp. 8–9.

[149] Judith Pascoe, 'Mary Robinson and the literary marketplace', in Paula R. Feldman & Theresa M. Kelly (eds.), *Romantic Women Writers: Voices and Countervoices* (Hanover, University Press of New England, 1995), pp. 260–4; Kimberley Crouch, 'The public life of actresses: prostitutes or ladies', in Hannah Barker & Elaine Chalus (eds.), *Gender in Eighteenth-Century England: Roles, Representations and Responsibilities* (London, Longman, 1997), pp. 73–5.

to say that she thinks that gender can be acted, put on and taken off like a suit of clothes; and therefore a woman can sometimes be feminine, sometimes masculine. As a former actress celebrated for her performance of breeches parts she might well be expected to see this. In the pages of her novels, her memoirs and her *Thoughts on the Condition of Women*, we encounter women with masculine minds, like her teacher Meribah Lorrington, and women who dress in male attire. There are men like Lord Daffodil who rouges, and Lord Powderwood who struts in front of mirrors and applies beauty patches to his face.

> Yet we should find a Lord of the Creation with a puny frame, reluctant to confess the superiority of a lusty peasant girl, whom nature had endowed with that bodily strength of which luxury had bereaved him.
> And would not a modern *petit maitre* have fainted beneath the powerful grasp of one of these rustic or domestic amazons?[150]

Walsingham is her most gender-bending work: '"Well, I confess," cried Lady Arabella, "that I should like of all things to peep out of my grave, and see what my great-grand-children are doing; I dare say affairs will be completely changed: men will make caps and puff ribands; and women forget their sex, to box and ride races."'[151]

Walsingham Ainsforth is the hero; when he plans to enlist as a soldier, Amelia Woodford, who loves him, proposes to dress in male attire and enlist too. But Walsingham has long been in love with Isabella. Walsingham's cousin, Sir Sidney Aubrey, comes back from Switzerland, where he has been brought up, and Isabella is much taken with him – for Sir Sidney is a model of manhood, polished, dashing, and brave. He extracts a promise from Isabella, that she will never marry Walsingham, and they go off together. Walsingham thinks that Sir Sidney has made Isabella his mistress, and they fight a duel. Walsingham misses; Sir Sidney discharges his pistol into the air, and honour is satisfied. To cut a long story short, Isabella tells Walsingham that she has never loved him. Then comes the dénouement, which must have taken every reader by surprise. Sir Sidney's father died just before his birth; his will provided that if he had no son, his estate should pass to his brother, Colonel Aubrey. Sir Sidney in fact is a woman; his mother concealed his gender so as to secure the inheritance, and had him brought up as a man. Sir Sidney is desperately in love with Walsingham, and that is why he made Isabella promise never to marry Walsingham. The novel ends with the marriage of Walsingham and the erstwhile Sir Sidney, who now puts on the other gender: 'Indeed, so completely is she changed, so purely gentle, so feminine in manners; while her mind still retains the energy of that richly-treasured dignity of feeling ... the effects of a masculine education.'[152]

150 Robinson, *Thoughts*, pp. 17, 20.
151 Robinson, *Walsingham*, iii, p. 243.
152 *Ibid.*, iv, p. 398.

Postmodern feminism has been concerned to show how women are imprisoned in a binary discourse of gender. Reading 'unsex'd' and 'proper' females
does not support this thesis in any obvious way. No doubt imaginative play
with Freudian/Lacanian repressions, Foucaultian disciplinary discourses and
Derridean silences can uncover or invent a prison. But a reading innocent of
such theories suggests that the bars had been bent, the walls undermined; a
stereotyped femininity had been comprehensively challenged, and if women
were forced to conform to a stereotype, that was not because discourses
offered no alternative. They offered a range of options for self-fashioning.
These options were not often simply options about gender (or genderless-
ness); for gender interweaves with class and status.

The birth of a middle-class subjectivity?

Do 'unsex'd' and 'proper' females give voice to a discourse of the kind identified by for example Elias and Kelly, one which is about the construction of
a middle-class subjectivity, or a professional middle-class subjectivity,
defined and elevated by contrast both with an aristocratic civilized self which
is merely polished surface without inner worth, and with a coarse lower-class
self? Do we witness in their writings confirmation of Armstrong's thesis that
this subjectivity first becomes hegemonic in the person of the middle-class
domestic woman? Criticism of what we would call 'high society' is certainly
standard and indeed clichéd. The target is persons of fashion, the 'haut ton',
the 'quality', the worldly, luxurious denizens of the metropolis and of fashionable watering-places, people who accord their respect to wealth and to
aristocratic birth. These are the people who in More's words are notoriously
guilty of the vices of 'ADULTERY, GAMING, DUELS and SELF-MURDER'.[153] In
the other direction lower-class lack of refinement is frequently deplored, but
the target is commonly the lower middle class rather than the very lowest –
the petty traders Mrs Mittin and Mr Dubster in Burney's *Camilla*, for
example. The rural poor are frequently idealized, for solid, uncorrupted
good-heartedness; class evaluations are complicated by a stock preference for
the country over the town.

An ideal of gentility is shared by many 'unsex'd' and 'proper' females,
and when *gentility* is associated with the *gentry* this ideal is partly to do with
leisured rural retirement. In a sense this is a middle-class ideal insofar as the
lesser gentry distinguish themselves from the quality, but it is a highly traditional one; neither the ideal nor the class is new. The class is constituted
without sharp boundaries between land, commerce and the professions.

153 More, *The Two Wealthy Farmers*, i, p. 18. For the debate about aristocratic
vice, see Donna T. Andrew, 'The code of honour and its critics: the opposition to
duelling in England, 1700–1850', *Social History*, 5:3 (October 1980), 409–34 and
'"Adultery à-la-Mode"'.

Indeed the class overlaps the aristocracy and greater gentry; in spite of the clichéd critique of aristocratic vice it is not clear that a class war is going on.[154] Slightly differing forms of this gentry ideal – which as *gentility* is a mode of subjectivity, a fashion of being – are to be found in Robinson, Smith, Burney, Radcliffe, West and Hays.

Macaulay Graham offers it in a form consonant with her own origins. Her forebears were London bankers and stockbrokers who purchased a landed estate and a grand country house in Kent – capitalists (but not industrial capitalists) turned landed gentry.[155] Her ideal is a life of elegant, rational luxury and liberal hospitality. A gentlewoman should not work too hard at perfecting any one accomplishment – musical performance, for example. That might be appropriate for someone in a dependent situation, but not for her; as Philip of Macedon remarked about Alexander's dancing, she would cry out that the young lady or gentlewoman performed too well.[156] Obviously Macaulay Graham is marking the difference between a professional or a governess who needs to work for a living, and a gentlewoman who does not; at the same time she is proposing that the ideal lies not in specialized outer accomplishments but in the cultivation of the whole self for its own sake. She is less relentless than other females about the need to be useful, being thankful for 'one of the great privileges of female life, which is the consent of the world, that we may amuse ourselves with trifles'.[157] Accordingly, unlike Wollstonecraft and Hays she recommends the traditional female activity of needlework. Macaulay Graham gives the impression of being confident and at ease with her own status. She is certainly an advocate of *Kultur* and inwardness, but at the same time her attitudes are those of a leisured aristocracy; she has no disdain for polish and refinement.

Wollstonecraft, who declares that the middle rank contains most virtue and abilities, is more of a class warrior.[158] In another place she remarks that 'With respect to virtue ... I have seen most in low life'.[159] She is critical of a status-system which recognizes birth and wealth, rather than virtue and ability, and is unremittingly hostile to the fashionable upper classes: 'In the superior ranks of life how seldom do we meet with a man of superior abilities, or even common acquirements?'[160] Elias's antithesis of *Zivilisation* and *Kultur* is well exemplified in the writings of Wollstonecraft.[161] In her history of the French revolution the court aristocracy are depicted as highly polished but without inner worth – sensual, luxurious, animal. There is a manifest

154 Vickery, *Gentleman's Daughter*, p. 23.
155 Hill, *Republican Virago*, pp. 4–7.
156 Macaulay Graham, *Letters on Education*, p. 63.
157 *Ibid.*, p. 65.
158 Wollstonecraft, *Vindication of the Rights of Woman*, p. 132.
159 *Ibid.*, p. 154.
160 *Ibid.*, p. 124.
161 Wollstonecraft, *Historical and Moral View*, p. 25.

intention in her writings to present herself as a superior person by virtue of qualities of mind, such as rationality, seriousness and freedom from prejudice. In her first novel, and in some of her later writings such as her *Scandinavian Letters*, her claim to status is based in part on her sensibility. In her 1797 essay on poetry, for example, she presents herself as a poet whose sensibility enables her to appreciate the beauties of nature, and thereby to communicate with nature's God. Even in the *Vindication* she asserts her superiority by reference to an aesthetic taste which has overtones of sensibility: 'With what a languid yawn have I seen an admirable poem thrown down, that a man of true taste returns to, again and again with rapture; and, whilst melody has almost suspended respiration, a lady has asked me where I bought my gown.'[162] She goes on to remark that men of the first genius and of cultivated minds – very obviously she is including herself in this select company – have the highest relish for the simple beauties of nature.

A decidedly middle-class voice, then, but certainly not one which can be associated with commerce, industry or the professions. To be sure, some of her vitriol against trade is to be attributed to her pain at the collapse of her relationship with the trader Imlay: 'Ah! Shall I whisper to you – that you – yourself, are strangely altered, since you have entered deeply into commerce ... Nature has given you talents, which lie dormant, or are wasted in ignoble pursuits.'[163] But her hostility is deeper and older than her resentment of him. In her *Historical and Moral View* she echoes Adam Smith's critique of the destructive effects of commerce on the character of the common people. But whereas Smith thinks that on balance economic advance is a good, Wollstonecraft longs for a rural arcadia, speculating that with the fall of the *ancien régime*, Paris will decay: 'In proportion as the charms of solitary reflection and agricultural recreations are felt, the people, by leaving the villages and cities, will give a new complexion to the face of the country.'[164] She had already lightly sketched such a utopia at the end of her *Vindication of the Rights of Men* and imagined the country gentleman taking paternal care of the rural poor.[165] Wollstonecraft is certainly employing a mode of subjectivity which she attributes to herself as a weapon in a status war against those she thinks have not recognized her worth. But she does not write from an identifiable socioeconomic position, nor does she target only the aristocracy and the lower orders.

No other 'unsex'd' or 'proper' female wages war against aristocracy with such unqualified gusto. Robinson is obsessive about neglected genius, citing Chatterton as an example and obviously thinking of herself; her novels give us writers who starve ignored in garrets while the society of brainless aristocrats is eagerly sought. Mental worth is what really counts, and the French

---

162 Wollstonecraft, *Vindication of the Rights of Woman*, p. 261.
163 Wollstonecraft, *Letters Written During a Short Residence*, p. 252.
164 Wollstonecraft, *Historical and Moral View*, pp. 518–21, 508.
165 Wollstonecraft, *Vindication of the Rights of Man*, pp. 59–61.

revolution was caused by an uprising of natural ability against hereditary nobility.[166] But though Robinson is demanding that women be valued for inner mental and moral qualities, she is not really promoting a middle-class consciousness of sober worth and virtue, nor does this former fashion icon despise glamour and splendour. Aristocrats populate the pages of her novels, and her heroes and heroines generally end up with titles. It is by no means clear that she is hostile to the aristocratic code of honour; in spite of occasional criticisms of duels, heroes and approved characters fight them in the pages of her novels and sometimes the tendency of the narrative is to commend the dueller. She puts a defence of duelling into the mouth of her hero Charles Belmont in *Angelina*, and in her *Thoughts on the Condition of Woman* suggests that women should be allowed to defend their honour in that way.[167] Robinson wants an aristocracy of birth and wealth to recognize and incorporate an aristocracy of talent and to patronize it; in *The Natural Daughter* there are fulsome tributes to the Duchess of Devonshire for doing just that, and the list of subscribers to the 1791 edition of her poems is stuffed with princes, dukes and duchesses, earls and countesses, viscounts and right honourables. Robinson can be snobbish about upstarts, her best example being the nabob Sir Hector Upas, later Lord Arcot in *The False Friend*, a former dustman who became pimp and pander to a nobleman before going to the far East to make his fortune.

Smith writes about class all of the time, in a complex discourse with some tension in it. Politically progressive, she criticizes those in the upper classes who are disdainful of trade, and in *Marchmont* when all seems disaster at the end of the novel a *deus ex machina* who has made a fortune in trade, Mr Desborough, comes along and opens his moneybags to put everything right. But Smith cannot entirely divest herself of the prejudices of gentility. Her heroes, for example Orlando in *The Old Manor House*, or Glenmorris in *The Young Philosopher*, have no relish for a career in trade or the professions (with the exception of the clearly gentlemanly profession of soldier). She is highly critical of those who are coarse and lacking in manners and sensibility. In other novels she finds plenty of those in the ranks of trade, for example in *The Old Manor House*. It would also be difficult to cite her as a spokeswoman for the professional middle classes; there are scarcely any admirable clergy in her novels, and her rage against lawyers knows no bounds. In her *Young Philosopher* she jeers at the accents of lower-middle-class attorneys who wish to elevate themselves into gentility (they always fail). She plainly writes from the point of view of the middling landed gentry.

Williams writes a set-piece scene in which her heroine Julia defends virtue in straitened circumstances against affluent society ladies who will have nothing to do with those they see as lower than themselves, and like

[166] Robinson, *Walsingham*, iii, pp. 261–2.
[167] Robinson, *Angelina*, iii, p. 392; *Thoughts*, pp. 5, 73–4.

Wollstonecraft she declares that the middle station is most favourable to improvement and to great and generous exertions.[168] But she is no enemy of polished manners, and there are satirical accounts of Mr Chartres, educated but gauche, and his upstart mother who insists on collecting a large party in lodgings far too small for a fashionable card assembly and *petit souper*. One of her charges against the jacobins is that in their rage for equality they affect a coarse vulgarity and a disdain for anything – including cleanliness and decent attire – that smacks of good breeding. Williams's ideal combines inner cultivation with outer polish, and the best men and women are marked by their delicacy, refinement and sensibility.

So far, then, I have failed to find in texts by 'unsex'd' females clear correlations between an ideal of inwardness, of *Kultur* as opposed to *Zivilisation*, and an anti-aristocratic consciousness of a rising commercial and professional bourgeoisie promoting domestic femininity. Nor is it to be found in the writings of the 'proper'. 'Proper' females take care to insist that their attack on fashionable dissipation is not an attack on aristocracy as such. Burney has one of her characters declare that 'if we have not as many women who are amiable with titles as without, it is only because we have not the same number from which to select them. They are spoilt or unspoilt, but in the same proportion as the rest of their sex'.[169] West, who most emphatically values inner qualities in women above superficial polish, ostentatiously refuses to present all aristocrats as bad.[170] Her ideal people are cast in a traditional mould – in *A Tale of the Times*, for instance, the Evanses who are rural clergy, and Sir William Powerscourt who is an old-fashioned squire. Both she and Hamilton oppose the arrogance and social exclusiveness of rank, but typically this is associated either with those newly arrived in the ranks of nobility, or with out-of-date semi-feudal aristocrats living in remote corners of the kingdom.[171]

'Proper' females share with 'unsex'd' an ideal of subjectivity characterized by inwardness which acts as a status-marker. But it would be inaccurate to characterize it as an ideal of middle-class domesticity; it is part of an ideal of refined and virtuous gentility which does not correlate precisely with economic class. The conception of gentility obviously has a status (perhaps status rather than class) component, but it is also about ethical and aesthetic ideals. In Radcliffe's *Udolpho* Emily's sensibility and refinement distinguish her not only from the good-hearted but unpolished servants, but also from her unfeeling wealthy uncle M. Quesnel with his aspirations to aristocracy, and from her wealthy but coarse *haute bourgeoise* aunt, Mme Cheron.

[168] Williams, *Julia*, i, p. 172.

[169] Burney, *Camilla*, p. 452; see also pp. 657, 707, 749.

[170] West, *Gossip's Story*, p. 116; *Advantages of Education*, i, pp. 196–7, ii, pp. 193–4.

[171] West, *Tale of the Times*, i, pp. 267, 284; Hamilton, *Hindoo Rajah*, pp. 122–3, 125–6, 194.

Discourse about gender cannot easily be disentangled from this discourse about gentility. Delicacy, refinement and sensibility mark the ideal woman, and she may have a ready excellence in these qualities. But they mark the gentlewoman, and the gentleman also, whether he be peer, squire, clergyman or merchant. Inner qualities are revealed by a highly cultivated style of self-presentation and behaviour, characterized by easy but unaggressive – indeed modest – sociability, genuine sympathy and sensitivity to the needs and feelings of others.[172]

The care of the self

If the world fails to satisfy us, we may seek to change it. If the barriers to change appear insuperable, we may overcome the tension by changing ourselves, by coming to terms with the world or by ceasing to care about its inadequacies. The latter strategy will appeal to women who recognize their lack of power to change the world in accordance with their wishes. Christianity offered late eighteenth-century women an ideal of self-transformation adapted to the powerless – as Nietzsche recognized in his hostile labelling of its morality as a morality for slaves.[173] Resignation of self-will, acceptance of trials and sorrows as sent by God, cultivation of indifference to worldly things and a turning towards a goal beyond this life added up to an ideal of subjectivity from which women were in no way precluded by their sex. The Christian ethic grew up in the shadow of stoicism, whose influence on eighteenth-century thought was also pervasive – a 'softened stoicism' which took from stoicism selectively, rejecting stoic apathy insofar as it meant a repression of benevolence and a lack of care for others.[174] Stoicism advocated a retreat into and a disciplining of the self, the cultivation of a subjectivity having value apart from engagement with the world, also therefore offering an ideal suited to women. It offered a kind of freedom and independence delivered by self-mastery and a detachment from bodily desires which might enslave the self to a world it could not control.

A preference for sensibility over reason sits ill with these ideals of selfhood because of their privileging of self-control, and therefore we find that, for example, Smith and Robinson are fairly critical of stoicism. Most other 'unsex'd' and 'proper' females promote it in some form. The inference that a woman must control her inner self because she cannot control her outer fate is enforced in the sermon penned by Mr Tyrold for Camilla:

172 Cf. L. E. Klein, *Shaftesbury and the Culture of Politeness* (Cambridge, Cambridge University Press, 1994).
173 Friedrich Nietzsche, *On the Genealogy of Morals* (*Zur Genealogie der Moral*, 1887) (New York, Random House, 1989), pp. 28–46.
174 Mark Roberts, *The Tradition of Romantic Morality* (London, Macmillan, 1973), pp. 63, 75–6, 80.

Struggle then against yourself as you would struggle against an enemy ... I
mean not to propose to you in the course of a few days to reinstate yourself in
the perfect security of a disengaged mind ... I can only require from you what
depends upon yourself, a steady and courageous warfare against the two
dangerous underminers of your peace and of your fame, imprudence and impa-
tience ... Good sense will shew you the power of self-conquest.[175]

Stoicism was best known to late eighteenth-century women through Mrs
Carter's translation of the works of Epictetus. West's *Tale of the Times* was
dedicated to Mrs Carter, and *The Advantages of Education* ends with a quotation from a poem by 'our female Epictetus'. That stoicism and Christianity
coincide for West is clear; she remarks that 'Humility, which inspires a
lowly mind and moderate desires, is the surest road to content'.[176] Humility
and lowliness were central Christian values. West would have a woman give
her life meaning by a kind of lesser heroism involved in the mundane struggle to control the self, so as to be ready to overcome the trials which
inevitably occur:

Now bend to reason's calm controul
Each rebel passion of the soul:
And from th'approving gods demand
Immortal glory's starry band.[177]

Among our 'unsex'd' and 'proper' females, the most explicit stoic was
Macaulay Graham. She recommends Cicero's *De Officiis*, Epictetus and
Seneca, and insists that there is no great difference between their teachings
and those of Christ. The compositions of the stoics may be regarded as
manuals of conduct enabling us to carry into practice the commands of the
Christian gospel.[178] Macaulay Graham's explication of a softened Christian
stoicism provides a consistent and distinctive ideal of subjectivity. She tells
her pupil/interlocutor 'Hortensia' that 'the only true excellence, [is] the
beauty of a well-regulated mind'.[179] In a sense then her ideal of personhood
is an aesthetic ideal whose aim is to produce a cultivated person who has
nobility, a beauty which stems entirely from inner qualities. Nobility in turn
may be specified in terms of self-control, self-possession, order, regularity,
tranquillity, freedom, independence. The two last values are to be achieved
in the stoic manner, by not caring too much about the world. Epictetus
argues that freedom is being in control, but we cannot control the world, nor
even our own bodies, which fall ill in spite of our wishes. The only thing I
can securely control is the inward, my own mind; I must find my freedom by
taking possession of and regulating that.

175 Burney, *Camilla*, p. 358.
176 West, *Advantages of Education*, ii, p. 235.
177 *Ibid.*, i, p. 122.
178 Macaulay Graham, *Letters on Education*, pp. 130, 446, 452.
179 *Ibid.*, p. 441.

Macaulay Graham endorses this ideal when she deplores 'the untutored, and the undisciplined mind, [which] is totally incapacitated for self government'.[180] 'Poise your desires so as to leave your understanding in the full possession of the field'[181] – be the mistress of your passions, not a slave to them. Christ declared that his service was perfect freedom, and Macaulay Graham agrees; both the empire of religion, and the empire of reason, liberate us from abject, ruinous and painful servitude to our passions.[182] The ideal explains the repudiation of the 'senseless course of dissipation',[183] of the restless round of luxury and worldly pleasures, which is standard in conduct books and novels of the period as well as in Macaulay Graham. For the dissipated self, pursuing one pleasure after another, is a fragmented, incoherent self. It also explains Macaulay Graham's rejection of 'those restless sensations which attend an impotent ambition' and her advice that children should not be encouraged to look forward to great joys in the future.[184] These mental habits are inimical to tranquillity; we should learn instead the stoic rules which teach us to maintain 'such a sovereignty over the mind and its desires, as should enable it to draw its happiness from the present moment'.[185]

In his *Genealogy of Morals* Nietzsche condemned this ethic as a morality of sour grapes, a morality for slaves (Epictetus was a slave). He advocated a contrary ethic of struggle and of self-assertion, of a Will to Power over the world including power over other humans. Does Christian stoicism appeal to Macaulay Graham precisely because, as she declares, it is an ethic attainable by everyone,[186] implicitly therefore including even the powerless and the socially subjugated, attainable even by women? Is it an ethic of defeat and abstinence, of making the best of a bad job, a dead end for women who should set themselves the goal of social and political emancipation, of capturing and controlling the world, rather than merely controlling themselves? Should women become Nietzschean blonde beasts and superwomen? Even if one could accept Nietzsche's revelling in thoughts of cruelty and destruction, it is by no means obvious that one should prefer an ethic attainable only by an elite, as Nietzsche's explicitly is. The values Macaulay Graham proposes – self-possession, self-mastery, integrity, tranquillity, contentment with the moment – are not despicable, servile values. They are moreover values detached from women's roles, values for a self thought of in isolation from social relationships. They offer to women a practice of fashioning the self free from feminine stereotypes.

180 *Ibid.*, p. 100.
181 *Ibid.*, p. 186.
182 *Ibid.*, pp. 422–3.
183 *Ibid.*, p. 13.
184 *Ibid.*, pp. 79, 108.
185 *Ibid.*, p. 80.
186 *Ibid.*, p. 81.

More offers a not dissimilar set of values and technology of the self, but oriented towards an evangelical Christian vision of life stressing the imperative to struggle against sinfulness. This system pervades the whole of her *Strictures*, and is especially apparent in the chapter 'On dissipation, and the modern habits of life'. Dissipation is all-engrossing, leaving no time for reflection and self-examination; it relaxes the soul and enslaves the heart.[187] More rests her ethic on a purely Christian basis; she would not build on Christianity and stoicism combined, because she wishes to enforce, presumably in reply to such as Macaulay Graham, a contrast between Christian and pagan values: 'Christian virtue differs *essentially* from Pagan.'[188] More is wrong here, for she has failed to distinguish between a classical republican ethic, which *is* very different from Christianity, and a classical stoic ethic, which is not. But three-quarters of a century before he wrote she has Nietzsche's perception of the difference between classical republicanism and Christianity. Humility is the appropriate grace of Christianity; the virtues of the Romans were founded in pride, and their language could only express humility in a bad sense, conveying the idea of meanness or vileness.[189] Of course More's evaluation of the two ethics is the reverse of Nietzsche's.

She has a strong conviction of the peculiar appropriateness of Christian ideals to women. She contends in her *Strictures* that Christianity – which occasionally More refers to as 'she' – was especially addressed by its founder to women, and that there were many pious women playing an important part in the early church. At the profoundest level Christianity teaches the equality of the sexes, for it maintains that the soul is unsexed and that salvation is equally available to women and to men. In addition she insists that the virtues of Christianity are such as women can develop, and that the nature and situation of women make them more receptive to its message – their feeling hearts, their readiness to depend upon a superior will, the quietness of their lives which gives them more time to ponder and to engage in introspection.[190] Is More saying in effect that the Christian ethic is a *feminine* ethic? It would be more accurate to describe the Christian ethic she proposes to women as ungendered. Christianity exalts the humble; women should acquire a submissive temper and a forbearing spirit, not 'on the low ground of its being decorous and feminine, ... but ... on the high principle of obedience to Christ', who was himself meek and lowly.[191]

Wollstonecraft in her *Vindication of the Rights of Woman*, like Macaulay Graham and More, is an enemy of dissipation and an advocate of self-control. To a certain extent she is closer to Macaulay Graham in that her self-possessed self is to be dignified with a strong sense of self-worth, rather than

187 More, *Strictures*, ii, pp. 154–5, 157.
188 *Ibid.*, ii, p. 249.
189 *Ibid.*, i, p. 250.
190 *Ibid.*, ii, pp. 30–2.
191 *Ibid.*, i, pp. 143–4.

meek and humble. Without doubt Macaulay Graham's ethic impressed her, though she does not follow Macaulay Graham in basing it explicitly on stoicism; I doubt whether her classical reading was as deep and extensive as Macaulay Graham's. For in another way she is closer to More: a particular Christian doctrine is the very cornerstone of her argument. Like many eighteenth-century Christians – her erstwhile friend and mentor Dr Price, for example – Wollstonecraft identifies the soul with reason. Unlike Dr Priestley, who believed in the resurrection of the body at the day of judgement, Wollstonecraft apparently thinks that immortality, and afterlife in heaven, is for the soul alone. From this follows an eschatological narrative of a human life on earth which orients it towards an afterlife in heaven and therefore takes as the main thread of the narrative the process of self-preparation for that afterlife. From her doctrine of the soul she infers that those who have cultivated their reason here on earth will be prepared for heaven after death. Those who have not done so will have no immortality, or a poorer one. She offers the most striking image of death and damnation as the plight of a soul which has not risen to reason, 'when the spirit is represented as continually hovering with abortive eagerness round the defiled body, unable to enjoy any thing without the organs of sense'.[192]

If this basis is granted, Wollstonecraft can go on to erect a most compelling argument for women's education, an education moreover as good as the best that men get, an education which trains the reason. A light and superficial one which fosters sensibility, or which imparts a few showy accomplishments, will never do; that would be an education for damnation. She must not be educated to please a man: 'Can she consent to be occupied merely to please him; merely to adorn the earth, when her soul is capable of rising to thee? – And can she rest supinely dependent on man for reason, when she ought to mount with him the arduous steeps of knowledge?'[193] Variants of this eschatological argument for women's education can also be found in Macaulay Graham's *Letters on Education*, More's *Strictures*, Hays's *Letters and Essays* and Hamilton's *Hindoo Rajah*.

Few commentators on Wollstonecraft have paid sufficient attention to this,[194] and perhaps they have been reluctant to do so, first, because this dimension of her thought fixes a gulf between her *Weltanschauung* and those of modern feminisms, and secondly, because as she moved away from orthodox religion in her last years, the removal of this dimension left her feminism without a philosophical basis – for as argued earlier, she never explored the philosophy of natural rights. When she wrote the *Vindication* she was not a

[192] Wollstonecraft, *Vindication of the Rights of Woman*, p. 137.

[193] *Ibid.*, p. 144.

[194] Exceptions are Barbara Taylor, 'For the love of God. Religion and the erotic imagination in Wollstonecraft's feminism', in Eileen Janes Yeo (ed.), *Mary Wollstonecraft and Two Hundred Years of Feminisms* (London, Rivers Oram Press, 1997), pp. 15–16, 24; and Myers, 'Reform or ruin'.

utilitarian either, for she did not think that earthly pleasure was the end of life. The underlying system is a perfectionist one, but perfection means cultivation of the reason/soul. Why should that be cultivated? Much of the book is a meditation on the purpose of human existence, and there is a reiterated insistence that it would be worthless without God and immortality. The whole argument of the *Vindication* has been made to rest on the eschatological narrative; if that were taken out, how would it stand? Other 'unsex'd' and 'proper' females who used this argument did not move away from Christianity as Wollstonecraft did. In any case, Macaulay Graham's ideal of the self does not rest on this alone but also has elements of utilitarianism and aesthetic perfectionism, concerned as it is with being a certain kind of noble and happy self here on earth. Thirdly, Wollstonecraft's ideal of subjectivity in the *Vindication*, her vision of a rational soul ready for heaven, does not sit square with that 'feminine romanticism' which some commentators have sought in texts of this period.[195] Her ideal is not about unity or community with others; it is an ideal of an ultimately solitary self, related primarily to God. It is undoubtedly a feminist vision, but of a particular kind. This woman's potentially immortal self is not exclusively or even primarily for fathers, husbands or children; it is for herself, and for her God. It is a Protestant individualist self.

I want to emphasize the significance of this in so many of the texts by both 'unsex'd' and 'proper' females. Perhaps this was their most important message to the women of their day. They encourage their contemporaries to avoid entrapment in a stereotyped, degraded femininity and to take control of their own self-fashioning. Through the cultivation of reason and self-control a woman is to become self-possessed. This process of *Bildung* is a salient theme especially of the conduct literature, such as Macaulay Graham's *Letters on Education,* Wollstonecraft's *Vindication*, More's *Strictures* and Wakefield's *Reflections on the Present Condition of the Female Sex*. It is narrated in some of the prose fiction also. For example, Smith's Althea in *Marchmont* grows in stature under the pressure of adversity. West's *Advantages of Education* is a *Bildungsroman* about the heroine, Maria Williams, whose development is contrasted with that of her friend Charlotte Raby. Nested within it is the flashback story of her mother's own *Bildung*. Until quite late on, Robinson's *False Friend* looks as if it is going to be a *Bildungsroman* in which Gertrude grows up to self-control, moderating her excessive sensibility. But *The False Friend* is Robinson's unhappiest novel, perhaps reflecting her own abandoned plight at the time, and Gertrude dies a victim of her own sensibility.

The rational self is not a stereotyped *feminine* self; but is it simply stereotyped in another way? Is it the production of an *individual* who lacks *individuality* in the sense of a strongly marked personality? Does self-control, as

[195] Cf. Mellor, *Romanticism and Gender*.

Barker-Benfield has argued, imply a negation of authenticity? To put it at its worst, is it an affair of *self-repression* rather than of *self-expression*? Or is there any sense of that process of *Bildung* described for example by Goethe, by which the individual unfolds and realizes a specific, personal essence or character? John Stuart Mill thought that *Bildung* in this sense was a discovery of the German *Goethezeit*;[196] if he was right, then we would not expect to find it in developed form in the writings of 1790s women about women, any more than we would expect it in writings by men about men. The intense Christian or post-Christian moralism of so much of the thought of the period favours virtue rather than variety. But there are some hints of an ethic of self-expression, growing out of a protestant esteem for the values of sincerity and authenticity.

These values are apparent whenever Wollstonecraft discusses writing, for example in her reviews for the *Analytical*. In a review of a play by Holcroft she writes, 'The characters in this comedy have that finished individuality, which quickly informs us that they are imitations of nature, and not servile copies of models, lifeless as the stone of which they are a transcript'.[197] This translates in the *Vindication* into critiques of those who slavishly conform to convention, and into occasional calls for individuality of character: 'Decorum, indeed, is the one thing needful! – decorum is to supplant nature, and banish all simplicity and variety of character out of the female world!'[198] More is no enemy of decorum, but she laments the tendency of fashion to efface variety of character; when a woman enters the giddy whirl of public resort, '*There* attrition rubs all bodies smooth, and makes all surfaces alike'.[199] The theme is played most often, however, by Hays:

> Female education, as at present conducted, is a complete system of artifice and despotism; all the little luxuriances and exuberances of character, which individualise the being, which give promise of, and lay the foundation for, future powers, are carefully lopped and pruned away; sincerity and candour are repressed with solicitude; and the terrors of *opinion* are set in array, and suspended over the victim, till the enfeebled and broken spirit submits to the trammels, and, passive, tame, and docile, is stretched or shortened (as on the frame of the tyrant Procrustes), to the *universal standard*.[200]

This 1797 article in the *Monthly Magazine* voices a complaint which might have come straight out of Mill's *Subjection of Women* of 1869, reminding us that Mill's own feminism was shaped not only by German ideals of *Bildung*, but also in the unitarian circles to which Hays belonged.

---

[196] John Stuart Mill, 'Coleridge', in *Dissertations and Discussions, Political, Philosophical, and Historical* (London, John W. Parker & Son, 1859), i, pp. 427–9.

[197] *Analytical Review*, 9 (January 1791), 44.

[198] Wollstonecraft, *Vindication of the Rights of Woman*, pp. 179, 85, 180.

[199] More, *Strictures*, ii, pp. 152, 166.

[200] *Monthly Magazine*, 3 (March 1797), 193; see also Hays, *Letters and Essays*, p. 55; *Appeal to the Men of Great Britain*, pp. 220–1.

Conclusion

This chapter has argued that women writers of the 1790s were not entirely imprisoned in a subjectivity created for them by male-authored discourses. They took the discourses available to them, and turned them to their own purposes. From their writings we may extract a composite picture of womanly subjectivity of considerable power. Most of them were reluctant to mount a head-on challenge to the gender binary, but they hollowed it out, undermined it, diminished its discursive power. From neoclassicism they took an aesthetic of the body concerned with simplicity and dignity, with essential qualities rather than with superficial decoration. The mental and historical philosophies of associationism and environmentalism gave them a basis for arguing that gender stereotypes were not inescapable and that modes of subjectivity, to use modern parlance, were to some extent a matter of choice. They could also argue from this basis that women had mental powers equal to those of men, and a potential for genius; they could back up their argument with examples of distinguished women writers. In prose fiction they presented images of intelligent, active, courageous and heroic women. They supplemented the discourse of sensibility by adding a component of reason and self-control, combining conventional masculine and feminine qualities, the thinking head with the feeling heart. A discourse of polite, refined gentility presented an ideal for men which women could realize too. The Christian doctrine of ungendered souls enabled them to claim equality at the most fundamental level. An ethic of the care of the self, having stoic and Christian roots, licensed them to engage in a process of self-fashioning independent of confining social roles.

7

Conclusion

As we have seen, the concerns and emphases of 'unsex'd' females do not mirror those of twentieth and twenty-first century feminism, nor even of the women's movements of the late nineteenth. They come close to the concerns of later female campaigners in their recognition of the importance of women's access to resources. Not only 'unsex'd' females such as Wollstonecraft, Hays and Robinson but also very 'proper' ones such as Mary Ann Radcliffe and Wakefield demand increased opportunities of income-earning work. Above all they are our precursors because of their sustained attack on a disabling and degrading gender stereotype. Only Wollstonecraft and perhaps Macaulay Graham wish to eliminate gender difference altogether; but there is a high degree of consensus among 'unsex'd' and 'proper' females for a reform of norms of womanly conduct so as to discourage affectations of weakness and timidity, and to encourage solid learning, rationality and strong-mindedness. It is their unanimous view that women should not be constructed as sexual objects, a view proposed with equal passion and power by the doyennes of propriety and radicalism, More and Wollstonecraft. There is a widespread awareness that sexual character is at least to some extent artificial and variable, and the variations are explored in the novels of Smith and Burney. Robinson appears to be moving towards a radical view of gender as enacted, subject to choice.

Political and civil rights are not ignored, but they are by no means central. Neither 'unsex'd' nor 'proper' females describe or propose a clear-cut separation of spheres, but at the same time they do not challenge the notion that the retired and the domestic is best for women (and for men). But women writers do enter the 'bourgeois public sphere' in some force by engaging in the debate on the French revolution, and 'unsex'd' females apply political concepts and parallels to their own situation and to the family. 'Unsex'd' and 'proper' females alike proclaim the value of romantic love and companionate marriage for women. Their criticisms are of men who want sex without love, of husbands who fail to make companions of their wives, and (on the part of 'unsex'd' females) of a moral and legal system which compels a woman to remain in a failed marriage. Only Wollstonecraft in her *Vindication of the Rights of Woman* and in *Maria, or the Wrongs of Woman*, and perhaps Fenwick in *Secresy* appear to be saying that the hope of happiness for women in love and marriage may be an illusion, and if this was Wollstonecraft's doctrine, she did not live her life in accordance with it. There is a substantial discourse about desire and eroticism going on in a veiled way in many of these texts; but it would be anachronistic to suppose that it was a half-concealed plea for free sexual expression. The main subject of this discourse about desire is in fact men: what kind of man a woman can love, what sort of conduct on his part will please her.

The writers we have discussed here are quite far removed from modern feminism in other ways too. For example, that ideology has a well-established view of the nineteenth century as a period when women were elevated onto a pedestal as it were, celebrated for their goodness. But a pedestal is a confined space on which to stand; twentieth- and twenty-first century feminists have wanted to come down. They are rightly unwilling to bear an unfair share of the burdens of morality. They cannot see why occasional lapses may be licensed for men, while women must be good all of the time. 'Unsex'd' and 'proper' females by contrast are engaged in the enterprise of *placing* women on that pedestal. Some authors think that women will have to be transformed before they will be fit for elevation; this is especially true of Wollstonecraft, but Macaulay Graham and Edgeworth are also very critical of women.

Others, though they may be calling for improvements in women's education, do not convey the impression that they think women morally inferior to men; they are fit for the pedestal already. Williams's *Letters from France* celebrates their self-sacrificing heroism; written across the period when Wollstonecraft was drafting her *Vindication*, their attitude towards women could hardly be more different. Something of the same could be said of Wollstonecraft's friend and disciple Hays, who apparently wishes to modify some of the judgements of her precursor. The *Appeal to the Men of Great Britain* denies 'that all, nor perhaps that most of the women of the past ages and the present, have been, and are, either vain and foolish, or insipid, or vicious'.[1] It invites its readers to compare the character and conduct of the men and women they know; women will have no cause to be ashamed of the comparison.[2] Women are less obstinate than men, more flexible and adaptable, better humoured. They are more chaste and modest; in this respect 'Nature has clearly given to women ... a most decided superiority'.[3] This text even claims, in flat contradiction of Wollstonecraft's *Vindication*, that a

[1] *Appeal to the Men of Great Britain*, p. 112.
[2] *Ibid.*, p. 41.
[3] *Ibid.*, p. 230.

great part of the education of women is good, tending to produce habits of order, discipline and application.[4] It goes so far as to claim, again in dissent from Wollstonecraft, 'that women in general possess even fortitude, that first of masculine virtues, in a much greater degree, and of a much superior kind, to that possessed by the men'.[5] Wakefield claims 'the superior purity of the morals of women, and the exquisite tenderness of mothers for their offspring'.[6] Robinson's *Thoughts on the Condition of Women* defiantly asserts women's superiority, even, in some cases, in bodily strength.

In prose fiction we encounter female role models, women of heroic virtue who are better than the men who love them: Smith's Celestina, her Geraldine in *Desmond* and Althea in *Marchmont*, Radcliffe's Emily in *Udolpho*, Hays's Mary Raymond in *The Victim of Prejudice*, Williams's Julia, Fenwick's Sibella in *Secresy*, Robinson's Martha in her *Natural Daughter* and her Angelina. Of the latter Wollstonecraft wrote in her review, 'In the portrait of Angelina we behold an assemblage of almost every excellence which can adorn the female mind, beaming mildly through clouds of affliction and melancholy'.[7]

We find occasional echoes, for example in Robinson's *Walsingham*, of the opinion of male authors such as Hume and Alexander that it is the mission of women to polish and civilize men. Rather than *claiming* this role, other women authors especially of prose fiction *perform* it by presenting an ideal of reformed, woman-friendly masculinity. Some 'unsex'd' and 'proper' females such as Hays and Wakefield claim a special role for women in leading moral reform: 'And in the reformation of manners so much talked about, and so loudly called for, let us catch the glorious enthusiasm, and take the lead!'[8] More calls them to this task too, claiming an influence for women which one male reviewer thought excessive.[9] The enlightenment grand narrative of the civilizing power of women is matched in importance by another, proposed for example by Wakefield, Hays, More, West and Hamilton, which connects the destiny of women with Christianity. Christianity was addressed by its founder as much to women as to men; it has played a key role in improving the lot of women, saving them from the oppression of brutal barbarism; it confers fundamental equality upon them by virtue of its doctrine that there is no sex in souls; and women have a role to play in setting an example of Christian piety.

All of this tends to distance 'unsex'd' and 'proper' females from their many times great-granddaughters of the present day, and it is tempting to regard it as a blind alley, a mistake, a self-inflicted burden of chains. But

---

[4] *Ibid.*, pp. 83–4.
[5] *Ibid.*, p. 175.
[6] Wakefield, *Reflections*, p. 107.
[7] *Analytical Review*, 23 (February 1796), 293–4.
[8] Hays, *Letters and Essays*, p. 157.
[9] *British Critic*, 13 (1799), 644.

historians of the early modern period have given us a vivid picture of the misogyny of that time, a kind of gender racism; to elevate the status of women, to defeat the view of them as disorderly, untrustworthy and irrational creatures of uncontrolled appetites was not the least achievement of women writers at the end of the eighteenth and beginning of the nineteenth centuries.

I hope that this study has given a sense of the common ground and of the language and assumptions shared by 'unsex'd' and 'proper' females. Conversely, I hope that it has revealed the differences among 'unsex'd' females, in the process decentring Wollstonecraft's *Vindication of the Rights of Woman*. So many of the opinions of that book were extreme, not shared by other radical women, or adopted in a much qualified form. On the basis of that one text, it would be possible to argue that Wollstonecraft was a misogynist. No other 'unsex'd' or 'proper' female is as critical of women as she is. No other woman writer, except perhaps Macaulay Graham, wishes to efface all gender difference in order to copy a masculine model. Though More, Edgeworth and West are critics of sensibility too, all other 'unsex'd' females are on balance advocates of it. If one were looking for central texts standing most securely on the common ground shared by most 'unsex'd' females and to a certain extent by 'proper' ones too, one would turn to Hays – not to her novels which so deeply offended conservatives, but to her *Letters and Essays* and the *Appeal to the Men of Great Britain* – the latter, protected by anonymity from association with the author of *Emma Courtney*, receiving a favourable review in the *Anti-Jacobin*.

'Proper' females by definition differ from 'unsex'd' ones by their rigid insistence on sexual propriety, and by their ostentatious repudiation of any flirtation with 'jacobin' philosophy. In other respects they are not so different. Passages could be lifted from More's *Strictures*, or Edgeworth's *Letters to Literary Ladies*, inserted into Wollstonecraft's *Vindication*, and a reader not deeply familiar with the text would not spot the intrusion. 'Proper' females are just as resolute for educated, rational women. They too wish to reform the gender stereotype, eliminating elements which they judge degrading to women. Their arguments for the moral equality of women, and substantial intellectual equality with men, effectively undermine the case for a secondary, subordinated status for their sex. Some of them demand enhanced access to resources with as much force as any 'unsex'd' female. Apart from Edgeworth, they all accord women important roles outside the domestic sphere. To some extent at least they all write *for* women, demanding gains in their status and conditions.

What was the appropriate voice in which to advocate the interests of women? Present-day judgements are all too likely to be swayed by present-day attitudes. Some present-day feminists will have difficulty sympathizing with attempts to conciliate and persuade late eighteenth-century men, and women who agreed with them because their consciousnesses had not been raised. From such a standpoint, 'proper' females will have the appearance of being imprisoned in 'patriarchal complicity', and Wollstonecraft's decidedly unconciliatory voice will win approval. On the other hand, an attempt to read with late eighteenth-century eyes, guided by what reviewers and other women writers thought, might deliver a different verdict. The *Appeal to the Men of Great Britain* is openly critical of Wollstonecraft's lack of tact.[10] By any standards there are problems with Wollstonecraft's chosen voice. She is perfectly explicit about it: she believes in sincerity and authenticity, directness and plainness, speaking her thoughts and feelings without reserve or concealment, expressing her *self*, disdaining all tricks of rhetoric. Once again some present-day feminists might be inclined to celebrate this as a distinctively *woman's* voice, different from cold, distanced, masculine rationality. Those who are not persuaded by the hypothesis of different gendered styles of thinking and speaking may conclude that this highly subjective mode of utterance fails in her novels because the characters and situations she creates never stand free of their creator; and that in her political-philosophical writings, it is better adapted to enthusing those who already agree with her, than to persuading those who do not. It works better for reviews, and best of all in her Scandinavian letters.

There were other ways of advancing the cause of women. To don the protective mantle of Christianity was a largely successful strategy, adopted by all 'proper' females except Edgeworth, adopted too by Hays in her *Letters and Essays* and by the *Appeal to the Men of Great Britain*. Wollstonecraft was still wearing it when she wrote her *Vindication of the Rights of Woman*, and this may help to explain why the attack upon her did not commence immediately in 1792. The armour of Christianity did not always offer complete protection, if it was the wrong kind; the *Monthly Review*, politically at odds with More, could bypass her shield by sneering at her closeness to methodism.

Wit and irony could also disarm criticism. Robinson's *Thoughts on the Condition of Women* is assertive, even aggressive, but very witty too. The conservative reviews did not bother to destroy it, and the *Monthly Review* was too amused to take it seriously. Hamilton gets away with a succession of radical comments, many of which could have come from the pen of a 'jacobin', in part because she writes ironically. The *Appeal to the Men of Great Britain* has a very clever, self-conscious and calculated rhetoric. The author adopts a modest and unassuming tone, lays very great emphasis on propriety, and then with gentle wit insinuates the subversive message. Little mines are exploded beneath the unwary reader, who has been lulled into a false sense of security. For example, at the end of a very effective exposé of the contradictions in 'What men would have women to be' she remarks:

[10] *Appeal to the Men of Great Britain*, 'Advertisement to the reader', and p. v.

Conclusion

You may indeed say to women, as the Scripture I believe does to us all, 'Be ye wise as serpents, and harmless as doves;' for these qualities of the mind are by no means at variance. ... But had the Bible itself said, as you do to women in as many words, Be ye wise as serpents, and foolish as turkey pouts; – why I really don't know well how we should have managed matters, – I believe we must have remonstrated a little.[11]

Were 'unsex'd' and 'proper' females imprisoned in male discourses? A great deal of recent work, especially by scholars of literature, has explored the ways in which, it is claimed, they were. This book has attempted to challenge that, and to put a contrary point of view. It has sought to present a 'revisionist' case in relation to women's writing akin to the revisionism of the historians who have explored women's actual engagement in economy, society and politics and their roles, power and status in the family. Indeed I would contend that, insofar as they were oppressed (and as historians of women's lives have demonstrated, not all women were oppressed, or oppressed to the same degree) the most intractable evils, the ones they could do least about, were not discursive and generic conventions but unequal political and civil rights and lack of access to money. My view has been that women writers of the 1790s had at their disposal a range of genres, voices, discourses, theories and narratives on which they could draw as bricoleurs in order to advance the interests of women; a woman who was prepared to think independently was not imprisoned by any one of them. They possessed cultural resources which enabled them to challenge constructions of gender, and to propose alternative ideals both for themselves and for their male partners. They could propose extensions to the scope of female activity. They could stand outside themselves, look with an appraising eye, and then embark upon the enterprise of self-fashioning. They offered women readers models of empowered, confident and assertive female subjectivity, through their prose fiction and non-fiction depictions of women, and in their own selves as represented and expressed in their writings.

11 *Ibid.*, p. 63; see for another example pp. 49–51.

Bibliography

Alexander, Meena, *Women in Romanticism: Mary Wollstonecraft, Dorothy Wordsworth and Mary Shelley* (London, Macmillan, 1989)

Andrew, Donna T., 'The code of honour and its critics: the opposition to duelling in England, 1700–1850', *Social History*, 5:3 (October 1980), 409–34

Andrew, Donna T., '"Adultery à-la-Mode": privilege, the law and attitudes to adultery 1770–1809', *History*, 82:265 (January 1997), 5–23

Anon., *Appeal to the Men of Great Britain* (London, J. Johnson, 1798) (probably by Mary Hays)

Armstrong, Nancy, *Desire and Domestic Fiction: A Political History of the Novel* (Oxford, Oxford University Press, 1987)

Armstrong, Nancy, 'The rise of the domestic woman', in Nancy Armstrong & Leonard Tennenhouse (eds), *The Ideology of Conduct: Essays in Literature and the History of Sexuality* (London, Methuen, 1987)

Armstrong, Nancy & Tennenhouse, Leonard (eds), *The Ideology of Conduct: Essays in Literature and the History of Sexuality* (London, Methuen, 1987)

Backscheider, Paula R. & Dykstal, Timothy (eds), *The Intersection of the Public and Private Spheres in Early Modern England* (*Prose Studies: History, Theory, Criticism*, 18:3, December 1995)

Ballard, George, *Memoirs of Several Ladies of Great Britain* (1752) (Detroit, Wayne State University Press, 1985)

Barker, Hannah, 'Women, work and the industrial revolution: female involvement in the English printing trades, c. 1700–1840', in Hannah Barker & Elaine Chalus (eds), *Gender in Eighteenth-Century England* (London, Longman, 1997)

Barker, Hannah & Chalus, Elaine (eds), *Gender in Eighteenth-Century England*: *Roles, Representations and Responsibilities* (London, Longman, 1997)

Barker-Benfield, G. J., *The Culture of Sensibility: Sex and Society in Eighteenth-Century Britain* (Chicago, University of Chicago Press, 1992)

Bass, Robert D., *The Green Dragoon: the Lives of Banastre Tarleton and Mary Robinson* (London, Alvin Redman, 1957)

Beard, Mary, *Woman as Force in History* (New York, Collier, 1946)

Bellamy, Liz, *Commerce, Morality and the Eighteenth-Century Novel* (Cambridge, Cambridge University Press, 1998)

Benhabib, Seyla, *Situating the Self: Gender, Community and Postmodernism in*

Contemporary Ethics (Cambridge, Polity Press, 1992)

Bennett, Judith M., '"History that stands still": women's work in the European past', *Feminist Studies*, 14:2 (1988), 269–83

Berger, John, *Ways of Seeing* (Harmondsworth, Penguin, 1972)

Boling, P., 'The democratic potential of mothering', *Political Theory*, 19:4 (1991), 606–25

Boos, Florence S., 'Catherine [*sic*] Macaulay's Letters on Education', *University of Michigan Papers in Women's Studies*, 2:2 (1976)

Brewer, John, 'This, that and the other: public, social and private in the seventeenth and eighteenth centuries', in Dario Castiglione & Lesley Sharpe (eds), *Shifting the Boundaries: Transformation of the Languages of Public and Private in the Eighteenth Century* (Exeter, University of Exeter Press, 1995)

Brown, Martha G., 'Fanny Burney's "feminism": gender or genre?', in Mary Anne Schofield & Cecilia Macheski (eds), *Fetter'd or Free?* (Athens, Ohio University Press, 1986)

Burke, Edmund, *Reflections on the Revolution in France* (1790) (Letchworth, Everyman, 1910)

Burney, Frances (Madame d'Arblay), *Camilla: or, a Picture of Youth* (1796) (Oxford, Oxford University Press, 1983)

Butler, Judith, *Gender Trouble: Feminism and the Subversion of Identity* (New York, Routledge, 1990)

Butler, Marilyn, *Jane Austen and the War of Ideas* (Oxford, Oxford University Press, 1975)

Butterfield, Herbert, *The Whig Interpretation of History* (London, G. Ball & Sons, 1931)

Calhoun, Craig (ed.), *Habermas and the Public Sphere* (Cambridge, Mass., MIT Press, 1992)

Cameron, K. N., *Shelley and his Circle 1773–1822* (Cambridge, Mass., Harvard University Press, 1961)

Castiglione, Dario & Sharpe, Lesley (eds), *Shifting the Boundaries: Transformation of the Language of Public and Private in the Eighteenth Century* (Exeter, University of Exeter Press, 1995)

Chalus, Elaine, 'Women, electoral privilege and practice in the eighteenth century', in Kathryn Gleadle & Sarah Richardson (eds), *Women in British Politics, 1760–1860: the Power of the Petticoat* (Basingstoke, Macmillan, 2000)

Chapone, Mrs, *Letters on the Improvement of the Mind Addressed to a Lady* (1773) (London, J. Walker, 1808)

Colley, Linda, *Britons: Forging the Nation 1707–1837* (New Haven, Yale University Press, 1992)

Conger, Syndy McMillen, *Mary Wollstonecraft and the Languages of Sensibility* (Cranbury, NJ, Associated Universities Presses, 1994)

Connors, Richard, 'Poor women, the parish and the politics of poverty', in Hannah Barker & Elaine Chalus (eds), *Gender in Eighteenth-Century England: Roles, Representations and Responsibilities* (London, Longman, 1997)

Copeland, Edward, *Women Writing about Money: Women's Fiction in England, 1790–1820* (Cambridge, Cambridge University Press, 1995)

Copley, Stephen & Whale, John (eds), *Beyond Romanticism: New Approaches to Texts and Contexts 1780–1832* (London, Routledge, 1992)

Bibliography

Cott, Nancy F., 'Passionlessness: an interpretation of Victorian sexual ideology, 1790–1850', *Signs: Journal of Women in Culture and Society*, 4:2 (1978), 219–36

Coward, D. A., 'Eighteenth-century attitudes to prostitution', *Studies on Voltaire and the Eighteenth Century*, 189 (1980), 363–99

Craft-Fairchild, Catherine, *Masquerade and Gender: Disguise and Female Identity in Eighteenth-Century Fictions by Women* (Pennsylvania, Pennsylvania State University Press, 1993)

Crouch, Kimberley, 'The public life of actresses: prostitutes or ladies', in Hannah Barker & Elaine Chalus (eds), *Gender in Eighteenth-Century England: Roles, Representations and Responsibilities* (London, Longman, 1997)

Cullens, Chris, 'Mrs Robinson and the masquerade of womanliness', in Veronica Kelly & Dorothea E. von Mücke (eds), *Body and Text in the Eighteenth Century* (Stanford, Stanford University Press, 1994)

Curran, Stuart, 'Romantic poetry: The I altered', in Anne K. Mellor (ed.), *Romanticism and Feminism* (Bloomington & Indianapolis, Indiana University Press, 1988)

Curran, Stuart, 'Mary Robinson's *Lyrical Tales* in context', in Carol Shiner Wilson & Joel Hafner (eds), *Re-visioning Romanticism: British Women Writers, 1776–1837* (Philadelphia, University of Philadelphia Press, 1994)

Curtin, M., 'A question of manners: status and gender in etiquette and courtesy', *Journal of Modern History*, 57:3 (1985), 395–423

Davidoff, Leonore & Hall, Catherine, *Family Fortunes: Men and Women of the English Middle Class 1780–1850* (London, Hutchinson, 1988)

Doody, Margaret Anne, *Frances Burney: The Life in the Work* (Cambridge, Cambridge University Press, 1988)

Dugaw, Dianne, *Warrior Women and Popular Balladry, 1650–1850* (Cambridge, Cambridge University Press, 1989)

Duncombe, John, *The Feminiad* (London, Cooper, 1754)

Dyer, George, *Poems* (London, J. Johnson, 1792)

Edgeworth, Maria, *Letters for Literary Ladies. To Which is Added an Essay on the Noble Science of Self-Justification* (1795) (London, J. M. Dent, 1993)

Elias, Norbert, *The Civilizing Process: The History of Manners* (1939) (Oxford, Blackwell, 1978)

Elias, Norbert, *The Civilizing Process: State Formation and Civilization* (1939) (Oxford, Blackwell, 1982)

Ellis, Markman, *The Politics of Sensibility: Race, Gender and Commerce in the Sentimental Novel* (Cambridge, Cambridge University Press, 1996)

Elshtain, Jean Bethke, *Public Man, Private Woman* (Princeton, Princeton University Press, 1981)

Epictetus, *Moral Discourses* (trans. Elizabeth Carter, 1758; London, Everyman, 1910)

Epstein, Julia, *The Iron Pen: Frances Burney and the Politics of Women's Writing* (Bristol, Bristol Classical Press, 1989)

Everest, Kelvin (ed.), *Revolution in Writing: British Literary Responses to the French Revolution* (Ballmoor, Open University Press, 1991)

Favret, Mary A., *Romantic Correspondence: Women, Politics and the Fiction of Letters* (Cambridge, Cambridge University Press, 1993)

Fenwick, Eliza, *Secresy; or, the Ruin on the Rock* (1795) (Peterborough, Ontario, Broadview Press, 1994)

Ferguson, Adam, *An Essay on the History of Civil Society* (1767) (Edinburgh, Edinburgh University Press, 1966)

Ferguson, Moira, *Eighteenth-Century Women Poets: Nation, Class and Gender* (Albany, State University of New York Press, 1995)

Ferguson, Moira, 'Mary Wollstonecraft and the problematic of slavery', in Eileen Janes Yeo (ed.), *Mary Wollstonecraft and Two Hundred Years of Feminisms* (London, Rivers Oram Press, 1997)

Fildes, Valerie, *Wet Nursing: a History from Antiquity to the Present* (Oxford, Blackwell, 1988)

Fitzgerald, Laurie, *Shifting Genres, Changing Realities: Reading the Late Eighteenth-Century Novel* (New York, Peter Lang, 1995)

Fletcher, Anthony, *Gender, Sex and Subordination in England 1500–1800* (New Haven, Yale University Press, 1995)

Fletcher, Lorraine, *Charlotte Smith: a Critical Biography* (London, Macmillan, 1998)

Flint, Christopher, *Family Fictions: Narrative and Domestic Relations in Britain, 1688-1798* (Stanford, Stanford University Press, 1998)

Forbes, Joan, 'Anti-romantic discourse as resistance: women's fiction 1775–1820', in Lynne Pearce & Jackie Stacey (eds), *Romance Revisited* (New York, New York University Press, 1995)

Fraiman, Susan, *Unbecoming Women: British Women Writers and the Novel of Development* (New York, Columbia University Press, 1993)

Fry, Carrol L., *Charlotte Smith* (New York, Twayne, 1996)

Furniss, Tom, *Edmund Burke's Aesthetic Ideology: Language, Gender, and Political Economy in Revolution* (Cambridge, Cambridge University Press, 1993)

Gifford, William, *The Baviad, a Paraphrastic Imitation of the First Satire of Persius* (London, R. Faulder, 1791)

Gilbert, Sandra M. & Gubar, Susan, *The Madwoman in the Attic: the Woman Writer and the Nineteenth-Century Imagination* (New Haven, Yale University Press, 1979)

Gilligan, Carol, *In a Different Voice: Psychological Theory and Women's Development* (Cambridge, Mass., Harvard University Press, 1982)

Gleadle, Kathryn & Richardson, Sarah (eds), *Women in British Politics, 1760–1860: the Power of the Petticoat* (Basingstoke, Macmillan, 2000)

Godwin, William, *Memoirs of the Author of* A Vindication of the Rights of Woman (London, J. Johnson, 1798)

Gonda, Caroline, *Reading Daughters' Fictions, 1709–1834: Novels and Society from Manley to Edgeworth* (Cambridge, Cambridge University Press, 1996)

Goodman, Dena, 'Public sphere and private life: toward a synthesis of current historiographical approaches to the old régime', *History and Theory*, 31:1 (1992), 1–20

Green, Katharine Sobba, *The Courtship Novel 1740–1820: A Feminized Genre* (Lexington, University of Kentucky Press, 1991)

Grimshaw, Jean, 'Mary Wollstonecraft and the tensions in feminist philosophy', *Radical Philosophy*, 52 (1989), 11–17

Gunther-Canada, Wendy, 'The politics of sense and sensibility: Mary Wollstonecraft and Catharine Macaulay Graham on Edmund Burke's *Reflections on the Revolution in France*', in Hilda L. Smith (ed.), *Women Writers and the Early Modern British Political Tradition* (Cambridge, Cambridge University Press, 1998)

Habermas, Jürgen, *The Structural Transformation of the Public Sphere: an Inquiry into a Category of Bourgeois Society* (Cambridge, Polity Press, 1989)

Halévy, Élie, *The Growth of Philosophic Radicalism* (1928) (London, Faber, 1972)

Hall, Catherine, 'The early formation of Victorian domestic ideology', in *White, Male and Middle Class* (Cambridge, Polity Press, 1992)

Hamilton, Elizabeth, *Translation of the Letters of a Hindoo Rajah* (1796) (Peterborough, Ontario, Broadview Press, 1999)

Hargreaves-Mawdsley, W. N., *The English Della Cruscans and their Time* (The Hague, Martinus Nijhoff, 1967)

Hawthorn, Jeremy, *Cunning Passages: New Historicism, Cultural Materialism and Marxism in the Contemporary Literary Debate* (London, Arnold, 1996)

Hays, Mary, *Letters and Essays, Moral, and Miscellaneous* (London, T. Knott, 1793)

Hays, Mary, 'Letter on A. B.'s strictures on the talents of women', *Monthly Magazine* (July 1796), 469–70

Hays, Mary, *Memoirs of Emma Courtney* (1796) (London, Routledge & Kegan Paul, 1987)

Hays, Mary, 'Letter on female education', *Monthly Magazine* (March 1797), 193–5

Hays, Mary, 'Obituary of Mrs. Godwin, late Mary Woolstonecraft' (*sic*), *Monthly Magazine*, 4 (September 1797), 232–3

Hays, Mary, *The Victim of Prejudice* (1799) (Peterborough, Ontario, Broadview Press, 1994)

Hegel, G. W. F., *Philosophy of Right* (*Naturrecht und Staatswissenschaft im Grundrisse: Grundlinien der Philosophie des Rechts,* 1821) (Oxford, Oxford University Press, 1952)

Hemlow, J., 'Fanny Burney and the courtesy books', *Publications of the Modern Language Association of America*, 65 (1950), 732–61

Henderson, Andrea K., *Romantic Identities: Varieties of Subjectivity, 1774–1830* (Cambridge, Cambridge University Press, 1996)

Henderson, Andrea, 'Commerce and masochistic desire in the 1790s: Frances Burney's *Camilla*', *Eighteenth Century Studies*, 31:1 (1997), 69–86

Hill, Bridget, *The Republican Virago: The Life and Times of Catharine Macaulay, Historian* (Oxford, Oxford University Press, 1992)

Honour, Hugh, *Neo-Classicism* (Harmondsworth, Penguin, 1968)

Howard, Stephen, '"A bright pattern to all her sex"; representations of women in periodical and newspaper biography', in Hannah Barker & Elaine Chalus (eds), *Gender in Eighteenth-Century England* (London, Longman, 1997)

Hume, David, 'Of the rise and progress of the arts and sciences', *Essays* (1741) (Oxford, Oxford University Press, 1963)

Inchbald, Elizabeth, *A Simple Story* (1791) (Oxford, Oxford University Press, 1988)

Inchbald, Elizabeth, *Nature and Art* (1796) (London, Pickering & Chatto, 1997)

Jaeger, C. Stephen, *Ennobling Love: In Search of a Lost Sensibility* (Philadelphia, University of Pennsylvania Press, 1999)

Janes, R. M., 'The reception of Mary Wollstonecraft's *A Vindication of the Rights of Woman*', *Journal of the History of Ideas*, 39:2 (1978), 293–302

Jebb, Ann, *Two Penny-Worth of Truth for a Penny; or a True State of Facts: With an Apology for Tom Bull in a Letter to Brother John* (London, 1793)

Johnson, Claudia L., *Equivocal Beings: Politics, Gender, and Sentimentality in the 1790s. Wollstonecraft, Radcliffe, Burney, Austen* (Chicago, University of Chicago Press, 1995)

Jones, Chris, *Radical Sensibility: Literature and Ideas in the 1790s* (London, Routledge, 1993)

Jones, Vivien, *Women in the Eighteenth Century: Constructions of Femininity* (London, Routledge, 1990)

Jones, Vivien, 'Women writing revolution: narratives of history and sexuality in Wollstonecraft and Williams', in Stephen Copley & John Whale, *Romanticism: New Approaches to Texts and Contexts 1780–1832* (London, Routledge, 1992)

Jones, Vivien, 'Placing Jemima: women writers of the 1790s and the eighteenth-century prostitution narrative', *Women's Writing*, 4:2 (1997), 201–20

Jump, Harriet Devine, *Mary Wollstonecraft: Writer* (Hemel Hempstead, Harvester Wheatsheaf, 1994)

Jupp, P. J., 'The roles of royal and aristocratic women in British politics, c. 1782–1832', *Chattel, Servant or Citizen: Women's Status in Church, State and Society*, Institute of Irish Studies, Queens University Belfast, Historical Studies 19 (1995), 103–13

Kaplan, Cora, 'Wild nights: pleasure/sexuality/feminism', in Nancy Armstrong & Leonard Tennenhouse (eds), *The Ideology of Conduct: Essays on Literature and the History of Sexuality* (London, Methuen, 1987)

Kelly, Gary, *The English Jacobin Novel 1780–1805* (Oxford, Oxford University Press, 1976)

Kelly, Gary, *Revolutionary Feminism: the Mind and Career of Mary Wollstonecraft* (London, Macmillan, 1992)

Kelly, Gary, *Women, Writing and Revolution* (Oxford, Oxford University Press, 1993)

Kerber, Linda K., 'Separate spheres, female worlds, woman's place: the rhetoric of women's history', *Journal of American History*, 75:1 (1988), 9–39

Klein, Lawrence E., 'Gender, conversation and the public sphere in early eighteenth-century England', in Judith Still & Michael Worton (eds), *Textuality and Sexuality* (Manchester, Manchester University Press, 1993)

Klein, L. E., *Shaftesbury and the Culture of Politeness* (Cambridge, Cambridge University Press, 1994)

Kowaleski-Wallace, Elizabeth, *Their Fathers' Daughters: Hannah More, Maria Edgeworth, and Patriarchal Complicity* (New York, Oxford University Press, 1991)

Kramnick, Isaac, *Republicanism and Bourgeois Radicalism* (Ithaca, Cornell University Press, 1990)

Landes, Joan B., *Women and the Public Sphere in the Age of the French Revolution* (Ithaca, Cornell University Press, 1988)

Lang-Peralta, Linda (ed.), *Women, Revolution, and the Novels of the 1790s* (East Lansing, Michigan State University Press, 1999)

Laqueur, Thomas, *Making Sex: Body and Gender from the Greeks to Freud* (Cambridge, Mass., Harvard University Press, 1990)

Lorch, Jennifer, *Mary Wollstonecraft: the Making of a Radical Feminist* (New York, Berg Publications, 1990)

Lucas, John, *Writing and Radicalism* (London, Longman, 1996)

Luria, Gina M., *Mary Hays: a Critical Biography* (New York, New York University dissertation, 1972)

Macaulay Graham, Catharine, *Letters on Education. With Observations on Religious and Metaphysical Subjects* (London, C. Dilly, 1790)

Macaulay Graham, Catharine, *Observations on the Reflections of the Right Hon. Edmund Burke, on the Revolution in France* (London, C. Dilly, 1790)

Mathias, Thomas James, *The Pursuits of Literature, or What You Will: A Satirical Poem in Dialogue, Part the First* (London, J. Owen, 1794)

McCreevy, Cindy, 'Keeping up with the Bon Ton: the Tête-à-Tête series in the *Town and Country Magazine*', in Hannah Barker & Elaine Chalus (eds), *Gender in Eighteenth-Century England* (London, Longman, 1997)

McGann, Jerome, *The Poetics of Sensibility: a Revolution in Literary Style* (Oxford, Oxford University Press, 1996)

Mellor, Anne K., *Romanticism and Gender* (London, Routledge, 1993)

Melzer, S. E., & Rabine, L. W., *Rebel Daughters: Women and the French Revolution* (New York, Oxford University Press, 1992)

Mews, Hazel, *Frail Vessels: Woman's Role in Women's Novels from Fanny Burney to George Eliot* (London, Athlone Press, 1969)

Midgley, Clare, *Women against Slavery: the British Campaigns 1780–1870* (London, Routledge, 1992)

Mill, John Stuart, 'Coleridge', in *Dissertations and Discussions, Political, Philosophical, and Historical* (London, John W. Parker & Son, 1859)

More, Hannah, *Village Politics. Addressed to All the Mechanics, Journeymen, and Day Labourers, in Great Britain. By Will Chip, a Country Carpenter* (London, F. & C. Rivington, 1792)

More, Hannah, *Sunday Reading. Bear Ye one another's Burdens, or the Valley of Tears: a Vision* (London, J. Marshall, 1795)

More, Hannah, *The Two Shoemakers* (London, J. Evans & J. Hatchard, 1795)

More, Hannah, *Black Giles the Poacher. Part II* (London, J. Marshall, 1796)

More, Hannah, *The History of Hester Wilmot; or, the New Gown* (London, J. Marshall, 1796)

More, Hannah, *Strictures on the Modern System of Female Education. With a View of the Principles and Conduct Prevalent among Women of Rank and Fortune* (London, T. Cadell, 1799)

More, Hannah, *'Tis All for the Best* (London, J. Evans & J. Hatchard, 1799)

More, Hannah, *The Two Wealthy Farmers; or, the History of Mr. Bragwell* (London, Rivington, 1799)

More, Hannah, 'A cure for melancholy: shewing the way to do much good with little money', in *The Works of Hannah More* (London, T. Cadell & W. Davies, 1818), vol. iv.

Morgan, Marjorie, *Manners, Morals and Class in England, 1774–1858* (Basingstoke, Macmillan, 1994)

Moses, Claire Goldberg, '"Equality" and "difference" in historical perspective: a comparative examination of the feminisms of French revolutionaries and utopian socialists', in S. E. Melzer & L. W. Rabine (eds), *Rebel Daughters: Women and the French Revolution* (New York, Oxford University Press, 1992)

Munslow, Alun, *Deconstructing History* (London, Routledge, 1997)

Murray, Penelope (ed.), *Genius: the History of an Idea* (Oxford, Blackwell, 1989)

Myers, Mitzi, 'Reform or ruin: "A revolution in female manners"', *Studies in Eighteenth Century Culture*, 11 (1982), 199–216

Myers, Mitzi, 'Hannah More's Tracts for the Times: social fiction and female ideology', in Mary Anne Schofield & Cecilia Macheski (eds), *Fetter'd or Free? British Women Novelists, 1670–1815* (Athens, Ohio University Press, 1986)

Myers, Mitzi, 'A peculiar protection: Hannah More and the cultural politics of the Blagdon controversy', in Beth Fowkes Tobin (ed.), *History, Gender & Eighteenth-Century Literature* (Athens, University of Georgia Press, 1994)

Myers, Sylvia Harcstark, *The Bluestocking Circle* (Oxford, Oxford University Press, 1990)

Newton, Judith Lowder, *Women, Power and Subversion: Social Strategies in British Fiction, 1778-1860* (London, Methuen, 1985)

Nietzsche, Friedrich, *On the Genealogy of Morals* (*Zur Genealogie der Moral*, 1887) (New York, Random House, 1989)

Nyquist, Mary, 'Wanting protection: fair ladies, sensibility and romance', in Eileen Janes Yeo (ed.), *Mary Wollstonecraft and Two Hundred Years of Feminisms* (London, Rivers Oram Press, 1997)

O'Day, Rosemary, *The Family and Family Relationships 1500–1900: England, France and the United States of America* (Basingstoke, Macmillan, 1994)

Offen, Karen, 'Defining feminism: a comparative historical approach', *Signs: Journal of Women in Culture and Society*, 14:1 (1988), 119–57

Okin, S. M., 'Women and the making of the sentimental family', *Philosophy and Public Affairs*, 11:1 (1982), 65–88

Orr, Clarissa Campbell (ed.), *Wollstonecraft's Daughters: Womanhood in England and France 1780–1920* (Manchester, Manchester University Press, 1996)

Outram, Dorinda, *The Body and the French Revolution* (New Haven, Yale University Press, 1989)

Pascoe, Judith, 'Mary Robinson and the literary marketplace', in Paula R. Feldman & Theresa M. Kelly (eds), *Romantic Women Writers: Voices and Countervoices* (Hanover, University Press of New England, 1995)

Pateman, Carole, *The Sexual Contract* (Cambridge, Polity Press, 1988)

Perry, Ruth, 'Radical doubt and the liberation of women', *Eighteenth-Century Studies*, 18:4 (1985), 472–93

Pocock, J. G. A., *Virtue, Commerce, and History: Essays on Political Thought and History* (Cambridge, Cambridge University Press, 1985)

Pocock, J. G. A., 'Catharine Macaulay: patriot historian', in Hilda L. Smith (ed.), *Women Writers and the Early Modern British Political Tradition* (Cambridge, Cambridge University Press, 1998)

Polwhele, Richard, *The Unsex'd Females: A Poem, Addressed to the Author of the Pursuits of Literature* (London, Cadell & Davies, 1798)

Poovey, Mary, 'Mary Wollstonecraft: the gender of genres in late eighteenth-century England', *Novel: a Forum in Fiction*, 15:2 (1982), 111–26

Poovey, Mary L., *The Proper Lady and the Woman Writer: Ideology as Style in the Works of Mary Wollstonecraft, Mary Shelley, and Jane Austen* (Chicago, University of Chicago Press, 1984)

Radcliffe, Ann, *The Romance of the Forest* (London, T. Hookham & Carpenter, 1791)

Radcliffe, Ann, *The Mysteries of Udolpho* (1794) (Oxford, Oxford University Press, 1980)

Radcliffe, Ann, *The Italian, or the Confessional of the Black Penitents* (London, T. Cadell & W. Davies, 1797)

Radcliffe, Mary Ann, *The Female Advocate; or, an Attempt to Recover the Rights of Women from Male Usurpation* (1799 reprinted in *The Memoirs of Mrs. Mary Ann Radcliffe; in Familiar Letters to her Female Friend*, Edinburgh, Manners & Miller, 1810)

Rajan, Tilottama, & Wright, Julia M. (eds), *Romanticism, History, and the Possibilities of Genre: Re-forming Literature 1789-1837* (Cambridge, Cambridge University Press, 1998)

Raphael, D. D., *The Moral Sense* (Oxford, Oxford University Press, 1947)

Rendall, Jane, *The Origins of Modern Feminism: Women in Britain, France and the United States, 1780–1860* (New York, Schocken Books, 1984)

Rendall, Jane, 'Virtue and commerce: women in the making of Adam Smith's political economy', in Ellen Kennedy & Susan Mendus (eds), *Women in Western Political Philosophy* (Brighton, Wheatsheaf, 1987)

Rich, Adrienne, *Blood, Bread, and Poetry: Selected Prose 1979-1985* (London, Virago, 1987)

Riley, Denise, *'Am I that Name?' Feminism and the Category of 'Women' in History* (Basingstoke, Macmillan, 1989)

Roberts, Mark, *The Tradition of Romantic Morality* (London, Macmillan, 1973)

Robinson, Mary, *Vancenza; or, the Dangers of Credulity* (London, 1792)

Robinson, Mary, *Monody to the Memory of the Late Queen of France* (London, T. Spilsbury & Son, 1793)

Robinson, Mary, *The Widow, or a Picture of Modern Times* (London, Hookham & Carpenter, 1794)

Robinson, Mary, *Angelina* (London, Hookham & Carpenter, 1796)

Robinson, Mary, *Hubert de Sevrac, a Romance, of the Eighteenth Century* (London, Hookham & Carpenter, 1796)

Robinson, Mary, *Walsingham; or, The pupil of Nature. A Domestic Story* (London, Longman, 1797)

Robinson, Mary, *The False Friend; a Domestic Story* (London, T. N. Longman & G. Rees, 1799)

Robinson, Mary, *The Natural Daughter. With Portraits of the Leadenhead Family* (London, T. N. Longman & O. Rees, 1799)

Robinson, Mary, *Thoughts on the Condition of Women, and on the Injustice of Mental Subordination* (London, Longman & Rees, 1799)

Robinson, Mary, *Memoirs of the Late Mrs. Robinson, Written by Herself* (1801) (published as *Perdita. The Memoirs of Mary Robinson*, London, Peter Owen, 1994)

Rogers, Katherine M., *Feminism in Eighteenth-Century England* (Brighton, Harvester, 1982)

Rogers, K. M., *Frances Burney. The World of 'Female Difficulties'* (Hemel Hempstead, Harvester Wheatsheaf, 1990)

Roper, Derek, *Reviewing Before the* Edinburgh, *1788-1802* (London, Methuen, 1978)

Rousseau, Jean-Jacques, *Émile ou de l'Éducation* (1762) (Paris, Garnier, 1964)

Rubin, Gayle, 'The traffic in women: notes on the "political economy" of sex', in Rayna R. Reiter (ed.), *Toward an Anthropology of Women* (New York, Monthly Review Press, 1975)

Sapiro, Virginia, *A Vindication of Political Virtue: the Political Theory of Mary Wollstonecraft* (Chicago, University of Chicago Press, 1992)

Bibliography

Schiller, Friedrich, *On the Naïve and Sentimental in Literature (Über naïve und senti-mentalische Dichtung*, 1795) (Manchester, Carcanet, 1981)

Schochet, Gordon, 'Vices, benefits and civil society: Mandeville, Habermas, and the distinction between public and private', in Paula R. Backscheider & Timothy Dykstal, *The Intersection of the Public and Private Spheres in Early Modern England (Prose Studies: History, Theory, Criticism*, 18:3, December 1995)

Schofield, Mary Anne, & Macheski, Cecilia, *Fetter'd or Free? British Women Novelists, 1670–1815* (Athens, Ohio University Press, 1986)

Scott, J. W., 'Gender: a useful category of historical analysis', *American Historical Review*, 91:4 (1986), pp. 1053–75

Scott, Joan W., 'The imagination of Olympe de Gouges', in Eileen Janes Yeo (ed.), *Mary Wollstonecraft and Two Hundred Years of Feminisms* (London, Rivers Oram Press, 1997)

Seward, Anna, *Llangollen Vale, with Other Poems* (London, G. Sael, 1796)

Shapiro, Ann-Louise, 'Introduction: history and feminist theory, or talking back to the beadle', *History and Theory*, Beiheft 31:4 (1992), 1–14

Shattock, Joanne, *Politics and Reviewers: the* Edinburgh *and the* Quarterly *in the Early Victorian Age* (Leicester, Leicester University Press, 1989)

Shevelow, Kathryn, *Women and Print Culture: the Construction of Femininity in the Early Periodical* (London, Routledge, 1989)

Shoemaker, Robert B., *Gender in English Society 1650–1850: the Emergence of Separate Spheres?* (London, Longman, 1998)

Smith, Adam, *An Inquiry into the Nature and Causes of the Wealth of Nations* (1776) (London, Everyman, 1910)

Smith, Charlotte, *Celestina* (London, T. Cadell, 1791)

Smith, Charlotte, *Desmond* (1792) (London, Pickering and Chatto, 1997)

Smith, Charlotte, *The Old Manor House* (1793) (Oxford, Oxford University Press, 1969)

Smith, Charlotte, *The Banished Man* (London, T. Cadell, 1794)

Smith, Charlotte, *Montalbert* (London, E. Booker, 1795)

Smith, Charlotte, *Marchmont* (London, Sampson Low, 1796)

Smith, Charlotte, *The Young Philosopher* (1798) (Lexington, University of Kentucky Press, 1999)

Smith, Charlotte, *The Poems of Charlotte Smith*, ed. Stuart Curran (Oxford: Oxford University Press, 1993)

Smith, Hilda L., 'Introduction. Women, intellect, and politics: their intersection in seventeenth-century England', in Hilda L. Smith (ed.), *Women Writers and the Early Modern British Political Tradition* (Cambridge, Cambridge University Press, 1998)

Soper, Kate, 'Naked human nature and the draperie of custom: Wollstonecraft on equality and democracy', in Eileen Janes Yeo (ed.), *Mary Wollstonecraft and Two Hundred Years of Feminisms* (London, Rivers Oram Press, 1997)

Spacks, Patricia Meyer, *Imagining a Self: Autobiography and Novel in Eighteenth-Century England* (Cambridge, Mass., Harvard University Press, 1976)

Spender, Dale, *Women of Ideas (And What Men Have Done to Them)* (London, Routledge & Kegan Paul, 1983)

Spring, Eileen, *Law, Land and Family: Aristocratic Inheritance in England, 1300–1800* (Chapel Hill, University of North Carolina Press, 1993)

Bibliography

Stafford, William, 'Dissenting religion translated into politics: Godwin's *Political Justice*', *History of Political Thought*, 1:2 (1980), 279–99

Stafford, William, 'Narratives of women: English feminists of the 1790s', *History*, 82:265 (1997), 24–43

Staves, Susan, *Married Women's Separate Property in England, 1660–1833* (Cambridge, Mass., Harvard University Press, 1990)

Steinbrügge, Lieselotte, *The Moral Sex: Woman's Nature in the French Enlightenment* (Oxford, Oxford University Press, 1992)

Stone, Lawrence, *The Family, Sex and Marriage in England, 1500–1800* (London, Weidenfeld & Nicolson, 1977)

Stott, Anne, 'Patriotism and providence: the politics of Hannah More', in Kathryn Gleadle & Sarah Richardson (eds), *Women in British Politics, 1760–1860: The Power of the Petticoat* (Basingstoke, Macmillan, 2000)

Straub, Kristina, *Sexual Suspects: Eighteenth-Century Players and Sexual Ideology* (Princeton, Princeton University Press, 1992)

Sutherland, Kathryn, 'Hannah More's counter-revolutionary feminism', in Kelvin Everest (ed.), *Revolution in Writing: British Literary Responses to the French Revolution* (Ballmoor, Bucks, Open University Press, 1991)

Taylor, Barbara, 'Mary Wollstonecraft and the wild wish of early feminism', *History Workshop*, 33 (1992), 197–219

Taylor, Barbara, 'For the love of God. Religion and the erotic imagination in Wollstonecraft's feminism', in Eileen Janes Yeo (ed.), *Mary Wollstonecraft and Two Hundred Years of Feminisms* (London, Rivers Oram Press, 1997)

Taylor, Charles, *Sources of the Self: The Making of the Modern Identity* (Cambridge, Cambridge University Press, 1989)

Tobin, Beth Fowkes, *Superintending the Poor: Charitable Ladies and Paternal Landlords in British Fiction, 1770–1860* (New Haven, Yale University Press, 1993)

Todd, Janet, *Sensibility: an Introduction* (London, Methuen, 1986)

Todd, Janet, *The Sign of Angellica: Women, Writing and Fiction 1660–1800* (London, Virago, 1989)

Todd, Janet, *Mary Wollstonecraft: A Revolutionary Life* (London, Weidenfeld & Nicolson, 2000)

Tomalin, Claire, *The Life and Death of Mary Wollstonecraft* (Harmondsworth, Penguin, 1977)

Tomaselli, Sylvana, 'The enlightenment debate on women', *History Workshop Journal*, 19 (1985), 101–24

Trumbach, Randolph, *The Rise of the Egalitarian Family: Aristocratic Kinship and Domestic Relations in Eighteenth Century England* (London, Academic Press, 1978)

Turner, Cheryl, *Living by the Pen: Women Writers in the Eighteenth Century* (London, Routledge, 1992)

Ty, Eleanor, *Unsex'd Revolutionaries: Five Women Novelists of the 1790s* (Toronto, University of Toronto Press, 1993)

Ty, Eleanor, *Empowering the Feminine: the Narratives of Mary Robinson, Jane West and Amelia Opie, 1796–1812* (Toronto, University of Toronto Press, 1998)

Van Sant, Ann Jessie, *Eighteenth-Century Sensibility and the Novel: The Senses in Social Context* (Cambridge, Cambridge University Press, 1993)

Bibliography

Veeser, H. Aram (ed.), *The New Historicism* (London, Routledge, 1989)

Vickery, Amanda, 'Golden age to separate spheres? A review of the categories and chronology of English women's history', *Historical Journal*, 36:2 (1993), 383–414

Vickery, Amanda, *The Gentleman's Daughter: Women's Lives in Georgian England* (New Haven, Yale University Press, 1998)

Wahrmann, Drohr, '*Percy*'s prologue: from gender play to gender panic in eighteenth-century England', *Past & Present*, 159 (1998), 113–60

Wakefield, Priscilla, *Reflections on the Present Condition of the Female Sex; with suggestions for its improvement* (London, J. Johnson, 1798)

Watson, Nicola J., *Revolution and the Form of the British Novel 1790–1825: Intercepted Letters, Interrupted Seductions* (Oxford, Oxford University Press, 1994)

Watts, Ruth, *Gender, Power and the Unitarians in England 1760–1860* (London, Longman, 1998)

West, Jane, *The Advantages of Education, or, the History of Maria Williams, a Tale for Misses and their Mammas* (London, William Lane, 1793)

West, Jane, *A Gossip's Story* (London, Longman, 1797)

West, Jane, *A Tale of the Times* (London, Longman & Rees, 1799)

White, Hayden, *The Content of the Form: Narrative Discourse and Historical Representation* (Baltimore, Johns Hopkins University Press, 1987)

Williams, Helen Maria, *Julia* (London, T. Cadell, 1790)

Williams, Helen Maria, *Letters from France* (1790–6) (facsimile reprint, New York, Delmar, 1975)

Williams, Raymond, *The Country and the City* (London, Chatto & Windus, 1973)

Wilson, Carol Shiner, & Haefner, Joel (eds), *Re-visioning Romanticism: British Women Writers, 1776–1837* (Philadelphia, University of Pennsylvania Press, 1994)

Wilson, Kathleen, *The Sense of the People: Politics, Culture and Imperialism in England, 1715–1785* (Cambridge, Cambridge University Press, 1995)

Wollstonecraft, Mary, *A Vindication of the Rights of Men, in a Letter to the Right Honourable Edmund Burke; Occasioned by his Reflections on the Revolution in France* (1790) (Cambridge, Cambridge University Press, 1995)

Wollstonecraft, Mary, *A Vindication of the Rights of Woman: with Strictures on Political and Moral Subjects* (1792) (Cambridge, Cambridge University Press, 1995)

Wollstonecraft, Mary, *An Historical and Moral View of the Origin and Progress of the French Revolution; and of the Effect it has Produced in Europe* (London, Joseph Johnson, 1794)

Wollstonecraft, Mary, *Letters Written During a Short Residence in Sweden, Norway and Denmark* (London, Joseph Johnson, 1796)

Wollstonecraft, Mary, *The Wrongs of Woman: or, Maria* (1798) (Oxford, Oxford University Press, 1980)

Works of Mary Wollstonecraft, ed. J. Todd & M. Butler (London, William Pickering, 1989)

Worthington, Kim L., *Self as Narrative: Subjectivity and Community in Contemporary Fiction* (Oxford, Oxford University Press, 1996)

Bibliography

Yeo, Eileen Janes, 'Introduction', in Eileen Janes Yeo (ed.), *Mary Wollstonecraft and Two Hundred Years of Feminisms* (London, Rivers Oram Press, 1997)

Zaczek, Barbara Maria, *Censored Sentiments: Letters and Censorship in Epistolary Novels and Conduct Materials* (Newark University of Delaware Press, 1997)

Index

Note: references to individual women authors who are the subject of this book are confined to longer or more specific discussions.

Index

Macaulay, Catharine *see* Graham,
    Catharine Macaulay
marriage 125–30
  arranged 58, 94–100
  companionate 55–8, 72, 111–12,
    155
    equality and 128–30
  radical views on 15–16, 23, 27, 33,
    217
'masculine' women *see* cross dressing;
    gender, transgression
masculinity 120–4
maternalism 150
Mathias, T.J. 3
matrophobia 68, 130–1
men, reformation of 62–3, 91,
    119–24, 218
modesty 139, 146, 148, 172, 183–4,
    196–200
money 80–1
More, Hannah (1745–1833) 29, 38,
    150–1, 180
motherhood 130–3, 173
  idealization of 54, 165–6

narratives of progress & decline
    39–45, 67–70, 72
neoclassicism *see* aesthetic
new historicism 43
Nietzsche, Friedrich 208, 210–11
novels, disapproval of 6–7, 32

objectification *see* beauty
ordinary life *see* spheres, separate,
    evaluation of

passionlessness *see* desire
passivity *see* weakness of women
patriarchy 40–4, 48, 55–8, 66–70, 129
  revolt against 94–100
  see also discursive imprisonment
pedestal, woman placed on 39–40, 66,
    217–19
philanthropy *see* social, role

poetry by women 5–6, 9, 23, 31, 70,
    191
politeness 62
politics
  gendered discourse 155–63
  interconnectedness of domestic &
    political 163–6
  women's involvement in 49–51,
    152–3
  see also bourgeois public sphere;
    discursive imprisonment;
    republicanism, classical
Polwhele, Richard 2–34 *passim*
'proper' females, list of 2, 31–3
property and property law 55–6, 86,
    92, 135
prose fiction, problems of
    interpretation 74–5, 84
prostitution 28, 81–3, 109–10, 142, 144
  marriage as legalized 126, 145
protection 80, 88, 102, 142
public and private writing 4–5
Pygmalion 76, 123

Radcliffe, Ann (1764–1823) 31
Radcliffe, Mary Ann (*c*.1746–*post*
    1810) 36
'radical' frameworks 40–4, 74
rape 78, 89
reason
  human 49, 158
  morality and 160
  political danger of when divorced
    from feeling 159–62
  sensibility and *see* sensibility, reason
    and
  women's lack of 48, 57, 61, 65,
    156, 158, 182
  women's possession of 51, 65, 106,
    130, 150, 163–5, 172–6
    passim, 188–90, 200, 210, 213
reformation of manners 150
  see also men, reformation of
religious role 129, 149–52